Studies in Major Literary Authors

William E. Cain, *General Editor*

Cormac McCarthy
and the Myth
of American Exceptionalism

John Cant

Routledge
New York & London

First published 2008
by Routledge
270 Madison Ave, New York, NY 10016

Simultaneously published in the UK
by Routledge
2 Park Square, Milton Park, Abingdon, Oxon OX14 4RN

Routledge is an imprint of the Taylor & Francis Group, an informa business

Transferred to Digital Printing 2009

Library of Congress Cataloging in Publication Data
Cant, John.
Cormac McCarthy and the myth of American exceptionalism / by John Cant.—1st ed.
p. cm.—(Studies in major literary authors)
"A Routledge Series"—T.p. verso.
Includes bibliographical references and index.
1. McCarthy, Cormac, 1933—Criticism and interpretation.   2. National characteristics, American, in literature.   I. Title.

PS3563.C337Z6 2007
813'.54—dc22   2007023587

ISBN10: 0-415-98142-5 (hbk)
ISBN10: 0-415-87567-6 (pbk)

ISBN13: 978-0-415-98142-2 (hbk)
ISBN13: 978-0-415-87567-7 (pbk)

Permissions

To Chris, Alison and Gillian

Contents

Acknowledgments

This book has been a number of years in the making and during that time I have enjoyed the stimulation and support of many admirers of Cormac McCarthy's work. Some of them will have influenced me without my knowing; the existence of a shared enthusiasm for a certain writer is a support in itself. Others will have given me ideas that I have been glad to use but, to my shame, forgetting the source over time, will have taken as my own; I can only plead their indulgence and hope that I may have repaid them in kind. Among those I am only too happy to acknowledge are Richard Gray, without whose support and encouragement I should not have undertaken this task in the first place. I must also mention Jackie Kaye, a formidable champion of McCarthy's work, Owen Robinson, Julia Firmin, Luke Whiting and Mike Gray. Rick Wallach, David Holloway and Dianne Luce have also played a part. I thank them all.

Finally I must acknowledge my wife who made the whole enterprise possible by supporting me at home and never objecting to my obsessive attention to the task.

Modified versions of the sections on *Wake for Susan* and *No Country for Old Men* have appeared in *The Cormac McCarthy Journal*; Vol. 3, No.1, 2003 and Vol 5, No. 1, 2006 respectively.

Part I

Preliminary

Chapter One

Introduction

All is telling. Do not doubt it.

—*The Crossing*

"The way is to the destructive element submit yourself, and with the exertions of your hands and feet in the water make the deep, deep sea keep you up."[1] Conrad's dictum for modern man, spoken in Germanic English by Stein, the revolutionary turned merchant, in *Lord Jim*, is perhaps appropriate to both my purpose in writing this book and the attitude of the writer who forms its inspiration.

My purpose is to write on the complete published literary output of the contemporary American author Cormac McCarthy. This consists of eight novels, two short stories, one TV screenplay and an unperformed play for the theatre.[2] Both the depth and extent of this output may be considered oceanic in itself. I intend to identify themes that unify McCarthy's texts and also to deal with the texts individually. In addition I shall trace lines of development that emerge when his oeuvre is considered as a whole.

Such largeness of ambition is, of course, as nothing compared to that shown by McCarthy himself. Whilst making it quite obvious that he places himself in the tradition of such diverse literary forbears as Melville, Faulkner, Joyce, T.S. Eliot, and a great many more besides, McCarthy has the confidence to seek to emulate their scale and profundity. In an age in which we have been made increasingly aware of the limits of language, of its inability to "signify the real," he makes clear his profound love of language, his confidence in its ability to do what he wants it to, and of his willingness to deploy it in many different modes—from the spare colloquialism of Tennessee mountain speech, through a lyricism that is uniquely his own, to the grand and musical cadences of the King James Bible. This mastery of language is deployed in the creation of texts that reveal a willingness to confront the most profound issues of human existence and to express implications that are neither comforting nor, in some cases, fashionable.

Whether or not McCarthy comes to be ranked alongside the great figures of the past on whom he draws so readily there seems no doubt that he has been prepared to dare to aspire to their scale, their scope, their heroic seriousness. This may, of course, appear to be hubris, or at least vanity. I suggest that the truth is that, for McCarthy, this largeness of purpose is an inescapable characteristic of literature; this is the destructive element in which he has immersed himself in a literary career that spans forty years. That this career is not yet necessarily over merely adds another unknown depth to the task that confronts those who, like myself, seek to consider his output "as a whole."

Although McCarthy has been publishing novels since 1965 his reputation was largely confined to specialized academic circles until *All the Pretty Horses* (1992) bought him belated and unexpected popular success. The publicity associated with this success had the effect of greatly increasing the level of critical attention paid to McCarthy, indicating that the market and the academy are more closely allied than either would perhaps care to admit. Certainly my own interest was initially stimulated by a chance encounter in a local provincial bookshop and the publisher's modest claim that *All the Pretty Horses* was "One of the greatest American novels of this or any time." During the period of his writing career so far only two full length works of McCarthy criticism by single authors have been published, Vereen Bell's *The Achievement of Cormac McCarthy* (1988), dealing perforce with what McCarthy achieved before the publication of The Border Trilogy, of which *All the Pretty Horses* was the initial volume and Robert Jarrett's *Cormac McCarthy* (1997) in Twayne's United States Authors Series. Jarrett dealt only with the novels and was faced with the invidious task of writing on The Border Trilogy when the final volume, *Cities of the Plain*, was not available to him. A number of book length editions of criticism of McCarthy's complete oeuvre do exist but these are all collections of essays by different authors and all of them deliberately set out to present a wide range of different critical points of view on McCarthy and to expose his work to a range of theoretical approaches. This book is therefore, I believe, the only work so far that aspires to present a single unified vision of McCarthy's output including his early short stories and the Border Trilogy as a whole. McCarthy does spend years rather than months over the production of an individual novel. However it is possible that my claim to represent a comprehensive, if individual, critical view of McCarthy's work may be undermined by an extension of that work.

Since the only way to avoid this possibility would be to wait for the author's death and since he and I are of about the same age there is no alternative but to proceed. That I may eventually be overtaken, as the other authors mentioned have been, would in fact be a welcome development, since it would mean that we had further McCarthy texts to enjoy.

Cormac McCarthy is one of the most eclectic of novelists. He claims to have read 300 different books in preparation for the writing of *Blood Meridian* alone.[3] In the first of only two published interviews, both with Richard B. Woodward, he commented that "The ugly fact is that books are made out of other books. The novel depends for its life on the novels that have been written."[4] However we may conclude that the "ugliness" involved has been insufficient to deter him from the extensive use of intertextuality throughout his work. Perhaps, like D.H. Lawrence, we must trust "not the artist but the tale." It has become a commonplace of contemporary criticism to equate eclecticism and postmodernism and a number of critics do regard McCarthy as a postmodern writer. Jarrett labels his chapter on *Child of God* and *Suttree*, "Postmodern Outcasts and Alienation" and sees him as undertaking the task of "rewriting" the South and, later, the Southwest. However it is my contention that labeling McCarthy's texts in this manner obscures as much as it illuminates. Postmodernism asserts the failure of the various "grand narratives" of western culture and I shall argue that one of the unifying themes of McCarthy's work is his depiction of the failure of the "grand narrative" of American Exceptionalism. However the postmodern critic also rejects the essentialist notion of a fixed human nature. McCarthy's depiction of various of his protagonists "in extremis" makes it clear that he believes in an all too powerful "essential" human nature and that violence is inherent to that essence. This is made very plain in *Blood Meridian*; the third introductory quote to that text notes that "a 300,000-year-old fossil skull . . . . . shows evidence of having been scalped." The implication is clear—since the scalp-hunters of *Blood Meridian* are nineteenth century white Americans, acculturated by Christianity and the Enlightenment, and living in the age of Darwin, such evolution as they may have undergone over the millennia has failed to remove them from a state of nature that owes more to Hobbes than it does to Locke. A *tabula rasa* it is not. Indeed McCarthy's reference throughout his texts to the existence of fossilized remains of extinct creatures and the symbols and broken artifacts of lost cultures "that seemed to have no referent in the world although they may once have"[5] makes clear his vision of humanity as of cosmic insignificance, and of modern man as the representative of a culture that will, like all others before it, become no more than "myth, legend, dust"—the final words of *The Orchard Keeper*.[6] Against this, the ultimate pessimism, McCarthy consistently asserts an existential antithesis, the inherent vitality of "ardenthearted" man.

> What he loved in horses was what he loved in men, the blood and the heat of the blood that ran them. All his reverence and all his fondness and all the leanings of his life were for the ardenthearted and they would always be so and never be otherwise.[7]

This also is an aspect of an essentialist view of human nature. The "dialectic of vitality and insignificance" is one of those common threads that unifies McCarthy's work. References to the heart occur throughout his texts and are always of great significance. Blood is a recurring emblem in his work and signifies both life and death, each defined in relation to its inescapable other. For McCarthy one might say that optimism comprises the notion that there is no death without life! The fact that social and cultural forces so often turn McCarthy's ardenthearted Americans to self-destructive and at times all-consuming violence is an aspect of his critique of American culture, and by extension, of Western culture as a whole.

McCarthy's eclecticism extends beyond the American concerns that Jarrett not unreasonably asserts, and is emphasized by his recurring references to Eliot, himself a deliberately and overtly eclectic writer. When Eliot claimed that "These fragments have I shored against my ruins,"[8] he was claiming descent from a literary and spiritual tradition that he believed to be both lost and of transcendent value. When McCarthy places the phrase "rock and no water"[9] unobtrusively in his most extreme denunciation of American culture he is not indulging in postmodern pastiche nor does he quote with playful irony. He also is claiming literary descent, from Eliot and by extension from Shakespeare, Dante, The Bible, Webster, Goethe, and all the sources of Eliot's "fragments". He is also asserting another of his unifying themes, that of the American Waste Land. In other senses however McCarthy refutes the Eliot who believed in the spiritual superiority of the past; McCarthy implicitly and consistently attacks the myth of the pastoral in all its forms, Southern, American, Western. Eliot recast myth in order to try to turn the modern world back to what he saw as the vision of a lost civilization. McCarthy recasts myth to attack what he sees as the false and destructive cultural constructs of American Exceptionalism in particular. He is what Matthew Guinn terms a mythoclast.[10] McCarthy also refutes Eliot in his obvious affection for the language of the everyday, in particular the everyday of the poor of Tennessee, Texas and Mexico. He deliberately and lovingly writes the voices of the excluded into his discourse of America; and he defiantly asserts the paradoxical value of language in all its forms, in particular the narrative form. "All is telling. Do not doubt it" says the storyteller in a ruined Mexican church.[11] That this church is ruined, like so many in McCarthy's texts, indicates that McCarthy's universe is without God. A number of critics point out the absurdist nature of this universe and draw parallels between the ceaseless wandering and repeated journeys of Billy Parham in *The Crossing* and Camus' absurdist existential reading of *The Myth of Sisyphus*.[12] Christine Chollier characterizes the Border trilogy as "baroque," pointing out that the term

> . . . expressed the world's and man's decentering (especially the decentering of humanity's vision), man's isolation from the *deus absconditus*, as well as the endless expansion and reflection of forms and lines which could break down the barriers between illusion and reality.[13]

If "All is telling" this is because man lives by telling stories and hearing the stories of others. He defines himself by telling himself what he hopes will be the true and happy story of his own life. He creates his history and his identity by telling his own story to others.[14] He witnesses and is witnessed. Thus is created the infinite matrix of human language, history, narrative. If Eliot saw the writer's task as one of persuading men to look back in despair at the great story of the past, McCarthy surely agrees with Emily Dickinson that an *ignis fatuis* is better than no light at all. Or rather he asserts that "no light" or rather "no story" is not a possibility. Man lives by story. His critique of America lies in the fact that he sees the "great story" that America has told her people in the same way that Eduardo sees John Grady Cole's story; "What is wrong with this story is that it is not a true story."[15] John Grady's story is indeed an American story, the American pastoral and Western myth that McCarthy seeks to deconstruct as a destructive lie. McCarthy is fully aware of the inescapability of myth; he realizes that language is not able to completely and unambiguously signify the world. Edwin T. Arnold, a longtime admirer and a frequent contributor of critical articles on his texts is one of the few scholars to have seen McCarthy's unpublished screenplay *Whales and Men*. He quotes as follows:

> . . . . language is described by the character Peter Gregory as "a thing corrupted by its own success. What had begun as a system for identifying and organizing the phenomena of the world had become a system for replacing those phenomena. For replacing the world . . . Everything that is named is set at one remove from itself. . . . Language is a way of

containing the world. A thing named becomes that named thing. It is under surveillance."[16]

The notion of unmediated experience is particularly alluring to the western post-enlightenment mind. The Christian mystics claimed unmediated experience of the divine and McCarthy, himself the product of a Catholic upbringing and education, seems to have constructed for himself a secular version of this ideal. Arnold again:

> As Garry Wallace recalled of a conversation with McCarthy, ". . . he thinks the mystical experience is a direct apprehension of reality, unmediated by symbol, and he ended with the thought that our inability to see spiritual truth is the greater mystery."[17]

It is this unmediated apprehension of reality that Billy Parham seeks in his emulation of the wolf in *The Crossing*. That the ideal remains unrealizable is made plain by Billy's experience, the fate of his "doomed enterprise,"[18] shown by McCarthy to be an aspect of the seductive, but ultimately pernicious myth of the pastoral. It is entirely characteristic of McCarthy that he should use the language and imagery of a particular mythology in order to create his own counter-myth. This is the essence of his "mythoclastic" method. This recreation of myth is another aspect of McCarthy's relation to Eliot. It reflects an acknowledgement of the inescapability, indeed necessity, of myth as a foundational element of any cultural matrix. This is an aspect of our reading of culture that has developed progressively during the period in which McCarthy has been writing. Barthes published his *Mythologies* in 1957, two years before McCarthy wrote his student short story *Wake For Susan*. Barthes pointed out the function of myth in convincing us that the ideological is the natural.

> Myth does not deny things, on the contrary, its function is to talk about them; simply, it purifies them, it makes them innocent, it gives them a natural and eternal justification, it gives them a clarity which is not that of an explanation but that of a statement of fact.[19]

Graves' *The Greek Myths*, published two years earlier, had begun the work of emphasizing the contemporaneity of myth by "reading" classical mythology in terms of the political and economic history of the time from which it emerged. Both these texts had the effect of accentuating the political dimensions of myth as opposed to the psychological readings that had become increasingly influential since Freud and which had been recently exemplified in Joseph Campbell's 1949 *The Hero With A Thousand Faces*.

In 1973 Richard Slotkin gave myth an American face; *Regeneration Through Violence* was sub-titled *The Mythology of the American Frontier, 1600–1860*. He begins his analysis by asserting that through mythology the values of the past are transferred to a present in which they are no longer viable, with negative results. He relates this to the myth of American Exceptionalism.

> The mythology of a nation is the intelligible mask of that enigma called the "national character." Through myths the psychology and world view of our cultural ancestors are transmitted to modern descendants, in such a way and with such power that our perception of contemporary reality and our ability to function in the world are directly, and often tragically affected.
>
> American attitudes toward the idea of a national mythology have been peculiarly ambivalent. There is a strong anti-mythological stream in our culture, deriving from the utopian ideals of certain of the original colonists and of the revolutionary generation, which asserts that this New World is to be liberated from the dead hand of the past and become the scene of a new departure in human affairs.[20]

It is my purpose in this book to argue that McCarthy deliberately sets out to give his texts mythic form and that he does so in such a way as to point out the destructive consequences of structuring the consciousness of individuals by means of powerful mythologies which they are not in a position to live out. He also critiques the myth of Exceptionalism in its various forms: the "redeemer nation" of Puritan ideology; the democratic "last best hope for mankind" of the revolutionaries who created the Republic; the pioneer "civilizers of the wilderness"; imperialist America's "manifest destiny" to bring Christianity and capitalist vitality to "lesser races" under the aegis of the expanding nation; the provider of the "more abundant life" for Europe's "huddled masses, yearning to breathe free"; and the "champion of the free world" against the "evil empire of International Communism". Beneath all these forms of Exceptionalism lies the pastoral conception of the New Adam. A number of critics read McCarthy's texts as elegies for a lost American Eden. I shall attempt to refute these readings; although it is clear that McCarthy characterizes the modern world as a waste land in both the literal and metaphorical sense it is clear that he depicts both the rural past and the wilderness as anything but paradisal. McCarthy's protagonists are consistently led astray by their search for an Adamic identity. Richard Gray remarks that ". . . McCarthy has marked all of his work with an indelible sense, not so much of evil (although that is certainly there) as of homelessness."[21] Gray also points out the relevance to McCarthy of Heidegger's notion of "the *unheimlich*."[22] A number of critics mention this term as singularly appropriate to McCarthy's wanderers. In this respect they share the experience of the Old Adam, rather than the New, and McCarthy makes it clear that the paradise which they seek to regain never existed in the first place.

"The critique of the myth of American Exceptionalism" and "the dialectic of insignificance and vitality" are the twin themes that will structure my account of McCarthy's output as a whole; and I read his texts as essentially mythic in themselves. The principal characters that occupy, and in some cases narrate, his tales are for the most part depicted in non-realistic modes. They tend to have exaggerated or enlarged aspects to their personalities and to be engaged in activities that are shown as beyond realism. Both the stories and the characters of his fiction lie in the American tradition of the "tall tale". They are the fictional and mythic relatives of Mike Fink, the master of the Mississippi flatboats, of Paul Bunyan, the mighty axe-man of the northern forests, of Jim Doggett, slayer of T.B.Thorpe's *Big Bear of Arkansas*, or John Henry, the "steel driving man" who built the railroads. They are frequently engaged on a quest, an essentially mythic project of some kind. Not infrequently they take the form of the anti-hero, that most American of all mythic outsiders, the "dangerous man", epitomized by Henry Wells (the *Stackalee* of the folk-song that immortalized him) who was hanged for shooting dead one Billy Wells in a quarrel over a stetson hat, or the Harpe Brothers, terrorizers of the Natchez Trace, who feature in Eudora Welty's mythic, "unhistorical historical novel"[23] *The Robber Bridegroom*. In classic deconstructionist mode, McCarthy writes in mythic form in order to deconstruct American mythology.

It is my contention that the above themes are the most significant for an understanding of McCarthy's work. He consistently displays a wide range of other characteristics and preoccupations that have been the subject of critical writing from many other sources. He consistently declines to take the reader into the mind of a character, or to offer authorial comment on his characters' motivation.[24] As Rick Wallach remarks, McCarthy is, "a narrator [who] inhabits every aspect of a story except the consciousness of its characters."[25] This produces a sense of detachment on the part of the reader. It is in keeping with McCarthy's rejection of systems of knowledge that purport to "explain" the world. He makes frequent reference to the impossibility of so doing. Luis, the old servant of Don Hector, tells John Grady Cole that "the notion that men could be understood at all was probably an illusion,"[26] while judge Holden is more comprehensive in his expression of the limitations of human epistemologies:

> Even in this world more things exist without our knowledge than with it and the order in creation which you see is that which you have put there, like a string in a maze, so that you shall not lose your way. For existence has its own order and that no man's mind can compass, that mind being but a fact among others.[27]

McCarthy's own dictum, "All is telling," makes it clear that his faith is in narrative rather than analysis. He suggests that human beings take their understanding of the world from the cultural matrix formed by the limitless range of tales, and that, since all tales find a place in this matrix, "Rightly heard all tales are one."[28] The converse of this idea is expressed by the mysterious storyteller who philosophizes narrative to an uncomprehending Billy Parham: "Where all is known no narrative is possible."[29] This avoidance of internalization by McCarthy is consistent also with the mythic form of his fictions. Mythic characters do not exist to be repositories for psychological motivation. They are representative of large generalized ideas, values and aspects of culture. In this respect McCarthy's fiction follows the tradition of American Romance, of Melville and Hawthorne; neither realism nor naturalism is of particular relevance to McCarthy.

This refusal of internalization could lead to superficiality; McCarthy avoids this by allowing action and dialogue to express character and relationships whenever these are appropriate. This method is particularly effective given McCarthy's eidetic style, his ability to make the reader "see." Vereen Bell writes that McCarthy "has the rare gift of a style that is photorealistic in its precision and yet charismatically rich and suggestive."[30] Flannery O'Conner, who resembles McCarthy in her use of the Southern gothic style, acknowledged the same aspiration, and quoted Conrad as her inspiration: "My task, . . . is by the power of the written word, to make you hear, to make you feel—it is, before all—to make you see. That—and no more, and it is everything."[31] Beside dynamic and, often, extremely violent action, McCarthy deploys his vivid descriptive powers to "make you see" landscape. This is consistent with his deconstruction of American mythology; landscape has always been an integral part of exceptionalist imagery. The wilderness offered the intrepid white man, whether Puritan or pioneer, the escape to freedom and the opportunity for conquest. Manifest destiny was powered in part by a vision of the sublime as depicted by the Hudson River School, a tradition continued into the twentieth century by the photography of Ansel Adams. Neil Campbell writes,

> Early visual images of the West came from painters like those of the Hudson River School led by Thomas Cole (1801–48) whose work blended detailed landscapes with moral themes, juxtaposing harmonious pristine wilderness and settlement as in his *The Ox Bow* (1836), presenting America as an Eden of possibility.[32]

> . . . . the towering presence of Ansel Adams in the presentation of the West cannot be overlooked, for it is in his work that the picturesque tradition continued to define the landscape, even of the twentieth-century West, as pristine and wild.

> . . . . he represented an ideal, of sublime wilderness of transcendent, aesthetic monuments.[33]

Some idea of the power and visual intensity of McCarthy's deconstructive response to this mythology can be gained from this description of part of the scalphunters' journey to the Colorado River:

> On the day following they crossed the malpais afoot, leading the horses on a lakebed of lava all cracked and reddish black like a pan of dried blood, threading those badlands of dark amber glass like the remnants of some dim legion scrabbling up out of a land accursed, . . . They crossed a cinderland of caked slurry and volcanic ash imponderable as the burnedout floor of hell and they climbed up through a low range of barren granite hills . . . A gravel flat stretched away to the horizon. Far to the south beyond the black volcanic hills lay a lone albino ridge, sand or gypsum, like the back of some pale seabeast surfaced among the dark archipelagos.[34]

What we "see" so vividly here is the counter-mythic landscape of the American Waste Land.

What we "hear" in McCarthy is dialogue, depicted sparingly, its intensity heightened by the economy with which it is represented, an economy accentuated by the absence of conventional punctuation. The exchange between John Grady Cole and an unnamed rider is typical:

I was supposed to get married in two days' time, the boy said.

The rider nodded but the boy said no more.

I take it you changed your mind.

The boy didn't answer. The rider looked off to the north and then
looked back again.

We might get some rain out of that.

We might. It's rained over in town the last two nights.[35]

By omitting quotation-marks McCarthy elides the distinction between dialogue and the rest of the text. His characters' voices take their place without
distinction alongside that of the author. This increases the dialogic nature of
the text. The precise identity of the "voice" in McCarthy is often difficult to
determine, a characteristic that will be considered in more detail in the sections dealing with *The Orchard Keeper* and *Suttree*.

In the Southwestern novels McCarthy renders sections of dialogue in
Spanish. Often these begin in Spanish but are continued in English. This
is done in such a way as to persuade the reader that the whole section is in
Spanish. This technique resembles that used by Faulkner in *As I Lay Dying*, to
render the complex thoughts and feelings of simple characters in a language
they could not possess. The following passage is from the gypsy's story:

La tercera historia, said the gypsy, es ésta. Él existe en la historia de las
historias. Es que ultimadamente la verdad no puede quedar en ningún
otro lugar sino en el habla.[36] He held his hands before him and looked
at his palms. As if they may have been at some work not of his own
doing. The past, he said, is always this argument between counterclaim-
ants. Memories dim with age. There is no repository for our images. The
loved ones who visit us in our dreams are strangers.[37]

The line "He held his hands before him . . ." serves to return the text to the
English in which it is to continue. McCarthy obviously needs to keep his text
intelligible to a monolingual readership. He uses this Faulknerian technique
to make clear the multi-lingual nature of the culture within which his text is
located. This is an extension of his depiction of varying modes of speech in his
previous texts, which have featured the educated and the colloquial, and the
accents of the Tennessee mountains and the Texas plains and borderlands. This
Bakhtinian polyglossia is itself a refutation of the monocultural exceptionalist
myth of America, and makes clear that neither past nor present can be represented in purely "Anglo" terms. Writing of *The Crossing*, Jarrett notes that,

The novel's *heteroglossia* establishes McCarthy as a writer with a masterful control of a unique literary language that merges the dialects of the South and the languages of the Southwestern United States.[38]

Another aspect of McCarthy's feeling for language is revealed in his choice of significant names for some of his characters. In this he resembles Dickens, who could create a character that has entered English consciousness as representative of a particular attitude to the education of children who existed as a *name* only. Mr. M'Choakumchild says and does nothing in *Hard Times*. He is simply there and named. McCarthy's frequent use of significant names is exemplified in *Suttree*.[39] "Cornelius Suttree" has a double significance. Cornelius was a third century pope "whose reign was marked by controversy over the lapsed".[40] Cornelius's leniency led to banishment, martyrdom (possibly) and his adoption as the patron Saint of the apostate, the condition of Suttree himself, and, of course, McCarthy also.[41] "Suttree" relates to Sut Lovingood, the comic anti-hero of G.W.Harris's *Sut Lovingood's: Yarns Spun*. Harris wrote in the mode of the Southwestern Humorists and McCarthy's Gene Harrogate can be read as an updated version of Sut. Like McCarthy and Suttree, Harris was himself a resident of Knoxville and McCarthy is reputed to be both familiar with and fond of his work. Many other examples of this kind of naming exist and will be mentioned in sections dealing with individual texts.

Throughout his career McCarthy has shied away from publicity of all kinds. He has given only two newspaper interviews and has consistently declined to attend prize presentations, even when he was to receive substantial sums of money and was himself in constant want of funds. He refuses to talk to academics or to discuss his work in public. He has impressed upon his family and friends that they should not do so either. For this reason the interpretation of his work in the light of his personal biography is even more conjectural than is usually the case. It is tempting to say that we have the texts and that should be enough. However who would deny that Keats's lines,

> Now more than ever seems it rich to die,
> To cease upon the midnight with no pain,[42]

gain in emotional impact and poignancy when the reader is aware that the poet was dying of tuberculosis, and knew it, and was very aware of the course that the disease would take? In the introduction to the section on the Tennessee novels I shall suggest that there is a particularly plausible connection between McCarthy's childhood in the Knoxville area and his family circumstances, and the setting and themes of the four novels set in that part of the world. It is obvious also that the paths followed by his protagonists, westward from Tennessee, match those taken by McCarthy himself as he has moved from East Tennessee to El Paso, Texas. Other personal factors of evident significance for his fiction include his Irish descent and Catholic upbringing and schooling. McCarthy's depiction of man in an absurdist universe is the product of a consciousness that has lost its religious belief but retained a religious cast of mind. Mention has already been made of the ruined churches that occur so regularly in his works. I shall argue that *Outer Dark*[43] is a deconstruction of Southern Protestant fundamentalism. The rejection of Catholicism in *Suttree* is quite overt. But the consistent representation in his texts of the dialectic of vitality and insignificance does mark McCarthy as a religious writer in a Godless world. His existential position is inextricably bound up with his love of language, despite it limitations, and of narrative, and is expressed in the words, "Each man is the bard of his own existence. This is how he is joined to the world. For escaping from the world's dream of him this is at once his penalty and his reward."[44] For McCarthy's heroes "the world's dream" is the American dream, the dream that has grown out of the myth of American Exceptionalism; most are destroyed by it; one or two escape, but not unscathed.

There is a continuous theme of conflict between father and son in McCarthy's fiction. In my view it rises in intensity throughout the Tennessee texts, reaches a peak in *Blood Meridian*, and gradually declines in the Border Trilogy. One would expect the roots of such a preoccupation to lie within childhood and familial relationships. On that we have no information. However the Oedipal theme is inherent in patriarchal epistemology, particularly in modern societies where rites of passage into adulthood have been lost. Such a conflict need not be interpreted in strictly Freudian terms, since Freud was himself the product of a deeply patriarchal culture. Harold Bloom expresses a similar idea with reference to Shakespeare:

> I never meant by "the anxiety of influence" a Freudian Oedipal rivalry,
> . . . . . A Shakespearean reading of Freud, which I favor over a Freudian reading of Shakespeare or anyone else, reveals that Freud suffered from a Hamlet complex (the true name of the Oedipus Complex) or an anxiety of influence in regard to Shakespeare.[45]

If power and authority are of central significance within a culture and if they lie with the male, then conflict between father and son is an inherent cultural characteristic. I shall suggest that this conflict can be taken as a paradigm for the struggle of the young writer to establish himself in a literary world dominated by the great figures of the Southern literary past, including predominantly William Faulkner. Jarrett writes:

> The weak, dead, absent or denying fathers of McCarthy's fiction point toward an imaginative repudiation of the central importance of the father and family in Southern culture and the South's heroic myth of its history figured in the revered patriarch—Robert E. Lee or Colonel Sartoris—of the Confederate Lost Cause.[46]

Jarrett seems to disregard the less than flattering portrait of Colonel Sartoris at the end of *The Unvanquished* but does go on to point out the further significance of patriarchy as expressed in Allen Tate's *The Fathers*. My contention is that McCarthy's concerns are wider than the South alone and that he addresses American culture as a whole. In some respects he goes beyond this and expresses universal concerns.

That Western society remains strongly patriarchal in character I take as axiomatic. A number of feminist critics point out the absence of significant female characters in McCarthy's texts and draw attention to the unhappy fate of most of those who do appear. That this is so cannot be denied. For feminists this is a serious weakness in McCarthy's vision of the world. However, from the mythoclastic point of view, the absence of the female is consistent with McCarthy's critique of American culture; by definition the "Waste Land" lacks the female principle of fertility. The fact that he very frequently associates the female with water and thus with fertility and the essentials of life itself gives the female a special mythic significance in his texts. This absence of the female contrasts with Larry McMurtry's depictions of the West in novels such as *Lonesome Dove* and *Dead Man's Walk*. In these texts women are granted agency and are frequently portrayed in dominant roles. McMurtry writes with self-conscious irony and knowingly parodies the clichés of the mythic West. His fiction has an unmistakable air of pastiche that places his revision of American history as postmodern in ways that contrast sharply with McCarthy's heroic seriousness and mythoclastic extremes.[47]

McCarthy makes reference to "the heathen" in several texts. The attribution is both biblical and Shakespearean. The heathen are so called because, like Lear, they are "on the heath," lost to God and family alike. This is the fate of McCarthy's characters; it is his vision of man on the American heath;[48] by implication it is his vision of modern man everywhere.

Throughout my analysis of his texts I shall try to relate their themes and preoccupations to the history of McCarthy's times. Born in 1933, he has lived through a period in which America has moved from the economic catastrophe of the Great Depression to a position of unchallenged hegemony. I believe that McCarthy's works are marked by the major events and changes of that period. As will be clear from the above, I suggest that he portrays an America in which material progress has not been accompanied by a spiritual or moral counterpart, that Americans are still being influenced by a national myth that is chimerical, and that man remains what he has always been, a fearful and therefore violent wanderer on the earth, his only guide and comfort lying in his tales; his ultimate tragedy is that too often his tales prove false.

Such is the grandeur of much that McCarthy has written that the words of Octavio Paz seem appropriate:

> History has the cruel reality of a nightmare, and the grandeur of man consists in making beautiful and lasting works out of that nightmare. Or, to put it another way, it consists in transforming the nightmare into vision; in freeing ourselves from the shapeless horror of reality—if only for an instant—by means of creation.[49]

Jarrett's final comment suggests the same conclusion:

> . . . McCarthy's fiction expresses a belief—a highly qualified belief—in narrative as a replacement for the older verities of divine narrative. If knowledge of the darkness of the world and the self is a perilous knowledge, what knowledge we can have must be expressed in the form of narrative: "All is telling." Beyond their considerable range of language and style, McCarthy's narratives gain their power largely through this belief in narrative and narrative alone.[50]

While McCarthy's mastery of language and narrative must speak for itself, I shall attempt to make clear the manner in which that mastery is used to express McCarthy's critique of the mythology that informs American culture and his own personal and pessimistic view of the nature of humanity and our place in the universe. His texts stand as his own vital and ardenthearted defiance of our cosmic insignificance.

Chapter Two
Personal and Literary Biography

Market Street on Monday morning, Knoxville Tennessee

—Suttree

McCarthy was born in 1933 at Providence, Rhode Island, the third of six children, three girls and three boys. His family were Catholic, of Irish extraction. He was named after his father, Charles Joseph McCarthy; how significant this naming was must be a matter for conjecture given the father/son conflict that characterizes so much of McCarthy's fiction. Suffice it to say that the son later chose to be known as "Cormac," the Gaelic equivalent of 'son of Charles'. According to some sources this change was inspired by a visit to Blarney Castle in County Cork, reputedly built in the fifteenth century by the Irish king Cormac Láidir McCarthy, whom the young American regarded as an ancestor. Other accounts suggest that "Cormac" was a name with affectionate connotations used within the McCarthy family during his childhood. Both could, of course, be true, although the latter would reduce the personal psychological significance of the change. Since the search for identity is an aspect of his fiction, this change of name does carry some weight in interpreting McCarthy's texts in my opinion. It is notable how closely the personal and the literary are paralleled, in this as in other ways; both the fiction and the public persona[1] of McCarthy are designed to eschew "psychological" interpretations.

In 1937 his family moved to Knoxville, Tennessee where McCarthy Senior took up a position as an attorney with the Tennessee Valley Authority. Cormac attended the Catholic high school in Knoxville, graduating in 1951. Some idea of his youthful character and intelligence may be gathered from his remarks made during his 1992 interview with Woodward:

"I was not what they had in mind," McCarthy says of his childhood dis-
cord with his parents. "I felt early on I wasn't going to be a respectable
citizen. I hated school from the day I set foot in it." Pressed to explain
his sense of alienation, he has an odd moment of heated reflection. "I
remember in grammar school the teacher asked if anyone had any hobbies. I was the only one with any hobbies, and I had every hobby there
was. There was no hobby I didn't have, name anything, no matter how
esoteric, I had found it and dabbled in it. I could have given everyone a
hobby and still had 40 or 50 to take home."[2]

There seems little doubt that these are the symptoms of what we would now
identify as the kind of frustration that can be experienced by the exception-
ally "gifted" child, an analysis borne out by McCarthy's subsequent literary career. This is also consistent with his extraordinary literary eclecticism,
the evidence within his fiction of his seeming to have read and absorbed
everything. There is also an indication of familial conflict, which it is tempting to relate to the fiction in the sense mentioned above. Whole and loving
families are conspicuous by their absence from McCarthy's fiction. He has
himself been twice divorced. On leaving school McCarthy spent one year
at the Knoxville campus of the University of Tennessee, enrolled as a liberal
arts major. In 1953 he joined the USAF and served four years. According to
Arnold and Luce he spent "half of that time stationed in Alaska where he
hosted a radio show."[3] On his return he re-enrolled at the University of Tennessee, which he attended from 1957 to 1960. He left the University without
graduating. However his subsequent literary achievements have resulted in
him featuring in the list of distinguished alumni, a fact marked by a plaque
in the University library. In fact his university career was not entirely without
distinction. His two short stories, *Wake For Susan* (1959) and *A Drowning
Incident* (1960)[4] were both published in The Phoenix, the literary supplement of Orange and White, the University magazine; for the first he was
listed as C. J. McCarthy Jnr. and for the second as plain C. J. McCarthy.
It was doubtless as a result of these that he was awarded the Ingram-Merrill
Award for creative writing in both years. Other prizes and awards were to
follow.

In 1961 McCarthy married fellow student Lee Holleman and they had
a son, Cullen. They divorced in 1964. Lee McCarthy has published a book
of her own poetry, *Desire's Door*, and some passages reflect the pain of a less
than successful relationship:

> It is snowing in El Paso where his father lives whose teeth
> are healthy but everything else has hit the rocks, gone on the
> skids. I hope it's a regular blizzard, that his teeth chatter.[5]

Others bear a distinct relation to her former husband's life and fiction:

> My son was named by his father. But his life shall re-name him a thou-
>   sand times.[6]
> My son, at an early age, learned how to ride a horse.
> My son, at an early age, heard the thunder of his own heart.
> My son's name was Siege.[7]

She uses an image from *The Orchard Keeper* to express her feelings about her own body:

> This body you see is not a museum. It's a shrine,
> a halfway house, a gazebo perched on the side of a cliff.[8]

This surely relates to the Green Fly Inn.

It is generally thought that McCarthy has declined the security of paid employment more or less throughout his career. However, according to Jarrett, McCarthy and his wife lived in New Orleans and Chicago for spells, where he had a series of odd jobs, "and wrote his first novel."[9] *The Orchard Keeper* was published in 1965 by Random House; McCarthy's editor there being Albert Erskine, who had performed the same function for Faulkner. As a consequence he was awarded a $5,000 fellowship by the American Academy of Arts and Letters, the William Faulkner Foundation Award for 1965 and a grant in 1966 from the Rockefeller Foundation. This reflected the novel's critical reception rather than its sales. McCarthy used this money to finance a trip to Europe, during which he made the aforementioned visit to Ireland. On the boat he met Annie DeLisle and they were married in England in 1967. The European trip lasted until December 1967. During this period *Outer Dark* was completed and it was published in 1968.

On their return to the United States the McCarthy's lived in modest circumstances, first in Rockford, near Knoxville and later in a converted barn in nearby Louisville, to which McCarthy added an additional room and stone chimney. These he built himself, using stones from the fields nearby and also bricks from a ruined house that had once been owned by James Agee. The relevance of this experience to *The Stonemason* is apparent from any reading of the play. It is also a practical metaphor for the intertextuality that McCarthy practiced so assiduously in creating his texts. Jarrett quotes Annie DeLisle in a manner that throws a little more light on McCarthy's character:

> [he] was such a rebel that he didn't live the kind of life anybody on earth lived.

> He knew everything that there was to do in life . . . We never had any money. We were always scrimping and scraping. He couldn't have had children, it would have driven him crazy.[10]

While the testimony of an abandoned spouse is not necessarily the most objective guide to a given personality, most of the little that we do know about McCarthy appears to support the view of him as a non-conformist who is unlikely to have been much influenced by the American Dream of materialistic success and the happy family, at least in his early life; this aspect of his persona appears to have undergone a change in his seventh decade. His avoidance of publicity regarding his work indicates that he also fears the fate of Hemingway's Robert Cohn, who "fell among literary people."[11] Despite the strong critique of American myth that runs through his work, McCarthy is quintessentially American in two ways. He is an individualist on a heroic scale and he believes in the possibility of moving on to reinvent the self. This belief is expressed by his own actions and also by those of certain of his fictional characters. The structure and outcome of *The Orchard Keeper* indicate that John Wesley Rattner has achieved this reinvention by "moving on". It is the theme of *Suttree*; the eponymous anti-hero comes at the last to realize that the possibility exists for him. Other characters fail in their attempted self-reinvention. Lester Ballard, John Grady Cole and Billy Parham all discover that their attempt is doomed. McCarthy presents this as a failure of American mythology. His young men's lives have been shaped by an American story but the real world of America denies them the opportunity to make the story true.

Despite his reluctance to talk about his writing it is obvious that he takes it profoundly seriously. His detailed descriptions of the painstaking perfectionism of conscientious craftsmen are metaphors for his own attitude to his craft, an attitude that is revealed in the reading of his texts.[12]

McCarthy was awarded another Guggenheim fellowship in 1969. When this money ran out he made ends meet by doing odd jobs while he worked on *Child of God*,[13] which was published in 1973. It is characteristic of McCarthy that he takes a long time to produce a novel. The pecuniary rewards were still not great. Jarrett records that "none of his Southern fiction would sell more than 2,500 copies in hardcover for Random House while Ecco Press's paperback reprints of 1984 would sell only 3000 to 5000 copies per novel."[14]

Throughout this period McCarthy attracted attention from professional critics. Not all of it was complimentary. The "New Criticism," although old by now, still had its devotees who were troubled by McCarthy's unconventional style. The most conservative among them failed to discern the essentially mythic nature of his work and felt that his subject matter was morally repugnant; it certainly did not present to the world a portrait of the South that they wished to acknowledge. Arnold and Luce quote a typical example of this type of critical response, written by Richard Brickner and relating to *Child of God*:

> [T]he carefully cold, sour diction of this book—whose hostility towards the reader surpasses even that of the world towards Lester [Ballard]—does not often let us see beyond its nasty 'writing' into moments we can see for themselves, rendered. And such moments, authentic though they feel, do not much help a novel so lacking in human momentum or point.[15]

Others were more perceptive: Jonathon Yardley wrote,

> McCarthy is perhaps the closest we have to a genuine heir to the Faulkner tradition. Yet he is not merely a skilled imitator. His novels have a stark, mythic quality that is very much their own . . . The sordid material of Lester Ballard's tale becomes more than an exercise in southern grotesque because of McCarthy's artistry. . . . *Child of God* is an extraordinary book.[16]

McCarthy's next project to reach completion was the screenplay for the TV drama *The Gardener's Son*.[17] This was undertaken in cooperation with the director, Richard Pearce, and the completed program was broadcast in January 1977. By this time McCarthy had left Annie DeLisle and Tennessee also. He moved to El Paso, Texas, and has lived there ever since. The couple were divorced a year or so later. Jarrett comments,

> Viewed in retrospect, McCarthy's move to the Southwest in early 1977 represents a sudden break with his past, including his family, wife, and career in Southern fiction.[18]

How complete this break with "Southern fiction" has been is a matter for debate. Perhaps it is associated with the question of how far "the Southwest" is distinct from "the South". The last of the Tennessee novels, *Suttree*, was published in 1979. It is reputed to have taken twenty years to write. It is also reputed to be McCarthy's most autobiographical text. Critical opinion remained divided, with some Knoxville locals being less than flattered by the portrait of their city. As usual they were interpreting the text in realist rather than mythic terms. It may be however that Knoxville's citizens were stung by the fact that they did indeed recognize the world that McCarthy had portrayed. The Appalachian region was one of the last to enjoy the rise in fortunes that occurred in America as it recovered form the Great Depression. Richard Marius, a young contemporary of McCarthy's, recalls Knoxville thus:

> It was a hand-to-mouth world where life for most was like the state of nature described by Thomas Hobbes—solitary, nasty, brutish and short.[19]

Other, more influential voices were raised in support of McCarthy; Shelby Foote and Saul Bellow both supported the award of a MacArthur fellowship in 1981. Worth $260,000 this financed the extensive research that McCarthy undertook in preparation for the writing of *Blood Meridian*, which was published in 1985. Critical opinion remained divided; Jarrett writes that Walter Sullivan "dismisses the novel as 'a single-minded celebration of rapine and slaughter, relieved only by a faint-hearted thrust at philosophy.'"[20] But other views were becoming more influential and *Blood Meridian* has become established as one of McCarthy's finest achievements, many would say *the* finest. Tom Nolan's comments, quoted by Arnold and Luce, are surely more illuminating than Sullivan's: he declared it "a theological purgative, an allegory of the nature of evil as timeless as Goya's hallucinations on war, monomaniacal in its conceptions and execution"[21] The reference to Goya is well chosen, since *Blood Meridian* is the first of McCarthy's texts to acknowledge the Spanish (and Mexican) influence in American culture.

From the point of view of the academic critic 1988 was a significant year for McCarthy since it saw the publication of Vereen Bell's *The Achievement of Cormac McCarthy*, published by Louisiana State University Press, and devoted to an analysis and evaluation of all the novels published to that date. Bell's stature as a respected Southern literary academic suggested that the world should take McCarthy seriously. For many writers, the serious attention and approval of such as Bell would have meant as much as the later commercial success; one suspects that McCarthy cared little for either. According to Woodward,

McCarthy would rather talk about rattlesnakes, molecular computers, country music, Wittgenstein—anything—than himself or his books. "Of all the subjects I'm interested in, it would be extremely difficult to find one I wasn't," he growls. "Writing is way, way down at the bottom of the list."

His hostility to the academic world seems both genuine ("teaching writing is a hustle") and a tactic to screen out distractions. At the McArthur reunions he spends his time with scientists, like the physicist Murray Gell-Mann and the whale biologist Roger Payne, rather than other writers. One of the few he acknowledges to have known at all was the novelist and ecological crusader Edward Abbey. Shortly before Abbey's death in 1989, they discussed a covert operation to reintroduce the wolf to southern Arizona.[22]

Bell initiated or formalized various critical debates regarding McCarthy's texts. Perhaps the most significant of these were McCarthy's relation to Faulkner, the reference in his work to the lost Southern pastoral and the question of the moral position implicit in the texts—the question of McCarthy's "nihilism." I shall expand on each of these in later sections of this book, arguing that the Faulkner influence can be exaggerated and does diminish, that the lost Southern past to which McCarthy refers was anything but Edenic and that his mythoclasm is "anti-pastoral", and that although McCarthy's concerns are not primarily moral at all, he does present in his fiction a vision of the good, albeit limited in both scale and efficacy.

Mention has already been made of the change in McCarthy's material fortunes that occurred with the publication of *All the Pretty Horses* in 1992. This success coincides with a change in the atmosphere of his work. However, given the intensity and radical nature of *Blood Meridian*, its combination of violence and philosophical metaphor, it is perhaps unlikely that he could have been expected to continue to write at quite that pitch or to produce works of such extreme singularity. There is a sense that, with the writing of this first Southwestern novel, McCarthy resolves some personal crisis, the precise nature of which can only be a matter of speculation. I shall attempt the speculation when I deal with the text in detail in Chapter 11. That McCarthy perhaps recognized within himself a self-destructive impulse which he was able to bring under control is suggested by his decision to stop drinking, since by that time many of his friends from the Knoxville days were dead and "The friends I do have are simply those who quit drinking."[23]

All the Pretty Horses sold 180,000 copies in hardback and 300,000 in paperback in two years. Reviews reflected this commercial success. Academic opinion, perhaps influenced by a suspicion of popularity, but also wrong-footed by the text's change of style, was less impressed and there has remained a view among certain sections of the academy that The Border Trilogy is a lesser body of work than the texts that preceded it. I do not share this view; to my mind these most recent texts comprise a remarkable extension of the range and depth of McCarthy's work and are a logical and indeed necessary development of his mythoclasm. No challenge to American Exceptionalist mythology would be complete without a deconstruction of the related myths of the frontier, the West and the cowboy. This new departure also gives McCarthy the opportunity to bring his analysis up to date and to address the most contemporary aspects of American culture, both political and intellectual, in a way that is quite outside the scope of the Tennessee works. In taking the road west McCarthy follows a historical thread that leads from Oak Ridge, site of the uranium processing plant powered by TVA generated electricity for the Manhattan Project, and a mere twenty miles from Knoxville,[24] to Alamagordo and the first atomic bomb test in *The Crossing*; and, in *Cities of the Plain*, the military requisition of dying range-land for the siting of nuclear missiles. In *The Crossing*, McCarthy makes plain his engagement with what David Holloway refers to as "the ideology of representation."[25] This engagement is metaphorical in *Blood Meridian* but much more overt in *The Crossing*.

Blood Meridian had been dedicated to Albert Erskine, who retired at about this time. McCarthy's new editor was Gary Fisketjon at Knopf; he also acquired a literary agent for the first time. It should not be thought that these changes account for the success of *All the Pretty Horses*, but they doubtless helped to maximize the commercial consequences of the book's appeal. This success has not been repeated by all the subsequent novels, although academic opinion has remained positive and *No Country for Old Men* has sold well.[26] McCarthy himself suggested to one acquaintance that the change in atmosphere in his later works was due to the fact that he had been working on a film-script and that this had resulted in certain changes in the way he wrote. This particular script in fact became the third part of the trilogy. However any reading of the three novels in sequence makes it quite clear that they were conceived as a unified whole, even though they are in fact very different in some ways. These texts also reflect the fact that the mythology on which they are founded and which they problematize was lodged in the American consciousness largely by the cinema and the western movie genre.

In 1991 McCarthy was one of seven writers to receive a grant from the American Express/John F. Kennedy Center Fund for New American Plays.

The result was *The Stonemason*,[27] published in 1994. The attempt to stage the play in New York proved unsuccessful. Some of those concerned considered it to be impracticable from a number of technical points of view. A group of African-American women members of the company expressed opposition to the project on the grounds of racism and sexism. McCarthy found the pressures of working in this environment difficult to accommodate—principally because technical modifications involved him in rewriting and he found it very difficult to write at the pace required in a working theatre. For whatever reason the attempt to stage the play foundered and has not been repeated to date.[28] The charge of racism is not substantiated in my view. Ironically McCarthy wished to show a black family as representative of America; his critics had not heard of him previously and were shocked to discover that he was not a young black man. They felt that the play portrayed African-Americans in a negative light and that the theatre should not be engaged in work of this kind. Anyone who had read *Suttree* would know that McCarthy was anything but racist. Certainly Papaw Telfair represents McCarthy's personification of an ideal, the craftsman of absolute integrity. The accusation of sexism has been mentioned previously; in my view its validity depends on whether or not one interprets McCarthy's work in mythic terms. Peter Josyph, himself a writer and actor, suggests that the play was not performed because it is technically impossible. Josyph admires the novels: "That Cormac McCarthy's first published play, *The Stonemason*, is a failure places him even more securely in the tradition of great novelists."[29] McCarthy's literary output to date has been completed by the publication of *The Crossing* in 1994, *Cities of the Plain* in 1998 and *No Country for Old Men* in 2005. The appearance of these novels has coincided with a growing number of critical writings of many kinds, of which this book aspires to become a small part. This scholarly recognition has been accompanied by other changes in McCarthy's circumstances. He has married for a third time and the couple have a son; he has a comfortable domestic establishment and, as an older man might, seems prepared to enjoy the security that commercial success has brought him.[30] He has a position as a 'writer in residence' at the Santa Fe Institute; whatever this position might involve it seems that McCarthy is at last able to pursue his extraordinarily wide-ranging interests among like-minded people, free of the limitations of self-imposed living hand-to-mouth.

The purpose of this outline has been to relate the publication of his texts to the bare outline of McCarthy's life. That such a man can be known in any truly enlightening way is clearly a false hope. However, as McCarthy himself would be the first to admit, we are unable to avoid the attempt, even though he wishes to deprive us of the material with which to accomplish the task. After all—"All is telling." In my view the works of Cormac McCarthy reflect the personality of a man who, although short of money, would refuse offers of $2,000 to speak at universities and who sent his publisher to the banquet at which the National Book Award was presented.

Chapter Three
Tennessee Background

East of Knoxville Tennessee the mountains start.

—The Orchard Keeper

"Man, it seems to me, is not *in* history: he is history."[1] The words of Octavio Paz express in a radical form the notion that personal and cultural identity exist in a dialectical relation to history. We are formed by history, and what we understand as history is formed by us. This dialectical relationship between the present and the past implies a degree of radical uncertainty about the relation between the culture of any given moment and the truth of what occurred in the past; and this is, of course, an aspect of the postmodern vision of the relation between culture and reality. It is also one of the strands that McCarthy weaves into his texts. It occurs in his very first published story, *Wake For Susan*. It is expressed by the Mexican Captain of police in *All the Pretty Horses*:

> We can make the truth here. Or we can lose it. But when you leave here
> it will be too late. Too late for truth. Then you will be in the hands of
> other parties. Who can say what the truth will be then?[2]

It is an essential theme of *The Crossing*. This uncertainty about the past, and thus about the present also, helps to account for the existence of that cultural space into which myth insinuates itself, like a hermit crab into an empty shell. The irony is that it is the crab that is alive. It is myth that energizes a culture, for good or ill. Paz concludes his essay "The Philanthropic Ogre" with the words,

> . . . before undertaking the criticism of our societies, their history and
> their actuality, we Hispanic American writers must begin by criticizing

ourselves. First, we must cure ourselves of the intoxication of simplistic and simplifying ideologies.[3]

In my view McCarthy pursues this aim. His texts are full of denials of the explicative powers of systems of thought, and criticisms of utopian gnosticism. These systems are often present in mythic mode and thus McCarthy's critique of American culture assumes a mythoclastic form. But of course he cannot assume a position that is detached from that culture; his critique has to come from within. Both myth and anti-myth exist within narrative and it is the creation of these deconstructionist narratives that is McCarthy's purpose and achievement.

It is therefore necessary to locate McCarthy within a version of the history of his own time and place. Given what I have said above it is perhaps only proper that I should first address certain aspects of my own point of view. I have tried to come to terms with the implications of the newness of the "New World". In my view the British have difficulty in appreciating the relatively short period that is encompassed by the history of the white man in America. We think of British history as existing in one form or another for well over two thousand years. The idea that we "began" in the 17th century would seem absurd. This is the beginning of "the modern period" of history, not of history itself. For the Americans the reverse is true. Even Spanish America can go back only to the late 15th century. For much of America "history" begins even later. The United States in its present continental form only came into complete existence in the 19th century and even during that period large areas remained uninhabited desert or semi-inhabited wilderness.[4] The "completion" of the nation was brought about by conquest, expropriation and racially motivated genocide. Within the boundaries of what was, or became, the United States, there occurred during the 19th century the Mexican War, the Civil War and the Indian Wars. The contrast with events in mainland Britain could hardly be more marked.[5] A central aspect of this difference, at least from the point of view of McCarthy's fiction, is the level of violence involved. My own values have been formed largely by the humanitarian left-wing thinking that arose partly out of the experience of the working class during the 1930s, and which received its most overt expression in the election of the Labour government of 1945, the creation of the post-war settlement and setting up of the welfare state. That this set of values was as much a product of Christian ideology as of Marxism helps to explain the particular resonance that exists for so many in McCarthy's texts. I have already argued that McCarthy remains a religious writer in a Godless world. He deploys very effectively that religious language which formed a central, if implicit, part of the education of my generation and which Flannery O'Connor refers to in her essay *The Catholic Novelist in the Protestant South*:

> Unfortunately, where you find Catholics reading the Bible, you usually find that it is the pursuit of the educated, but in the South the Bible is known by the ignorant as well, and it is always that mythos that the poor hold in common that is most valuable to the fiction writer.
>
> When the poor hold sacred history in common, they have ties to the universal and holy, which allows the meaning of their every action to be heightened and seen under the aspect of eternity. The writer who views the world in this light will be very thankful if he has been fortunate enough to have the South for his background, because here belief can still be made believable, even if for the modern mind it can not be made admirable.[6]

McCarthy attacks the Southern Protestant ability to "allow the meaning of their every action to be seen under the aspect of eternity", especially in *Outer Dark*. Unlike O'Connor he does not adhere to the "faith of his fathers;" he reverses the process that she describes—implying that belief cannot still be made believable and that, on the contrary, in an absurdist world, it is unbelief that is admirable. This locates McCarthy in an intellectual universe that I recognize and which I believe many now share. However, there are other aspects of McCarthy that are a challenge to the culture that I inhabit. The most obvious of these is his "Hobbesian" view of the essential savagery of mankind. It is in this respect that one becomes most acutely aware of the difference between the British and American experiences of "modern history." Of course it can be persuasively argued that the American experience is much closer to that shared by most of the rest of the world, Continental Europe included, and that English humanitarianism is a product of an atypical history, or even of historical myopia. My difficulty in this respect is greatly moderated by my disinclination to read McCarthy in any but mythic terms. Once the implications of realism and naturalism can be discounted from the interpretation of his texts, their violence takes on a different set of meanings, particularly when read as an anti-mythology. Read in realist terms *The Metamorphoses* of Ovid would constitute a superstitious catalogue of murder, rape, incest, violence and degradation. Both their form, content and cultural tradition make it clear that to do so would be grossly inappropriate. It is an understanding of myth that makes their nature and meaning clear. In my view the same is true of McCarthy.

The other aspect of America which the British find hard to fully appreciate is its sheer scale. The Continental United States is approximately 2,700 miles wide from East to West (at its greatest) and 1,600 miles from North to South. It has an area of 3,718,000 square miles. This makes it about 83 times the size of England. McCarthy's "home state" of Tennessee itself has an area equal to that of England. The literary implications of this need to be taken into account when thinking about American fiction, much of which reflects a concern with the relationship between national and regional identity. This has been of particular concern in the South for obvious historical reasons. In my view it has powerful geographical reasons also and sheer size is one of the most significant. It is for this reason of scale that so much American writing is regional rather than national. Mention has already been made of the likes of G.W.Harris and T.B.Thorpe, both so called "local colour" writers and "Southwestern Humorists" and both creators of the tradition that informed McCarthy. Flannery O'Connor never had the slightest hesitation in considering herself "Southern"; indeed, as we have seen above, she regarded it as a distinct advantage in important ways. The writers of the American Renaissance tended to be associated with New England although Melville and Whitman strove to address the wider nation in overt terms. Even Faulkner, while concerned with universal themes such as the dialectic between past and present that I mentioned at the beginning of this chapter, was quintessentially Southern, not to say Mississippian, and wrote of the South in order to wrest it from its twin mythologies of race and "the lost cause". The new generation of American writers, Doris Betts, Harry Crews, Rick Bass, Frederick Barthelme, Joan Didion, McCarthy himself, either retain unmistakable regional identities or, in an attempt to shake off the limitations of one region, migrate, in fictional terms, to another.[7] Crews remains indelibly southern; Betts, Bartheleme and McCarthy go West. Didion ranges far and wide but remains a Californian. Bass heads for the hills, to inhabit the region "American Wilderness". It is appropriate and indeed, if my argument is valid, inevitable, that this should be so. For surely the overriding task of American culture is to create, at least in terms of some adequate minimum, "One Nation" from the enormous diversity and scale of its land and people, to literally make a "United States" of America. That this task falls to a culture that would regard itself as being little more than 200 years old, in my view helps to explain the continued regionalism of American literature.[8]

The myth of American Exceptionalism is one of those aspects of its culture that has been propagated to provide a common sense of identity for Americans. Perry Miller has made clear the extent to which this aspect of American ideology is rooted in the beliefs and literature of the Puritan colonists of the 17th century and in their theological notion of the Redeemer Nation. In texts such as *The American Puritans: Their Prose and Poetry* and *Errand Into the Wilderness*, Miller traces in the writings and preaching of Hooker, the Mathers, et al the origins of the belief that America is to be a place in which the world can be made anew, as an example for the rest of humanity. Sacvan Bercovitch presents the Puritans as the founders of American identity, an idea inherent in the title of his 1975 text, *The Puritan Origins of the American Self*. McCarthy makes clear both the decidedly unredemptive nature of much of American history and also the extent to which Bercovitch's thesis is unduly racially restrictive, suggesting as it does that "American" is indeed synonymous with "White Anglo-Saxon Protestant."[9] Winthrop's words, "For we must consider that we shall be as a city upon a hill, the eyes of all people are upon us,"[10] have taken their place in the rhetoric of America, to be brought out by national politicians whenever it is felt advantageous to reassure Americans that they are still irrefutably "exceptional". Bercovitch and Perry Miller both argue that Exceptionalism and the Puritan notion of Divine Providence have resulted in a reading of American history that sees the success of various national projects, particularly that of expansion, as being divinely sanctioned, indeed Providential. The idea of the Redeemer Nation has also been associated by these writers with the notion of America as the place where the individual may embark on the process of self-redemption, of the remaking of the individual and his fortunes by his own effort in a world that places no artificial barriers of birth or privilege in his path. All of these notions McCarthy challenges in his various texts.

In *American Exceptionalism*, Deborah Madsen analyses the manner in which the myth of Exceptionalism has evolved to form an ideological underpinning for successive American national projects. The Revolutionaries portrayed America as the "Last best hope of mankind", the model nation which would represent to the world the unmistakable benefits of republican government and democratic institutions, the model which all would then choose to follow. The Exceptionalist vision is expressed in the icon of the Statue of Liberty and the accompanying text, addressed to the "huddled masses yearning to be free." Once again America was to offer the common man the opportunity that Europe could not. McCarthy portrays the outcome for those who came fleeing destitution in Russia or Ireland only to find it duplicated in the isolated hamlets of the Appalachian Mountains.

I have already indicated that both McCarthy's life and his literary output can be reasonably divided into two sections—that related to Tennessee, and the later Southwestern period. The majority of critics appear to regard historical background as of greater consequence for the latter texts than the former.[11] This is, I think, because *Blood Meridian* is set in the mid-nineteenth century, a moment of the greatest significance for the American nation, or at least for its mythology. In my view it is a mistake to underestimate the importance of Tennessee and its history for McCarthy and his fiction. I would suggest that the formative influence of his childhood experiences are, if anything, even more important than is the history of the Southwest. If this is a truism, it is one that seems to have been ignored by many of those who have engaged with McCarthy's work.

Since "Geography is the mother of History," and given the importance of landscape to McCarthy, it is necessary to consider both these aspects of his Tennessee background. The State of Tennessee occupies an area approximately the size of England, a fact that I mentioned previously in connection with what I consider the inescapable regionalism of American fiction. It is located to the west of the Appalachian Mountains and is bounded by the crest of that range, the Great Smoky Mountains, in the east and by the Mississippi River in the west. Its northern and southern boundaries are, largely, the northerly lines of latitude 36.5 and 35 degrees approximately. These boundaries perfectly express the manner in which American history has involved the imposition of abstract Enlightenment notions of order on natural landscape. To east and west are great natural barriers that it took centuries to overcome; to north and south "lines" that exist in theory alone.[12] These boundaries also mark Tennessee out as a border state in two distinct senses, and this geography is indelibly inscribed in the state's history. The Appalachians were the barrier to western expansion for the first 200 years of white settlement in America. They formed the natural boundary for the Thirteen Colonies. Crossing them involved a combination of heroic endeavor and determined extirpation of the Native Americans. This process was delayed, in both senses, by the British who found the consequent Indian Wars a drain on resources already stretched by conflict with the French. One of the motivations for the American Revolution was the desire to cross the Proclamation Line and "open up" the West. This process was accelerated by the success of the Revolution and resulted in the expansion westward of the state of North Carolina. It was this process that brought into existence the State of Tennessee. The part played in this process by North Carolina politicians such as Blount and Sevier is marked by the naming of counties after these two, whose maneuverings resulted in their own personal enrichment through the acquisition and profitable resale of the public lands. Sevier County is the location of much of *The Orchard Keeper* and *Child of God*. Lester Ballard "crossed the mountain into Blount County one Sunday morning in the early part of February."[13] The territory west of the Great Smokies was ceded to the Federal Government in order that North Carolinians, like Colonial Americans before them, should be able to pass on to the Government the cost of the Indian Wars that the expansion had provoked. The creation of the State of Tennessee in 1796 was a consequence of this. At this time the Mississippi River was both a north-south highway for the flatboats from Ohio and Kentucky down to New Orleans and a barrier to further westward expansion. The great river thus doubled the "border" aspect of Tennessee's relation between east and west.

By the time of the Civil War the State's position in relation to North and South became of greater significance. In this respect also Geography had a profound formative influence. The mountainous nature of the eastern part of the state meant that neither its climate nor its terrain were suitable for plantation agriculture. Consequently slavery was virtually unknown in the East and blacks made up a low proportion of the population. This accounts for the absence of the theme of race from McCarthy's Tennessee fiction,[14] already mentioned as one of the features that distinguishes him from Faulkner and indeed much other Southern writing. Mary Dorthula White relates the same notion in Mildred Haun's *The Hawk's Done Gone*: ". . . I never have seed a Negro. But I've heard tell of them. Ad sees them sometimes when he goes to Newport."[15] In the Mississippi plain of the western part of the state the situation was precisely the reverse. Thus Tennessee was a divided State in 1860. It seceded only after Lincoln's call for volunteers. It sent regiments to fight for both sides (as did every Southern State except South Carolina). Of those who did fight for the South there were perhaps many who came to share the disillusion expressed by Sam Watkins, who "enlisted in Company H of the First Tennessee Regiment in 1861 and fought at Shiloh, Murfreesboro, Chickamauga and Atlanta. . . . He was one of only seven who survived."[16] In 1882 he published his memoir of the War, quoting the common soldier's belated recognition of an ideology that excluded his interest, "rich man's war, poor man's fight."[17] He records that at Corinth,

> Our troops were in no condition to fight. In fact, they had seen enough
> of this miserable yet tragic farce. They were ready to ring down the cur-
> tain, put out the footlights and go home. They loved the Union any-
> how, and were always opposed to this war.[18]

The men of East Tennessee remained resolutely for the Union. The Tennessean Andrew Johnson maintained that secession was illegal throughout. He became Lincoln's Vice-President in 1864, succeeded him on the assassination and presided over Radical Reconstruction.

The Unionist and Republican loyalties of East Tennessee are clearly portrayed by Mary Noailles Murfree[19] in her stories set in that region. Although Murfree's tales tend to present a romanticized view of the life and people of the mountains she does at times capture the ambivalence that is so characteristic of a State that finds it difficult to know quite how it should locate itself in American life. In *The Bushwhackers* Hillary Knox joins the Southern Army despite the fact that "the majority of the mountaineers of East Tennessee were for the Union."[20] Hillary makes his choice not on the basis of personal conviction or family loyalty but because he is dazzled by the uniform, the dash and color of the Cavalry. "His heart kept pace with the hoofbeats of the horses."[21] It is characteristic of Murfree's ideological stance that the young man comes to see the war as morally confusing and to believe that it had no ideological context. It proves not even to be a valid context for personal heroism. Murfree's portrait of the mountaineers is idealized especially when compared with that depicted by McCarthy. However she does indicate both the backwardness and violence of the region in tales such as *The Panther of Jolton's Ridge*,[22] which features the conflict between moonshiners and the Baptist Minister who preaches against whisky and has his church burned about his ears.[23] There is death and darkness in this story as well as an indication of the conflict between the old ways of the mountain folk and the new world that is being brought in by the railroad. Despite her tendency to romanticize the mountains and their inhabitants Murfree's fiction is both serious and in touch with some of the intellectual currents of her age. *The Prophet of the Great Smoky Mountains* is not only a portrait of a typical self-proclaimed backwoods religious enthusiast but also a powerful representation of the religious doubt that haunted the 19th century consciousness. Pa'son Kelsey expresses the paradox in memorably paradoxical fashion:

> 'I hev los' my faith!' he cried out, with a poignant despair. 'God ez gin it—ef thar is a God—hev tuk it away. You-uns kin go on. You-uns kin b'lieve. Yer paster believes, an' he'll lead yer tey grace,—leastwise ter a better life. But fur me thar's the nethermost depths of hell, ef'—how his faith and his unfaith tried him!—'ef thar be enny hell. . . .;' nothing like this had ever been heard in all the length and breadth of the Great Smoky Mountains, ...[24]

In this text, published in 1885, one senses that the voices of Nietzsche and
Darwin are being heard in the Great Smokies, albeit faintly. They are much
more clearly distinguishable in the works of Murfree's heir, if McCarthy can
be so regarded.[25] The world she portrays seems quite recognizable in *Outer
Dark*. Although Murfree cannot be regarded as a major literary figure she has
some significance in that she does write of a people who previously had not
received serious literary treatment. The only writers to feature them at all had
been the humorists such as G.W.Harris. Murfree does incorporate the dialect of the mountain people in her texts but like the humorists she "frames"
their speech with formal, educated language which has the effect of patron-
izing her erstwhile subjects. She is a "local colour" writer who exemplifies
the 19th Century literary ideal of providing a morally improving and uplift-
ing tone to her work, the tendency against which the realists and naturalists
reacted. Despite her weaknesses however Murfree does occupy a place among
the very small band of writers who preceded McCarthy in writing about this
particular part of the world, and she is, I think, the first to do so seriously.
There are a good many distinguished Tennessee writers but few venture "East
of Knoxville."

A single exception is the little known Mildred Haun, herself a mountain woman, a native of Cocke County, Tennessee, and an inheritor of the
tradition of the "Granny Woman" whose role it was to act as midwife to the
community and to dispense the traditional remedies of a culture that was
rooted in pre-enlightenment epistemology and continued to feature superstition, isolation, illiteracy and the blood feud. Haun determined to bring
modern medicine to her isolated world. She pursued her education, attended
Vanderbilt, and discovered that her talents were literary rather than scientific.
Encouraged by Donald Davidson she turned to writing, became a journalist,
collected folk songs and worked in the information section of the Depart-
ment of Agriculture, at that time a part of the New Deal. From 1940 to
1968 she wrote a series of stories expressive of the traditional culture of the
mountain communities. These were published as a single volume under the
title, *The Hawk's Done Gone and Other Stories*. This is a remarkable collection.
All the tales are told in the first person narrative voice and wholly in the dialect of the time and place.[26] The narrator is herself a central character, Mary
Dorthula White (Kanipe by second marriage), the "Granny Woman" of the
mountain community. The tales have a form and content which makes clear
the mythic nature of the culture from which they spring. In this regard they
are a distinct precursor of McCarthy although I have encountered no indication that he was ever aware of their existence. Chapter 4 tells the story of

"Barshia Kanipe (born April 30, 1862)"[27] and is entitled *"Barshia's Horse He Made, It Flew."* Barshia is Ad Kanipe's "oldest boy by his first old woman."[28] He has a compulsive movement of the foot and rarely travels far from home. He spends most of his time hand-working in wood. Some idea of the general tenor of all these stories is conveyed by Mary Dorthula's account of Barshia:

> He made us crack walnuts and pick out the kernels for him. One time he got so mad at Amy because she didn't get the boy's britches out whole that he grabbed the hammer and hit her on the head with it. He knocked the breath plumb out of her. That was before she was yet four years old. I thought he had kilt her and it near scared the daylights out of me. Barshia didn't do a thing but set there and grin like a 'possum all the time I was working with her. Amy has still got the scar on her face. None of us ever told the truth about that scar. We always just said she bumped into the crib door over there.[29]

The level of violence, especially by men towards women, is truly extreme and, at its height, matches anything in McCarthy. In *Wild Sallet*, Linus Kanipe agrees to keep both the twin babies born of another man to his sister Meady. On changing his mind he burns one of them on the kitchen fire:

> She heard flesh spewing and crackling in the other room. Like ham meat frying, she [Meady] said. Smelled like it too—sort of. She heard something pop like a rifle. The bones. The smell and sound of a cholery hog being burnt. And she had cut the wood to burn it.[30]

Only when read as mythic can Haun's tales be encountered with anything but horror. These tales are an antidote to the romanticized view of the mountain folk created by Murfree. The mythic quality of Haun's stories is made quite clear as the tale of Barshia unfolds. He uses his skill as a wood-worker to make himself a horse, with wings made of "'possum hide". The horse flies with fatal consequences for Barshia:

> Them 'possum wings, they begun to flop. Sure enough they could flop. Up and down. Old Maud,[31] she begun to move. Just sliding a little, I thought. But she got her front feet to the edge. I held my breath. He kept working the pedal, you know. It looked like Old Maud went straight up. Up into the air. And them wings a-flopping. "Amy, it is going up. It is," I yelled. I shut my eyes.

When I opened them again, I saw it going down. Head foremost down. Down to the ground on its head. His head too, I guess. I didn't look at him. I didn't want to see it all. "Amy, he's kilt," I said.[32]

That Barshia is Haun's Tennessee mountain Icarus seems clear. She presents her tales from the point of view of Mary Dorlutha who "sees" the world through the medium of a mythic epistemology untouched by Enlightenment modernity. It is this culture that informs Ather Ownby in *The Orchard Keeper*, who can tell John Wesley Rattner "Knowed a man oncet had a cat could talk."[33]

Even allowing for their mythic quality there is no denying the disturbing violence of Haun's texts. That they were rooted in the experience of a violent society, seems indisputable. That some remnants of this violence must have still been in existence during McCarthy's childhood seems inevitable. Richard Marius, a youthful Christian doing "good works" in the Knoxville of 1953, writes:

> I climbed up and down the steep streets and muddy alleyways, visiting the sick and the drunk in hovels that stank of old urine, feces, sweat, vomit, and an indefinable damp rottenness left in the wood by the merciless decades. I found kids born of incest living in basements on dirt floors. . . . I visited men and women imprisoned in the various jails of Knoxville and Knox County.[34]

All the writers of the region portray violence in one form or another. Vigilante violence was a commonplace of the South and existed in various forms in different places. The Deep South had the Ku Klux Klan; the Nightriders terrorized Kentucky and Virginia. Sevier County suffered the depredations of the "White Caps" whose activities are described by Knoxville local historian Mike Gibson, his account based on the *White Cap Book* originally published in 1899 in the name of Tom Davis, the schoolteacher turned sheriff whose efforts brought "White-Capping" to an end. Gibson writes,

> For five turbulent years in the 1890s, that small county in the shadow of Appalachia was beset by a tide of unrestrained vigilantism. . . . bands of masked avengers rode the . . . dales . . . of Sevier, enforcing . . . their own myopically drawn code of righteousness. The results were predictably calamitous, as the movement mutated from an irreparably flawed instrument of homespun justice to an outright sanctuary of criminal self-interest.[35]

The White Caps' original motivation was the enforcement of what was seen as sexual propriety but, as Gibson points out, this rapidly deteriorated into violent criminality and personal vendetta. McCarthy makes direct reference to the White Caps in *Child of God*. An aged resident of Sevierville recalls them as "lowlife thieves and murderers"[36] and this echoes Gibson's comment:

> The local White Caps, begun as a remote association of self-appointed moral arbiters, would eventually reach a chaotic magnitude of influence, granting *de facto* legal sanction to all variants of criminal activity, dividing a once placid region according to divergent loyalties.[37]

As Gibson notes, Pleas Wynn and Catlett Tipton were the last of the White Caps, hanged in July, 1899. The name of Tipton occurs in both *The Orchard Keeper* and *Suttree*. Agrarian violence is, of course, a characteristic of isolated and impoverished areas. The theme of change and its destructive effect on the mountain folk who cannot adapt is present in Haun's tale *God Almighty and the Government*.[38] Pharis Drennon and his family had subsisted on his mountain holding for generations. The Federal Government appropriates his land as part of its creation of the Great Smoky Mountain National Park and the Drennon family is destroyed by this loss. The same theme appears in *The Orchard Keeper*. Like McCarthy Snr., Mildred Haun was an employee of the Government that carried out these projects, both creative and destructive at the same time. The dilemmas of "progress" are bound to be considered by serious writers when they locate their fictions in areas such as East Tennessee.

Some critics have pointed out that James Agee writes of the mountain people in *A Death in the Family*. This is true, but only to a limited extent The members of "the family" on which he focuses are either not mountain people, like Mary Follet, or have left the mountains and their ways behind like her husband Jay. They are striving to live lives of security and respectability in the Knoxville of 1915. Their only contact with the mountains comes in a visit to those distant family members who, it is clear, inhabit not only another place, but another time. On the journey Jay speaks of his mountain family and their past. He says of his Great-Grandmother, "She's a hundred and three years old. Hundred and three or hundred and four. She never could remember for sure which". He recounts that during his own youth, "There were cats back in these mountains, Mary—we called 'em painters, that's the same as a panther—they were still around here when I was a boy. And there is still bear, they claim."[39] It seems clear that this text and *The Orchard Keeper* draw on the same cultural sources. Ather Ownby tells John Wesley tales of the painter, and Murfree's human panther has his painter counterpart in *The Panther of Jolton's Ridge*. Agee wrote with great sympathy of the Southern rural poor in *Let Us Now Praise Famous Men*, but his subjects were the share-croppers of Alabama rather than the mountain men of Appalachia. *A Death in the Family* expresses a sympathy and affection for the mountain people but the main focus is elsewhere.

No account of the literature concerned with the mountain people would be complete without some mention of George Washington Harris. Harris was himself a resident of Knoxville in the mid. 19th century and he belongs to the local color school of Southwestern humorists. Like all the writers of this genre he frames his dialect narrative in his own "educated" speech in order to "tame" the wild excesses that his humor exploits. What Harris depicts is wildly funny at times, but, like other writers of this genre, his tales also express racial prejudice of all kinds, take a delight in extremes of violence and drunkenness and describe a world of sexual license that, in retrospect, exposes the darker forces at work in the Southern culture of the period. *Sut Lovingood's Tales* were published over a number of years in magazines and were extremely popular. McCarthy himself was familiar with Harris' work and it is not difficult to see the feckless Sut reflected in Gene Harrogate, the seducer of melons, in *Suttree*. The significance of the name Suttree has already been alluded to. There exists also in Harris' tales the same conflict between father and son that is so characteristic of McCarthy. In *Sut Lovingood's Daddy Acting Horse* the family is without a horse for ploughing. Sut's "Dad" solves the problem by taking the horse's part himself. Sut puts him to the work:

> I shoulder'd the gopher plow, an' tuk hole ove the bridil. Dad leaned back sulky, till I sed cluck wif my tongue, then he started. When we cum tu the fence I let down the gap, an' hit made dad mad; he wanted tu jump hit on all fours hoss way. Oh geminy! what a durn'd ole fool kin cum tu ef he gins up tu the complaint.[40]

The atmosphere of *Suttree* is in fact very different from that of *Sut Lovingood* despite their obvious connections. McCarthy expresses an essential respect for his mountain men—comics, victims and criminals alike. This is quite lacking in Harris. If McCarthy writes in recognition of Harris he also writes in redress.

Just as East Tennessee enjoys a different geography, history and local culture to the Western part of the State, so the literatures of the two sections have different atmospheres. Peter Taylor is a native of West Tennessee and many of his stories are set in the Memphis area. His own background is distinguished; his grandfather was both Governor and Senator for the State. His novels are the sophisticated product of an educated mind. He portrays his bourgeois Tennesseans with an affecting combination of sympathy and sadness. The sufferings of his people cannot be accounted for by isolation or deprivation. They are both modern and Southern, afflicted by their inability to forge a satisfactory identity from their vision of the past. Their social pretensions reflect the divided identity of Tennessee itself. He entitles his novel of the cycle of generations of a distinguished family *In the Tennessee Country*, perhaps a reference to Murfree's *In the Tennessee Mountains*. The narrator describes an aspect of the family's history:

> His family had come from Upper East Tennessee, near Bristol, where the Solid South was not so solid, and a good many soldiers had fought on the Other Side. They were always careful to speak of the Confederacy as Our Side and sometimes of the War for Southern Independence. His father had fought with General Kirby-Smith and General Longstreet in their efforts to take East Tennessee for the Southern Cause. He seemed ashamed, my father used to say, of the *r*'s that crept into his accent and the flat *a* sounds, and so he took every opportunity to use the Tidewater diphthong. But there still remained something always about the *r*'s in his speech and a certain harshness to remind everyone that no matter how genteel his people, they *were* from the mountains.[41]

Taylor's style and the world that he portrays contrast sharply with those of Harris, Murfree, and Haun, not to mention Sam Watkins. Agee is closer to Taylor in some ways but his focus is still on the other end of the social scale. McCarthy and Taylor inhabit different literary worlds.

The group of writers who deal with the people of the mountains of East Tennessee therefore constitute the small *local* tradition within which McCarthy may be located. His achievement has been to place within this tradition the diverse influences of the literature of a wider world; of the South, of America as a whole, and of Europe. He also relates his tales of Sevier County to the literatures of many ages, including those of Dante, Shakespeare, and the Bible, the great figures of the 19th Century, the modernists and their successors.

Such is the peculiar and individual nature of the geography, history and culture of this area in which McCarthy spent most of his childhood. Just as Tennessee is on the border of North and South, so McCarthy's fiction is within the Southern tradition in its gothicism and its almost sensuous enthusiasm for language, but is distinguished from it in other ways. For reasons which should already be clear, McCarthy's Tennessee fiction is little concerned with race. Of the novels only *Suttree* features black characters.[42] Suttree himself mixes with black and white indifferently. Often it is impossible to tell a character's color. For McCarthy it is not an issue although he is far from indifferent to the racism existing in the Knoxville of the day. In the ironic words of the indomitable Ab Jones, "Bein a nigger is a interestin life."[43] It is Jones who makes the profoundest of remarks to Suttree; "You got a good heart, Youngblood. Look out for your own."[44] It takes Suttree the whole of the novel to recognize the fundamental importance of these words. When Jones is killed by a white policeman Suttree strikes back by stealing the policeman's car and running it into the Tennessee River.[45] In the mountain communities blacks are rare indeed. Race becomes much more of a theme in the Southwestern novels, although even here it is implicit rather than foregrounded. This is perhaps the greatest difference between McCarthy and Faulkner, with whom he is so frequently compared.

The ambivalence that I have suggested characterizes much of Tennessee's history has continued to be evident in the twentieth century in ways that are reflected in McCarthy's work. Tennessee played a prominent part in the campaign to introduce Prohibition. The disastrous effects of the Prohibition era have been well documented. The efforts of the moonshine whisky runner are a staple of Southern culture.[46] Marion Sylder notes that ". . . his job had gone off the market December fifth 1933."[47] He continues to "run" whisky for the traditional reason of avoiding the excise man. In addition, as Richard Marius points out in recalling the time of his (and McCarthy's) youth: "Bootleggers and Baptist preachers combined forces to keep the town legally dry."[48] He adds, expressing the ambivalence that I have suggested characterizes Tennessee attitudes, "In Knoxville you learned to live with contradiction and paradox."[49] The political impetus for Prohibition came initially from the Southern Baptists whose Calvinist fundamentalism McCarthy attacks so vigorously in *Outer Dark*. They were, and are, the source of the opposition to the teaching of the theory of evolution in American schools, their influence currently more powerful than ever. The "Scopes Trial" of 1925 was another episode that illustrated Tennessee's position on a border, this time between modernity and atavism. Suttree encounters one of the principles of the Scopes trial in the streets of Knoxville:

> Morning, Dr. Neal, he said.
> The old tattered barrister halted in his tracks and peered at Suttree from under his arched brows. Who'd been chief counsel for Scopes, a

friend of Darrow and Menken and a lifelong friend of doomed defen-
dants, causes lost, alone and friendless in a hundred courts.[50]

McCarthy suggests that time and Tennessee had not been kind to a man who
attempted to defend the South against unreason.

The lawless turbulence of the 1930s was, of course, greatly exacerbated
by the catastrophic effects of the Great Depression. The effect of this was to
deepen the poverty and intensify the isolation of the mountain region and of
the South as a whole. The New Deal was the Roosevelt Administration's program aimed at alleviating the enormous deprivation and social breakdown
that the Depression occasioned. This program had a particular effect on Tennessee because, of course, its centre-piece was perhaps the creation, in 1933,
of the Tennessee Valley Authority. The principle function of the TVA was the
generation of electricity by means of water power. The construction of dams
in the valleys of the region, ideally suited to the purpose, but necessitating
the drowning of some mountain communities, enabled hydro-electric generation to begin the task of modernizing and developing the area. The process
is still in operation. On a visit to Knoxville I was informed by a local construction engineer that the TVA was the catalyst for the current development
of the region. Members of the English faculty at the University explained
that the Authority was still unpopular in the area, not because of the "socialist nature" of the project, nor because it was of Federal origin, but because it
was the work of a Democrat administration and this was still, as in Civil War
times, a Republican area. American politics retains a tribalist character that is
sometimes difficult for British observers to understand. There was ideological
opposition to the TVA at the time of its inception, as there was to the New
Deal as a whole. T.H.Watkins notes:

> Writing in the October-December, 1934, issue of *Sewanee Review*, James
> R. McCarthy took exception to what he called Morgan's "patronizing"
> tone and suggested that the natives of the region "resented the implica-
> tion that Washington was the seat of government which regarded the
> valley as a colony."[51]

Given the Agrarian sentiments of those associated with *Sewanee Review* at
this time these views are hardly surprising.

As already noted McCarthy Senior took up a position as an attorney
with TVA in 1934, thus occasioning the move to Knoxville of Cormac and
the rest of the family. It is possible to associate the action of *The Orchard
Keeper* with opposition to the TVA; Ather Ownby's target is the "government

tank" of unspecified purpose that he perceives as an intrusion into his domain. I shall explore this and the associated theme of father/son conflict that is implied for the author in the later section on this text. All critics agree that the theme of modernization and change is strong in the Tennessee novels; there is less unanimity over the interpretation of McCarthy's treatment of the theme. That it is related to his family circumstances seems beyond contradiction.

Today's Knoxville bears scant resemblance to the town described with such resonance by McCarthy. Such is the economic activity of the region that the City boasts a new and wholly modern airport and a characteristic American freeway system that bears the usual unceasing traffic. Areas of Knoxville that were rebuilt in the 60s to replace the dereliction described by McCarthy have been demolished again to make way for the endlessly new. The twin tower blocks of the TVA headquarters still dominate the townscape. But "East of Knoxville. . . . the mountains start" as ever.[52] The mountains retain much of their natural character. The area is covered with hundreds of square miles of still dense forest. Deer and other wild animals can still be commonly encountered even by the roadside. It is hard to resist the notion that much of this forest is still in the condition of the original American wilderness. It is easy to see how it could for so long have supported what Fennimore Cooper so aptly described as "the people of the forest." Even the dams of the TVA with their generators and electric power lines add a certain grandeur to their locations, especially through the formation of their associated lakes. It is strange to speculate that McCarthy may have left this extraordinarily green and beautiful area in part because it could not be for him a metaphor for the waste land that he felt America to be.

McCarthy's vision of the old Knoxville of the 1950s and the isolated mountain communities of the 30s and 40s seems to be a gothic nightmare, owing its atmosphere to the Southern literary tradition of Faulkner, Katherine Anne Porter and Flannery O'Connor. He depicts a world that we recognize from *Light In August* and *As I Lay Dying, Noon Wine* and *Pale Horse, Pale Rider, Wise Blood* and *The Violent Bear It Away*. It would be tempting to see this gothicism as a purely literary conceit. However this is far from being the case. The popular culture of the period was deeply rooted in the traditional music and song of the South, and particularly of the mountain people. Richard Marius recalls brief meetings with the young McCarthy in which:

> We spoke about country music. . . . this was before country music
> became generally popular or even noticed or even before it was called
> "country music." We called it hillbilly; so did the musicians. It was the

music of the common folk of East Tennessee, of the mountains, or more accurately perhaps, the nostalgic music of the uprooted who had migrated to the city from the mountains and lived homesick for kith and kin in the blue hills and green coves that they had forsaken.[53]

The critic Greil Marcus writes of this music and of its inheritors, particularly Bob Dylan who played a major part in the "folk revival" of the 1960s.[54] In McCarthy and Marius's Knoxville this music did not need "reviving" since it had never expired. It can still be heard in its form of the twenties and thirties on the *Harry Smith Anthology of American Folk Music*. The voices and playing of Bascom Lamar Lunsford, The Carter Family, Uncle Dave Macon, Blind Lemmon Jefferson,[55] Dock Boggs, The Memphis Jug Band et al live in these recordings and demonstrate to us that the gothic was the popular form as well as the literary. Marcus writes of "The Old Weird America" in his chapter on the Smith Anthology and its influence:

> Here is a mystical body of the republic, a kind of public secret: a declaration of what sort of wishes and fears lie behind any public act, a declaration of a weird but clearly recognizable America within the America of the exercise of institutional majoritarian power.[56]

The world of Cormac McCarthy's Tennessee novels is clearly recognizable in such songs as *Ommie Wise*—(the pregnant Naomie Wise is drowned by her lover who has tired of her affections), *Charles Giteau*—(the murderer of President Garfield tells his own story) and *Henry Lee*—(a young man is murdered by a jealous girl).[57] The folk-gothic is expressed most powerfully in *Oh Death*: Dock Boggs' version contains the following:

> What is this that I can see, with icy hands takin hold of me.
> I am Death none can excell, I'll open the door to heaven or hell.
> . . .
> Oh Death! Oh Death! Can't you spare me over 'till another year.
> . . .
> I'll fix your feet so you can't walk, I'll lock your jaw so you can't talk,
> Close your eyes so you can't see, This very year come go with me.
> Death I come to take the soul, leave the body and leave it cold.
> To drop the flesh off of the frame, the earth and worm both have a
>   claim.
> Mother come to my bed, place a cold towel upon my head.
> My head is warm, my feet are cold, death is moving upon my soul.

. . .

Oh the young, the rich or poor, all alike to me you know.
No wealth, no land, no silver, no gold, nothing satisfies me but your
   soul.

. . .

Oh Death! Oh Death! Can't you spare me over 'till another year.[58]

This world is characterized by violence and death, murder, betrayal and the blood feud. Here lovers are abandoned and husbands languish in jail. Despite the harshness of the life depicted in these songs the music itself sounds a defiantly spirited note. Here in simple but powerful form is the folk equivalent of McCarthy's dialectic of insignificance and vitality. Within this culture lies his inspiration, as much as in the great literary works already alluded to.

I have tried in this chapter to indicate some of the historical and geographical factors that have influenced McCarthy's work. The contradictions that his early texts express are, in part, reflections of the contradictions within the history and geography of the State of Tennessee. They are compounded by those of his own life, as a Northerner come to live in the South, a Catholic family in the bible belt, and as a lover of the natural world whose father works for the great modernizing, industrializing institution of the TVA. He was also a member of a comfortable, affluent family in the poverty stricken deprivation of Depression Appalachia. His father was an employee of a Democrat government in a fiercely independent Republican area, and a man who must have fought many legal battles for the TVA against the opposition of local interests. Small wonder that McCarthy's texts express the search for identity and are characterized by a profound sense of the *unheimlich*. Given the history of the South in general and of East Tennessee in particular it is small wonder also that such a keen and discerning intellect as McCarthy's should perceive and criticize the Exceptionalist myth of America. In the words of the South's most distinguished historian,

> The experience of evil and the experience of tragedy are parts of the Southern heritage that are as difficult to reconcile with the American legend of innocence and social felicity as the experience of poverty and defeat are to reconcile with the legends of abundance and success.[59]

Part II
The Tennessee Texts

Chapter Four
Wake For Susan and
A Drowning Incident

As he entered this forgotten resting place,
the rich and lonely haunted feeling thickened in the air

WAKE FOR SUSAN

Wake For Susan is McCarthy's first known published work. It appeared in the
October 1959 edition of *The Phoenix*, the literary supplement of *Orange and
White*, the magazine published by the University of Tennessee. Not surpris-
ingly it has received very little critical consideration. It is not commercially
available[1] and most critics tend to assume that it will be little more than
typical undergraduate juvenilia. I have found only two who have paid it serious attention. Rick Wallach and Dianne Luce both deal with it in essays
contributed to *Myth, Legend, Dust*. Wallach is rather dismissive of the story,
finding that it "blurs the line between nostalgia and sentimentality on several
occasions."[2] In my view it is the protagonist, Wes, who displays sentimentality; the complexity of "voice" in the story, clearly identified by Luce, enables
us to "read" McCarthy rather differently from Wes. Luce is generally more
appreciative of the story and sees it as a metaphor for "the artist's creative
awakening."[3]

In fact McCarthy was 26 when the story was published, and had spent
the previous four years in the USAF, during which time he had embarked on
that process of self-education that was to make him familiar with an extraordinarily wide range of literature and ideas. In my view the story is cleverly
conceived and uses language and metaphor in ways that are both vivid
and economical. It also contains themes that are to appear in McCarthy's
more extended texts and which, indeed, run through his work as a whole. I

therefore consider it worth while devoting attention to this story and to its companion of the following year.

The atmosphere of *Wake for Susan* is set by the introductory quotation from Sir Walter Scott:

> "Who makes the bridal bed,
> Birdie, say truly?-
> "The grey headed Sexton
> That delves the grave duly."[4]

Walter Scott's works were immensely popular in 19th and early 20th century America, particularly in the South where his romantic pseudo-medievalism and blurring of the distinctions between the ersatz aristocratic world of his fiction and the realities of modernity, perfectly expressed the escapism of the myth of the Old South. Samuel Chamberlain, writing of his youth in the 1840s, speaks for more than one generation when he relates that he "got hold of Scott's immortal works. What a glorious new world opened up before me, how I devoured their pages and oh how I longed to emulate his heroes!"[5] Mark Twain was more perceptive:

> Sir Walter Scott is probably responsible for the Capitol building (in Baton Rouge); for it is not conceivable that this little sham castle would ever have been built if he had not run the people mad, a couple of generations ago, with his mediæval romances. The South has not yet recovered from the debilitating influence of his books.[6]

Twain belongs to that mythoclastic tradition in which I suggest McCarthy should be located.

Scott's romanticism also informed America's image of the western hero, the cowboy; it is this mythology that McCarthy deconstructs in his Border Trilogy. The verse quoted here expresses that other romantic trope, the equivalence of love and death. It is a verse from *Proud Maisie*,[7] sung by "Madge Wildfire"[8] on her deathbed in *The Heart of Midlothian*. As the editors of *Romantic Prose and Poetry* remark, "it is in the tradition of the mad song,"[9] Madge is beautiful Margaret Murdochson, seduced, betrayed and driven mad by the murder of her infant love-child. She lies on her deathbed having been set upon by the mob and half drowned in the ducking pool "according to their favourite mode of punishment."[10] The parallel with the gothic folk-songs of what Marcus called "the Invisible Republic", the "Old, Weird America,"[11] is very clear. This is the world of the White Caps of Sevier

County and Mary Dorthula White rather than that of quiet, loving domesticity that is to inform the tale as Wes imagines it. Thus at the very first moment of his career as an author McCarthy places on his work the stamp of the gothic; death and madness take the place of beauty and love.

The world of the forest in which Wes walks, hunts and imagines, is, superficially, a site of the Edenic pastoral; but McCarthy's reference to Scott has already subverted that mythology, and in a way that will prove to be strongly characteristic of his later texts. Scott has been quoted in a manner that also subverts the romanticism that he appears to express. McCarthy inverts Scott as he was to invert so much else in the future. What Wes is to create in his first act as an "imaginative artist," in the first tale that he tells himself, is a romantic myth that is at odds with the world of Madge Wildfire, dying mad; and with the "minor tragedy" of the chipmunk, scratched to death by the fox and left "for the smaller carnivores."[12] It is this subversion that Wallach fails to discern when he describes McCarthy's tale as "sentimental." It is Wes's tale that is sentimental, and the Scott quotation makes it clear that Wes is the first of those McCarthy heroes that America sends into life informed by a myth, a story rendered false by the elision of the true nature of the world and of the people in it. The full significance of the Scott verse is made clear when one considers the end of Wes's tale. He casts himself as the lover, but one that is either bashful or considerate of Susan's reputation. He imagines her as the more sensual and sexually forward of the two: "After a while she would look up at him, rather boldly he thought, . . . At the door her kiss would be full of meaning and he would tumble out into the sharp night air and run most of the way home. . . . she would carry the lamp into her room and look at herself to see what there was about her that made her such a delicate piece of china."[13] The irony is compounded by the fact that Wes's tale has been inspired by the long abandoned grave of a girl dead at seventeen in 1834. "How had she died? The mute stone left no testimony. There were so many ways."[14] In fact the stone has perhaps left a clue: ". . . the Source of Life has reclaimed His own . . ."[15] This straightforwardly religious sentiment may acquire another meaning when one considers that Madge Wildfire had proved herself a "source of life." Susan Ledbetter could have died under similar circumstances to Margaret Murdochson in which case her lover would have lived in an altogether darker tale than that imagined by Wes.

If the subversively gothic atmosphere of his first story is characteristic of McCarthy's work as a whole the same is true of other aspects of this initial text. Clearly the Scott quotation is crucial to its overall meaning, and the story as a whole illustrates the place of intertextuality in literary creation, since Wes creates his tale around the "fragment" of text that is inscribed on Susan's gravestone. Indeed the grave and its stone are themselves fragments that are woven into Wes's text, as are the woods and the landscape generally. His initial act of "telling" is sparked by the discovery of spent musket-balls on the forest floor. Dianne Luce suggests that they were from shots that missed their mark, just as Wes has done in trying to shoot a squirrel "that came slithering down the tree directly in front of him"[16] If Susan was a Margaret Murdochson as McCarthy hints, then Wes's tale misses its mark also. The creation of tales from the texts of the past is not only the process with which McCarthy consciously engages, it is the process by which history itself, and indeed the whole matrix of a given culture, is created according to the vision contained in *The Crossing*. As a means of mediating our experience of the world this matrix is at once our only guide and a source of stories that are "not true;"[17] and this is the central thrust of McCarthy's fiction.

Wake for Susan also gives us our first experience of McCarthy's technique of combining narrative voices in an ambiguous manner. This is the method used in *The Orchard Keeper* and *Suttree* in particular. As Luce points out "As in many of McCarthy's more mature works . . . the narrative voice . . . is ambiguous, the line between removed authorial voice and an involved narrator deliberately blurred."[18] The transformation of voices is achieved in a subtle, almost un-noticed manner:

> 1834, for instance, was a year one could remember. In this year, a stone said, the Source of Life has reclaimed his own—one Susan Ledbetter. Susan had lived on the earth a full seventeen years.
>
> From a simple carved stone, the marble turned to a monument; from a gravestone, to the surviving integral tie to a once warm-blooded, live person. Wes pictured Susan:
>
> She was blue-eyed and yellow-haired, soft and bright in her homespun dress. (1834 was a year one could remember; not like 1215, or 1066, but a real year.) Susan sat at the table with her parents and brothers and eyed with pardonable pride the meal she and her mother had prepared.[19]

The first paragraph of this passage is in the authorial voice. The wording on the gravestone is "written" by McCarthy. In the second a transition takes place: "Wes pictured Susan." In the third the voice has become that of Wes himself—it is his imagination that "pictures" the scene and creates the story. He writes himself into it as Susan's lover. But three paragraphs later we read,

> They discussed death and bass-fishing and square dances, and the epic
> of life around them seemed to unfold. They imparted to each other a
> great deal of understanding.[20]

The vocabulary has become that of the author again. The ambiguity is deliberate and recalls the Faulknerian technique mentioned previously,[21] used to
enable unsophisticated characters to express complex feelings of a kind they
might experience but be unable to articulate. Luce interprets this as McCarthy using Wes as his own surrogate and thus deploying the story as a metaphor for "the artist's creative awakening" as noted at the beginning of this
section. This is a persuasive reading but I also feel that Luce's response to the
outcome of Wes/McCarthy's creativity is unduly sunny. She feels that the
story ends on a note of optimism and that Wes has "experienced catharsis"[22]
after weeping for "all the lost Susans" by the gravestone: "Wes smiled, and
walked home. Towering even among the lean trees."[23] As I have already
argued, Scott's introductory verse suggests that Wes's optimism as he moves
towards the future may prove to be illusory.

The logic of Luce's position is that Wes represents McCarthy's own
progress toward his future as a writer. Certainly this short text contains a
number of embryonic characteristics that will become fulfilled in later, more
substantial works. In particular *The Orchard Keeper* features the story of John
Wesley Rattner who "becomes" the narrator as he sits beside a grave (his
mother's). Throughout McCarthy's fiction young men travel in isolation and
are, for the most part, "without women" in the sense invoked by Hemingway. Also the gothic atmosphere of McCarthy's texts is consistently punctuated by passages of lyrical prose:

> Winds were about. A little band of leaves jumped up beneath his feet
> and frolicked and tumbled ahead of him, then did a disorderly right
> oblique and scampered crazily down a sunny woodland corridor, leap-
> ing and dancing before the wind in a travesty of life.[24]

The assumption that these woods are located in East Tennessee will be confirmed in McCarthy's first three novels. Language is used in ways that belie
a surface simplicity. The word "Wake" in this context has a double meaning, and the simple "perhaps" in "Perhaps her thoughts were too much taken
with a tall lean and dark-eyed man . . ."[25] reminds us that neither of our
possible narrators can be thought of as omniscient. The line "1834 was a
year one could remember; not like 1215 or 1066, but a real year"[26] has a

double complexity. Magna Carta and the Battle of Hastings are events in English history; by 1834 America has a "history of its own"; but the story begins with a quote from English (or Scots) literature. Throughout McCarthy's work blood has the greatest significance; it is the emblem of both life (Susan was "a once warm-blooded, live person" [27]) and death (The fox "scraped and clawed the chipmunk until it was bloody and lifeless" [28]) and is emblematic of the continuing dialectic of vitality and insignificance that is one of his fiction's defining characteristics.

Above all *Wake for Susan* begins McCarthy's journey as a writer exploring the essential nature and purpose of narrative and the manner of its creation from and within a cultural matrix existing in the present but created from the language and artifacts of the past and carrying myths that may prove to be both beguiling and destructive at the same time. The Faulknerian aspect of such a project is clear and is emphasized by the fact that the text is focused on the unattainable female. Thus, despite the fact that East Tennessee is "different", McCarthy's literary origins are of the South.

The full version of *Proud Maisie*[29] emphasizes the atmosphere of madness, grief and death that McCarthy invokes with this, his initial literary quotation:

> 'Proud Maisie is in the wood,
>   Walking so early.
> Sweet Robin sits on the bush
>   Singing so rarely.
>
> "Tell me thou bonny bird,
>   When shall I marry me?"
> "When six braw gentlemen
>   Kirkward shall carry ye."
>
> "Who makes the bridal bed,
>   Birdie say truly?"
> "The grey-headed sexton,
>   That delves the grave duly."
>
> The glowworm o'er grave and stone
>   Shall light thee steady;
> The owl from the steeple sing,[30]
>   "Welcome proud lady." '

A DROWNING INCIDENT

McCarthy's second story, appearing in the March 1960 edition of *The Phoenix*, seems at first sight a stronger piece of work than the first. Certainly this is Wallach's opinion. ". . . McCarthy seems to have banished sentimentalism as well as any hint of casual narrative sprawl, and the voice of the mature author suddenly becomes audible."[31] However, in my view the second story lacks the narrative complexity of its predecessor and relies for its power on the contrast between McCarthy's vividly convincing (eidetic) descriptions of the natural world and the overtly gothic nature of the actions of the small boy in the tale. The complexity of structure and meaning of the first story is absent from the second. The authorial voice is unchanging throughout and remains detached from both the text and the action. There is no intertextuality here, either direct, as in the Scott quotation, or implied, as in Wes's use of Susan's epitaph. In addition the gothic tenor of the tale is not oblique, as in the first story, but direct and extreme. If, as I have suggested, *Wake for Susan* is primarily about narrative—its creation and function—then the gothic aspect of the tale is of secondary significance and is thus relegated to a position in which its impact on meaning is oblique, a function of the very intertextuality that relates to the story's principal meaning. In the case of *A Drowning Incident* precisely the opposite is the case. The focus of the story is the small boy. His consciousness is undeveloped, ". . . his mind a dimensionless wall against which only a grey pattern, whorled as a huge thumbprint, oscillates slowly."[32] The boy, un-named as the kid of *Blood Meridian* will be, cannot become the narrator of his own tale, he lacks the wherewithal to accomplish such a task. His innocent destructiveness becomes the subject of the tale and the source of its horror. It is his unconscious that is to be the subject of this narrative.

The contrast between the pastoral beauty of the setting and the boy's actions provide us with another glimpse of McCarthy's characteristic mythoclasm. In the fecund Eden of Suzy and "her dugs no longer dragging to the ground",[33] we have the black widow spider waiting to paralyze and devour. The ideal of "home" as a place of love and security is subverted from the very beginning; there are "huge untended hedges"[34] and the "outhouse"[35] has a rotted door, "the planks were warped and velveted with a pale green patina."[36] This is the place in which Suzy has given birth to her pups and in which the spider lurks. The fact that the boy "peered down the hole . . . to the gloom below"[37] suggests to us that we may seek a Freudian meaning to the story, a suggestion that is powerfully confirmed as the narrative unfolds. The notion of the impossibility of innocence, even in a small child, contradicts the American optimism that believed in the new Adam and his place in the New World. The story begins with an act of disobedience as the boy leaves the house—". . . he rounded the corner of the house so as to be out of sight, then ran for the woodshed and put it between himself and the house. He was not to go far away."[38] The possibility of psychological conflict is conveyed with McCarthy's characteristic simplicity and economy, "The baby was taking its nap."[39] The contradiction of "childhood innocence" is powerfully conveyed as the boy steps on the cricket in the outhouse: "It was still kicking one leg in slow lethargic rhythm; a thick white liquid was oozing from it."[40]

The effect is reinforced as the boy ". . . dropped it down the hole and bent to watch."[41] His childish cruelty is confirmed as he drops a "huge drop of spittle"[42] on the spider.

Having established the overtly gothic atmosphere of the story and associated it with the unfeeling cruelty of the small boy, McCarthy changes the mood of the narrative as the boy's truancy carries him into the idyllic setting of the summer woods. Certainly the lyricism evident in the first story is rendered more intensely in the second:

> The creek was shallow and clear. The floor of the pool was mottled brown and gold as a leopard's hide where the sun seeped through the leaves and branches overhead. Minnows drifted obliquely across the slow current. Through the water-glass he watched the tiny shadows traverse the leopard's back silent and undulant as a bird's flight. He found some small white pebbles at his elbows and dropped them to the minnows; they twisted and shimmered slowly to the bottom trailing miniscule bubbles that stood in the brief tendrils before rising and disappearing. The minnows rushed to inspect. He folded his arms beneath his chin. The sun was warm and good on his back through the flannel shirt.[43]

But the interlude gives way immediately to an image of death: ". . . a small puppy, rolling and bumping along the bed of the creek, turning weightlessly in the slow water."[44] The sense of unease thus conveyed is intensified to the level of trauma as the boy's investigations reveal the sack in which all Suzy's pups have been drowned. "He sat down slowly, numb and stricken. . . . He had no tears, only a great hollow feeling which, even as he sat there, gave way to a slow mounting sense of outrage."[45] The rest of tale details the manner in which the boy uses resourcefulness and skill to retrieve the decomposing corpse of the last puppy from the stream. We receive an intimation of the horrors that will be recounted in later texts—*Outer Dark, Child of God,*

Blood Meridian—the remaining puppy is trapped in the sack by the bricks that have weighted it down and it has,

> . . . a large crawfish tunneled half through the soft wet belly. He hooked his wire into the crawfish and pulled it out, stringing behind it a tube of putrid green entrails. He tried to push them back with the toe of his shoe.[46]

The extreme nature of the child's emotional alienation is conveyed with compelling intensity as he expresses both rage against a betraying father and an associated sibling rivalry. The sack and corpse are placed in the cot with the baby sister: "He remembered vaguely seeing the green entrails oozing onto the sheet as the blanket fell."[47] The story is completed with a single concession to narrative complexity. The tense changes from past to present for the final paragraph which concludes with "He is waiting for him to come home."[48]

Even at this early stage in his career I would suggest that McCarthy is the kind of self-aware writer who deploys no overt technical narrative device without a reason. This final paragraph implies that the conflict expressed has not been resolved. There is ample evidence in McCarthy's subsequent texts to bear out this assumption. The conflict between father and son is one of the constant themes that run through the whole of his oeuvre, albeit with an intensity that gradually abates after the extremes of *Blood Meridian*. In a number of cases this conflict is associated with the image of a dog or puppy, and the young men who McCarthy sends out into the world, often from less than happy homes, seek, and not infrequently find, surrogate fathers, for good or ill, and encounter dogs in one form or another. That this theme of oedipal conflict is quite overt in McCarthy is made clear in this initial story. I shall indicate its relevance to each of the subsequent texts in their own chapters.

I have made it clear that I do not share Wallach's view of *Wake for Susan*. I feel that he under-estimates the significance of that text's narrative complexity. Consequently I do not share his estimate that *A Drowning Incident* represents an improvement on the earlier story. In my view such comparisons are not instructive. The two stories have different structures because they seek to address different narrative concerns. The first reveals a modernist preoccupation with the very nature, significance and limitations of narrative itself. The second seeks to express what is for McCarthy the inexpressible, the inner consciousness of the individual human being. By making his protagonist a child McCarthy removes the possibility of articulate self-consciousness from the subject of the text. He was to refuse to enter his character's consciousness consistently in his later works, referring repeatedly to the impossibility of knowing what such a consciousness might be and how his character's actions might be explained. In this he expressed his skepticism regarding systems of knowledge and belief.[49]

In my view these two short stories can be considered together as a complementary pair. Between them they give clear indications of the style and concerns that are to characterize McCarthy's fiction as his career develops. The density of allusion and meaning that they convey together with their emotional intensity clearly mark them as the work of a young writer of unusual promise. The manner in which they derive mythoclastic significance by combining lyrical and eidetic descriptions of the beauties of the East Tennessee woods with gothic intimations of conflict, violence and death mark them as the works of a writer who will align himself with the harshest critics of American mythology.

Chapter 5
The Orchard Keeper

No avatar, no scion, no vestige of that people remains.
On the lips of the strange race that now dwells there their names are
myth, legend, dust.

McCarthy's first novel is a product of the 1960s. The growth of affluence and rapid technological change that followed the end of the Second
World War produced cultural, social and political change in all the indus-
trialized societies of the West. The culture of that decade continued to be
influenced by the modernist notion that art needed to find new forms in
order to express new insights regarding human beings and their world. The
French film director Jean Luc Godard, a leading figure of the *nouvelle vague*,
spoke quite seriously when he informed the world that a film should have
"a beginning, a middle and an end, but not necessarily in that order." Reading *The Orchard Keeper* one gains the impression that for McCarthy, what
was true for film was also true for the novel. The action of the first page of
the text is in a place and time that only becomes apparent on the very last
page. Both sections of text belong in time to the end of the story. I have
mentioned already the Faulknerian aspect of this theme of "the past in the
present". I have also suggested the powerful and continuing influence of
Eliot in McCarthy's work. In this case we are confronted with a key theme
from *The Four Quartets*:

Time past and time future
What might have been and what has been
Point to one end, which is always present.[1]

Matthew Guinn writes:

> Modernist narrative technique shapes the intertwined stories of Arthur (sic) Ownby, John Wesley Rattner, and Marion Sylder, providing an epistemological structure of fragmented viewpoints by which the plot is pieced together.[2]

Only at the conclusion of the tale do we discover that John Wesley Rattner has been "present" in the text from the very beginning and that he occupies the same relation to the story, in time and place, as the narrator. As mentioned in the section on *Wake For Susan*, Dianne Luce suggests that we may identify *The Orchard Keeper* as John Wesley's story and that in a sense he may be considered its narrator. However it would be an exaggeration to claim that Luce puts forward this idea in as definite a manner as this. John Wesley is like Wes in that he finds inspiration for his thoughts in a graveyard but his relation to the narrative voice is less clear cut than in Wes's case (whose own position was not without its complexity). As previously stated, Luce correctly identifies the narrative voice as "ambiguous."[3] It is clear that much of the prose of *The Orchard Keeper* could not have emanated from John Wesley. Indeed the Tennessee mountain boy can only be the narrator of the text if he is, like Wes, read as a surrogate for McCarthy himself. That we should so read him is entirely consistent, both with the structure of the novel, the precedent of *Wake For Susan*, and what we know about McCarthy's own boyhood in East Tennessee.

The narrative complexity of *The Orchard Keeper* is indeed considerable. The "framing" of the tale itself by the episode of the tree cutters in the Knoxville graveyard is just the most overt example of a structure that presents the reader with real difficulties. It requires very careful examination to work out the timescale of events depicted and the historical context of the action, both in detail and as a whole. Clues regarding these matters are scattered thinly throughout the text and the reader's attention is hardly drawn to them in most cases. It was only as a result of careful and deliberate consideration that I was able to calculate the period of the tale. John Wesley buys four traps in Knoxville and agrees to take eight more "prior to Jan. 1, 1941"[4] thus placing this action in 1940.

"On the twenty-first of December"[5] of that year (significantly the date of the winter solstice) Ather places the seventh annual cedar branch over the pit in which Rattner's corpse was hidden. Thus he had placed the first in 1934 and this must have been the date of Rattner's return and killing. Sylder had been returning to Red Branch in that year since "his job had gone off the market December fifth 1933,"[6] the date of the repeal of prohibition. He was able to operate as a whisky runner from Red Branch since

Knoxville remained "dry." It is 1941 when John Wesley visits Ather in the "crazy house" and the old man comments on the year, "I look for this to be a bad one. I look for real calamity before this year is out."[7] The attack on Pearl Harbor took place on December 7th. of that year. Mrs. Rattner's gravestone informs us that she died in 1945 and the text informs us that this had been "three short years" ago.[8] Thus we may place the story in time between 1934 and 1948, although details from an older time are revealed on occasion. In the case of Sylder and Kenneth Rattner they are given in the authorial voice. Ather's past is revealed through the tales he tells or by means of internalized narrative in the form of memory flashes that occur to the old man, often without having any particular relevance to the action of the moment. These latter are rendered in italics.

The "difficult" time structure of the narrative of *The Orchard Keeper* can be considered a weakness in my opinion. Narrative complexity is justified in such a text since it seems clear that McCarthy wishes to convey the complex nature of the experience of interaction within even a small group of individuals. He deliberately declines to present the tale from a single point of view and he makes it clear that different individuals not only experience the "same" events differently but mediate them by means of different cultures and epistemologies. Indeed the overall theme of the text is that of the interaction of mutually uncomprehending cultures. Thus it is quite legitimate for McCarthy to present his narrative, not as a structure with a logical development in time and a single point of view with which the reader can identify (or not as the case may be), but as a patchwork of different experiences involving different characters of undifferentiated significance and with mutually exclusive points of view. The narrative that is so formed bears a closer relation to the infinite complexity of actuality, the matrix of human experiences with all their characteristic mis-readings, ignorances and failures to connect, than would a conventional Jamesian narrative. However the fullest meaning of the text can only be gained by the reader if the year dates are interpreted correctly. Any reader coming to *The Orchard Keeper* for the first time, and not forewarned, would be very unlikely to follow this aspect of the tale and would lose something thereby. In this respect McCarthy has perhaps indulged his narrative intelligence to excess and this is a failure of over-ambition and inexperience. It is not complexity as such that is at fault; that is of the essence. It is the excess of one particular aspect of that complexity.

There are other aspects of this particular text that demonstrate a young man's ambition. McCarthy is at pains to convey to the world his love of language and his remarkable ability to create passages that are clearly intended to be read as a pleasure in themselves. This might easily have led a lesser writer to disaster and have resulted in self-consciously "purple passages" which were at odds with the bulk of the text. It is a measure of McCarthy's ability that such is not the case. Instead these passages take their places in the patchwork that is the tale as a whole and add to the richness and variety of the experience that is afforded to the reader. John Wesley's experience of a Red Branch evening is rendered in terms that create a prose-poem of elegaic beauty:

> From somewhere in the darkness came the sound of a banjo, tentative chords . . a message . . what news? Old loves reconsummated, sickness, a child's crying. Silence now in the houses. Repose. Even to those for whom no end to night could bring rest enough. And silence, the music fled in the seeping amber warmth of innumerable dreams laid to death upon the hearth, ghostly and still . . The morning is yet upon the nether end of the earth, and he is weary. Bowing the grass in sadness the dew followed him home and sealed his door.[9]

This lyricism is contrasted with the bravura gothic of the description of Knoxville market:

> *He went up the far side of the square under the shadow of the market house past brown country faces peering from among their carts and trucks, perched on crates, old women with faces like dried fruit set deep in their hooded bonnets, shaggy, striated and hooktoothed as coconut carvings, shabby backlanders trafficking in the wares of the earth, higgling their goods from a long curb and freighted with fruits and vegetables, eggs and berries, honey in jars and boxes of nuts, bundles of roots and herbs from sassafras to boneset, a bordello of potted plants and flowers. By shoe windows where shoddy footgear rose in dusty tiers and clothing stores in whose vestibules iron racks stood packed with used coats, past bins of socks and stockings, a meat market where hams and ribcages dangled like gibbeted miscreants and in the glass cases square porcelain trays piled with meat white-spotted and trichella-ridden, chunks of liver the color of clay tottering up from moats of watery blood, a tray of brains, unidentified gobbets of flesh scattered here and there.[10]*

In addition the text is punctuated with vivid and original imagery that conveys mood with brilliant economy, as when Sylder and his mountain girl pick-up copulate in the abandoned Negro church:

> *Their steps ghostly on the warping boards, rousing an owl from the beams, passing over them on soundless wings, a shadow, ascending into the belfry*

like an ash sucked up a flue and as silently. She gripped his arm. Together to
the mourners' bench. O Lord, O Lord. Witnessed by one nightbird.[11]

These typical passages are not mere authorial flourishes; they are essential
to McCarthy's method of making the reader "see" and "hear", to his eidetic
style. The variations in voice and language that occur so frequently throughout the text are consistent with the changes of focus and point of view already
mentioned. The inextricable interpenetration of different lives and cultures
within this complex novel are prefigured in its initial image, that of the elm
tree and the iron fence, through which the workmen try in vain to cut their
way. Even the clash of epistemologies is expressed in this metaphor: for the
workmen the iron "*Growed all up in that tree.*"[12] and the relation between the
works of nature and the works of men will be yet another theme of the text
and one of growing significance in later novels.

Virtually all critical responses to *The Orchard Keeper* point out its elegaic quality and this raises the issue of the relation of McCarthy's texts to
America's version of the myth of the pastoral. It is a commonplace that this
mythology played (plays still) an especially significant and long-lasting role
in the life of the South. The development of the "New South" was proposed
as the answer to the region's manifest problems from the late 19th. century,
indeed immediately after the end of the Civil War. The New South was slow
in coming but by the 1960s its development was accelerating sufficiently
to begin to affect areas such a Sevier County and the fringes of the Appalachians. Opposition to the effects of this change had been given literary
expression by reactionary groups of which the Agrarians were the most influential. The central metaphor for what they saw as their identity as a civilization was that of the pastoral. It is not therefore surprising that McCarthy's
first novel should be read by some as an elegy for a lost pastoral way of life.
Even Matthew Guinn, who correctly identifies McCarthy as a mythoclast,
writes of ". . . the philosophical influence of the Agrarian tradition that,
together with the modernist prose style, places the novel in the tradition of
Southern Renascence fiction,"[13] and goes on to describe Ownby as "a nearly
anachronistic figure from an earlier South, an Adamic figure sustained by the
soil of a southern Arcady."[14] In my view this is a misreading of this particular
text and of McCarthy's writing in general. It is clear that *The Orchard Keeper*
is indeed concerned with the passing of a way of life. The concluding passage
of the text states this in the plainest terms:

They are gone now. Fled, banished in death or exile, lost, undone. Over
the land sun and wind still move to burn and sway the trees, the grasses.

No avatar, no scion, no vestige of that people remains. On the lips of the strange race that that now dwells there their names are myth, legend, dust.[15]

But the notion that the way of life that has been lost was in any way Edenic is dispelled by McCarthy in his account of the lives of Ather Ownby and the community of Red Branch. Pastoralism is associated with the notion of the edenic garden. Ather is not a gardener. It is true that he is the "keeper" of the orchard, but it has long since been abandoned. Its peaches are "small and hard;"[16] McCarthy states that they were "his peaches"[17] but the orchard had degenerated to the point where the fruit are no longer suitable for the kind of "trade" whereby Ather makes his precarious living; ginseng and other roots are all that he can take to Eller's Red Branch store. Ather has no garden. John Wesley and the boys of Red Branch learn the skills of fishing, hunting and trapping. For them, as for Ather, it is closeness to nature that defines their being. They do not cultivate, but see themselves as members of a predatory nature; they trap muskrat and mink, shoot rabbits and hunt raccoon with hounds. The young Ather's attempt to establish himself as a farmer ended in disaster. His fragmentary and arbitrary recollections, mostly conveyed "internally," reveal to us that his young wife deserted him for "*That goddamned bible drummer*"[18] and that as a result his grip on life slipped away:

> He stayed for five more days, wandering about the house or sitting motionless, sleeping in chairs, eating whatever he happened to find until there wasn't any more and then not eating anything. While the chickens grew thin and the stock screamed for water, while the hogs perished to the last shoat. An outrageous stench settled over everything, a vile decay that hung in the air, filled the house.[19]

The labeling of the bible seller as a wife stealer deserving of damnation adds an element of black humor to this gothic recollection. In letting his stock starve Ather committed the farmer's cardinal sin; nothing could be further from the pastoral ideal. As the world impinges on Ather's isolation, in the forms of Rattner's corpse in his peach pit and the government tank above his orchard, he longs for flight:

> If I was a younger man, he told himself, I would move to them mountains. I would find me a clearwater branch and build me a log house with a fireplace. And my bees would make black mountain honey. And

I wouldn't care for no man.—Then I wouldn't be unneighbourly neither, he added.[20]

Ather's means of avoiding unneighborliness, Red Branch's (and McCarthy's)
cardinal sin, is to avoid having any neighbors at all. When the social worker
describes Ather as anomic he speaks no less than the truth.

The citizens of Red Branch are depicted as leading lives of penurious
insecurity, their poverty made more acute by the catastrophe of the Depression and the isolation of their mountain location. McCarthy uses gothic
imagery to dispel any notion of Red Branch as another Eden:

> Under the west wall of the mountain is a community called Red Branch.
> It was a very much different place in 1913 when Marion Sylder was
> born there, or in 1929 when he left school to work briefly as a carpen-
> ter's apprentice for Increase Tipton, patriarch of a clan whose affluence
> extended to a dozen jerrybuilt shacks strewn about the valley in unlikely
> places, squatting over their gullied purlieus like great brooding animals
> rigid with constipation, and yet endowed with an air transient and hap-
> penstantial as if set there by the recession of floodwaters. Even the speed
> with which they were constructed could not outdistance the decay for
> which they held such affinity. Gangrenous molds took to the founda-
> tions before the roofs were fairly nailed down. Mud crept up their sides
> and paint fell away in long white slashes. Some terrible plague seemed
> to overtake them one by one.[21]

Like their social centre, The Green Fly Inn, the citizens of Red Branch cling
to a precarious place in American life. The Inn is a fitting metaphor for their
situation, supported on the mountainside by an inadequate structure, partly
natural (the pine tree) and partly man made, insecure, relying for its success
on the faith of its denizens in the notion that what has been will continue to
be. Its demise, burning like a pagan festive fire celebrating the return of the
light at the winter solstice, serves to provide the ever eager celebrants with a
final bacchanal.

Certainly the culture of Ather Ownby, "lover of storms,"[22] "watcher of
the seasons and their work,"[23] his hickory pole "hewed . . . octagonal" and
"graced . . . with hex-carvings—nosed moons, stars, fish of strange and pleis-
tocene aspect,"[24] represents the mythic, pre-enlightenment epistemology of a
people about to vanish at last from American life, to become "myth, legend,
dust." But McCarthy makes two things clear; that this is not the loss of an
edenic pastoral, and that, in the fullness of the earth's time, all things come

to dust. As in all his texts, McCarthy uses geological and scientific phenomena as images for the mutability of every form of life and culture:

> Light saw him through the thick summer ivy and over windfalls and limestone. Past the sink where in a high bluff among trilobites and fishbones, shells of ossified crustaceans from an ancient sea, a great stone tusk jutted.[25]

It is clear therefore that although McCarthy recognizes the role of myth in conveying the values of a culture, and in providing the system of belief by which experience is mediated, his first novel does not feature the characteristics of myth itself. In this respect it is different from all the novels which follow. All the characters in the text remain believable human beings, unlike so many of those of the later texts whose deliberately exaggerated stature and characteristics mark them out as mythic in the "tall tale" American tradition. The action of the story is also entirely believable in a way that is not true, or meant to be true, of later texts. Although *The Orchard Keeper* attacks America's myth of the pastoral it is not in itself an anti-myth.

Like all McCarthy's novels, *The Orchard Keeper* illustrates the author's concern with the primacy of culture in motivating human behavior. McCarthy does not afford us the possibility of psychological insight into the motivations of his characters. They are moved to act in accordance with what they believe and understand, factors that are determined by the culture they have acquired from their social experience. Ather's experience, constrained by mountain isolation and rooted in the archaic past, fails to enable him successfully to mediate the modern world. Marion Sylder, a younger man who has traveled far from Red Branch and experienced the wider world is able to accommodate himself to modernity. He is the master of the motor car and had adapted its speed and power to the traditional needs of the whisky runner. He is the master of both machine and situation as he avoids capture on the road:

> The lights had come to rest straight back down the road and he already had the shiftlever up in second, the tires whining, inching forward, when the cruiser leapt over the hill before him. Then the tires bit and he was gone, raking the fender of the other car with deliberate skill.[26]

The crash that leads to his meeting with John Wesley is the result of a burst tyre and his eventual arrest comes about through rain-water having got into Eller's petrol at the pump. These are the hazards of his occupation, accepted as unavoidable, and worth the risk. Sylder and Ownby share at least two elements of a common traditional culture however. Both hunt in the woods and both are "ag'in the government." Sylder's opposition, as a bootlegger, is primarily economic. But Ather's opposition, represented by his shooting up of the "government tank" has a moral ambivalence that most critics have not acknowledged. Ather's action, seemingly a defense of the pastoral, has implications that are only available if the "meaning" of the tank is explored beyond its mere symbolism of industrial, anti-natural modernity. There are, in my view, two interpretations of the tank that may inform a more complex reaction to Ather's act. In Sevier County the Government means primarily the Tennessee Valley Authority, the agency that instituted the modernization of the area and by whom McCarthy senior was employed. The attack on the tank could therefore be considered an element of that father/son conflict that informs much of McCarthy's work. However Robert Jarrett puts forward a much more challenging possibility: he refers to ". . . a government tank holding atomic waste atop a nearby mountain—like an ironic cathedral tower announcing itself to a fallen world."[27] This interpretation would probably not occur to anyone understandably confused by the time-scale of *The Orchard Keeper*. It was only after my calculation of that aspect of the novel that I was able to disabuse myself of the notion that Jarrett's idea was a chronological impossibility. In fact the Manhattan Project, and its Oak Ridge installation were in place by 1940, the year in which the tank is attacked. Oak Ridge was associated with the TVA, whose operation made available the electrical power needed for the Oak Ridge process. This interpretation is strengthened by the knowledge of McCarthy's concern with the nuclear theme and its appearance in *The Crossing* and *Cities of the Plain*. The fear of nuclear annihilation was particularly strong in the 1960s, when the nuclear arms race was under way. The revival of interest in traditional folk music at this time was associated with the longing for a simpler, safer, more "authentic" world. The fear was understandable (and should not have diminished) but the escape to a past without "the bomb" was a refusal of history of the kind that McCarthy attacks by his anti-pastoralism. In historical context Ather would be attacking something he could not be expected to understand, and which would have been secret anyway, but whose importance in a time of war when a ruthless enemy might have developed such a weapon first, could hardly be exaggerated. Ather's action thus may have implications that go far beyond those associated with the interpretations of those critics whose sympathies lie with the pastoral vision of an American Eden. When the authorities come to apprehend Ather, as come they must, he responds by opening up with the shotgun and three officials receive wounds of unspecified seriousness.[28]

These actions are interpreted sympathetically by most critics but in my view McCarthy is more complex in his representation of Ather. Sylder witnesses the shooting of the tank:

> There was something ghastly and horrific about it and he had the impression that this gnomic old man had brought with him an inexhaustible supply of shells and would cease his cannonade only when he became too weary to lift the gun.[29]

Informed by his more contemporary and pragmatic culture Sylder overcomes the problem of government "encroachment" on his affairs by unbolting the gate at the hinge end, and bolting it up again after he has passed through. Ather's actions and reactions take on an altogether more sinister aspect when they are seen as a product of that American cultural tradition in which the citizen bears arms in order to protect himself from the tyranny of government. The consequences of this have been seen in an extreme form in Oklahoma City and in the activities of extremist militias. The moral complexity of McCarthy's text matches its narrative structure and reflects the difficulty of establishing cultural, and hence moral cohesion in a changing world.

Critics frequently refer to *The Orchard Keeper* as a *Bildungsroman*. To the extent that John Wesley Rattner provides one of the three main foci of the text this is, of course, true. We encounter a few incidents of John Wesley's life, scattered over the whole period of the text's seven years. What McCarthy focuses on is the culture that John Wesley acquires by means of his contact with the various adults in his life at this age when the child's mind is beginning to adopt the lessons that the world has to teach. Most critics interpret this aspect of the text in accordance with the notion of government's and modernity's assault on the pastoral. But as I have already argued John Wesley's boyhood pursuits are anything but pastoral, those of his friends even less so. Warn Pulliam keeps a buzzard on a string. Johnny Romines catches a bullfrog in a mousetrap for a bet. The two of them blow up the birds in Johnny Romines' yard:

> I told Warn to thow the switch. Goddamn but it come an awful blast, said Warn. I eased the switch over and then BALOOM! They's a big hoop of snow jumped up in the yard like when you thow a flat rock in the pond and birds goin ever which way but mostly straight up. I remember we run out and you could see pieces of em strung all out in

the yard and hangin off the trees. And feathers. God, I never seen the like of feathers. They was stit fallin next mornin.

Lord, whispered Boog, I'd of liked to of seen that.[30]

However one responds to this episode, and one may well find it comic, horrific or both, it certainly is not "pastoral."

Georg Guillermin interprets McCarthy in the light of a broader interpretation of the pastoral; for him the natural world as a whole is the pastoral space:

McCarthy's pastoralism is ecopastoral not just because it respects the ecological quality of all creatures and favors undomesticated nature over agricultural land, but, moreover, because it equates the external wilderness of nature with the social wilderness of the city and the internal wilderness of the human mind.[31]

Guillermin associates this interpretation of pastoral with melancholy and locates this melancholy in the narrative voice of much of McCarthy's work. However in my view the South out of which McCarthy grew, and in whose culture it is rooted, found its pastoral ideal in the notion of the sacred (edenic) garden and it is in the light of this vision that I interpret McCarthy's southern works. There is no doubt that Guillermin is correct in finding McCarthy's characteristic landscape as 'wilderness' in all respects. Given the importance to American mythology of the mission to domesticate that wilderness, this characteristic of McCarthy's vision may be interpreted as an aspect of his mythoclasm.

As in so many of McCarthy's tales, family plays a less than positive part in shaping the young John Wesley. His father is probably the most lamentable of all McCarthy's failed patriarchs. Kenneth Rattner forsakes his family, robs the fallen as the platform of the Green Fly Inn collapses and presents Marion Sylder with "a profound and unshakeable knowledge of the presence of evil."[32] He has already stolen from a roadside store and we may presume that the billfold and contents that he discards after removing its cash has also been stolen, quite probably after murdering the driver who gave him a lift to Atlanta. When Mrs. Rattner claims that she knew of a platinum plate in her husband's head, the result of a "war wound," by means of "a vision", the lugubrious Gifford reveals both his worldliness and an unexpected wit: "Wonder if she had a vision of him bein wanted in three states."[33] Rattner's murderous assault on Sylder results in an unlamented demise. In this fragmented narrative he is the only link between the three main characters. For John Wesley he is little more than a disembodied idea; for Sylder a mortal assailant and inconvenient corpse; for Ather an unwelcome visitor from the world of the dead whose unquiet spirit resides in the "flying cat" that so puzzles Eller, and whose presence must be hidden from authority for a mythic seven years.[34]

Rattner is replaced in John Wesley's life by Sylder, the real father's killer. Neither of them is aware of this fact, nor does it acquire any significance in the narrative. The rakish bootlegger rewards John Wesley for helping him out of the car-wreck by befriending him, taking him hunting, and acting as his protector against Gifford. He advises the boy against his own beliefs in an attempt to keep him out of trouble with the law—indicating his awareness of the unsatisfactory nature of his own way of life. Above all he gives John Wesley McCarthy's talisman of true fatherhood—the puppy. When his mother urges on him the duty of the blood feud and demands that he find and kill his father's killer (although at that time she does not know that he is dead) John Wesley remains unaffected. His mother interprets her situation in the light of the old patriarchal mythology but it means little to the boy since his father is little more to him than a photograph on the wall. His values and view of the world are influenced principally by his mentors Ather Ownby and Marion Sylder. From them he has learned that the principal virtue is "neighborliness." He has also learned to distrust the law and its officers and that the government is a distant, official other that may be legitimately cheated by representing a sparrowhawk as a chickenhawk in order to claim the bounty: "*Is it a chickenhawk? Yesm, he said. It's a youngern.*"[35] This deception is consistent with the moral complexity that is inherent in McCarthy's narrative. It undermines the virtue of John Wesley's returning of the hawk bounty as he rejects the authority that can "thow people in jail and beat up on em.[36] . . . And old men in the crazy house."[37] Critics who find John Wesley to have imbibed a nobler sense of values from his adult guides are perhaps victims of pastoral delusion or at least have taken an over-simplified view of McCarthy's vision of the world. What we do find in *The Orchard Keeper* is the first sign of McCarthy's attempt to create a narrative that escapes the confines of anthropocentrism and makes the world of nature, animate and inanimate, an equal principal in his epistemology.

The Orchard Keeper features other McCarthy characteristics. Some names have significance: Ownby is the most obvious in this case. The head of the Tipton clan is named "Increase". The irony is twofold: the clan's numbers increase without check but their wealth remains inadequate. Kenneth Rattner, besides being the "dangerous man" of the text, is also interpreted by Jarrett as a metaphor for Faulkner, the patriarch of southern literature, from whom all later southern writers must emancipate themselves and who McCarthy therefore delights in killing off. This may seem a fanciful notion but "Ratt-ner" is an amalgam of "Ratliff," Faulkner's surrogate in the Snopes Trilogy, and of "Faulkner" itself. Like Faulkner, Rattner has a mythic war wound and an equally mythic platinum plate in his head. Legwater's demented efforts to dig up this "treasure" recall the efforts of Armstid, Bookwright and Ratliff to dig up Flem Snopes "treasure" in *The Hamlet*. Such intertextuality would be entirely in keeping with McCarthy's literary method. Of course in "dispos-ing" of Faulkner, McCarthy draws attention to him. It is easy to see Sevier County as McCarthy's Bakhtinian chronotope, his Yoknapatawpha. It is in his subsequent novels that McCarthy draws increasingly further away from Faulkner's example. Other details that are to be encountered consistently in subsequent texts include the flood, resulting from the storm in which Ather is felled, and his subsequent "return from the dead." There is also the repre-sentation of the spontaneous power of life and its recurring metaphor, the beating heart:

> It rained and the pond went blood-red and one afternoon he caught a bass from the willows in water not a foot deep and cleaned it and held the tiny heart in the palm of his hand, still beating.[38]

For Faulkner's Vardaman Bundren the fish is an image of death. McCarthy recasts the metaphor in a more complex, paradoxical form, the "still beating" heart made available to the boy by death but retaining its vital characteristic and thus remaining an image of life. The power of the metaphor is intensi-fied by having the fish caught from water that has turned "blood-red."

By the end of the text we have learned that John Wesley's boyhood home has become an abandoned house and that he is without family in the world, mother and father both dead. This is to prove the fate of all McCa-rthy's future protagonists; they all set out on the quest for identity, meaning, home. Their quests are defined for them by American mythology and their fate provides McCarthy with occasions to create in various forms his Ameri-can anti-myths. That all his heroes pursue in vain shelter from the experience of the *unheimlich* is one of the characteristics that give McCarthy's fiction a significance that goes beyond both regional and national boundaries.

In *The Orchard Keeper* therefore, McCarthy takes the people of a forgotten region, the mountain people of isolated Appalachian Tennes-see, and writes them into the discourse of America in a way which no-one had previously attempted. Mildred Haun appears to have written more as an anthropologist than as a creative artist.[39] Mary Murfree's vision of the mountain people was largely sentimental and romanticized.[40] Although she did deal with serious themes she failed to make her vision of East Tennessee essentially different from the overall fictional representation of the rural America of her day. Only McCarthy has made this unique way of life his metaphor for America and the world at large. Given the narrative complexity and depth of multi-layered significance of *The Orchard Keeper*, together with its wide ranging inter-textuality, powerful human appeal, extraordinary command of language and range of expression, it is small wonder that this first novel was taken up by academic critics and hailed as the work of a great new talent. Its "difficulty" no doubt greatly restricted its popular appeal but it is not hard to see why prizes and grants should have accrued. Emboldened by this intellectual success McCarthy embarked on the writing of his next novel with the intention of taking a more radical turn and of further establishing his own literary persona. But the seeds of what was to come are to be found in his remarkable first work.

Chapter Six

Outer Dark

I believe it's a hard enough case to give Jehovah hisself the witherins.

McCarthy's second novel was published in 1968, the year when youthful and rebellious protest was as vigorous and unsuccessful on American college campuses as at the universities of Paris and London. The riotous tumult of Paris, Berkeley and the London School of Economics may seem far removed from McCarthy's Appalachia in geographical, social, economic and political terms. I suggest however that *Outer Dark*, and McCarthy's work in general, does reflect two aspects of what is now seen as a crucial period in the life of the West. The revolt of what was mainly a student (male) class in 1968 appeared then to have more to do with the clash between youth and age than with the overthrow of capitalism and the emancipation of the working class. Of course there were social and economic forces at work that energized the various movements of protest. Many young Americans felt that the requirement to fight in Vietnam was not motivated by a rational need to defend American interests. The Civil Rights movement still found that progress towards racial justice had as yet not matched expectation. A decade of growing affluence and technological development had seen a radical change in attitudes towards sexuality, drugs, authority and materialism generally, especially among the young and this had produced tensions in conservative societies such as America, Britain, France and Germany. This conservatism was matched, ironically, in the countries of Eastern Europe, which also experienced political protest, although of a much more serious, but less successful nature (in the short run).

In my view the involvement of youth in the disturbances of 1968 served to give these events an oedipal character at least in part. I have already argued that this aspect of conflict is inescapable in a patriarchal culture and that McCarthy's work is informed by powerful and continuing oedipal concerns. I believe it to be as revealing as it is distasteful that the expression "motherfucker" has come into general use in the interim. In addition cultural theorists, adrift of their moorings at the failure of Marxism so vividly illustrated after the '68 events, began to announce the postmodern and to identify among its characteristic assertions the failure of the metanarratives of western culture. I argue in this thesis that McCarthy's entire oeuvre can be read as an anti-myth, as attack on the American metanarrative of exceptionalism, and that this attack consistently takes the form of deconstruction, of subversion from within. McCarthy takes the language, symbols and images of his culture and inverts their meanings in order to illustrate the destructive consequences of following narratives that are "false."

Although *Outer Dark* bears some superficial resemblance to *The Orchard Keeper*, being set in the Appalachians and involving characters whose speech identifies them as mountain folk, this second novel is radically different from its predecessor. The realism of the former is resolutely abandoned and the adoption of mythic form is overt and clearly "announced."[1] The concern with narrative form noted in the previous section is replaced by a uniform authorial voice. Authorial comment and explanation are non-existent. The affectionate portrait of the beauties of the natural world that balanced the darker aspects of *The Orchard Keeper* are absent from *Outer Dark*. Time continues to be a central concern of the text, but it is approached from different point of view. The gothic atmosphere predominates and is greatly intensified. The shadow of Faulkner continues to fall across the work. Above all one gains the impression that, encouraged by having achieved his first publication and doubtless urged forward by Erskine, McCarthy determined to give full rein to his mythoclastic imagination and his formidable powers of expression.[2] The first page of *Outer Dark* is one of those italicized passages with which McCarthy structured the temporal punctuation of his first novel. This second text is similarly punctuated but the temporal structure is straightforwardly linear, the murderous trio thus early introduced reappearing at regular intervals of time and narrative. Nevertheless time is still a subject of this text in ways which I will seek to make clear subsequently. The text's second page begins with characteristically simple, "realistic" and eidetic lines:

> She shook him awake in the quiet darkness. Hush she said. Quit hollerin.
> He sat up. What? he said. What?[3]

This apparent and convincing realism is a source of confusion for many readers and not a few critics of McCarthy's work. Duane Carr suggests that

> . . . . many of his characterizations are neither sympathetic nor dispassionate, as has been claimed, but rather some of the most blatant stereotypes of Southern "rednecks" in contemporary American fiction.[4]

It seems odd that so many who must surely be familiar with *Moby Dick* and *The Scarlet Letter* should fail to discern the character of a text which follows this vividly "real" beginning with:

> She shook him awake from dark to dark, delivered out of the clamorous rabble under a black sun and into a night more dolorous, sitting upright and cursing beneath his breath in the bed he shared with her and the nameless weight in her belly.[5]

Shortly we discover that "she" is his sister. The original impression thus made is that here is a radical inversion of the myth of southern womanhood, the myth expressed in so many texts of the kind exemplified by F. Hopkinson Smith's *Colonel Carter of Cartersville*. The Colonel's Aunt Nancy is a case in point. A maiden aunt of course and no longer young:

> She had the same silky gray hair—a trifle whiter, perhaps; the same frank, tender mouth, graceful figure; and the same manner—its very simplicity a reflex of that refined and quiet life she had always led. For hers had been an isolated life, buried since girlhood in a great house far away from the broadening influences of the city, and saddened by the slow decay of all that she had been taught to revere. But it had been a life so filled with the largeness of generous deeds that its returns had brought her the love of every living soul she knew.[6]

It is not difficult to see Rinthy Holme as the anti-myth of Aunt Nancy. The blunt assertion of incest shocks as it is meant to do and also suggests Faulkner's Caddy Compson, that other female embodiment of a southern ideal. However it quickly becomes clear that other mythologies are being called to serve McCarthy's fictive purpose. A male child is born:

> The head had broken through in a pumping welter of blood. He knelt in the bed with one knee, holding her. With his own hand he brought it free, the scrawny body trailing the cord in anneloid writhing down

the bloodslimed covers, a beetcolored creature that looked to him like a skinned squirrel. He pinched the mucus from its face with his fingers. It didn't move. He leaned down to her.

Rinthy.

She turned her head. Far look and slow flutter of her pale lashes. I'm done ain't I? she said. Ain't I done?[7]

As ever blood is a powerful and prominent image for McCarthy, in this case signifying life in its most elemental form. The child's blood will signify death in even more horrific fashion at the novel's end. The un-named child is taken by his father who abandons him in the forest from which he is recovered by an itinerant tinker. The mythic reference could not be plainer, especially in a South still familiar with claims to be inheritors of the values of classical civilization. Thus McCarthy makes quite clear the mythic, non-realistic nature of his text, and, at the same time, concentrates his gothic atmosphere and imagery at a new level of intensity. Oedipal imagery occurs throughout the text. Like Oedipus, Culla wanders through the world although he finds no Colonus at the end of these wanderings, no sacred grove, but only a swamp. By then he has his own limp and encounters a blind man, as do so many of McCarthy's wanderers. Indeed it cannot be said that Culla's wanderings do come to an end. His journey is existential, the novel that it structures is picaresque. Like the kid in *Blood Meridian* the illiterate Culla is virtually without culture. In this sense the Holmes,[8] living alone and unconnected to the world in their forest isolation, suggest a wider American mythoclasm; they are Adam and Eve, but existing in a realm that enjoys neither the bliss of innocence nor the consolation of culture. They are figures of the anti-pastoral, a theme that connects with other aspects of the text in ways which I shall deal with below.

The Adamic motif is, as already noted, a product of America's Puritan origins. Protestant fundamentalism is an inherent part of that Puritanism and its Southern Baptist form has proved to be particularly destructive of cultural openness. Perry Miller points out the inescapable nature of the society formed by the original Puritans. In their desire for "freedom" they felt constrained to create:

> . . . a political regime, possessing power, which would consider its main function to be the erecting, protecting and preserving of this form of polity. This due form would have, at the very beginning of its list of responsibilities, the duty of suppressing heresy, of subduing or somehow getting rid of dissenters—of being, in short, deliberately, vigorously and consistently intolerant.[9]

Whilst the theocracy did not survive the forces of history it did bequeath to American culture a religious strain in which the Manichean vision of a world contended by the real and coequal forces of good and evil maintained its influence. It was this influence that Faulkner attacked in *Light In August*, a text with which *Outer Dark* is frequently associated. Faulkner also gave certain of his characters significant names—in this case the violent, self-righteous and iron-willed patriarch McEachern. The figure of the Baptist preacher appears in *Outer Dark*, urging death on Culla for no other reason than his own enthusiasm for violence. "Don't flang him off the bluff, boys, the preacher said. I believe ye'd be better to hang him as that."[10] But McCarthy deploys religious imagery in a far more radical, subversive, and mythoclastic manner than this. The "murderous trio" have puzzled many critics. I have argued already that "the dangerous man" is a characteristic feature of McCarthy's texts; these three belong to that category, in a text that features a number of such characters whose taste for death and violence seems both arbitrary and extreme. For Terri Witek they are "three evil magi figures."[11] Jarrett identifies "the bearded outlaw" as "representative of patriarchal judge and providing father."[12] However William Spencer faces up squarely to the full implications of McCarthy's use of inverted religious imagery: "This terrible trio, this unholy trinity, parodies the theological concept of a triune God."[13] That McCarthy is indeed referring to the Christian notion of the Trinity is made clear enough. On the text's first page we read ". . . light touching them about the head in spurious sanctity . . ."[14] At the assassination of the snake-hunter the three combine "in consubstantial monstrosity, a grim triune . . ."[15] As the use of theological language indicates, there is little difficulty in identifying the bearded patriarch who dominates the trio as the Father and the ironically named "Harmon" as the Son; the inversion of religious mythology is completed by the demented wordless third as Holy Spirit. It is surely impossible to imagine a more radical and extreme attack on the beliefs and imagery of "that old time religion" than this. McCarthy himself refers to this aspect of his text in the exchange between Culla and the preacher at the encounter with the hog-drovers:

What place of devilment you hail from mister? he asked.

Holme looked at him wearily. I don't come from no place of devilment, he said. I come from Johnson County.

Never heard tell of it. You a christian?

Yes.

I cain't say as you've much took on the look of one.

It ain't marked you a whole lot to notice neither, Holme said.

Don't disperge the cloth son, the preacher said. Don't disperge the cloth.

Cloth's ass, Holme said.

Well now, said the preacher, what have we here. I believe it's a hard enough case to give Jehovah hisself the witherins.

Holme didn't answer.[16]

It is also surprising that great controversy was not created by what is to the faithful nothing short of the most extreme blasphemy. In fact I have not encountered any reaction to this particular aspect of McCarthy's work; this is no doubt due to the still limited readership of his earlier texts.[17]

The wholly arbitrary manner in which the parodic trinity "harvest" the squire and their other victims is perhaps one of the aspects of the novel that puzzles some critics. Vereen Bell sparked an on-going debate by commenting that:

> *Outer Dark* . . . is as brutally nihilistic as any serious novel written in this century in this unnihilistic country.[18]

The mythic interpretation that I am suggesting for his texts deals with the issue of McCarthy's nihilism by pointing out that the moral grounding of myth is strictly implicit. Ovid's metamorphoses may feature incest, rape and murder but they are not meant to be read literally, but rather as metaphors of transformation—social, cultural, historical. If they have a moral ground it is a belief in the coincidence of goodness and beauty. McCarthy's moral ground is suggested by the concept of neighborliness, a concept that unites biblical Christian, socialist and existentialist alike.

Thus we find in *Outer Dark* two mythic strains, the oedipal and the biblical. They are however united in particular ways. As Jean-Joseph Goux makes clear in his interpretation of the Oedipus myth, *Oedipus Philosopher*,[19]

Oedipus's initial act was to solve the riddle of the Sphinx. In so doing he employed reason, became "the first philosopher," and cast down the Sphinx, a manifestation of the Great Goddess of antiquity and the female image of the holistic culture that predated patriarchy.[20] In the Oedipus myth the epistemology of the Mother is superceded by that of the Father, with violent results. As Octavio Paz writes, "In all civilizations, God the Father becomes an ambivalent figure once he has dethroned the feminine deities."[21] As well as embodying "the generative power, the origin of life, . . . he is also the lord of the lightning bolt and the whip; he is the tyrant, the ogre who devours life."[22] The Bible consistently expresses the continuing struggle of patriarchal religion to win the people away from the worship of the Goddess, the Old Testament myth of Eden being only one example of this. In the New Testament the appearance of St. Paul, a Jew, in Ephesus, creates uproar among the people: ". . . all with one voice about the space of two hours cried out Great is Diana of the Ephesians . . . what man is there that knoweth not that the city of Ephesus is a worshipper of the great goddess Diana, . . ."[23] In placing reason at the centre of Patriarchal epistemology Oedipus also institutes the linear conception of time as opposed to the "female", natural, cyclic conception associated with holistic matriarchal culture. This aspect of the myth represents the creation therefore of the notion of death as an end, rather than as a stage on the unending cycle of nature; it also mythicises the inception of the notion of "history." This conception of time and, therefore, death also informs both Old and New Testaments, as death involves not a return to the natural cycle but a transfer to the supernatural realm. It is this temporal aspect of the twin myths that McCarthy invokes in *Outer Dark* and that give the text its American mythoclastic significance. This has been most clearly noted by John M. Grammer in his perceptive essay in *Perspectives on Cormac McCarthy*. He points out that:

> These menacing riders, armed with farming tools, are of course figures of *time*, reapers who move through the novel, leaving a trail of violent death behind them; the farm tools they carry will indeed become weapons as their spree commences. Thus they embody the deadly threat which history poses to the pastoral realm. And yet they are themselves pastoral figures, or at least parodic versions of such figures, bearing spades and brush hooks through a barnyard, frightening the stock. Whatever threat they represent, that is, emerges in some sense *from* the pastoral realm they scourge; they are that community's nightmare, the seed of destruction that lurks within the pastoral dream.[24]

Grammer enlarges on this theme of the pastoral dream as "an escape from history"[25] and quotes Pocock's assertion that the South has been imprisoned

> . . . within a "Machiavellian moment:" the moment when the republic, conceived as a civic order created in defiance of history, begins to recognize its mortality.

and

> . . . to theorize some social transformation which will effect an escape from history; the pastoral myth of the plantation has served this purpose admirably . . . I think that we will discover in McCarthy's southern fiction a profoundly serious interrogation of this oldest cultural impulse in southern history. This is to say that McCarthy participates in the South's second-oldest intellectual tradition, that of the anti-pastoral.[26]

These passages give more formal and authoritative expression to the notion of the anti-pastoral that I have used to characterize the texts of the previous sections of this book, particularly *The Orchard Keeper*. This theme informs all McCarthy's work in my view, and is one of the unifying features of his oeuvre.

It is also entirely characteristic of McCarthy that he should maintain, and, if anything, intensify the density of allusion that his work shares with that of T.S. Eliot. The brush-hook wielded by the murderous triune is a version of the scythe, traditional symbol of both time and his inevitable companion, death. The men who meet their end at the trio's hands all have a particular attitude or relation to time. The first victim is the squire whose readily consulted watch enables him to "tell the time" with precision:

> The squire hauled by its long chain a watch from somewhere in his coat, snapped it open and glanced at it and put it away. It's near six o'clock he said. Likin about three minutes. How much time would you say you put in on that job?[27]

The squire's attitudes towards Culla, his work, the black servant and his property in general are puritanical in their harsh self-righteousness:

> . . . shiftlessness is a sin, I would judge. Wouldn't you? . . . Yes. The bible reckons. What I got I earned. Daybreak to backbreak for a Godgiven dollar.[28]

Blinded by the certainty of his own righteousness and the permanence of the pastoral realm which he has created for himself, the squire is taken all unawares by the murderous three, who cut him down with his own stolen brush-hook. The snakehunter, disembowelled by his smiling assassin, has also referred himself to time: "If I live to see the fifth day of September I'll be sixty three years old . . ."[29] His attitudes are crudely patriarchal: "I had a wife one time used to run off. Like a dog. Best place to hunt 'em is home again."[30] His significance is heightened by his occupation as a hunter of snakes for money. The snake was an emblem of the Goddess; its ability to shed its old skin and emerge as new made it a symbol of rebirth.[31] Clark, the man of power of Preston Flats, uses time as an instrument of domination:

> Easy now Bud, he said. It's a warm day. Tell you what. I'll see what the law can do.

> Law's ass. You are the law . . .

> Law takes time, the other said. Yours is an unusual case. We don't want to jump too fast here and do the wrong thing do we? I think maybe another day or two and we'll be able to handle your problem. It's kindly good advertisin for the public peace just now. Ain't it?[32]

The "*problem*" is the disposal of the corpses of the two victims of the lynching. Clark's cynicism is answered with irony. His corpse, identifiable by its dusty white suit, soon hangs by the other two, his fate sealed by his temporal dominion:

> Clark lifted an enormous watch from the pocket of his coat and looked at it. Tell you what I'll do Holme, he said, addressing the face of the watch.[33]

Two other figures are associated with time:

> The lawyer tucked a long forefinger into his waistcoat pocket and flashed forth a watch. He snapped it open, looked at it, looked at the sun where it rode darkly as if to verify the hour in that way. He won't be in till about one-thirty, he said. It's ten till now. He snapped shut the watch-case and slipped it into his vest once more. Is it urgent? he said.[34]

He is referring to the doctor who gives Rinthy his time freely. Neither of these is visited by the temporal murderers. The lawyer appears to need to check watch time against sun time. Their kindliness towards Rinthy places them outside the murderers' orbit. As educated professional men they are not identified with the pastoral mythology. As the lawyer remarks, "We get a lot of rain here in the fall, . . . After it's too late to do any good."[35]

If the oedipal Culla represents linear time, the time that can only be "accounted for" by his existential quest in the realm of the *unheimlich*, and whose journey can be finally terminated by death alone, it is unsurprising that McCarthy remains true to the full extent of his mythic form by representing cyclic, holistic, natural, matriarchal time in the person of Rinthy. This is, of course, most obvious in her position as a loving mother in unceasing quest of her lost child. Her continued lactation in the absence of the child renders her a symbol of maternal plenitude. She is associated with nature in a most direct manner:

> Butterflies attended her and birds dusting in the road did not fly up when she passed. She hummed to herself as she went some child's song from an old dead time.[36]

The "old dead time" is the archaic pre-patriarchal past. Her attitude to linear time is imprecise. She does not mark the time of the child's birth by the month, but the other way around: "Just March or April. I forgot."[37] Her own journey is cyclic in form; she returns to the nature with which she is so "at home"—the opposite of her brother. McCarthy associates her with words that carry mythic significance; she is "cradled in a *grail* of jade and windy light;"[38] she steps softly "in a frail agony of *grace*."[39] Despite her inability to recognize the charred remains of her "chap" in the glade she remains a curiously uncompromised figure at the end of the novel: "Shadows grew cold across the wood and night rang down upon these lonely figures and after a while little sister was sleeping."[40]

The temporal theme is also relevant to that other enigmatic figure of the text, Dietch, the tinker, the alien representative of peripatetic commerce who bitterly declares,

> I give a lifetime wanderin in a country where I was despised. . . . I give forty years strapped in front of a cart like a mule till I couldn't stand straight to be hanged. . . . I been rocked and shot at and whipped and kicked and dogbit from one end of this state to the other . . .[41]

The tinker is the Wandering Jew, the mythic scapegoat for the death of Christ. The tinker's temporal "transgression" has been to rescue the child, thus becoming the "surrogate father" of the text. But his killing is doubly ironic for death was the release that was forbidden the Wandering Jew. He was trapped for ever in time; and the patriarch's slaughtering of the child mirrors the paranoid Christian myth of the Jew as a cannibalistic child killer. The Jew's corpse, hanging in a tree and devoured by the vultures, returns to the natural order:

> Black mandrake sprang beneath the tree as it will where the seed of the hanged falls and in spring a new branch pierced his breast and flowered in a green boutonniere perennial beneath his yellow grin.[42]

McCarthy's interest in the theme of time thus takes a different and more esoteric form than in *The Orchard Keeper*. The latter demonstrated a concern with the relationship between present and past and related this in turn to the narrative form of the text. *Outer Dark* is altogether more metaphysical in its concern with time, and with the implications of our temporal epistemologies. Unlike *The Orchard Keeper*, *Outer Dark* has no chronotope. Johnson County, the most north-easterly corner of Tennessee is the only identifiable place mentioned in the text, and that is the place from which Culla has traveled and which most of the people he meets have never heard of. The historical period of the action is also indefinite. It seems to be before the existence of the automobile but features "store bought bread" and bottles of "dope," both indications of the twentieth century, even in Appalachia. Grammer points out that:

> In fact the book's temporal setting is not only vague but contradictory: the band of marauders seem a kind of Murrell gang, figures from the antebellum days of frontier settlement; . . . The temporal setting is strange and surreal, emphasizing the novel's general sense of displacement in time.[43]

This deliberate refusal of specific time and place strengthen the mythic character of the text and emphasize the existential nature of the state of being of its protagonists.

It should be remembered that we still mediate our experience with reference to both linear and cyclic notions of time. Historical time is linear; the discrete individual comes into being at birth and ceases to be at death.

Societies, cultures, species, even landscapes are born and die in this sense, as McCarthy never ceases to remind us. Years are "numbered." But clock time is cyclic, as are the days of the week, the months of the year, the natural seasons, the cycle of vegetation; and, signifying the Goddess and the female principle, the phases of the moon. There is a growing interest in the possible ecological and environmentalist implications of McCarthy's work, with Dianne Luce prominent in this respect. There is a complexity in McCarthy's work in this regard as in most others: he combines a respect for the life and time of nature with a warning against the delusions of the pastoral refusal of history.

The allusiveness of McCarthy's text, his use of intertextuality, is further illustrated by the remarkable passage in which Culla encounters the great herd of hogs as they are swept off the bluff by their own momentum, taking a drover with them. This is a characteristic McCarthy literary *tour de force*, spread over two pages of the most vivid and dynamic description which never loses its grip on the appalled reader. The passage is too long to quote in full but a brief section conveys the energy and horror of the whole:

> Drovers were racing brokenly across the milling hogs with staves aloft, stumbling and falling among them, making for the outer perimeter to head them from the cliff. This swept a new wave of panic among the hogs like wind through grass until a whole echelon of them careering up the outer flank forsook the land and faired out into space with torn cries. Now the entire herd had begun to wheel wider and faster along the bluff and the outermost ranks swung centrifugally over the escarpment row on row wailing and squealing and above this the howls and curses of the drovers that now upreared in the moil of flesh they tended and swept with dust had begun to assume satanic looks with their staves and wild eyes as if they were no true swineherds but disciples of darkness got among these charges to herd them to their doom.[44]

In this passage McCarthy demonstrates once again both his ability to "make us see" vivid and compelling action, but also to develop the atmosphere of a passage rapidly but almost imperceptibly from one level to another. In this case we are taken from the physical to the metaphysical in the single line: "Now the entire herd had begun to wheel . . . no true swineherds but disciples of darkness got among these charges to herd them to their doom." The power of the language is such that the transformation seems entirely apposite. The impression is strengthened by the clear reference to the story of the Gadarene Swine.[45] This is a further typical example of McCarthy's use of mythic imagery in an inverted form; it is not only a representation of the anti-pastoral but is also part of his attack on the associated mythologies of patriarchy and Protestant fundamentalism. As ever, McCarthy remains a religious writer in a godless world, and a novelist working in a culture steeped in religious language and mythology. His characteristic allusiveness is compounded by yet another correspondence; the destructive rush of the hogs recalls The Reverend Hightower's waking dream of the great cavalry charge of the mythic Old South, one of several correspondences between *Outer Dark* and *Light In August*.

Outer Dark represents a further development of McCarthy's fictional ambition in that it is the first of his texts in which a philosophical concern with language is introduced, an interest that will be greatly expanded in *Blood Meridian, The Crossing* and *Cities of the Plain*. This initially appears as an almost comic illustration of the enigmatic quality of language and the difficulties that can inhibit human communication as Culla and the pair of gravediggers fail to distinguish between the words "two" and "too":

Howdy' he said. You sure you diggin in the right place?

Yessir, the seated one said.

You ain't diggin two are ye?

Yessir. I just waitin on him a minute.

Where's the other one?

They ain't but just us.

Holme looked at him blankly. Where's the other hole at? he said.

The two negroes looked at each other. The one digging said: we wasn't told to dig but one.[46]

Later the patriarch deepens the discourse:

. . . I wouldn't name him because if you cain't name somethin you cain't claim it. You cain't talk about it even. You cain't say what it is.[47]

I have referred previously to McCarthy's acknowledgement of the "ugly fact . . . that books are made out of other books."[48] This suggests a further level of meaning for the grave robber of Cheatham. The body in the coffin "wore a white shirt and a necktie but no coat or trousers". A local comments, "I reckon whoever done it will be wearin a black suit."[49] Seven pages on we encounter an anonymous figure: "He wore a dusty suit of black linen that was small on him . . . he wore neither shirt nor collar. . . ."[50] This powerful patriarchal figure, obviously the grave-robber, has no difficulty in whipping the gullible locals into a lynch mob and in provoking the death of "two itinerant millhands"[51] whose only crime was that they were strangers. The significance is two-fold yet again. Lynching is an image of the anti-pastoral and a grim fact of southern social history; the grave robbing is McCarthy's acknowledgement that, as a writer, he is wearing a dead man's clothes.

The most obvious "dead man" in this case, leaving aside ancient classical and biblical authors, is Faulkner. If McCarthy sought to dispose of him in *The Orchard Keeper*, he here acknowledges that such an effort is neither possible nor, perhaps desirable. After all it is himself that he casts as the grave-robber. Mention has already been made of the parallels between *Outer Dark* and *Light In August*, referred to by various critics, but usually only in general terms. Both novels feature a biblical parallel; both have a sacrificial victim; both are concerned to make clear the destructive power of a false mythology; both castigate the inhuman violence and intolerance inherent in Protestant fundamentalism. The most obvious and oft-quoted parallel is that between the two goddess figures, Lena Grove and Rinthy Holme, both of whom have significant names,[52] represent maternal fecundity and produce babies. McCarthy does not share Faulkner's preoccupation with race but he acknowledges the presence of that all-important theme in the text upon which he has reflected; the white corpse in the plundered coffin is not alone:

> Across the desiccated chest lay a black arm, and when Holme stood on his toes he could see that the old man shared his resting place with a negro sexton whose head had been cut half off and who clasped him in an embrace of lazarous depravity.[53]

The other southern writer with whom McCarthy is most frequently identified is Flannery O'Connor. The gothic atmosphere of *Outer Dark* and its treatment of Protestant fundamentalism in all its passionate unreason, is similar to that of *The Violent Bear It Away*. Both texts conclude with the death of a child, both deaths caused by figures associated with destructive religious extremes. But McCarthy's version is a contradiction of that of O'Connor. The latter's faith in the power of Divine Grace to operate despite the "intentions" of those concerned enables us to read the drowning of Bishop as a baptism. But the slaughter of Rinthy's "chap" by the "unholy trinity" is an act of mythic destructiveness that has no redeeming connotation:

> The man took hold of the child and lifted it up. It was watching the fire. Holme saw the blade wink in the light like a long cat's eye slant and malevolent and a dark smile erupted on the child's throat and went all broken down the front of it. The child made no sound. It hung there with its one eye glazing over like a wet stone and the black blood pumping down its naked belly. The mute one knelt forward. He was drooling and making little whimpering noises in his throat. He knelt with his hands outstretched and his nostrils rimpled delicately. The man handed him the child and he seized it up, looked once at Holme with witless eyes, and buried his moaning face in its throat.[54]

At this moment we encounter McCarthy at his most mythoclastic. The drinking of the child's blood recalls the mass and in this passage McCarthy expresses his rejection of the religious mythology of the culture into which he was born and from which he seeks to emancipate himself. Culla Holme is the most extreme of the failed fathers of all McCarthy's texts. He makes no attempt to save his son and seems largely unaffected by the infant's death. With the parodic trinity, the assorted preachers, squires and rabble-rousers of this text, Culla presents us with a comprehensive condemnation of the excesses of patriarchal values as they have been expressed not only in the poor-white Appalachian South, but in the America of pastoral delusion and in the patriarchal West in general. The child himself has a two-fold significance, as we have come to expect in this complex and densely allusive text. The incest of which it is the product is the classic motif of inward-looking societies that, through either choice or circumstance, find themselves cut off from the wider world. Appalachia, through physical isolation and economic dereliction found itself in this condition in the long period that that was ending at the time of McCarthy's youth. The South as a whole, isolated economically, politically and morally by its dependence on slavery, chose its own exclusion, made a virtue of its supposed necessity, and centered its mythology on the pastoral refusal of history. *Outer Dark* parodies both these myths of regional identity and deploys religious and literary images in inverted form to construct the anti-myth, depicting the existential isolation of modern man in linear, historical time. But the classical reference so clearly deployed in *Outer Dark* also suggests to us the Ovidian interpretation of the incest image. Seen in such mythic terms the child represents the synthesis of two forms of time, both of which remain necessary to us in creating a meaningful temporal structure within our own epistemology. That synthesis is made impossible by an excessive dependence on patriarchal values. This is the final meaning for this mysterious and many layered work. If it strikes us as radical in its imagery it could also be read as reflective of a violent and rapidly changing period and also prophetic of a growing need to recognize the importance of the natural world to our chances of survival and our need to emancipate the female in both political and cultural terms.

Chapter Seven
Child of God

Saxon and Celtic bloods. A child of God much like yourself perhaps.

If *Outer Dark* is McCarthy's most radically metaphysical text, *Child of God* is his most determinedly naturalistic. While there can be no mistaking the essential drives within Lester Ballard, troglodyte, murderer, necrophiliac, he is also presented as an American archetype in the typical McCarthy manner. He is informed by American mythology and values and compelled by his culture to seek a way of life that his American circumstances deny him. In characteristic McCarthy fashion Lester's tale is told in a manner that relates the text to clearly discernable literary forebears, Faulkner still prominent among them. The literary method employed differs quite markedly from that of the two earlier novels although the social milieu remains the same; *Child of God* closes the sequence of Appalachian novels.[1] There is an overt concern with "history" although it would have to be regarded as local rather than national in character. This makes the text less overtly mythic than is McCarthy's other work, a characteristic emphasized by the naturalism mentioned above. However both the form and content of the text display a concern with the relation between history and myth and Lester Ballard's literary and cultural antecedents are mythic in themselves. If this seems contradictory, I shall try to make the distinction clear in the analysis that follows. Despite the ghastly nature of his crimes Lester Ballard never entirely loses our sympathy; he remains a human figure to his awful and inevitable end. He is at one and the same time an inverted American hero and "A child of God much like yourself perhaps."[2]

The narrative form of *Child of God* is unique in McCarthy's oeuvre. The text is in three sections; the first of these, comprising almost half the novel, consists of twenty-five chapters, all of them short, some less than a page in length. Of these, eighteen are given in the authorial voice and the remaining seven in the voices of unspecified members of the community of which Lester was, in some sense, a part. These chapters feature the mountain vernacular and are in the form of personal reminiscence or "common knowledge." In one case the reader is cast as a member of a listening group: the account of Lester's grandfather and his claim to a Union pension, despite not having fought in the Civil War, concludes with the lines,

> Talkin about Lester . . .

> You all talk about him. I got supper waitin on me at the house.[3]

The abbreviated length of these chapters conforms to the fragmented nature of the community's knowledge of Lester and to their laconic mode of speech. The story is built up gradually by means of these fragments of narrative, many of them in the form of vignettes. At the same time they are united by a continuous narrative thread. The effect is to present the text in the form of a ballad, a folk tale whose dark and violent content conforms to the gothic, anti-pastoral atmosphere of the Appalachian folk songs of Marcus's ". . . weird but clearly recognizable America."[4] The choice of the name "Ballard" is surely significant in this respect. The format also provides McCarthy with an opportunity to explore the relation between history, narrative and myth. The text provides us with both Lester's history and his community's reaction to it. It hints at the way in which that history may be mythicized when the community needs to tame the terrible story, to domesticate it, to make it "safe," even to find within its extremes a source of pride. One of the anonymous representative voices comments:

> I'll say one thing about Lester though. You can trace em back to Adam
> if you want and goddamn if he didn't outstrip em all.

The response is in the affirmative:

> That's the god's truth.[5]

This concern with the relation between history and myth is given further significance by the knowledge that the story is based on actual events. Nell Sullivan quotes Dianne Luce to the effect that "Lester Ballard's genesis [lay] in the historical person of James Blevins of North Georgia, who was accused of a number of murders in 1963 similar in nature to Ballard's."[6] McCarthy was to use the name of Blevins for the dangerous man (boy) of *All the Pretty Horses*; he compounded the ironic joke by declining to make clear whether this was his real name, and by making his "real" Jimmy Blevins a radio evangelist. That the events of *Child of God* are related to actuality in this way poses the question of motivation, a question to which McCarthy responds by couching this aspect of his tale in naturalistic terms. Lester Ballard is driven by the irresistible appetite of sexuality; this is a staple of the Naturalism of Zola and Norris,[7] as is his propensity to violence. The fact that his economic, social and personal circumstances combine to deny Lester any living human outlet for his sexuality is not sufficient to suppress it altogether; that his response is both violent and perverse is in keeping with the tenets of both Zola and Freud.

McCarthy's concern with history is emphasized by his inclusion in this text of an account of the "White Caps of Sevier County." This episode took place at the end of the 19th. Century and bore the characteristics of agrarian violence and vigilantism familiar to impoverished and isolated rural communities, and by no means confined to Appalachia or indeed the United States. The details of this episode were recounted in *The White Cap Book*,[8] originally published in 1899 and written by Tom Davis, the man who more than anyone else suppressed the outbreak. Although authoritative historical accounts of "White Capping" probably do not exist there is no doubt that such an episode did occur. The lack of authoritative historical record is probably due to the fact that the locals preferred that it be forgotten. Writing in *Knoxville Local History Magazine*, Mike Gibson notes that:

> Even today, the County historian Beulah Linn affirms, with some understatement, that "it's still a very touchy topic. I never mention it in my writings." A local history student, upon researching the topic, was told that he "did not want to ask questions about *that*."[9]

McCarthy's text echoes this sentiment:

> Here's a man can tell ye about the White Caps, said the sheriff.

> People don't want to hear about that, said the old man.[10]

It is surely characteristic of the mythoclastic McCarthy that he should defy this taboo. His judgment on the White Caps is a powerful fragment of his anti-pastoralism:

> They was a bunch of lowlife thieves and cowards and murderers. The
> only thing they ever done was to whip women and rob old people of
> their savins. Pensioners and widows. And murder people in their beds
> at night.[11]

It seems likely that White Capping began as a moralistic movement by the
community to enforce conventional standards of sexual propriety[12] and
degenerated rapidly into a form of collective criminal violence. McCarthy
has hinted at the existence of this history, before drawing our attention to
it in detail: "I had a uncle was a White-Cap, Johnny Romines said."[13] while
part of the condemnation of Lester Ballard's grandfather was that, far from
being a soldier in the Civil War "He was a by God White Cap."[14] His reference to the White Caps is not only an aspect of McCarthy's assault on the
myth of the pastoral, it is also an aspect of his desire to write into American
discourse forgotten, ignored or suppressed aspects of American history. It
seems clear that Appalachia was the site of an appreciable segment of this history, although not by any means the only one. Suppression could be regarded
as a concomitant to mythicization; thus the representation of the suppressed
becomes a necessary aspect of the anti-myth.

The "ballad like" aspect of the first of the text's three sections also
enables McCarthy to introduce a subtle temporal complexity into what at
first sight seems a straightforward narrative. The sections given in the authorial voice recount the events of the tale in the order in which they occur. For
the most part the past tense is used:

> The High Sheriff of Sevier County came out through the courthouse
> doors and stood on the portico surveying the gray lawn below with the
> benches and the Sevier County pocketknife society that convenes there
> to whittle and mutter and spit.[15]

Occasionally the present tense is employed:

> Ballard in a varnished oak swivelchair. He leans back. The door is peb-
> ble-grain glass. Shadows loom upon it. A deputy comes in and turns
> around. There is a woman behind him. When she sees Ballard she
> begins to laugh.[16]

The effect of this is to heighten the impression that we are following a story
as it unfolds in time, that we are in the hands of a professional story-teller.
But the chapters given by the members of the community are otherwise.

They express points of view based on an evident knowledge of Lester's story as a whole. I have already mentioned the opinion that Lester had managed to "outstrip em all" even "back to Adam." Occasionally the folk-narrator mentions an aspect of the story with which we, as readers, have yet to be acquainted:

> I don't know what he had on Waldrop that Waldrop never would run him off. Even after he burned his old place down he never said nothin to him about it that I know of.[17]

We do not encounter the burning of the hut until seventy pages later. An even earlier account has informed us that Lester ". . . didn't look so pretty hisself when Greer got done with him."[18] Not until page 173 do we learn from the author that Lester's arm is blown off by a blast from Greer's shotgun. In neither of these cases do we have the least idea of what the earlier story-teller is referring to. This creates for the reader the sense that he is being introduced to a history of which the community is already aware. It also adds a touch of folk "authenticity" to the sections of narrative delivered by voices "other than the author." They betray a lack of appreciation of the story-teller's art, an impression strengthened by digressions such as the account of "crazy Gresham's wife's funeral,"[19] "the Trantham boy's oldtimey oxes,"[20] or Sheriff Fate Turner's dealings with the young man on an assignation "got his britches on inside out."[21] Or rather these sections of narrative are conversation pieces among the citizens themselves, "overheard" for us by McCarthy. They read like the verbatim transcribed tape recordings of an Appalachian Studs Terkel. But their anonymity conveys the sense of folk-narrative, of collective rather than individual memory. This is profoundly ironic for reasons which should shortly become apparent.

They also recall the method employed by Faulkner in *As I Lay Dying*. But the parallel is inverted. Faulkner's tale is concerned with a family, which, despite the most unpromising of circumstances, holds together and survives. The Bundren's journey is an epic of sheer unthinking indomitability. They may lose a member here or there to death or madness, but they return to their home with a new matriarch and a new Bundren waiting to be born. Lester's family has ceased to exist before the text even begins. His efforts to create familial continuity are brought to naught by his lack of appeal to the local females. His is a family of the dead. He has more in common with Mink Snopes than with any of the Bundrens. His other literary antecedents include Rip Van Winkle, who also slept under the mountain with his rifle at his side. Irving satirized the Jeffersonian ideal of the self-sufficient yeoman farmer, the individualistic hero of the American pastoral ideal. Jefferson wrote "Those who labor in the earth are the chosen people of God, if ever He had a chosen people, whose breasts He has made his peculiar deposit for substantial and genuine virtue."[22] Jefferson espoused the Lockean view that those who worked the land created their own entitlement to it. The relevance of this to the fate of Lester Ballard, and to McCarthy's mythoclastic intent, is clear and profound as Grammer has emphasized in his previously mentioned discussion of McCarthy's anti-pastoralism.[23] Grammer's location of pastoral as a refusal of history places McCarthy's concern with history in its fullest context.

McCarthy pursues the same satiric end as Irving, but in a much more radical and extreme fashion. Lester loses his farm through no particular fault of his own. The loss of farms due to the inability to pay taxes was a commonplace of rural America during the Depression. This is the final dispossession visited upon Lester. He had no brothers or sisters: "They was just the one boy. The mother had run off, I don't know where to nor who with."[24] Lester is no more fortunate with his father than any of McCarthy's other protagonists:

> They say he was never right after his daddy killed hisself. . . . . He come in the store and told it like you'd tell it was rainin out. We went up there in the barn and I seen his feet hangin. . . . He just stood there and watched, never said nothin. He was about nine or ten years old at the time. The old man's eyes was run out on stems like a crawfish and his tongue was blacker'n a chow dogs.[25]

Lester's opposition to the auction of his farm is met with brutal finality.

> Lester Ballard never could hold his head right after that. It must of thowed his neck out someway or another. I didn't see Buster hit him but I seen him layin on the ground. I was with the sheriff. He was layin flat on the ground with his eyes crossed and this awful pumpknot on his head. He just layed there and was bleedin at the ears. Buster was still standin there holdin the axe.[26]

Thus Lester is deprived by circumstance of the identity, means of sustenance and place of status that the founding myth of his culture regards as his birthright. Under these circumstances all that remains for him is to adopt that other American mythic role, that of the heroic pioneer, the lone individual surviving in the wilderness with only his resourcefulness and his rifle to sustain him. The myth demands that Lester become a Daniel Boone. Instead he expresses the rage at his dispossession and the frustration of his sexual rejection by becoming James Blevins. If we followed cultural parallels we would say that rather than becoming Natty Bumpo, the celibate rifleman hero of the wilderness, he becomes Norman Bates, the cinema's first hero/victim as serial killer, in Hitchcock's *Psycho*, and surely "quoted" by McCarthy:

> He'd long been wearing the underclothes of his female victims but now he took to appearing in their outerwear as well. A gothic doll in illfit clothes, its carmine mouth floating detached and bright in the white landscape.[27]

Just as McCarthy goes to the extreme in his inversion of religious mythology in *Outer Dark*, so he creates of Lester Ballard an American folk anti-hero, a mythic figure whose radical individualism is carried to the extreme of solipsism and whose needs can only be met in an underworld of his own creation. Instead of the self-sufficient, ruggedly individualistic American pioneer hero, Lester becomes the "dangerous man" of the text, a mythoclastic inversion that is, perhaps, uncomfortably closer to the solipsistic reality of the American hero as isolate.

The account of Lester's gradual descent into utter deprivation, madness, murder and necrophilia is contained in the second and third sections of the novel and is given exclusively in the authorial voice. This intensifies the sense of Lester's isolation; the solitariness of his later pursuits necessarily removes the possibility of community witness that has been present before his dispossession and exile to the mountain. As ever, McCarthy constructs his text by a combination of his own feeling for language and references to other texts, both ancient and modern.

> He laid queer plans. His shuffling boot tracks trampling out the prints of lesser life. Where mice had gone, or foxes hunting in the night. The dovelike imprimatur of a stooping owl.[28]

The final sentence of this passage is in the unmistakable McCarthy voice. But images from classical mythology are also deployed, acknowledging the narcissism inherent in Lester's isolation:

> Kneeling in the snow among the fairy tracks of birds and deermice Ballard leaned his face to the green water and drank and studied his dishing visage in the pool. He halfway put his hand to the water as if he would

touch the face that watched there but then he rose and wiped his mouth and went on through the woods.

    Old woods and deep.[29]

The "deep woods" in snow refer to Robert Frost.[30] The reference to Narcissus must be accompanied by that to Echo, similarly trapped in solipsistic isolation, doomed to nothingness:

> There for a moment he flailed wildly, his hand scrabbling along the concrete, his eye to the river and the tracks there which already he was trailing to the end of his life. Then his hand closed upon the stock of the rifle. He fetched it down, cursing, his heart hammering. You'd try it, wouldn't ye? he wailed at the tracks in the snow. His voice beneath the arches of the bridge came back hollow and alien and Ballard listened to the echo of it with his head tilted like a dog and then he climbed the bank and started back up the road.[31]

Lester views from afar as the boar and hounds fight to the death:

> Ballard watched this ballet tilt and swirl and churn mud up through the snow and watched the lovely blood welter there in its holograph of battle, spray burst from a ruptured lung, the dark heart's blood, pinwheel and pirouette, until shots rang and all was done.[32]

Blood remains McCarthy's emblem of both life and death. Lester sits like Aphrodite on Mount Erymanthus as Adonis hunts the boar. Characteristically the image is inverted: the boar it is that dies. Like Adonis, Lester's sexuality seems ambivalent. Like Adonis he goes down into the underworld, the world of the dead. Unlike Adonis, the corn god, he will not be annually reborn, but will meet a final extinction at the hands of modern science:

> His body was shipped to the state medical school at Memphis. . . . . He was laid out on a slab and flayed, eviscerated, dissected. His head was sawed open and the brains removed. His muscles were taken from his bones. His heart was taken out. His entrails were hauled forth and delineated and the four young students who bent over him like those haruspices of old perhaps saw monsters worse to come in their configurations. At the end of three months when the class was closed Ballard was scraped from the table into a plastic bag and taken with others of his kind to a cemetery outside the city and there interred.[33]

The reference to haruspices, the ancient Roman officials who divined the future by reading the entrails of slaughtered beasts, reinforces McCarthy's acknowledgement of his classical roots while at the same time expressing his skepticism regarding scientific gnosis. The passage reads more like the medieval torture and execution of some grievous heretic than the practices of modern science. McCarthy manages to make this dehumanized treatment of Lester's mortal remains seem as horrific as has been Lester's treatment of the bodies of his own dead victims. The power of the passage is reinforced by the sense that Lester is presented as a human being throughout, in spite of his murderous perversity. This is, of course, another of McCarthy's continuous themes. The potential for violence and perversity is an inescapable part of human character; it is a part of our badge of humanity. "You think people was meaner then than they are now? the deputy said. The old man was looking out at the flooded town. No, he said, I don't. I think people are the same from the day God first made one."[34] In this sense, for McCarthy we can each be seen as "a child of god."

I have already mentioned the aptness of the name "Ballard" for this text; "Lester" is also significant. Erskine Caldwell's *Tobacco Road* features the degenerate poor white Jeeter Lester. This Lester also sets fire to his house through his own carelessness; he perishes in the flames as does his wife.[35] Ballard survives, but loses his first beloved corpse. Despite these similarities however, McCarthy does challenge Caldwell's attitude towards his poor-white characters. Jeeter is destroyed by weakness but Lester Ballard is anything but weak. He is the mythic individualistic American hero in his resourcefulness and power of endurance. It is his own violence that consumes him in the end.

Sexuality features more prominently in *Child of God* than in any other McCarthy text.[36] As I have already mentioned it is this aspect of the tale that emphasizes the naturalistic character of McCarthy's approach and reflects a Freudian influence. This is especially so with regard to Lester's rifle, which has clear phallic significance; his prowess with the gun is a substitute for sexual success. This is particularly clear in the fairground sequence where his marksmanship wins him two mohair teddy bears and a tiger, the kind of trophies one would give to a girl. But for Lester this cannot be:

> And you could see among the faces a young girl with candyapple on her lips and her eyes wide. Her pale hair smelled of soap, womanchild from beyond the years, rapt below the sulphur glow and pitchlight of some medieval fun fair. A lean skylong candle skewered the black pools in her eyes. Her fingers clutched. In the flood of this breaking brimstone galaxy

she saw the man with the bears watching her and she edged closer to the
girl by her side and brushed her hair with two fingers quickly.[37]

Lester's sexual frustration and isolation are heightened by the enthusiastic
sexual plenitude that surrounds him; the couples in their cars at the turn-
around on Frog Mountain, the dumpkeeper's promiscuous daughters, the
old prostitute encountered at the roadside. However the dumpkeeper's incest
reminds us that this plenitude is anything but innocent and the production
of idiot children is the inevitable consequence. That these children feature
so frequently in McCarthy's texts is another consistent feature of his mythoclastic assault on America's vision of itself. For the rejected and frustrated
Lester the rifle apes the phallic function when he shoots his female victims,
it represents for him the essential first stage of sexual conquest. His retreat
under the mountain also has Freudian significance. The entry is via a narrow
place where only the emaciated Lester can pass; he follows "the stream" and
"the narrow gorge through which it flowed," until he reaches "a tall and bell
shaped cavern. Here the walls with their softlooking convolutions slavered
over as they were with wet and bloodred mud, had an organic look to them,
like the innards of some great beast."[38] Lester has returned to the womb. I
have already mentioned the allusion to the classical myth of the underworld;
this is combined with an image from contemporary religion: "Here in the
bowels of the mountain Ballard turned his light on ledges or pallets of stone
where dead people lay like saints."[39] In this manner McCarthy expresses in
Freudian terms the psychic linking of religion, sex and death. The manner
in which Lester is impelled to express his sexuality is, of course, absolutely
divorced from any possibility of reproduction. Lester's couplings are expres-
sions of the aridity of the American Waste Land, another of McCarthy's consistent themes.

    I have already pointed out McCarthy's propensity for the expression
of philosophical concerns within his texts. Although no Oedipus, Lester is
given moments of philosophical reflection:

> Coming up the mountain through the blue winter twilight among great
> boulders and the ruins of great trees prone in the forest he wondered at
> such upheaval. Disorder in the woods, trees down, new paths needed.
> Given charge Ballard would have made things more orderly in the
> woods and in men's souls.[40]

This recalls the celebrated remark attributed to Alfonso the Wise, King of
Castile in the 13th century: "If I had been present at the creation I would

have given some useful hints for the better arrangement of the Universe." In his cave Lester watches the bats fly out ". . . fluttering wildly in the ash and smoke like souls rising from hades. When they were gone he watched the hordes of cold stars sprawled across the smokehole and wondered what stuff they were made of, or himself."[41] As Lester crosses the flooded river McCarthy interpolates metaphysical speculation:

> He could not swim, but how would you drown him? His wrath seemed to buoy him up. Some halt in the way of things seems to work here. See him. You could say that he's sustained by his fellow men, like you. Has peopled the shore with them calling to him. A race that gives suck to the maimed and the crazed, that wants their wrong blood in its history and will have it. But they want this man's life. He has heard them in the night seeking him with lanterns and cries of execration. How then is he born up? Or rather, why will these waters not take him?[42]

There is a hint here of McCarthy acknowledging that Lester is a literary construct; I suggest that this is an example of literary reflexivity. If Lester "Has peopled the shore with them calling to him." then he is writing his own story, becoming his own author, albeit momentarily. McCarthy also seems to be acknowledging that America seeks to destroy the physical actuality of the monstrous killers that it has spawned, but, at the same time, preserve them in mythic form as in some way free of the moral limitations that inhibit those of us who live lives of quiet obscurity.[43] *Child of God* challenges that myth.

Other consistent McCarthy themes are readily discernable. The nobility and value of good work is powerfully expressed in the axe-sharpening passage. Three entire pages are devoted to a detailed account of the smith's hardening, sharpening and tempering of the axe; this in a text in which most of the many chapters are considerably shorter. At each stage the smith gives a clear account of his craft, which not only affords him a living and gives him status and identity but also carries with it an implication of moral worth that inheres in the craft itself when it is practiced by a master. The meaning of the episode is lost on Ballard: the chapter concludes with a brief exchange,

> Reckon you could do it now from watchin? he said.
> Do what, said Ballard.[44]

However Lester does display mastery and care in one aspect of his life:

> He sits and dries the rifle and ejects the shells into his lap and dries
> them and wipes the action and oils it and oils the receiver and the barrel
> and the magazine and the lever and reloads the rifle and levers a shell
> into the chamber and lets the hammer down and lays the rifle on the
> floor beside him.[45]

Lester's devotion is to his only remaining possession. The rifle, with all that
it signifies in American life, is all that he can care for and is the agent of
destruction—his victims' and his own.

There is the usual reminder of the insignificance of human society in
the timescale of the earth:

> He passed a windfelled tulip poplar on the mountainside that held aloft
> in the grip of its roots two stones the size of fieldwagons, great tablets on
> which was writ only a tale of vanished seas with ancient shells in cameo
> and fishes etched in lime.[46]

It is the essence of McCarthy's dystopian satire that Lester's vitality, the
antithesis of this insignificance, is channeled by his American circumstances
into violent, destructive and perverse ends.

As ever the horror of the action in the text is contrasted by the power
and vivid originality of the language and imagery by which it is expressed.
As Lester's adopted cabin is destroyed by fire "The flames ran down the bat-
boards and up again like burning squirrels."[47] Interrupted in his coupling
with a freshly killed corpse,

> He leaped up hauling at his breeches and tore through the brush toward
> the road.
>   A crazed mountain troll clutching up a pair of bloodstained breeches
> by one hand and calling out in a high mad gibbering, bursting from the
> woods and hurtling down the gravel road behind a lightless truck reced-
> ing half obscured in rising dust.[48]

There are even moments of grim humor that throw into contrast Lester's
bleak descent into his solipsistic hell. His first step towards ultimate degradation is taken opportunistically. The asphyxiated couple's car radio is still playing: "The man on the radio said: We'd like to dedicate this next number to all
the sick and the shut-in." The response is sardonic: "On the mountain two
crows put forth, thin raucous calls in the cold and lonely air."[49] The "next
number" is charged with bitter irony:

Gathering flowers for the master's bouquet.
Beautiful flowers that will never decay.[50]

The irony is compounded by the song's overt meaning: the "flowers" are souls of the dead, the master is God, and his bouquet is to be presented in heaven. Lester is gathering flowers from the dead for a hellish bouquet of his own.

Perhaps the most telling aspect of Lester's abandonment and desolation, at least in the terms that McCarthy has established in his earlier texts, is that he has no surrogate father and not even a dog. These are the ultimate deprivations in the McCarthy scale of human needs. In the person of Lester Ballard we find both the absolute failure of patriarchal care and responsibility and the absolute corruption of patriarchal power. Within this context American mythology has promised Lester the right to work his own land and make his own way while American capitalism and government, in the person of the county auctioneer, have taken it away. The tale's only figure of order and responsibility is Fate Turner, the "High Sheriff of Sevier County." His dignity, judgment and purpose run through the text like a quiet promise of eventual resolution. When the resolution does occur it is indeed "fate" that reveals it. The text concludes with the sheriff driving away with "seven bodies bound in muslin like enormous hams"[51] in the trailer of his jeep. "As they went down the valley in the new fell dark basking nighthawks rose from the dust in the road before them with wild wings and eyes red as jewels in the headlights."[52] Both aspects of the imagery recall *Psycho* once again. Norman Bates is a keeper of stuffed birds of prey and the film concludes with a car being drawn from the swamp at the rear of the Bates Motel; the corpse of Marion Crane is in the boot.

There is a double sense of finality at the end of *Child of God*. McCarthy has set his first three novels in the mountains of East Tennessee. He has written the lives and speech and experience of the mountain people into the discourse of America in a manner that has not been done before. He has made this world in all its "American weirdness" and natural beauty a site for a devastating critique of America's mythology of exceptionalism, presenting it instead as an anti-pastoral waste land in flight from history. In creating his own anti-myth he has focused on pastoral delusion and hinted at the threat of modern gnostic utopianism, lambasted traditional Southern religion and, finally, exposed the solipsistic extremes of individualism. In so doing he has drawn on a wide variety of Southern and other literary sources, the dominant figure of Faulkner prominent among them. His attempt to move out from Faulkner's shadow has met with only partial success but he has undoubtedly found his own distinctive voice. In order to broaden his vision and critique of American life and culture he must now move away from the mountains and forests of Appalachia and, inevitably, go west. But first he must pass through the city of Knoxville and recount the tale that he has been creating at the same time as this initial trilogy, the possibly autobiographical story of Suttree.

Chapter Eight
Suttree

The murengers have walled the pale, the gates are shut, but lo the thing's inside and can you guess his shape?

The "story" of *Suttree* in brief: three years commencing 1951: Cornelius Suttree, formerly student of the University of Tennessee, alienated from his catholic family and their bourgeois values, frequents the stews of Knoxville's McAnally Flats and subsists by catching fish from the Tennessee River. He carouses with the roisterers and whores of the city, black and white, hetero- and homosexual, blind, crippled, halt and lame. He "does time." He loses two lovers, one to death and the other to his own emotional detachment. He survives typhoid fever. He leaves the city on the western road.

Of course such an outline reads like a simplification, recalling Conrad's remark that, "approached with sufficient detachment," the entire history of the human race could be expressed in a single phrase, "They were born, they suffered, they died."[1] Conrad was able to declare that he was not capable of such detachment and neither is McCarthy, or any novelist. Conrad was objecting to a critical judgment that his novel was "too long." *Suttree* is by far the longest of McCarthy's novels. It comprises some four hundred and seventy-one pages, fifty or so more than his next longest, *The Crossing*, and two hundred and seventy-four more than *Child Of God*. It is reputed to have taken him twenty years to write. Never the-less-the above outline is fairly exhaustive. It follows therefore that "the devil is in the detail," doubly so since the eponymous Suttree, being an educated, reflective and self-aware individual, allows McCarthy the freedom to take us within this protagonist's consciousness, to provide us with experiences of his emotional life, to give us indications of his motivation, to see his hallucinations, suffer his deliriums and inhabit his dreams. The text is also rich in detail to an extent that goes well beyond anything in McCarthy's other works, details of everyday life, of the actions of the many other characters of the text, of Knoxville and its environs, of the Tennessee River, of the surrounding mountains and woods. *Suttree* therefore is quite different to McCarthy's other novels in significant ways. At the same time it is informed by characteristic McCarthy themes and preoccupations and remains very clearly related to the works that both precede and follow it.

One of the most significant aspects of *Suttree* lies in its literary antecedents; McCarthy is considered by most critics to be writing predominantly in the Southern literary tradition and I have indicated some of his most significant and self-consciously adopted antecedents. At the same time I have suggested that McCarthy's eclecticism is wider, more international in scope than the purely Southern,[2] and have identified the influence of T.S.Eliot as being of particular relevance. *Suttree* draws on still wider antecedents:

> [He] believed that a writer's first duty might be to insult rather than to flatter national vanity. He wished to shock his compatriots into a deeper awareness of their self-deceptions.[3]

The words might have been written about McCarthy. In fact they are from Declan Kiberd's introduction to *Ulysses* and *Suttree* is surely related to Joyce's great work in a number of ways. At the simplest level McCarthy makes his reference plain by using significant names in his characteristic fashion; the Greek who runs Comers restaurant is called Ulysses and the name of Suttree's prostitute lover is Joyce. The parallels go much further however. Knoxville and Dublin occupy positions of similar significance in their respective texts. Both are clearly identifiable by reference to actual locations; both stand on rivers with which they are particularly identified; both are places from which to escape. For both protagonists Catholicism is one of the forces from which escape is necessary, as is Christianity in general. Both are long works in which "plot" is secondary to detail, especially quotidian detail. Both are related to myth and seek to create anti-myth. Both use the works of the past as palimpsests; Joyce, of course, produces his text over that of Homer and McCarthy over that of the Gospel story of the life of Christ. Within these contexts both display the broadest eclecticism.

There are direct intertextual examples of the relationship. In *Suttree* a corpse is hauled from the Tennessee with a boathook:

> As the fisherman passed they were taking aboard a dead man. He was very stiff and he looked like a window-dummy save for his face. The

face seemed soft and bloated and wore a grappling hook in the side of it and a crazed grin. They raised him so, gambreled up by the bones of his cheek. A pale incruent wound. He seemed to protest woodenly, his head awry. They lifted him onto the deck where he lay in his wet seersucker suit and his lemoncolored socks, leering walleyed up at the workers with the hook in his face like some gross water homunculus taken in trolling that the light of God's day had stricken dead instanter.[4]

In *Ulysses* the corpse comes from Dublin's harbor:

Found drowned. High water at Dublin bar. Driving before it a loose drift of rubble, fanshoals of fishes, silly shells. A corpse rising saltwhite from the undertow, bobbing landward, a pace for a pace a porpoise. There he is. Hook it quick. Sunk though he be beneath the watery floor. We have him. Easy now.

Bag of corpsegas sopping in foul brine. A quiver of minnows, fat of a spongy titbit, flash through the slits of his buttoned trouserfly. God becomes man becomes fish becomes barnacle goose becomes feather-bed mountain. Dead breaths I living breathe, tread dead dust, devour a urinous offal from all dead. Hauled stark over the gunwale he breathes upward the stench of his green grave, his leprous nosehole snoring to the sun.[5]

Quite apart from the obvious correspondence of the incident we may note other striking similarities between the two passages; the unexpected use of language—"incruent wound," "silly shells;" the conjoining of words—"lemoncoloured," "fanshoals," "saltwhite," "corpsegas." The work of both writers exhibits deep erudition and a playfulness regarding words, a refusal to be bound by linguistic conventions, and a determination to use all aspects of language as fully as possible and without any regard for the strictures of "minimalism." Both display a wide ranging eclecticism regarding the speech of those around them, and their literary traditions. Both have an insouciant confidence in the creation of neologisms, the meanings of which remain clear—often clearer than "regular" words such as "gambreled." Both are happy to elide the distinction between poetry and prose. These are, I believe, the characteristics of writers motivated by their great love of language itself; I feel this most powerfully when reading these two texts and believe this to be characteristic of all McCarthy's work. Joyce also forgoes the use of inverted commas to denote speech, a characteristic of all McCarthy's texts and which I have commented on previously. Both passages refer to the deity; both are haunted by death; both are concerned with the elemental conflict between the forces of life and death. Joyce was writing against the values and mythology that he saw as formative of the useless slaughter of the First World War and opposing it with a counter mythology of the quotidian heroic. McCarthy identifies death with the Christian religion, at least in the forms that Knoxville has made familiar to him. Suttree flies from death, or rather from the fear of death; his consciousness is structured by the Christ narrative and it is this that he must learn to recognize and from which he must free himself.

In some respects however *Suttree* and *Ulysses* differ completely. Joyce wrote against the myth of the "naturally belligerent" Irishman. McCarthy writes of the incorrigibly violent American. Kiberd writes that "Ulysses is an endlessly open book of utopian epiphanies."[6] The eponymous Suttree experiences his own individual existentialist epiphany at the last, but McCarthy writes against the utopian gnosticism that he identifies as lying at the heart of the myth of American Exceptionalism. As ever McCarthy acknowledges his source but expresses the inverse of its meaning.

Suttree is the final text in McCarthy's sequence of "Tennessee" novels and, in scale and ambition at least, it is the culmination of that sequence. It emphasizes McCarthy's desire to relate himself to the great figures of modernism, to Faulkner, Eliot and Joyce. McCarthy's purpose in so doing has a number of different facets. He accepts the modernist's assertion that the texts of the present cannot be created as if those of the past did not exist; the novel, like the language and culture in which it is created, can only be constructed in relation to what has gone before. He acknowledges that it is dependent on the cultural matrix from which it is generated and of which it will, in turn, become a part. He pays homage to his literary forebears; he hears what Bakhtin called "the voice of the fathers."

The theme of father-son conflict that is so strongly characteristic of these McCarthy texts is also a metaphor for the contemporary writer's struggle to find his own voice, to fulfill his ambition of taking his place alongside the great figures of the past. A work on the scale of *Suttree* suggests that, unlike O'Connor,[7] McCarthy does not wish to avoid a confrontational comparison with the dominant figure of the literary past. Far from avoiding the "Dixie Limited" one gains the impression that he wants to be a different train going in the opposite direction.

It would be easy to create the impression that McCarthy's recognition of and challenge to the great modernists was little more than personal literary ambition. However I think that I have already made it clear that McCarthy's challenge to the past exists at a more fundamental level than this. The modernist wish to "make it new" carried with it an implicit promise that the world could be remade, that the myths of the past could be recast in forms that would enable us to reinvigorate an exhausted culture (Eliot) or divest ourselves of false visions (Faulkner, Joyce). McCarthy challenges both these notions. His texts do not assert a faith in the ability of new forms to say new things, but rather they assert that the old forms may be redeployed in ways which enable an individual voice to be heard, but a voice which, in McCarthy's case, asserts that the violence and destructiveness of man is as old as man himself and that this aspect of human nature is unchanging. It is this pessimism that underlies his vision of human history as a nightmare[8] and which motivates his challenge to the various forms of the myth of American Exceptionalism as I have traced it throughout his work so far.[9] In the novels subsequent to *Suttree* McCarthy focuses more and more on the role of narrative in both reflecting and re-creating discourse. He asserts more strongly the notion that discourse shapes perception, that myth informs vision and that systems of belief, provisional at best, are relative to the culture they inhabit. These novels bear a less striking resemblance to those of the modernists, although Eliot's image of the waste land continues to appear and is still McCarthy's dominant metaphor for America. In *Suttree* therefore, I suggest that McCarthy finally comes to terms with his need to honor, accommodate and supplant "the voice of the fathers," in as much as the "fathers" were the three great modernist writers most readily reflected in his work.

I began this chapter by referring to the great length and wealth of detail in *Suttree*. Like its forebear it could well provide material for a complete study of its own—a full *Suttree* commentary. This is not the place for such a work. I shall therefore confine the rest of this section to a consideration in more detail of the main themes of the text and of how it relates to McCarthy's work as a whole.

Two interlinked themes dominate the mood of *Suttree*. Family conflict, especially between father and son, a prominent theme throughout McCarthy's oeuvre; and the metaphysical conflict between the spirits of life and death. Suttree is alienated from all sections of his family. He rejects his father's vision of the world:

> In my father's last letter he said that the world is run by those willing to take responsibility for the running of it. If it is life that you feel you are missing I can tell you where to find it. In the law courts, in business, in government. There is nothing occurring in the streets. Nothing but a dumbshow composed of the helpless and the impotent.[10]

The text continues, "From all old seamy throats of elders, musty books, I've salvaged not a word."[11] Suttree's rejection of parental values leads him to espouse the life of the streets in all its colour and variety, but also in all its poverty, drunken despair and arbitrary violence. The "good hearts from McAnally,"[12] beat ardently and are filled with that vitality that McCarthy espouses, but their vitality is turned to destructive ends. They defy death in their desperation but in so doing pursue it to an inevitable conclusion:

> He seized the whiskey and drank, his slack gullet jerking. When he lowered it his eyes were closed and his face a twisted mask. Pooh! He blew a volatile mist toward the smiling watchers. Lord God what is that?
>   Early Times, Nig, cried J-Bone.
>   Early tombs is more like it.[13]

The "voice" of the initial quote above, "In my father's last letter . . .," raises the question of the possible autobiographical nature of the text, since the passage immediately prior is in the authorial voice. There is no indication that Suttree is "speaking" these words. As a lawyer for the TVA McCarthy's own father could well be read into the text at this point and this heightens the impression that the author is writing of his own experience to a considerable degree. McCarthy was indeed a young man in Knoxville during the period and it is clear that *Suttree* is based on a good deal of personal experience. But much of this would have been common to most young men in similar times and places. It is a commonplace that such a novel would draw on a great deal of personal experience. It is not the case that McCarthy has severed ties with his family. There are other details of the text that are clearly the product of imagination only; McCarthy had neither grandfather nor Southern family mansion in the Knoxville area, coming to the city as he did at the age of four. Also the phrase ". . . from musty books I've salvaged not a word" is the very opposite of the case for McCarthy himself. Therefore there is reason to regard *Suttree* as informed by McCarthy's early experiences in Knoxville and no doubt the novel reflects his own personal conflicts and family tensions—how could it be otherwise? But the extent of its status as autobiography is difficult to ascertain and therefore easy to exaggerate; this difficulty is intensified by McCarthy's reluctance to expose his life to public scrutiny. In my view there is little to be gained in reading *Suttree* as anything but fiction; on the contrary, it is as fiction that it gains its resonance and power.

    As readers of a fictional text we are free to read the "my father's letter" passage in more complex ways. McCarthy frequently indulges in arbitrary changes of voice and tense. In this case we could regard Suttree as having become the author of his own text, in the manner mentioned in the section on *Wake For Susan* and deployed by Faulkner in *As I Lay Dying* and *Absalom, Absalom!* This reflects another aspect of McCarthy's concern with narrative, expressed in the words "Each man is the bard of his own existence,"[14] an idea to be dealt with at greater length in a later chapter. If self-authorship can only be achieved by inverting the narratives received from a patriarchal culture, the father-son conflict so characteristic of McCarthy texts becomes the essential metaphor of this process. Not only is Suttree alienated from his father, he fails as a father himself by reason of the failure of his marriage. This alienation is compounded by his son's death, a loss that intensifies Suttree's fear of mortality. There is a sense in which Suttree becomes a surrogate father for Gene Harrogate,[15] but even in this role he fails; his commitment to his young friend is too weak. He is unable to influence the naive "country mouse" to abandon any of his absurd schemes. Defrauding the telephone company leads inevitably to arrest and jail, to Brushy Mountain and a life irretrievably lost to crime. The relationship between Reese and his son Willard is also fraught with conflict. In the end Reese reports that:

> Willard run off. . . . I never did understand that boy. I never would get to where I could just talk to him but what he'd up and do some hatefulness and not a bit of use in the world in it.[16]

McCarthy combines the comic and the macabre in the relationship between Leonard and his dead father, the latter's corpse being kept at home for six months in order not to lose his relief money. Leonard insists that Suttree help him in finally disposing of the old man in the river. Suttree likens this to a burial at sea but neither can find any words to say as the decomposing corpse sinks into the Tennessee, weighed down by chains. Even this episode expresses the contest between life and death within Suttree himself; this errand onto the river of death draws him away from a night with a girl on his houseboat. The outcome is ironic for eventually "the sea gives up its dead" in parody of the resurrection and Leonard has to report "He come up, Sut. Draggin all those chains with him."[17] The reply expresses the inherent conflict: "Fathers will do that, said Suttree."[18]

The eclecticism so characteristic of McCarthy is exemplified in remarkable fashion in the rhetorical passages that frame the main text. The first of these, in italics as in *The Orchard Keeper* and *Outer Dark*, is a little over two pages in length. It features rolling cadences reminiscent of Shakespeare and the King James Bible. The text commences thus:

Dear friend now in the dusty clockless hours of the town when the streets lie black and steaming in the wake of the watertrucks and now when the drunk and the homeless have washed up in the lee of walls in alleys or abandoned lots and cats go forth highshouldered and lean in the grim perimeters about, now in these sootblackened brick or cobbled corridors where lightwire shadows make a gothic harp of cellar doors no soul shall walk save you.[19]

The address to the individual reader recalls Eliot's

Let us go then, you and I,
When the evening is spread out against the sky
Like a patient etherised upon a table;
Let us go, through certain half-deserted streets,
The muttering retreats
Of restless nights in one night cheap hotels
And sawdust restaurants with oyster shells:[20]

and the tone of the passage refers back to Joyce's descriptions of the night-town scene, also italicised:

Snakes of river fog creep slowly. From drains, clefts, cesspools, middens arise on all sides stagnant fumes. A glow leaps in the South beyond the seaward reaches of the river.[21]

Each of these texts is concerned with the theme of death. McCarthy makes his concern quite plain from the outset: we read of "*Thin dark trees through yon iron palings where the dead keep their own small metropolis.*"[22] The gothic style expresses this deathly preoccupation.

Old tins and jars and ruined household artifacts that rear from the fecal mire of the flats like landmarks in the trackless vales of dementia praecox. A world beyond all fantasy, malevolent and tactile and dissociate, the blown lightbulbs like shorn polyps semitranslucent and skullcolored bobbing blindly down and spectral eyes of oil and now and again the beached and stinking forms of foetal humans bloated like young birds mooneyed and bluish or stale gray.[23]

The theme is expanded in a manner that transforms the horrific into the strangely lyrical:

The night is quiet. Like a camp before a battle. The city beset by a thing unknown and will it come from forest or sea? The murengers have walled the pale, the gates are shut, but lo the thing's inside and can you guess his shape? Where he's kept or what the counter of his face? Is he a weaver, bloody shuttle shot through a timewarp, a carder of souls from the world's nap? Or a hunter with hounds or do bone horses draw his deadcart through the streets and does he call his trade to each? Dear friend he is not to be dwelt upon for it is just by suchwise that he's invited in.[24]

The reference to the pale, bordering that eastern part of Ireland beyond which the King's writ did not run, is one of several Irish references in *Suttree*: Irish Long[25] the fighting philanthropist, Billy Ray Callaghan, the jovial belligerent, and the names of McAnally Flats and Suttree himself.[26]

The "thing unknown" is the fear of death, rather than death itself. Suttree experiences this fear but an authorial interjection points up his weakness:

He sees them stoop to read some quaint inscription and he pauses by an old vault that a tree has half dismantled with its growing. Inside there is nothing. No bones, no dust. How surely are the dead beyond death. Death is what the living carry with them. A state of dread, like some uncanny foretaste of a bitter memory. But the dead do not remember and nothingness is not a curse, far from it.[27]

That such interjections are rare in McCarthy's other works is a reminder that *Suttree* is indeed different. The final passage of the novel completes the process of "framing." It is much shorter than the first and is in the same form as the text as a whole. It is not detached although it does revert to the poetic rhetorical style. As Suttree leaves the changing Knoxville a waterboy gives him a drink of pure water:

When he looked back the waterboy was gone. An enormous lank hound had come out of the meadow by the river like a hound from the depths and was sniffing at the spot where Suttree had stood.

Somewhere in the gray wood by the river is the huntsman and in the brooming corn and in the castellated press of cities. His work lies allwheres and his hounds tire not. I have seen them in a dream, slaverous and wild and their eyes crazed with ravening for souls in this world. Fly them.[28]

The drink of pure water is life giving, in contrast to the deathly "splo" whis-key that has slaked the thirsts of the residents of McAnally. It recalls the restorative water encountered at the end of *The Waste Land.* The huntsman is death, symbolizing that religious epistemology that makes the fear of death and judgment its principal weapon in the task of controlling the minds of men. The hound reminds us of the patriarchal significance of the dog for McCarthy. This is not the puppy that may be loved by the child, but rather the symbol of that patriarchal power that must be overthrown if the child is to become his own man. As a Catholic McCarthy would be familiar with the notion of the hound of heaven, the image of Christ who refuses ever to give up his pursuit of the soul of the sinner. Francis Thompson expressed the notion in the lines:

> I fled Him, down the nights and down the days;
> I fled Him, down the arches of the years;
> I fled Him, down the labyrinthine ways
> Of my own mind; and in the midst of tears
> I hid from Him, and under running laughter.[29]

McCarthy inverts the metaphor since he rejects a religious vision of the world. For him death and Christianity are coterminous. In the first framing passage he refers to the Protestant Tennessee mountain men as the descen-dants of:

> . . . *old teutonic forebears with eyes incandesced by the visionary light of a massive rapacity, wave on wave of the violent and the insane, their brains soaked with spoorless analogues of all that was, lean aryans with their abrogate semitic chapbook reenacting the dramas and parables therein and mindless and pale with a longing that nothing save dark's total restitution could appease.*[30]

The Bible, "their abrogate semitic chapbook" is directly related to their desire for "dark's total restitution." Catholicism fares no better. Suttree recalls his youthful religious education:

> . . . cold mornings in the Market Lunch after serving early Mass with J-Bone. Coffee at the counter. . . . Lives proscribed and doom in store, doom's adumbration in the smoky censer, the faint creak of the taber-nacle door, the tasteless bread and draining the last of the wine from the cruet in a corner and counting the money in the box. This venture into

the world of men rich with vitality, these unwilling churched ladling cream into their cups and watching the dawn in the city, enjoying the respite from their black clad keepers with their neat little boots, their spectacles, the deathreek of the dark and half scorched muslin that they wore. Grim and tireless in their orthopedic moralizing. Filled with tales of sin and unrepentent deaths and visions of hell and stories of levitation and possession and dogmas of semitic damnation for the tacking up of the paraclete. After eight years a few of their charges could read and write in primitive fashion and that was all.

Suttree looked up at the ceiling where a patriarchal deity in robes and beard lurched across the cracking plaster. Attended by fat infants with dovewings grown from their shoulderbones. He lowered his head to his chest. He slept.[31]

Vereen Bell, whose chapter on *Suttree* is the most comprehensive and revealing section of McCarthy criticism that I have yet encountered, comments that Suttree "like Stephen Dedalus, is an imperfectly lapsed Catholic, left impaled upon the wrong end of a coherent theological dogma in which the world can only be a place of death and suffering and, at best a dangerous obstacle to salvation."[32] As I have already argued McCarthy remains a religious writer in a Godless world. He opposes the annihilating notion of human insignificance, of nihilism, with the assertion of subjective meaning that is motivated by man's inherent vitality. It is this that Suttree has to discover as he wanders bereft of faith and meaning in the Knoxville of his youth.

McCarthy's use of framing passages reflects that employed by the Southwestern humorists of the 19th Century.[33] They employed it to contain and tame the wildness of their frontier protagonists, whose violence and lack of civility they rendered in comic terms and in the dialect of the region, often so broadly as to be difficult for the contemporary English reader to comprehend. The framing passages, by contrast, performed their function of containment, of making safe for the genteel Eastern reader, by the use of strictly correct and formal language, the language of the "civilized." McCarthy's framing has a different purpose. Its highly wrought and poetic language contrasts with that of the main body of the text which is much more contemporary in tone and renders the tale in mainly naturalistic terms.[34] The function of these framing passages is to make clear the metaphysical context in which *Suttree* is to be read.

George Washington Harris, himself a Knoxville man, was one of the most popular writers of the Southwestern humorist genre. His character Sut Lovingood, is surely the inspiration for Gene Harrogate, whose harum-scarum adventures are certainly comic but are given the depth of tragedy also as the "country mouse" fails in his various doomed schemes to gain the wealth that will render him a "city rat." The connection between "Sut" and "Suttree" is another characteristic McCarthy use of significant names.[35] The original Sut also lived a life in conflict with his "Dad."

Suttree is much the most scatalogical of McCarthy's texts. This is not simply a more accurate reflection of the actual speech of most of his characters. The text is full of references to excrement. The McAnally Flats are composed of "fecal mire."[36] There are "gouts of sewage"[37] in the river. Suttree contemplates drowning in the Tennessee:

> To fall through dark to darkness. Struggle in those opaque and fecal depths, which way is up. Till the lungs suck brown sewage and funny lights go down the corridors of the brain, small watchmen to see that all is quiet for the advent of eternal night.[38]

Mother She describes the effect of one of her curses:

> She has bored a keep in a treebole and hid therein the dung of her enemy and plugged it shut with an oakwood bung. She leans to them in terrible confidence: His guts swole up like a blowed dog. He couldn't get no relief. His stool riz up in his neck till he choken on it and he turn black in the face and his guts bust open and he die a horrible death a screamin and a floppin in his own mess.[39]

Harrogate's favorite expletive is "Shit fire;" he has plenty of occasions to use it, not least when he is regaled by the mad evangelist from his window overlooking the Flats:

> The viperous evangelist reared up, his elbows cocked and goat's eyes smoking, and thrust a bony finger down. Die! he screamed. Perish a terrible death with thy bowels blown open and black blood boiling from thy nether eye, God save your soul amen.
>
> Shit fire, said Harrogate, . . .[40]

Harrogate's expedition into the caves under Knoxville in search of bank vaults and easy fortune ends with him covered in excrement as he blows not a bank but a sewer: ". . . he was covered in dried sewage. True news of man here below. . . . I thought I was dead. I thought I'd die in this place."[41] Suttree goes down into this underworld to rescue his young friend, his surrogate son. These references, individually and collectively, make clear the meaning of the metaphor; it is the association of excrement and death. The persistence of this metaphor and its linking also with money and perverted religion are an illustration of the coherence and density of theme and image in McCarthy's long and variegated narrative. This coherence in variety is one of the signs of his mastery of the form. The text concludes with a final example in which Suttree's resolution of his deathly obsession is made clear. It combines simplicity, economy and power to great effect. Two negro boys comment on the removal of the decayed corpse from Suttree's houseboat. "Shit, one said. Old Suttree ain't dead."[42] Norman O. Brown's *Life Against Death* enjoyed a considerable vogue in the 1960s and '70s. It contains a section on the excremental vision, focusing on Swift in terms that could well have influenced the writing of *Suttree*, directly or otherwise. He quotes Lewis Mumford: ". . . the last stage of the polis is Nekropolis,"[43] as Gene Harrogate discovers in the caves under Knoxville.

Death haunts Suttree throughout the tale. He feels his existence compromised by the fact that his twin brother was still-born. He believes that he recalls his father holding him up to see his dead brother in his burial robes. He was a "mirror image"[44] of this dead twin. "On the right temple a mauve halfmoon."[45] Suttree has "a like mark on his left temple"[46] He is the "Gauche carbon."[47] His heart is therefore on the right: "A dextrocardiac, said the smiling doctor. Your heart's in the right place."[48] Meant as a joke, the doctor's remark unwittingly expresses the essence of McCarthy—the ardent heart is all-important. Ab Jones expresses the same sentiment: "You got a good heart, Youngblood. Look out for you own."[49] This is the lesson that Suttree has to learn. He feels that death has already claimed his double and has therefore already claimed him. The doppelganger is associated with the notion of death in Conrad's *Secret Sharer* and Suttree remains haunted by this fearful shadow. In the forest of the Great Smokies,

> . . . each glade he entered seemed just quit by a figure who'd been sitting there and risen and gone on. Some doublegoer, some othersuttree eluded him in these woods and he feared that should that figure fail to rise and steal away and were he therefore to come to himself in this obscure wood he'd neither be mended nor made whole but rather set mindless to dodder drooling with his ghostly clone from sun to sun across a hostile hemisphere forever.[50]

Suttree's identification with his twin and death is intensified by meeting identical twins Fern and Vern at Reece's family camp-fire on the French Broad. Their apparent ability to communicate at a distance without speech[51] raises again his fear of the loss of individual identity that undermines his sense of his own life. Their appearance is immediately followed by the death of Wanda, Suttree's Eve, in the rock-fall caused by incessant rain.

When his mountain wandering first begins Suttree rests by a river and recalls one of those folk-ballads telling of death and mentioned in previous sections:

> In an old grandfather time a ballad transpired here, some love gone wrong and a sabletressed girl drowned in an icegreen pool where she was found with her hair spreading like ink on the cold and cobbled river floor. Ebbing in her bindings, languorous as a sea dream. Looking with eyes made huge by the water at the bellies of trout and the well of the rimpled world beyond.[52]

The romantic image, linking love and death, is followed very shortly by a recollection of sheer bizarre horror. A horseman rode under a nearby bridge; his horse came out the other side:

> The rider did not appear. They found him dangling by his skull from a steel rod that jutted from the new masonry, swinging slightly, his hands at his sides and his eyes slightly crossed as if he would see what was the nature of this thing that had skewered his brains.[53]

By the end of the tale death has claimed too many of Suttree's people. The ragpicker has got his wish at last: "They say death comes as a thief in the night, where is he? I'll hug his neck."[54] Callaghan and hoghead[55] are both shot; Ab Jones beaten to death by his enemy, the cop Tarzan Quinn; Quinn himself killed by ". . . the fiddler little Robert,"[56] Wanda, Leonard's father, Suttree's own son, all are gone. Death himself is the "dangerous man" of this McCarthy text, "the huntsman in the brooming corn," the stuff of Suttree's nightmare:

> By the side of a dark dream road he'd seen a hawk nailed to a barn door. But what loomed was a flayed man with his brisket tacked open like a cooling beef and his skull peeled, blue and bulbous and palely luminescent, black grots his eyeholes and bloody mouth gaped tongueless. The

traveler had seized his fingers in his jaws, but it was not alone this horror that he cried. Beyond the flayed man dimply adumbrate another figure paled, for his surgeons move about the world even as you and I.[57]

His obsession leads him to hallucinate the loss of epistemelogical order:

> Seized in a vision of the archetypal patriarch himself unlocking with enormous keys the gates of Hades. A floodtide of screaming fiends and assassins and thieves and hirstute buggers pours forth into the universe, tipping it slightly on its galactic axes. The stars go rolling down the void like redhot marbles. These simmering sinners with their cloaks smoking carry the Logos itself from the tabernacle and bear it through the streets while the absolute prebarbaric mathematik of the western world howls them down and shrouds their ragged biblical forms in oblivion.[58]

Suttree's vision, the product of the delirium of typhoid fever, is a drama of the insignificance of man in the timescale of the earth and of the emptiness of his culture in a godless universe. And yet throughout the text Suttree has received reminders of that vitality that needs no eschatology. It is evident in the wild energy of his McAnally friends, their self destructiveness being a product, in part at least, of their history of American poverty and of their uprooting from their mountain communities and migration to the city. His black friends owe their alienation to slavery and racial prejudice: as the mighty Ab Jones remarks "Bein a nigger is a interestin life."[59] The perennial Micawber-like optimism of Reece, so often endorsed by a mixture of cunning and good fortune—even his unflinching resolve in continuing to strive, after losing both Wanda and Willard, stands in permanent opposition to Suttree's despair, as does the hair-brained resourcefulness of Harrogate. The warmth and sensual generosity of his lovers, Wanda and Joyce, points up Suttree's detachment. Their love is matched, if not exceeded by that of J-Bone, who braves typhoid to get Suttree into hospital.

There are the usual McCarthy emblems of insignificance:

> It was overcast and there were no stars to plague him with their mysteries of space and time.[60]

> He'd lie on his back in the shallows and on these nights he'd see stars come adrift and rifle hot and dying across the face of the firmament. The enormity of the universe filled him with a strange sweet woe.[61]

Willard . . . came back . . . lugging a goodsize spoonbill catfish, relict of devonian seas, a thing scaleless and leathery with a duck's bill and the small eyes harboring eons of night. Suttree shook his head. Some like spirit joined beast and captor. Looky here, called the boy. Suttree sat in the boat with his head in his hands. Darkness settled on them before they'd rowed halfway back to the camp.[62]

A dark stone disc. He reached and picked it up. In his hand a carven gorget. He spooned the clay from the face of it with his thumb and read two rampant gods addorsed with painted eyes and helmets plumed, their spangled anklets raised in a dance. They bore birdheaded scepters each aloft.

Suttree spat on the disc and wiped it on the hip of his jeans and studied it again. Uncanny token of a vanished race.[63]

But the dialectic is balanced as before:

A sole star to the north pale and constant, the old wanderer's beacon burning like a molten spike that tethered fast the Small Bear to the turning firmament. He closed his eyes and opened them and looked again. He was struck by the fidelity of the earth he inhabited and he bore it sudden love.[64]

He found pale newts with enormous eyes and held them cold and quailing in his palm and watched their tiny hearts hammer under the blue and visible bones of their thimblesized briskets.[65]

The spontaneity of life is the lesson that Suttree must learn; but he can only do so when he overcomes his denial of his fear of death:

Suttree felt the terror coming through the walls. He was seized with a thing he'd never known, a sudden understanding of the mathematical certainty of death. He felt his heart pumping down there under the palm of his hand. Who tells it so? Could a whole man not author his own death with a thought? Shut down the ventricle like the closing of an eye?[66]

The implicit answer is, of course, No!

In order fully to incorporate the religious nature of Suttree's inherited cultural dilemma into the text, McCarthy structures the narrative of Suttree's life in parallel with that of the life of Christ. Thomas D. Young Jnr. refers to ". . . the novel's rich and adumbrated Christology, . . ."[67] Suttree is a fisherman, although he declines to be a "fisher of men" from the Tennessee river. He also declines to "be about his father's business." He consorts with publicans and sinners. Joyce is his Magdalen. He encounters a baptism by the river but declares that he is not saved. He wanders the wilderness of the Great Smoky Mountains, starved but untempted by the powers of this world, departing in late October and emerging on December third. McCarthy directs our attention to the length of this ordeal; the text asks the question, "How long is that?"[68] It is about forty days and forty nights. The coal-vendor's horse is named "Golgotha." Suttree's mother's name is Grace. The Goat-man's wagon bears the legend "JESUS WEPT;" he reminds Suttree that this was for the dead Lazarus. Suttree goes down into hell in his typhoid delerium. Above all he is "resurrected" having received the last rites and been given up for dead.

Suttree's final visit to the world of the dead takes place under the influence of Mother She's conjuring. His visit to her represents an abandonment of his educated rationality but is also an acknowledgment that rationality alone is not enough to sustain him in life. Drug induced or spell induced, Suttree's hallucination helps to free him from the burden of the past. "A door closed on all that he had been."[69] He glimpses the possibility of ". . . things known raw, unshaped by the constructions of a mind obsessed with form."[70] This is another McCarthy reference to the possibility of the mystic's direct experience of the world. The reference to Mother She as "portress of hell-gate"[71] could be thought to be condemnatory but previous texts, particularly *Outer Dark*, have made us aware of McCarthy's acknowledgement of the pre-patriarchal epistemology of the Goddess. The Great Mother was typically represented in three manifestations, nymph, matron and crone. Suttree encounters all three; Wanda is the nymph, Joyce the matron and Mother She the crone. The latter is the Queen of the Underworld; the Goddess presides over both life and death, each passing into the other continuously. It was the loss of this epistemology that brought to man the need for "resurrection," the conquest of death.

But Suttree does not simply escape untimely death. He comes to a profound realization of himself and emancipates himself from his dream of mortality. He learns that "Nothing ever stops moving." and that "There is one Suttree and one Suttree only."[72] He casts off the "othersuttree" that was his dead twin and realizes that life is movement, action, change. He comes to accept the words of the sheriff who runs him out of his wife's home town, and in so doing abandon his death-haunted nihilism. Suttree remarks "No one cares. It's not important."[73] The Sheriff replies:

> That's where you're wrong my friend. Everything's important. A man
> lives his life, he has to make that important. Whether he's a small town
> country sheriff or the president. Or a busted out bum. You might even
> understand that some day I don't say you will. You might.[74]

He does. The sheriff is another of those representatives of order that occur
throughout McCarthy's texts. This one is a philosopher who goes directly
to the heart of Suttree's malaise. The phrase ". . . he has to make that important," expresses the existential notion that meaning is an act of creative and
imaginative will. Like Camus' Sisyphus, Suttree will accept the responsibility of creating his own meaning for life, abandoning the old mythic forms,
now empty of significance in a godless world, and setting out to create his
own existential narrative, leaving the Knoxville necropolis behind him. In so
doing he accepts that he must "become the bard of his own existence" and
cast off the myths of patriarchal religion that inhabit the myth of America.
However he does conform in one respect to American mythology, as did
McCarthy himself. He will seek to remake himself in another image and in
order to do so he will leave on the road to the west.

Because of its urban setting *Suttree* is less concerned with America's
myth of the pastoral than the other Appalachian texts, but it does intensify
the critique of religious mythology, characterizing it as death-haunted, and
seeks to replace it with the anti-myth of the existential hero who chooses life.
This extends the novel's concerns beyond the purely American and places it
in the purview of western culture as a whole.

As I have intimated earlier in this section, *Suttree* is a long book, filled
with detail. It is the text that is most likely to have been influenced by the
author's direct personal experience. There are points of interest and learned
literary, mythic, theological, scientific and historical details in the greatest
abundance. I have tried to include in this account those that I considered
most important to the individual text and also those which were most significant in terms of the continuity of theme in McCarthy's work as a whole.
Much has had to be omitted, all of it adding to the fascination of the text.
The scale of the novel, in such great contrast to those that preceded it,
enlarges our awareness of the scope of McCarthy's ambition and of the powers he brings to bear on its realization. In my view it would be appropriate to reappraise critical evaluation of *Suttree*. The novel has been relatively
neglected within the field of McCarthy scholarship. I believe that it may
come to be regarded as one of his most interesting works; it certainly stands
apart from the other novels in the sense that it is more obviously rooted in
the consciousness of its chief protagonist. McCarthy's courage in attacking

his culture's most cherished beliefs is manifest. His confidence in placing his work in association with that of the acknowledged masters of the art will, for many, seem justified. Above all his determination to express his love of language without inhibition, to use it in as great a variety of ways as possible, stands in paradoxical contrast to his powerful critique of the culture that has placed this language at his service. That language has this power to transform its own world is perhaps the final meaning of the art produced in a universe in which "Nothing ever stops moving."

Chapter Nine

The Stonemason

We have nothing to sustain us but the counsel of our fathers.

I am dealing with McCarthy's novels in chronological order of publication but his two dramatic works do not fit easily into this structure. Although *The Stonemason* was written several years earlier it was not published as a text until 1994. It has, as yet, never been performed in public in its published form:[1] it thus becomes difficult to place the play in the sequence of McCarthy's texts. The fact that it has not been possible to see a production makes analysis more difficult. There is no way of knowing how the play might have been modified in practice, possibly by McCarthy himself. Therefore analysis and evaluation must be related to the only available text. For this reason I am dealing with the play as a short, relatively unimportant segment of McCarthy's work, and placing it with *The Gardener's Son* at the end of the sequence of works set in the South.

The fact that it has never been successfully performed indicates that there is something amiss with *The Stonemason*. It is fairly obvious what this might be: Ben Telfair physically occupies two places simultaneously within the context of a single role. He stands at a podium "At far stage left"[2] throughout the action, commenting on what transpires and speaking the words his character speaks in that action. To have such a figure "outside" the action and able to comment is not in itself a difficulty. It is, of course, as old as drama itself, although the Greek Chorus was not a single individual. Brecht employed a similar device, the Singer, in *The Caucasian Chalk Circle*, and Thornton Wilder began *Our Town* with the figure of the stage director explaining the *mise-en-scene* directly to the audience. But McCarthy goes far beyond these examples as the initial stage directions indicate:

*It is important to note that the Ben we see onstage during the monologues is a double and to note that **this double does not speak**, but is only a figure designed to complete the scene.*[3]

Herein lies the central weakness of *The Stonemason* as a drama. Ben is at the centre of the action in almost every scene and, therefore, almost all the dialogue. But the Ben taking part in the action and the Ben speaking the words are in different places, both in space and time. Thus the very means whereby the drama can come to life, the emotional interaction between the characters as created and represented in their verbal intercommunication, is completely undermined: "This double does not speak." I believe that McCarthy has underestimated the extent to which this device contradicts the dynamics of collective performance. The announcement of the proposed Clear Lake production stated that "the play will not be "presented in monologue by Ben the Stonemason . . .'"[4] Clearly some radical restructuring was called for but it seems clear that the essential flaw in the play's structure had to be addressed before production could become a realistic proposition.

McCarthy's reasons for structuring the play in this way are made clear in his further stage directions. Regarding the doubling of Ben he states:

The purpose, as we shall see, is to give distance to the events and to place them in a completed past.[5]

This recalls the narrative strategy adopted, at least occasionally, in *Wake For Susan*, *The Orchard Keeper*, *Suttree* and even, momentarily, *Child of God*, in which the narrative voice becomes that of the protagonist. This aspect of the play is strengthened by the stage direction, "*The podium is lit. Ben comes forward to take his place there. As he begins to speak, his double, seated at the table onstage **begins to write**.*"[6]

McCarthy wishes to contrast the action with Ben's consciousness of that action:

What must be kept in mind is that the performance consists of two separate presentations. One is the staged drama. The other is the monologue—or chautauqua[7]—which Ben delivers from the podium. And while it is true that Ben at his podium is at times speaking for—or through—his silent double on stage, it is nevertheless a crucial feature of the play that there be no suggestion of communication between these two worlds. In this sense it would not even be incorrect to assume that Ben is unaware of the staged

*drama. Above all we must resist the temptation to see the drama as some-
thing being presented by the speaker at his lectern, for to do so is to defraud
the drama of its rightful autonomy. One could say that the play is an artifact of history to which the audience is made privy, yet if the speaker at his
podium apostrophizes the figures in that history it is only as they reside in
his memory. It is this that dictates the use of the podium. It locates Ben in a
separate space and isolates that space from the world of the drama on stage.
The speaker has an agenda which centers upon his own exoneration, his own
salvation. The events that unfold upon the stage will not always support
him. The audience may perhaps be also a jury. . . .*[8]

The sheer length of this stage direction, which in its entirety runs for almost
two pages, is an indication that McCarthy is grappling with the limitations of
theatrical realism. The deployment of "two Bens" reinforces this impression.
McCarthy's intention is clear enough. His consistent theme is the relation
between the world as it is, and the world as our consciousness experiences it;
and he is above all concerned with the structures of belief imposed on that
consciousness by culture, especially in its mythic forms. It is this that dictates
to him the need to contrast the action with Ben's separately rendered version
of it: ". . . *if the speaker at his podium apostrophizes the figures in that history it
is **only as they reside in his memory**.*"[9]

As a novelist McCarthy has consistently shown a willingness to challenge the conventions of a form still heavily influenced by realism and naturalism. In so doing he has been able to express philosophical and metaphysical
concerns in a manner that has become characteristic of his oeuvre. *The Stonemason* attempts something similar with theatrical form. The insistence that
". . . we must resist the temptation to see the drama as something presented
by the speaker at his lectern . . ." is a direction to the audience while "The
speaker has an agenda which centers on his own exoneration, . . ." indicates
that these stage directions are as significant to the text as the dialogue itself,
and that this significance must somehow be conveyed to the audience by
means that go beyond what is apparent from the action and dialogue itself.
To some extent this is a challenge to be met by the director and actors as best
they may. At the same time there is a sense in which *The Stonemason* appears
to be a text to be read as well as a play to be performed. Although I shall consider some of the difficulties that confront those engaged in a performance—
this is a stage play after all—I shall spend most of this chapter discussing the
play as a text to be read.

The text contains a number of other stage directions that challenge
the practical limits of the form. When Ben and Papaw visit the farmhouse

which they are rebuilding, the stage direction requires that there be "... *a low partial wall of actual stone* ..."[10] Quite what the relevance here of the word "actual" might be is hard to fathom, nor is it obvious how the audience might be made aware of this actuality. Of course the play expresses the notion of the craft of the stonemason being a metaphor for authenticity and integrity, but the theatre conveys its truths through commonly accepted illusions of the real. When Big Ben first enters "*He has three or four very expensive rings that he wears when he is not working.*"[11] Once again there is no mention of these details in dialogue or monologue and they must therefore remain incommunicable to the audience, despite the fact that they are significant in revealing something of Big Ben's character, in contrast to that of Papaw in particular. There are other moments that are perfectly ordinary as text but would be extremely difficult to achieve on stage:

Ben opens the door.

MAMA   And let Bossy out.

BEN   (*To the dog*) Let's go.

The dog looks at him.

BEN   Let's go I said.

The dog climbs slowly out of the box and goes to the door and looks out.

BEN   Hit it.

The dog goes out.[12]

If *The Stonemason* were to be *filmed* many of these difficulties would disappear and it is perhaps significant that the proposed Clear Lake production is also billed as a "multi-media performance with video, slides ..."[13]

Leaving aside such practical difficulties of performance, *The Stonemason* does contain a good deal that is of interest and, considered as a text, brings into focus a number of themes that have been present in the Tennessee novels with varying degrees of intensity. All McCarthy's texts refer to the idea of the family; as noted previously happy families are conspicuous by their absence. *The Stonemason* is the one work that concentrates its whole attention on the members of one family and which presents us with a variety of characters in a good deal of detail, rather than, as in *Suttree*, an alienated individual member of dispersed families, families we only get to know through Suttree's subjective report. The location of the play in Louisville, Kentucky, a town that straddles the border with Tennessee, justifying the inclusion of the text in the "Southern" category. The Telfair family is black but the play is not about race;[14] the Telfairs are representative. Their difficulties are located within a culture that relates to black and white alike. One senses that this is McCarthy's implicit rejection of racism; the Telfairs are a conventional American family, making their own way in the world and conscious of their social position and respectability. They also regard the family as a place of refuge from the world and a source of tradition, identity and values.

Within this familial context *The Stonemason* foregrounds the father-son conflict in its most intense form. The "happy family" and the loving father-provider are powerful aspects of America's mythology[15] and the representation of both, presented in McCarthy's texts in general, and *The Stonemason* in particular, are essential aspects of his mythoclastic project. The sense of the family as a unit that in some sense inhabits a world of its own creation, a small world within a world, is, of course, well suited to the stage drama form. One gains a sense that McCarthy is well aware of this and has chosen the subject to fit the form, but that he is somewhat ill at ease without his landscapes (and cityscapes in *Suttree*). It is perhaps for this reason that he fills his stage set with so many different sites, some of them outside the Telfair family home. The physical environment is always so full of meaning for McCarthy that the household interior seems too limited for his imagination to work with.

Despite these inhibiting factors McCarthy does create a powerful portrayal of the family as the site of a destructive patriarchal mythology. Four generations of Telfairs are represented in the play. In each case son rejects the values of father and reacts against patriarchal power. In each case the result is destructive. Papaw is the craftsman, who finds his justification in the mastery of his craft. His is the old attitude of the powerless who find dignity in their labour and whose pride is more than satisfied by the knowledge that their work is well done:

PAPAW   The man's labor that did the work is in the work. You
               caint make it go away. Even if it's paid for it's still
               there. If ownership lies in the benefit to a man then
               the mason owns all the work he does in this world and
               you caint put that claim aside nor quit it and it dont
               make no difference whose name is on the paper.[16]

His son, Big Ben, cannot match his father's pride in work and does not find it possible to exist in the world as a man of business without compromising the old man's perfectionist values. To Big Ben the "name on the paper" makes all the difference. His pride is in his appearance (the four expensive rings) but he is undermined by the fact that he is not the true master in his own house, nor of his wife's affections. The coldness between husband and wife is expressed with a powerful economy in a simple moment on his first appearance:

> *He . . . goes to the stove and pours coffee from the percolator.*

MAMA   That ain't done perkin.

> *He continues to pour and then takes his cup and takes his watch out of his pocket although there is an electric clock on the stove and another clock on the wall. He puts his watch back in his pocket and shuffles back across the kitchen and out the door.*[17]

The distance between man and wife is implied in the lack of exchange over the coffee, while the reference to his own watch rather than the family clocks reinforces the sense of Big Ben as a man in isolation. That he has been driven to live outside his own family home by the emotional and cultural dominance of his own father becomes increasingly clear as the play progresses. Ben the son loves his grandfather, not his father. He espouses the old man's values and cannot account for the fact that his own father does not. Mama is the same and therefore also dotes on the son:

MAMA   Well, you waitin on me to peck holes in Benny you
              better make yourself comfortable, that's all I got to
              say.

BIG BEN   You don't need to tell me that. Nooo. You sure don't
              need to tell me that.[18]

For a man of power Big Ben's family situation is all but intolerable:

BEN   I give you forty hours a week. Every week. Papaw
              worked on the job every day till he was ninety-two
              years old. What do you want?

BIG BEN   Dont make no difference what I want. I aint goin to
              get it. Not even in my own house. Under my own
              roof. Never could and never will.[19]

Big Ben succumbs to his sense of alienation. His espousal of values that completely contradict those of his father results in debts, incurred for unspecified purposes. His pride is destroyed by the knowledge that his financial losses will cost the family their home and in consequence he shoots himself.

Ben is the central figure of the play. It is his consciousness that is most strongly represented, both in the dialogue and the action in which it is contextualized, and in the monologues in which Ben delivers his interpretation of events and philosophical ruminations. Ben is a tragic figure in the classic sense; his failure to perceive his own limitations helps to bring disaster to those he loves. As the representative of the third of the four generations of Telfairs he occupies a position of crucial patriarchal significance. His identification with his grandfather is a rejection and betrayal of his own father, repeating the pattern that Big Ben has followed. Of course this rejection is seen by McCarthy as inherent within patriarchal epistemology; maleness is about power. The fourth generation is represented by Soldier, Ben's nephew. The generational conflict is both continued and intensified in Soldier. His father has deserted the family and the boy's anger is in part a response to this abandonment. At the same time his alienation is deepened by the treatment he receives. We learn eventually that Soldier is a nick-name. It carries connotations of manhood. But he is treated within the family like a mixture of child and servant:

SOLDIER *enters the kitchen. He is Ben's sister's son, aged fifteen.*

MAMA   You just the man I want to see. Get them plates and
                set the table.

Soldier drags himself to the cupboard and takes down the plates.

MAMA   And when you get done with that holler upstairs at
                Big Ben.[20]

When Soldier's manoeuvre with the telephone is exposed we perceive the anger and violence that lie just below the surface of the family's relationships:

The phone rings again. Carlotta reaches Soldier first.

MAMA   Fool. If I dont put a knot on your head.
SOLDIER   There's something wrong with this phone.

Carlotta snatches the phone from him and raps him on the top of the head with it.

SOLDIER   Ow!

. . .

Soldier goes wide around Mama, who is taking her place at the table again. He is holding the top of his head.

SOLDIER   Shit.
BIG BEN   What did you say?

Soldier mutters something that no one can hear. Big Ben reaches down the table and takes a swipe at him. Soldier ducks and the chair goes to the floor. Big Ben stands up to deal with him further and Mama stands up and takes Big Ben by the arm.

MAMA   Dont hit him on the ear you'll make him deaf like
               they done Edison in the movie.

Across the table Papaw is eating peaceably.[21]

The family blames Soldier's alienation on the boy himself although there is also a recognition of the effect on him of Landry's desertion. What is not recognized is the extent to which the family refuses to accommodate Soldier as a youngster on the verge of manhood. Too late Ben comes to see the truth:

MAVEN   Somewhere else is where he got to be the way he is
               now.
BEN   (*Shaking his head*) No he didn't. He got that way right
               here. In this family. Nowhere else.[22]

The previous passage expresses two other significant ideas that are central to the play and to McCarthy work as a whole. The cause of Edison's deafness "is not definitely known—it could have been a result of an early childhood illness or the result of a "boxing" of his ears by a rail conductor, possibly a myth."[23] McCarthy refers to the place of myth in our culture and the way in which this plays a part in shaping our understanding of, and reaction to experience. He points out the significance of the cinema in disseminating myth. I have already referred to the (inappropriate) cinematic character of the play. But even more significant is the fact that Papaw, "eating peacefully," remains entirely detached from the events going on before him. The great irony is that it is this old man's position as the repository of wisdom, authenticity of experience and pure values—his symbolic status as The Stonemason, that places on his family the unbearable burden of a perceived perfection. This is the core of McCarthy's vision of patriarchy. Just as he himself struggles to match the achievement of the great literary fathers so, he suggests, the archetypal American family struggles under the burden of the deeds and values of its own mythic patriarchs.

While Big Ben and Soldier are destroyed by this burden and by the frustration of their need to become themselves "the man," Ben himself is corrupted by this mythology and becomes an agent in the downfall of the family that he believes he can and must preserve. The deaths of his father and nephew and the loss of the family home are the context in which we have to judge Ben's espousal of what he believes his grandfather to stand for.

> The arc of the moral universe is indeed long but it does bend towards justice. At the root of all this of course is the trade. . . .

> The trade was all they had, the old masons. They understood it both in its utility and in its secret nature. We couldnt read or write, he says. But it was not in any book. We kept it close to our hearts and it was like a power and we knew it would not fail us. We knew that it was a thing that if we had it they could not take it from us and it would stand by us and not fail us. Not ever fail us.[24]

As McCarthy indicates in the initial stage direction quoted at the beginning of this chapter Ben is concerned, particularly in these monologues, to justify his own actions and values. His philosophizing on the value and meaning of the stonemason's craft reflects those passages in other McCarthy texts in which the details of a task are described in loving detail and to which I have referred several times before. But the values of work are not enough. They do not apply when the task in hand is that of father, husband, son. Living in the family is not a craft, nor even a philosophy. It is a matter of emotions and loving understanding and enabling others to be. Ben comes to realize this at the last:

> The work devours the man and devours his life and I thought that in the end he must somehow be justified thereby.

. . .

I lost my way. I'd thought by my labors to stand outside that true bend of gravity which is the world's pain. I lost my way and if I could tell you the hour of it or the day or how it came about I should not have lost it at all.[25]

In his dream of judgment he relates that:

I stood with my job-book under my arm in which were logged the hours and the days and the years and wherein was ledgered down each sack of mortar and each perch of stone and I stood alone in that whitened forecourt beyond which waited the God of all being and I stood in the full folly of my own righteousness and I took the book from under my arm and I thumbed it through a final time as if to reassure myself and when I did I saw that the pages were yellowed and crumbling and the ink faded and the accounts no longer clear and suddenly I thought to myself fool fool do you not see what will be asked of you? How He will lean down perhaps the better to see you . . . And ask as you stand there alone with your book—perhaps not even unkindly—this single question: Where are the others? Where are the others. Oh I've had time in great abundance to reflect upon that terrible question. Because we cannot save ourselves unless we save all ourselves. I had this dream but I did not heed it. And so I lost my way.[26]

"The others" are gone. Big Ben has shot himself. Soldier has died of a heroin overdose, the drug bought with money given him by Ben in an effort to buy him off and protect the family from corruption and grief. His sister, Soldier's mother, has left with her new husband, ironically named "Mason,"[27] unable to forgive her brother for the deception that prevented her from seeing her son again before he died. Papaw alone has died a peaceful and natural death. The irony of the play is compounded because Ben remains unaware of the role the old man's apparent perfection has had in the tragedy of all their lives.

Ben is unable to "save the others" because he has believed the patriarchal myth of the provident father as all knowing and all wise. He has arrogated to himself the role of provider, protector, philosopher, spokesman and curer of all ills. He is both educated and a worker, thinker and craftsman. As his sister truly says, "You think you can fix everything. You cant."[28] His arrogance has contributed to Soldier's alienation: "Well, I see you ain't changed.

Still know everthing."[29] Even in his moment of revelation Ben fails to see that no-one can answer the question "Where are the others?" without experiencing grief and acknowledging failure.

While the relation between Ben and the other members of the family provides the bulk of the action and hence of the thematic development of the play, other ideas are inherent in the text and familiar McCarthy images and textual characteristics also appear. Mama and Carlotta dispute the role of women; their focus is Maven who is training to be a lawyer:

MAMA	Aint nobody badmouthin nobody. She's a sweet girl. Couldn't ask for no better hardly. She just got a lot of high tone ideas, that's all. Life'll smack a few of em out of her before it gets done with her. Beside's, Benny's the one ought to be the lawyer. He'd be a dandy too. Smart as he is.
CARLOTTA	Well I declare, Mama. I don't believe I'm hearing this. You're jealous of her on Ben's part.
MAMA	Aint done no such a thing. Just statin the facts, that's all.
CARLOTTA	Well in any case she's here more than Ben, that's for sure.
MAMA	She's supposed to be.
. . .	
CARLOTTA	You think that men are born with rights that women don't have. That they can come and go like migratory birds and its perfectly natural . . .
MAMA	It is natural. Tryin to change nature. Women has babies. You cain't get around that. That's the plan the good Lord laid down and you wont change it. You can make up your own plan if you want to, and you can read it in ruin.[30]

Mama has lived her life according to the traditional patriarchal plan but she lives to "read it in ruin" as far as her own family is concerned. A play that questions patriarchy must perforce consider "the woman question." It is clear that Mama's innocent complicity in patriarchal values has contributed to the pressures within the family and her refusal to acknowledge the existence of failures enables those pressures to create a crisis. Carlotta's rejoinder, "Well it wasn't the good Lord's plan for men to gone all hours of the day and night."[31] is a veiled reference to Big Ben, who we later learn has a mistress with whom his true affections lie. Mama suppresses this: "You watch yourself girl. You hear? You just watch yourself."[32] Of course Mama's stoic refusal to admit the truth is a product of her powerlessness as a woman in a traditional family.

Such sequences of dialogue illustrate McCarthy's gift for representing speech and reflecting its rhythms and inflections in a compelling manner. This aspect of the play is particularly convincing and makes one regret that he did not choose to present the entire text in this form. The dialogues are so much more direct and powerful, in their characteristic economy and simplicity, than the monologues which seem like sermons and which rely on a poetic rhetoric that does not resonate in this otherwise realistic context.

I have mentioned the significance of the dog in McCarthy's texts whenever it has occurred. The Telfair's dog has already been mentioned for his theatrical unsuitability. He is however a symbol of the family itself. The early sense that all is not well with the Telfairs is strengthened by Ben's reaction to the dog's reluctance to move:

BEN	Mama what are you going to do about this dog?
MAMA	Aint nothin wrong with that dog.
BEN	He raises his leg to take a pee and then falls over in it.
MAMA	You don't need to go worryin bout that dog. That dog's just fine.[33]

Mama's reaction is another example of her refusal to face the truth. After the fall of the Telfairs, Ben recounts the tale. He speaks of the house, now empty and deserted:

| BEN | The big elm tree died. The old dog died. Things that you can touch go away for ever. I dont know what that means. I dont know what it means that things exist and then exist no more. Trees. Dogs. People. *Will* that namelessness into which we vanish then taste of us?[34] |

The reference to namelessness reflects McCarthy's consistent use of significant names. This is an aspect of his understanding of the nature of language. Naming relates word to thing, calls it into consciousness but at the same time limits it and, ultimately, remains its double, its other, necessary but not sufficient. Nothingness, non-existence and namelessness are coterminous for McCarthy. Telfair is ironically chosen; the family have struggled to survive by telling fair instead of true. Their discourse has been informed by a false mythology. Benjamin[35] was the favorite youngest son of Jacob in the Genesis story of the generation of the twelve tribes. Not only is this part of the founding patriarchal myth of Judaism it is also a tale of family conflict and sibling jealousy. After Soldier's[36] death the family acknowledge him as their own and we learn that he too was named Benjamin. The passing on of the name reflects the patriarchal nature of the Telfair's American conception of family. Papaw's real name was Edward and this is the name given to Ben's new son. This naming reflects the burden of the mythic past from which McCarthy's protagonists struggle to free themselves but to which they are bound by the ties of family identity. I have already mentioned the ironically coincidental "Mason."

The Stonemason then is a play that poses practical difficulties that inhibit possible stage performance. These might be remedied most readily by an imaginative production in another medium; television and the cinema both possess a flexibility that could accommodate McCarthy's creation in a way that realistic theatre must find difficult if not impossible. The dialogue sections would readily come alive and even the divided presence of Ben could be accommodated. The monologue sections would be difficult to render in a convincing manner since they lack the living immediacy of the dialogue and the lyrical intensity of the rhetorical passages of the novels. I have suggested that McCarthy adopts this radical form as part of his own personal attempt to transcend the limitations of realism in the theatre, something that he has successfully accomplished in his novels.

Considered as a text *The Stonemason* deals powerfully with characteristic McCarthy themes. In Ben Telfair McCarthy has created a man in love with a mythic past who believes that this mythology of the stonemason's craft, in tune with "the warp of the world"[37] will provide him with the philosophy and values that enable him to fulfill the role of the patriarch, the *paterfamilias* able to protect his dependents from all ills. His efforts fail. Death and dispossession leave the Telfairs bereft. Ben's mythology of work is inadequate. His understanding of human beings is incomplete. Patriarchal power relations create conflict between father and son, a conflict that undermines all the Telfair men. As the teenage Jeffrey realises: "Man I dont know how old you are. All I know is you livin in the past. I'm livin in the past. History done swallowed you up cept you dont know it."[38] Ben comes to the end of the play still unable to free himself of this "history," this mythology represented by the grandfather he has idealized:

BEN   . . . we are embarked on a journey to something unimaginable. We do not know what will be required

of us, and we have nothing to sustain us but the counsel of our fathers.

. . .

Papaw materializes out of the fog upstage just at the edge of the headstones.
He is naked.

BEN   He came out of the darkness and at that moment
             everything seemed revealed to me . . . and I knew that
             he would guide me all my days and that he would not
             fail me, not fail me, not ever fail me.[39]

Ben's declaration of faith is rendered ironic by what has gone before. The
patriarchal myth of the family still holds him in its grip. But the truth has
been spoken, not by a man, and not by a member of the family, but by its
unspoken and unacknowledged other, Mary Weaver, lover of Big Ben:

. . . That's why you here aint it? Cause you caint get around that daddy?

Caint get around that daddy.[40]

Chapter Ten

The Gardener's Son

Everbody that aint got a say so, dont mean they dont care.

The Gardener's Son ought to be evaluated and analyzed as a television film. This was the form in which it was conceived and indeed brought into being. The project, originated by Richard Pearce and created by Pearce and McCarthy jointly,[1] was completed successfully and broadcast on American television in January 1977. In order to perform this critical task adequately it would be necessary to have access to repeated viewings of the film itself, but this is not possible. A video does exist but copyright conditions are such that it is not available, even to academics. The Cormac McCarthy Society has been able to show it at conferences and I have seen it once.[2] The conditions for viewing left something to be desired but I was able to form an overall impression of the film, to gauge its atmosphere and respond to the actors' performances. However it would be quite inappropriate to base a detailed response on this one experience and I shall not attempt to do so. Instead I shall base this chapter on the screenplay published by Ecco Press in 1996. The film as broadcast does vary slightly from this text, but the differences do not seriously alter the overall meaning of the piece or the way in which its is structured. The details of these variations are contained in Dianne Luce's 1993 article on the production.[3] My own viewing confirmed the impressions gained from the screenplay that *The Gardener's Son* exhibits those concerns that have provided the thread of continuity I have traced in all McCarthy's "Tennessee" or "Southern" works.

It is unlikely that many readers of my text will have had the opportunity to see the film; some idea of its style and mood can be gained from the knowledge that the part of Robert McEvoy is played by Brad Dourif and that his performance is very like that he gave as Haze Motes in the 1979 film of *Wise Blood*.[4] It is, of course, impossible to determine how much the published screenplay[5] is influenced by Pearce and, conversely, how much the broadcast film was influenced by McCarthy. My working hypothesis is that the screenplay is the writer's work, and that the director is responsible for the film. I contend therefore that my basing of this chapter on the screenplay alone is justified by more than mere necessity; *The Gardener's Son* can be read as a Cormac McCarthy text.

The continuing theme of the rebellious son and his relationship with his father is what first strikes one about the film, but closer analysis reveals it to be interwoven with a number of other concerns which make it a complex and satisfying work of considerably more depth than *The Stonemason*.

The Gardener's Son has received little in the way of critical attention. However Dianne Luce has written two extensively researched and perceptive articles on the text.[6] In the first of these she makes clear the process by which Pearce and McCarthy evolved the eventual film. She refers to the "seven 'research newsletters' that Pearce sent to the Alicia Patterson Foundation in New York,"[7] Pearce's copies of which are housed in the library of the University of South Carolina, and which detail the historical research undertaken.[8] These make clear the fact that the text is based on actual events—the killing of James Gregg by Robert McEvoy in the South Carolina town of Graniteville in 1876, McEvoy's trial for murder and his consequent conviction and execution. In this article Luce draws attention the theme of the problem of historical authenticity, "Times past are fugitive . . ."[9] and reminds us that history is written by the articulate and for the powerful. She makes the point that McCarthy is concerned to give a voice to the inarticulate, to create in his various texts[10] a version of "history from below" (not Luce's phrase). She also points out the differences that exist between the published screenplay and the broadcast film and gives some indication of the way in which Pearce's newsletters explain the changes made and which led to the eventual shooting script.[11]

Luce expands on the theme of historical authenticity in her second article which relates *The Gardener's Son* to those other works in which the main part of the text is "framed" in such a way as to call into question the "authorship" and therefore the point of view of the teller of the tale. There can be no doubt that this is a central concern of *The Gardener's Son* and that any serious critical discussion of the text must deal with this aspect of its meaning. It will be clear from the above that my account of this aspect of the text concurs with that of Luce and it can be assumed that it is informed throughout by her reading. Other aspects of the analysis are my own, particularly those regarding the father/son conflict and the notions of the relation of the text to aspects of Southern mythology.

As previously noted *The Gardener's Son* is set in Graniteville, South Carolina, in the year 1876. The very beginning of the screenplay creates Luce's textual "framework," the full meaning of which is only revealed at the very end of the film. The initial scene is set:

> *Interior. Old Office of the Graniteville cotton mill. Daylight through dusty windows. An old desk. Boxes and crates standing about the floor.*[12]

In such a location one encounters the artifacts of the past. These artifacts are of questionable meaning and dubious historical value however:

> TIMEKEEPER (*os*)[13] God knows what all is in here. I'd watch where I
> put my hands.
> That was the . . . . I don't know what that was.
> . . .
> Old papers and stuff. What aint eat up.[14]

The Timekeeper is addressing a young man who is revealed as an inquirer into the past—the history of the death of James Gregg. McCarthy uses his great gift for dialogue with telling economy and subtlety even at this early point to make clear that memory as well as artifact have a part to play in the recreation of the past:

> TIMEKEEPER Oh yes. I remember him. I was just a kid. My daddy
> was the supervisor and we went to the funeral over in
> Augusta. The wind blowed my brother Earl's hat in
> the street and a horse stepped on it.[15]

The Timekeeper's recollection of the funeral is focused on a triviality but he recalls what was vivid to him at the time. His recollection is subjective, that of a child for whom the embarrassment of a brother has more emotional impact than the burial of a prominent man. Even though he is now an old man, details of his own family are what are important to him. There is perhaps a hint of sibling rivalry in his focusing on his brother's public discomfort—family conflict being one of the text's principal themes. This simple framework passage establishes the context of the screenplay as an attempt to discover the history of an event. It makes clear the fact that such an endeavor is inherently impossible. The two sources of "history", artifact and memory, are themselves in need of interpretation. The whole notion of the subjects of history—on whom this history is to be focused, and the question of by whom and for whom is it to be written—will be called into question by the action of the film. The introductory "framework" scene expresses the "problem of history" succinctly:

> TIMEKEEPER   You wont find it here.
> YOUNG MAN   What wont I find?
> TIMEKEEPER   They're just boxes of records. There's some old picher albums here somewheres. Mill used to keep.
>
> *The young man shuffles through a box, idly looking at papers that turn up.*
>
> TIMEKEEPER   They aint the thing. Old papers or pichers. Once you copy something down you dont have it any more. You just have the record. Times past are fugitive. They caint be kept in no box.[16]

At the end of the text we discover that the young man, William Chaffee, is the nephew of James Gregg and that he is investigating an episode of his family history. His desire to uncover the past has been provoked by his recognition that his "family history" lacks the power to convince: "It was just a family story. It was like something in a book. It didnt seem like real people."[17]

The main action however enacts the events themselves. It should not be thought that McCarthy is presenting his version of these events as the truth, since this would be to contradict the very assumption on which the text is based. What he does do is present a version that contradicts the official history and that suggests that the distinction between history and fiction is blurred to say the least. It places Robert McEvoy's killing of James Gregg in a different context, a context that takes into account the possibility that both history and justice are owned by the powerful and that fiction may be used to subvert this cultural hegemony. McCarthy expresses the need of the voiceless to be heard in the words of one of the very humblest of his characters, a black man hired to dig a grave for Mrs. McEvoy:

> 1ST BLACK   Everbody that aint got a say so, dont mean they dont care. In this life or out of it.[18]

Luce interprets McCarthy's text as a response to this need of the voiceless to have their version of history made known. My interpretation complements this idea; I argue throughout this thesis that McCarthy confronts myth with counter-myth. For me the significance of *The Gardener's Son*[19] lies in the manner in which it makes clear the way in which economic and political power are used to shape the myth in the first place.

Broadus Mitchell's biography of William Gregg, the founder of the Graniteville cotton mill, contains an account of the events depicted in the film and Luce quotes an extensive passage. It is this account that the film challenges. It is a myth of simplicity, of the elision of cause and effect, a myth of political innocence. Robert McEvoy is simply "bad." "The bad boy of the village was Bob McAvoy. (sic)."[20] Significantly the name is misspelt, an indication of the absence from the historical record of the voices of the Robert McEvoys of this world. The story is told of Robert's loss of his leg and of Mrs. Gregg's solicitude in caring for him at her own home. The killing of James Gregg is presented as beyond explanation: ". . . nobody knows why . . ."[21] The "official" version takes its cue from Mrs. Gregg who "recorded in the family Bible that her son was murdered in cold blood."[22] However Mitchell also recorded the fact that Robert's attack was not upon an unarmed man: "One may still see the hole in the door frame torn by the bullet which Gregg sent after him."[23] It is highly unlikely that Mitchell, writing in South Carolina in 1928, would have interpreted the circumstances of James Gregg's death in terms emanating from Marx and Freud. At the same time it is equally unlikely that "nobody" knew, or thought they knew, why the killing had taken place. *The Gardener's Son* recreates these events in fictional form, but in such a way as to make possible interpretations that Mitchell could not or would not attempt. It also brings into the world the voices that Mitchell excludes.

The interpretations of the killing of James Gregg that McCarthy represents in his text arise from class and family conflict. A one-dimensional political drama would concentrate on the former of these two forces and a conventional leftist piece would make Robert McEvoy the simple victim of an oppressive class system. But the portrait of Robert and his family circumstances is such that we become aware that he is that recognizable McCarthy figure the "dangerous man." Thus personal and familial factors must be taken into account when "explaining" Robert's actions and this gives the drama an added level of complexity. This complexity is compounded by the fact that James Gregg is also an alienated son. The Gregg family is subject to the same internal tensions and conflicts as the McEvoys. James is also a "dangerous man" whose alienation and egotism contribute as much to his own death as does that of Robert. The irony of *The Gardener's Son* lies in the fact that both families are destroyed by the actions of their violent sons. Robert is the actual gardener's son, his father being employed to beautify the factory by making its grounds into a garden. But William Gregg himself is also a gardener in the sense that it is his desire, will and resources that ensure the garden's creation. Thus James is also the "Gardener's Son," and this doubling emphasizes the importance that McCarthy places on this aspect of the drama. By now we recognize this preoccupation with conflict between father and son as a central McCarthy concern and this locates the screenplay in relation to those texts discussed in previous chapters.

The class structure that the Graniteville mill has imposed on the town's citizens is made clear from the outset. The McEvoys are disturbed by the prospect of the doctor's visit:

MARTHA	I seen him. The doctor. He's here.
MRS. McEVOY	Lord save us, he aint to the house is he?
MARTHA	No. He was headin towards Kalmia.

Mrs McEvoy is flustered. She looks around at the state of her house. She pats her hair distractedly.[24]

However the doctor's first call must be on the Greggs. Both families are threatened by death. William Gregg is beyond help but the doctor is solicitous of this important man anyway. Robert McEvoy is threatened by a gangrenous leg but he must wait. For Mrs. Gregg the doctor's visit can be met with the confidence that social superiority affords, a superiority indicated by the existence in her house of a hallway, a stairway and servants:

Exterior. Evening. The doctor's carriage arriving at the house of William Gregg. A boy comes to take the horses in hand.

Interior. The doctor in the hallway of the house handing off his coat and hat to the servant Daphne. . . . . Mrs. Gregg comes down the stairway to greet him.

MRS GREGG	Good evening Dr Perceval. Thank you for coming.
DR PERCEVAL	Not at all. How is your husband?
MRS GREGG	I'm afraid he's much the same.[25]

We gather from their conversation that the dying man, the creator of the source of the town's employment, was imbued with those values that the Puritans brought to America:

DR PERCEVAL He's beyond my or any man's practise.
MRS GREGG   I prayed for God to take him. Is that wrong?
DR PERCEVAL No. Thats not wrong.
MRS GREGG   He hated sickness.
DR PERCEVAL I guess he despised any kind of idleness.
MRS GREGG   Yes. He wouldnt tolerate it.[26]

Mrs. Gregg prays that her husband may be relieved by death but she will not permit Robert the same release from the dreadful prospect of a life with only one leg. It is clear that she arrogates to herself the power of life and death itself over the mill's employees and their families, and that she does this as a function of the power inherent in the class system that the mill creates. She accompanies the doctor on his visit to the home of the McEvoys. There can be no question of her needing an invitation. She is ruthless in her self-righteousness as she imposes her will on Robert:

DR PERCEVAL Mrs Gregg, I dont think he'll listen. He swore at me.
MRS GREGG   He'll not at me.

. . .

MRS GREGG   Robert, what Dr Perceval says is true. You must have
                     the operation.
ROBERT   I'd rather be dead.
MRS GREGG   Life is a precious gift from God. No one has the
                     right . . .
ROBERT   Its up to him.

She looks at him. She does not understand what he means.

ROBERT   If God put the rot in then let it rot off.[27]

This reply is McCarthy's characteristically spare but effective way of show-ing us that Robert is not only "difficult" but also intelligent and thoughtful, albeit in an untutored manner. This is one of the sources of his discontent. He perceives the inadequacy of Mrs Gregg's understanding of the ways of God just as he sees the injustice of his social situation. Mrs Gregg imposes her will and her relentless logic on Robert:

Robert McEvoy is very much afraid. He shakes his head rapidly from side to side. She takes hold of the bedlinen on the far side of the bed and pulls it back. He half rises up in the bed to stop her.

ROBERT   No.

She jerks away the covers. He struggles. . . . His legs lie revealed. The injured one is loosely swathed in bandages through which discolored stains have seeped and his whole lower leg and foot are perfectly black. She turns her head aside at the odor. He falls back sobbing. She recovers him and puts her hand to his face.

MRS GREGG   I know it's very hard. I know. I'll stay with you.

The kitchen. The doctor and the family are waiting. Mrs. Gregg enters. The two men rise.

MRS GREGG   Dr Perceval, I think you may fetch in your assistant
             now.[28]

There is an unmistakable sense of symbolic castration present in this sequence; the young man in bed, the pulling back of the bed-clothes, the revealing of the legs—and of course the cutting off of the limb. The castration is symbolic of the political, social and economic impotence of Robert and his class, an impotence that is contrasted with Mrs. Gregg's irresistible power. She imposes the relentless medical logic of the situation on Robert just as her husband has imposed economic logic on the town. The historical Gregg wrote "An exclusively agricultural people, in the present age of the world, will always be poor . . . They want cities and towns, they want diversity of employment."[29] This is the "New South" argument and it surely represented the lesser of two evils for the region in the post-bellum period. McCarthy's text acknowledges as much, William Gregg's eulogist points out that:

> There are many among us today who can remember what life held in the way of promise before this man came among us. Too many of us were raised in hunger and poverty ever to forget. To see what he has wrought, the neat homes, the churches and schools, the gardens and lovely grounds and last but not least the massive factory structure with its beautiful and perfect machinery, these things seem created by magic.[30]

It is too easy to dismiss this kind of rhetoric as the idealization of a brutal and dehumanizing system. McCarthy accepts the complexity of an imperfect world. He contrasts the condition of those who live and work in the Graniteville mill with the rural destitute who cannot find industrial work:

James Gregg goes past the man to the door and looks out. Standing along the edge of the road are a band of filthy and ragged people with bales of bedding and sorry household effects, nearly all barefooted, some appearing to be albinos, a couple of emaciated hound dogs, a few crates of chickens. They are staring hungrily towards the office.[31]

What undermines the moral authority of the industrial system presided over by William Gregg, and more particularly his son, is the fact that it serves the interests of the Gregg family first and places them in positions of power over their fellow citizens. It is characteristic of McCarthy's mythoclasm that he insists on confronting utopian projects with the harsh realities that invariably undermine their claims to perfectibility. In this case both industrialism and agrarianism are so confronted.

William Gregg's paternalism dies with him. His son imposes the logic of capitalism on the Graniteville mill and its employees in a manner that will prove to be self-destructive. He brings to an end the factory gardens, forcing Mr. McEvoy to lose his avocation and become a mill worker:

GREGG   . . . This company is in the textile business. We have stockholders to answer to. We're not in the flower business.[32]

He uses his position to exploit the factory girls sexually as the scene between James and Martha makes plain:

JAMES GREGG . . . You got a boyfriend?
MARTHA   No sir.
JAMES GREGG Dont have a boyfriend?
MARTHA   No sir.
JAMES GREGG Well I dont know why not.

Martha is nervous, but she gives a sort of toss of her head to clear her hair from her face. James Gregg smiles.

JAMES GREGG Maybe you're just too feisty for these young boys.[33]

Such exploitation is always common knowledge. Robert's drinking companions make this clear. They do not labor the point—it is something that goes without question:

PINKY	It's kindly slack times here. Reckon it is everywheres.
FIRST MAN	You reckon to get on at the mill?
McEVOY	I aint lost nothing down there.
PINKY	I hear ye. Only way to get ahead down there is to get your wife knocked up by the boss. Give ye a little leverage.[34]

The linking of power and sexual predation in the person of James Gregg contrasts with Robert's political and economic impotence, already given a sexual connotation through his symbolic castration by the powerful female.

The confrontation between James and Robert that lies at the heart of the story also reflects the class gulf between the two men and their families. Robert is more aware of it than James; it is part of the text's complexity that he seems the more intelligent of the two:

GREGG	Did you want to see me?
McEVOY	I was huntin my father.
GREGG	Your father.
McEVOY	He was the gardener.
GREGG	I know who he was.
McEVOY	No you dont.
GREGG	What do you mean I dont?
McEVOY	You might know his name is all.[35]

The text's enactment of Robert's trial has a two-fold significance. It makes clear the manner in which the administration of "justice" is concerned to protect the interest of the governing class. Robert is prevented from speaking for himself by his own lawyers who are mindful of their need to keep on the right side of the Greggs:

MR McEVOY	I dont see why Bobby caint testify for hisself.
. . .	
JORDAN	Worst mistake in the world, McEvoy. Worst mistake in the world. We wont get anywhere in an attempt to blacken the Gregg name. People dont want that. We've agreed with Mrs Gregg to call no female witnesses[36] and I dont have to tell you that we have exacted every consideration in exchange. Her anxiety to protect the family is one of the things most in our favor.

. . . .

JORDAN   All the law dont go on in the courts, McEvoy. And
                I'm sure I dont have to tell you that.[37]

The second aspect of the trial's significance lies in the fact that it is an image of the process by which "history" is written. Neither activity, judicial process nor the writing of history, is free of the constraints imposed by the power of those who run society. Neither is free of the epistemological assumptions on which the interpretation of events is based. Robert's indictment, given in the actual words of the real trial as contained in the court record, expresses the contemporary notion of the motivation of evil deeds:

PROS. ATTORNEY   That Robert McEvoy, not having the fear of God
                   before his eyes, but being moved and seduced
                   by the instigation of the devil . . .[38]

The judicial and historical narratives of the killing of James Gregg are shown to be false. The circumstances of that event have been made clear to us through the action described in the text. It was a confused event in which violence was provoked by a mixture of mutual antagonism and misunderstanding. There is no indication of "malice aforethought" on Robert's part but we know that he is a "dangerous man," a characteristic that James shares to a considerable degree. It is clear that the conflict and misunderstanding between them would not have had fatal results had not both been armed with pistols. The script indicates that it is James who first reaches for his gun; possibly each thinks that the other is about to shoot, although we cannot be certain about even this:

Gregg reaches into his top pocket and brings forth some coins. He selects a ten dollar gold piece and flips it onto the desk in front of McEvoy.

GREGG   Take it and get out.

McEvoy stares at the gold piece. When he looks up his eyes are filled with hatred. Gregg looks at McEvoy and then looks at the coin and then looks at McEvoy again. Then his face drains. He jerks suddenly at the top drawer of his desk. McEvoy snatches the pistol from his belt.

McEVOY   Dont.

> *Gregg scrabbles in the desk drawer for his pistol and McEvoy fires. Gregg is knocked back sitting in his chair. He reaches again for the drawer and McEvoy fires again. Gregg reels in the chair. He puts his hand to his side and rises.*[39]

Since there are no witnesses to this episode, and Robert is not permitted to testify (nor to write his own history) it follows that neither trial nor researcher can discover what transpired. It is only the subsequent action that is witnessed by Captain Giles, who testifies truly enough to the little that he does see. The whole episode is created in a way which suggests that only imaginative fiction can produce narratives that match the complexity of real events and that the "whole truth" of such events must lie forever beyond our grasp. It also illustrates the idea of the overlap between historical and fictional narrative; the first can never be created without employing the second—at that point where knowledge gives place to conjecture.

The "history" of the deaths of James Gregg and Robert McEvoy inevitably forms a part of that wider history of their time and place. McCarthy makes this wider historical context an implicit aspect of the text. The period is that of the Reconstruction, that period which the South regarded as even more shameful and outrageous than the defeat of the Civil War. The myth of the period was promulgated by the Redeemers as they worked to overturn the changes that Reconstruction brought about. It featured the carpetbagger, an exploitative and opportunistic northern intruder, and the scalawag, a black rogue arrogating to himself privileges to which only the white man was entitled. *The Gardener's Son* subtly contradicts both these stereotypes. William Gregg is the man who has picked up the threads of commerce in Graniteville but he is himself a southerner, the Gregg's hailing from Charleston, and his efforts begin to draw the impoverished and defeated South out of its state of destitution. The only reference to a "carpetbagger" is deeply ironic:

> *. . . Train arriving at the outskirts of Graniteville. A solitary figure riding the last boxcar. The train slows. Robert McEvoy sits atop the boxcar with his crutch and a tattered carpetbag.*[40]

The black characters occupy positions at various levels. The humble laborers who dig a grave are respectful, not to say fearful of Robert McEvoy. From this simple source comes the profound idea that the voiceless are not the unconcerned.[41] Dr. Perceval's "man" is sufficiently trusted and proficient to assist the doctor in the removal of Robert's leg. Both prosecution and defense at Robert's trial have white and black lawyers, the latter being shown as educated and, in terms of McCarthy's text, indistinguishable from their white counterparts. This, more than anything else, is the historical detail that places the action in the Reconstruction period. The jury comprises nine black and three white jurors. It is made quite clear that, far from having an undue influence on the trial, the presence of blacks within the judicial process has no effect at all on the Gregg's control of events. Even the drinkers in the doggery are less than obsessed with the question of race:

> SECOND MAN Never thought I'd live to see the day. Niggers runnin
> crazy killin folks. Right in ye own country.
>
> *He drinks.*
>
> PINKY   Don't get him started on the niggers, for God's
> sake.[42]

In a passage reminiscent of Faulkner's "Pantaloon in Black" Mrs. Gregg's black driver expresses the most profound idea of the whole text:

> BLACK   Night my Ella died I went to the cardhouse and got
> drunk. I laid in my own vomit. That's what I thought
> of the hand of the Lord. Lay dead drunk in ye own
> vomit like a dog. I aint proud of it, but I give up lyin
> same as I done drinkin.
> ROBERT   What did it get ye?
> BLACK   What get me?
> ROBERT   What did it get ye? To give up drinkin and lyin.
> BLACK   It aint what it got me. It's what it got me from.
> ROBERT   And what was that?
> BLACK   Death. I seen his face. I know where he uses. How he
> loves the unready.[43]

There is a poetic ring to this last line which goes to the heart of the drama and which reinforces the portrayal of blacks as insightful and morally significant, in contrast to the mythic stereotype.

The key to Robert's character is revealed in his response to the black driver's profound awareness of death: "He loves us all."[44] Robert is a man of death. Denied it initially by the power of Mrs. Gregg, he accepts it at last as his silence at the end of his trial makes clear:

JUDGE   . . . by a jury of thy peers and I do solemnly demand
                 that thou show cause, if any thou hast, why execu-
                 tion of the judgment established by law for the state
                 should not be passed upon thee.

Robert McEvoy does not answer.

JUDGE   He saith nothing. . . .[45]

Although this is a representation of the denial of voice that is a major theme
of the text, in my view it is also an example of the complexity of McCarthy's
treatment of the tale. Robert's acquiescence in his own death is an existential
choice for one who wishes to escape from an intolerable life. Crippled physically, socially and emotionally he seeks in death an escape from a world he
can no longer tolerate. He feels that he has been denied the chance to express
those elements of his character that his culture leads him to believe to be his
birthright. His intelligence, initiative, energy and "ardentheartedness" have
been frustrated and turned to destructive ends by poverty, impotence, misfortune and the restrictions imposed upon his class. He speaks his own bitter
epitaph:

McEvoy . . . I was never born to be hung. I could have been
somebody.[46]

His calm and stoic acceptance of his fate in the final scenes of the drama
confirm the sense that in meeting death he is coming home at last. Unlike
Suttree, Robert's fate has been too harsh for him to "choose life." His final
words say as much: "Yes. I'm ready."[47]

As I have suggested already, Robert's alienation is not solely a function
of his powerless position within the class structure; it is also rooted in his
family circumstances. As in all McCarthy's texts it is his relationship with
his father that is crucial to him. One senses in *The Orchard Keeper* and *Suttree* that the sons revolt against the father's power, finding the dominating
patriarch an obstacle to the establishment of their identities. But Robert, like
Lester Ballard, is made aware of his father's powerlessness, and his violence
and waywardness are a result of his refusal to accept a similar impotence
without some expression of his frustration. The loss of his leg, in a sense at
the hands of Mrs. Gregg, thus becomes an intolerable outrage. He is made
aware that his family cannot prevent her from entering their home and taking over the conduct of their affairs, even in a matter of life and death. The

tenor of Robert's conduct and his father's open acknowledgement that he cannot control the wayward boy is made apparent in terms that echo Reese in *Suttree*. The family are at supper, the family meal being a central emblem of unity and mutual affection; significantly Robert is not present:

> MARYELLEN   Mama where's Bobby at tonight?
> MR MCcEVOY   Gone to run crazy in the woods like an Indian. If you
> all aint hungry just pass it up this way.
> MARTHA   Is he still goin to work of a mornin?
> MR McEVOY   So they tell me.
>
> *He helps himself to beans, to cornbread. They are at passing the bowls up the table and around. Mr McEvoy pauses and stares off down the table.*
>
> MR McEVOY   I dont understand that boy. Dont understand nothin
> about him. Some of the things he says. They make
> sense, but they sound . . . I dont know what goes on
> in his head.[48]

This poignant speech makes us aware that Robert's isolation is increased by his intelligence. His deeper understanding of the world makes it more difficult for him to communicate with those nearest to him who do not share his perceptions or values. His father recognizes in the boy an anguish that he cannot comprehend:

> MARTHA   Bobby says they's caves all in under Graniteville.
> Where Indians has been.
> MR McEVOY   Well maybe he's took to livin down there in em.
> Maybe there's still Indians hid out down there. Him
> and the heathen can rage together.[49]

Mr McEvoy struggles to describe Robert's alien knowledge in the only language that he has at his disposal. The reference to the heathen is one that I have commented in other chapters. The notion of being "on the heath" is the Shakespearean equivalent of the *unheimlich*. McCarthy's use of "heathen rage" is a reference to Psalm 2:

> Why do the heathen rage and the people imagine a vain thing?[50]

The full significance of the reference is made apparent by the last verse:

Kiss the son lest he be angry, and ye perish in the way,
when his wrath is kindled but a little.[51]

Mr McEvoy realizes that his description of his son is inadequate and acknowledges his own confusion:

MARYELLEN   Is Bobby a heathen ? Daddy?
MR McEVOY   No. Eat your supper. He aint no heathen. He's just got
            a troubled heart and they dont nobody know why.[52]

Robert's alienation provokes him to run away from home, to become literally *unheimlich*. His two year absence does nothing to soften his anger. On his return, *"He is older and harder looking and he wears a scar."*[53] His return is prompted by the news of his mother's illness. He discovers that he is too late, and that she has just died. His rage is such that he turns the watchers out of the house. He blames Graniteville in general and the mill in particular for her death, telling Martha "I wish you hated this place like I do."[54] But one gains a strong sense that his outbursts are also an expression of his own sense of guilt at failing to be in time for his mother's passing. He refuses to countenance her burial in the graveyard owned by the mill. His belief that she should be "took back up home"[55] for burial recalls *As I Lay Dying*. Billy Parham has the same conviction regarding his brother's bones in *The Crossing*. But Robert is unable to complete the task that the Bundrens and Billy accomplished in such heroic fashion. It is after learning of his mother's death that Robert goes in search of his father at the mill. His failure to find him is due to the father's moral collapse: Martha tells Robert "He cant stand it. Bobby. He's just tore up."[56] This is another example of the father's weakness betraying the son: instead Robert has his fatal encounter with James Gregg.

Mr. McEvoy therefore suffers three grievous blows. He loses his position as the gardener, a job for which he has a gift and which gave him an identity outside the ordinary; he loses his wife; and he sees his son arrested for the murder of the most important man of the town. His inability to stand up to these losses is reflected in his failure in the matter of his wife's burial. He cannot oppose his son's will even in this matter. The neighbor's complaining of the smell of the decomposing corpse also refers to *As I Lay Dying*. Mr McEvoy's solution to the problem has an apocalyptic character:

He goes to the woodpile and commences carrying armloads of kindling, then stovewood, then logs, to the center of the yard. He piles the wood up into a great heap and takes the lamp and takes off his cap and uses it to grip the

hot lampchimney and removes the chimney and throws it on one side and
kneels with the lamp and lights the pile of wood at the bottom. When it is
going he returns to the house. . . . he commences to drag the coffin across the
floor toward the door.[57]

In this sequence McCarthy places his drama firmly in the southern gothic tradition and emphasizes the extent to which this is a history in which the struggle between life and death was settled in favor of the latter.

I have drawn attention to the parallel between Robert and James at various points in the above analysis and this applies to their family situations also. James is relieved of the burden of the patriarch at an early stage of the drama, the death of William Gregg following immediately on the amputation of Robert's leg. Thus, as Robert suffers in impotence, James takes up his position of power. But in taking over his father's position James shows all too clearly his rejection of the old man's values. He abandons the paternalism that had mitigated the harshness of the mill's regime. For William ". . . was himself born in indigent circumstances,"[58] but his son has been insulated from hardship from the outset. James also rejects his father's Puritanism: "That son of a bitch will take a drink."[59] I have already noted his sexual exploitation of the mill girls. Above all he abandons the cultivation of the factory garden, symbolically and physically announcing his rejection of his father's philosophy. His egotism is one of the principal factors in provoking his own demise. The hostility of these two rebellious sons brings down both families. Mrs. Gregg, seemingly so strong and stable, descends into her own gothic world of death in life: in a bourgeois parody of the Bundrens' epic task she has all her family dead exhumed and removed from Graniteville to her place of origin, Charleston.

The text concludes with William Chaffee's conversation with Martha in the Columbia State Hospital. This is the closure of the textual frame to which Luce alludes. There is a temptation to suppose that Chaffee has been told the story that has been contained in the preceding text as this is conventional in films that employ "flashback." In fact this is not the case. Chaffee learns only what he has gathered from the old records (and "they aint the thing") and what Martha has been able to tell him. This latter is very little and is confined to matters of which she had first hand knowledge. This, of course, is the whole meaning of the structure of the text.

The Gardener's Son therefore can be located as one of McCarthy's southern texts. It exhibits something of the gothic atmosphere that is so often associated with such texts. It deals in convincing fashion with the profound theme of the nature of history, of historical truth as essentially unknowable and of the relation between power and both history and justice. It presents narrative fiction as the only means of expressing something that approaches the complexity of actual human lives and historical events. It places the story of the deaths of Robert McEvoy and James Gregg in the context of the historical dilemma of the "New South" and subtly undermines the South's myth of Reconstruction. The location of the action, both in time and place, enables McCarthy to deal with the subject of race in a way that his East Tennessee locations do not.[60] The characterization of blacks in the text is significant in that they are presented as inherently the same as the whites, a radical departure from the mythic depictions of the 1870s and a reflection of the change in attitudes that was taking place in America one hundred years later as a result of the civil rights movement. This is achieved by including educated blacks in the action and placing them in positions that are superior to those of some whites, as in the case of the lawyer Whipper and Mr. McEvoy. The text deals with the continuing theme of father/son conflict and places it in the wider context of the family. It contrasts the power of the Greggs with the impotence of the McEvoys but hints that they share the tensions that are inherent in the structure of patriarchal power. It demonstrates the destructiveness of both insensitive power and self-conscious impotence and shows how the clashing egos of two "dangerous men" can bring down families, especially in a society in which the violence that is never far below the surface of life can readily express itself through the use of the gun. All this is expressed within the matrix of McCarthy's characteristic gift for the creation of convincing dialogue and in a manner that has great emotional impact.

We have seen that McCarthy has tended to adopt radical and unconventional approaches to narrative in his novels and his stage drama. The television film imposes a more conventional and accessible narrative method on its screen-writers. McCarthy has been able to accommodate his radical instincts to the demands of the medium and through his characteristic use of convincing dialogue and subtle suggestiveness has created a dense and richly meaningful text that rewards close reading and exhibits a complex interweaving of profound themes beneath a seemingly simple and melodramatic surface. It is tempting to believe that the creation of *The Gardener's Son* made McCarthy more aware of the potentialities of a narrative form that owed less to literary heritage and more to the potentialities of a popular medium. The form and style of the novels of the Border Trilogy lead one to suppose that this may have been the case.

Part III

The Southwestern Texts

Chapter Eleven
Blood Meridian

Where does a man come by his notions?

I argue throughout this book that McCarthy's texts can be read as comments upon the mythology of American exceptionalism in one form or another and that these comments are expressed as a series of anti-myths. It may therefore be considered inevitable that the setting of his novels should move at some point from East Tennessee to "the West." Of course from a historical point of view Tennessee is itself part of the American West. But the mythic west, the west of the dime novel and the Hollywood movie, constitutes that area lying across the Mississippi River that became part of the United States largely as a result of events of the nineteenth century. Exceptionalist ideology rationalized the process of expansion, conquest and expropriation as "Manifest Destiny," thus linking imperialist ambition with that "divine purpose" that had inspired the Puritans to found the "redeemer nation" and the revolutionaries to establish the democratic "last best hope of mankind." Like the British "white man's burden" it legitimized the cultural and material extirpation of the indigenous population as a divine mission to civilize the savage. It extended the myth of the pastoral onto the great plains as a domestication of the wilderness. Above all it imposed the will of the economically and technologically powerful in the name of racial superiority. That such a history should be characterized by violence was, of course, inevitable and nowhere was this violence more radical than in the Southwest—in what is now Texas, New Mexico and Arizona.[1]

As already noted, by the late nineteen-seventies McCarthy had left the Knoxville area and, after a period of traveling the country, was living in the Texas border town of El Paso. This change of personal location matches that of his fiction. His three Appalachian novels[2] had been relatively short and had drawn their imagery from communities that had been largely excluded from

American discourse. Their scale was such as to permit an intimacy that made clear the extent to which Greil Marcus's "old weird America" still remained in the mountains and woods of East Tennessee, unobserved by the nation as a whole, and providing an appropriate setting for the kind of anti-myth that McCarthy wished to create. But this intimacy was in itself limiting, relying as it did on the very "strangeness" of the mountaineers' culture, its smallness, its American otherness; the Appalachian texts lack the epic dimension that has to be incorporated into any examination of American mythology. In writing in and of the Southwest, McCarthy finds the landscape and the mythology of American epic and his texts begin to express the necessary largeness of an American scale. Guillemin comments on this change of fictional location by quoting Tim Poland to the effect that,

> Rather than a landscape [the South] that exists as a setting for human action and is imprinted with human qualities, the landscape of much western writing functions more like a character in itself and imprints on the human characters its own qualities.[3]

Blood Meridian is the text that most tellingly expresses this sense of a harsh landscape as a "character in itself" whose propensity to "imprint its own qualities on human characters" implies a move away from an anthropocentric cultural standpoint, the grievous consequences of this change being greatly increased by the West's largeness of scale. The action of the tale ranges from East Tennessee[4] to the Pacific Ocean, matching the mythic journey across the continent that led to the establishment of the United States as a transcontinental entity, the very heart of the project of Manifest Destiny. It takes us from the north Texas plains to Chihuahua, Mexico. The whole vast area features a landscape comprising "mountain, creosote bush, chaparral and desert".[5] Thus McCarthy chooses to locate his post-Tennessee novels in that region of America that contrasts his former locale in flora and fauna as well as scale. Gone are the woods and creeks, the raccoon and bass of Sevier County. In the arid country on either side of the Rio Grande and at the high tide of imperialistic expansion McCarthy finds his American chronotope.[6] The tale of slaughter that he recounts has a bleakness that matches this arid landscape; both aspects of the text express the mythoclastic notion of America as a "waste land." The bulk of the action takes place in "the year eighteen and forty-nine,"[7] a year of significance in American mythology through its association with the Californian gold rush and all that it signifies of mythic optimism, intrepid pioneering and the promise of immediate riches.

The exploits of the scalphunters inform a different discourse. If American idealism has its basis in Lockean notions of man as the rational animal whose proprietary entitlement is vested in his own efforts and abilities, the vision expressed in *Blood Meridian* is of a Hobbesian war of all against all, carried to an extreme in which the warrior eventually turns his aggression against himself. Thus even the revisionist reading of the history of the period is challenged by McCarthy's depiction of the Native Americans as in no way morally distinct from their Anglo-Saxon or Mexican rivals, especially with regard to a propensity for homicidal violence. In my view the violent tenor of *Blood Meridian* and the unrelieved atmosphere of death that permeates the text from start to finish reflect an underlying mood in the America of the period in which the text was written. It is possible that McCarthy spent the best part of a decade researching and writing his text. Prior to the seventies America had witnessed the assassinations of John and Robert Kennedy, Martin Luther King and Malcolm X, to mention only the most prominent few. The murder of Sharon Tate and her companions by Charles Manson's acolytes associated bloody ritual killing with the notion of American "family." The Vietnam war brought actual slaughter onto the television screen and into American homes with an impact that words could rarely match. The My Lai massacre[8] took place in 1969. Film of a South Vietnamese general shooting a prisoner in the head at close range provided one of the defining images of the conflict, one that McCarthy was to incorporate into his text:

> The woman looked up. Neither courage nor heartsink in those old eyes. He pointed with his left hand and she turned to follow his hand with her gaze and he put the pistol to her head and fired.

> The explosion filled all that sad little park. Some of the horses shied and stepped. A fistsized hole erupted out of the far side of the woman's head in a great vomit of gore and she pitched over and laid slain in her blood without remedy.[9]

In my view the violence of *Blood Meridian* expresses an aspect of contemporary American life that many would have preferred to have suppressed.

Blood Meridian has enjoyed little in the way of commercial success but its reputation in academic circles is high. Many critics regard it as McCarthy's masterpiece. Leo Daugherty writes,

> McCarthy's greatness lies most centrally and most obviously in the fact that, in "progressing over the plain," he has become our finest living

tragedian. . . . In major consequence of his mastery of the high tragedian's art, McCarthy has become the best and most indispensable writer
of English-language narrative in the second half of the century.[10]

However, if one defines tragedy as the destruction of a noble character in
consequence of some single fatal flaw, it is difficult to see how *Blood Meridian*
can be classified in this way. The scalphunters evince no hint of nobility and
their characters are uniformly homicidal. Indeed so devoid are they of moral
sensibility that they do not actually appear to be realistically human at all.
This sense of unreality is heightened by the fact that for the most part they
care no more for themselves than for anyone else. Dana Phillips declares that
Blood Meridian is McCarthy's "most noteworthy book."[11] Harold Bloom has
said, "I yield to no-one in my admiration for *Blood Meridian*. I think there
is no greater work by a living American."[12] Those who praise the work with
most enthusiasm seem to me to judge it on aesthetic grounds only. Critical
articles on this text greatly outnumber those on any of McCarthy's other
works. In my view this is due to the challenge to our sensibilities of the contrast between the unrelenting violence of the text and the sumptuous language in which it is depicted. There is even a comic aspect to the inevitable
succession of atrocities that the scalphunters both suffer and commit. It is
the comedy that arises from a sense of the absurd and from the fact that we
are not able, or indeed required, to identify with any of the book's characters.
Blood Meridian is a text almost wholly devoid of emotion; even our horror
at the sanguinary outrages that constitute its action is diluted by the richness
of language already mentioned. As readers we sit in god-like detachment:
the victims of the slaughter seem to us "as flies to wanton boys." Some critics have been led to question the book's moral position for this very reason.
Denis Donoghue writes:

> The experience of reading *Blood Meridian* is likely to be, for most of us,
> peculiarly intense and yet wayward. The novel demands that we imagine
> forces in the world and in ourselves that the Enlightenment and Chris-
> tianity, rarely in agreement on other issues, encourage us to think we
> have outgrown. We have not outgrown them, the book challenges us
> to admit. These forces are primordial and unregenerate: they have not
> been assimilated to the consensus of modern culture or to the forms of
> dissent which that culture recognizes and to some extent accepts. They
> are outside the law. The difficult beauty of McCarthy's run-on sentences
> arises from the conflict between these dire forces and the traditions of

epic, tragedy, elegy and lyric which have been devised to appease them. Or to sequester them, if they cannot be appeased.[13]

If, as I suggest, the text gives the reader a wholly detached view, a detachment without which the tale would indeed be unendurable, then Donoghue's criticism seems overstated. For the same reason some of the most generous praise of this particular text seems to be informed by a fascination with the experience of "seeing" violence without "feeling" it. To my mind all of these aspects of the text are illustrated in what has become perhaps its best known, or most notorious passage, the "death hilarious"[14] sequence of the massacre of the filibusters:

> Now driving in a wild frieze of headlong horses with eyes walled and teeth cropped and naked riders with clusters of arrows clenched in their jaws and their shields winking in the dust and up the far side of the ruined ranks in a piping of boneflutes and dropping down off the sides of their mounts with one heel hung in the withers strap and their short bows flexing beneath the outstretched necks of the ponies until they had circled the company and cut their ranks in two and then rising up again like funhouse figures, some with nightmare faces painted on their breasts, riding down the unhorsed Saxons and spearing them and clubbing them and leaping from their mounts with knives and running about on the ground with a peculiar bandylegged trot like creatures driven to alien forms of locomotion and stripping the clothes from the dead and seizing them up by the hair and passing their blades about the skulls of the living and the dead alike and snatching aloft the bloody wigs and hacking and chopping at the naked bodies, ripping off limbs, heads, gutting the strange white torsos and holding up great handfuls of viscera, genitals, some of the savages so slathered up with gore they might have rolled in it like dogs and some who fell upon the dying and sodomized them with loud cries to their fellows. . . .[15]

The "run on" nature of the above sentence helps to create the dynamism of action in a way that recalls the "gadarene swine" passage in *Outer Dark*. This dynamism also sweeps us through the action but denies us the necessity of contemplating the subjective horror of the experience from the victims' point of view, or indeed from that of the perpetrators.

In my view too many critics have misread *Blood Meridian*, regarding it as a realist text when it is nothing of the kind. I have argued throughout that

McCarthy is a creator of myth. *The Orchard Keeper* is a realist work although it features a recognition of the existence of mythic epistemologies. *Outer Dark* dispenses with the conventions of realism altogether and is wholly mythic in character, although it manages to retain sympathetic human dimensions for some of its characters (Rinthy, Deitch). *Blood Meridian* has the same mythic, non-realistic form but has completely dispensed with sympathetic human characters.[16] In short it is an intellectual exercise, almost wholly metaphorical in character. I shall attempt to justify this assertion and to interpret the metaphor in what follows.

I have drawn attention to the complex narrative structures present in a number of McCarthy's earlier texts. The manner in which John Wesley Rattner or Cornelius Suttree can be read as the narrators of their own stories is characteristic of McCarthy's debt to literary modernism with its reflexivity and concern with the notion of "voice." I have suggested that this parallels the author's preoccupation with freeing himself from the "voice of the [literary] fathers." In *Blood Meridian* such complexities are completely absent.[17] The narrative voice is that of the omniscient author, albeit this is an omniscience that refuses to reveal the full extent of its vision and which maintains its position of detachment to the extent of refusing all but the most fleeting glimpses of the motivation of its characters. Of the kid, whose peregrinations provide the thread of continuity of the tale, we are told merely that "in him broods already a taste for mindless violence. All history present in that visage, the child the father of the man."[18] This disinclination to offer theoretical "explanations" of character is consistent with McCarthy's rejection of systematic accounts of human behavior. What he does offer us is a brief portrait of a youth who sets off into the world, and into the mythic west, in something approaching a "state of nature:"

> See the child. He is pale and thin, he wears a ragged linen shirt. . . . His folk are known as hewers of wood and drawers of water . . .

> The mother dead these fourteen years did incubate in her own bosom the creature who would carry her off. The father never speaks her name, the child does not know it. He has a sister in this world that he will never see again. He watches, pale and unwashed.[19]

It is made clear that the "nature" in which state the child exists is devoid of the female element. Once again the female principle is referred to, *in absentia*, as an aspect of a living fertility without which patriarchal power generates an arid waste land and the vitality of the "ardent-hearted" male is filled with the aforementioned "taste for mindless violence." It is significant for my reading of the text that the child is also devoid of all but the most the most rudimentary culture:

> . . . in truth his father has been a schoolmaster. He lies in drink, he quotes from poets whose names are now lost.

> He [the child] can neither read nor write . . .[20]

With neither the creative power of the female nor the consolation of culture, man "in the state of nature" finds the terrible burden of his cosmic insignificance too much to bear. His inherent vitality sends him on a mythic existential quest—*Blood Meridian* is an account of the outcome of such a quest.

That many critics have read *Blood Meridian* in realist terms is no doubt due in part to McCarthy's "photorealistic style":

> They rode down from this country through a deep gorge, clattering over the stones, rifts of cool blue shade. In the dry sand of the arroyo floor old bones and broken shapes of painted pottery and graven on the rocks above them pictographs of horse and cougar and turtle and the mounted Spaniards helmeted and bucklered and contemptuous of stone and silence and time itself.[21]

One can indeed see the riders, the landscape and the pictographs, hear the clattering hooves and feel the sudden cool of the shade. The "realism" makes the experience tangible. But at the same time the lyrical prose creates a sense of the poetic that goes beyond realism. The shade is "blue," and the pictographs express contempt for "stone and silence and time itself." This characteristic McCarthy reminder of the fragility and impermanence of men and their cultures states the unmistakably metaphysical. It also suggests Eliot's "fragments" and reminds us that McCarthy himself is engaged in creating his own works by deploying those of the past. Realist readings are also promoted by the fact that the text features characters and events that have a degree of historical authenticity. Filibusters did indeed "invade" Mexico in the manner of Captain White. Scalphunters operated in the territory; they were hired by the Mexican authorities to hunt and kill Indians. The taking of the scalp was an earnest of the kill and therefore the item for which payment was made. That McCarthy was familiar with a large number of contemporary accounts of the conflict in the Southwest is clear from the references to historical figures of which Glanton and Holden are the most easily discernable.

It is clear that McCarthy was familiar with Samuel Chamberlain's *My Confession*, a source which mentions both men.[22] A degree of skepticism is necessary when reading the whole of Chamberlain's memoir, the general tone of which is highly romanticized. He writes of the early influence on his mind of Walter Scott:

> Then I got hold of Scott's immortal works. What a glorious new world opened up before me, how I devoured their pages and oh how I longed to emulate his heroes! I took pride in all athletic exercises and was anxious for a chance to use my strength and skill in defence of oppressed beauty.[23]

Chamberlain writes of his experiences as a regular soldier campaigning in Mexico in the 1840s. The memoir is retrospective and its writing was curtailed in 1861 when Chamberlain returned to service as an officer in the Union army. It was not published until 1956, the manuscript being discovered in a Baltimore antique shop at some point in the 1940s. For all its romanticism *My Confession* contains accounts of bloody massacres committed by all involved, Americans and Mexicans, regulars and volunteers, soldiers, rangers and citizens alike.[24] There seems little doubt that the all-pervading violence of *Blood Meridian* expresses a mythicized version of such events with the intervening periods of civilized order omitted. In the final chapters of his text Chamberlain describes his adventures in the Southwest on leaving the army. He learns of the activities of the scalphunters and decides to join them in an attempt to make his way to California. He writes:

> The band was known as the "Scalp Hunters" and was commanded by John Glanton of Texas, the desperado of the Bexar Exchange.[25]

Chamberlain informs his friend Tom Hitchcock of his plan to ". . . join Glanton's company. He with much bluntness advised me to 'join Satan and go to H--l at once . . .'"[26] He writes that "Glanton was paid fifty ($50) [sic] dollars for every Apache scalp brought in . . ."[27] McCarthy has clearly drawn on two Chamberlain passages in particular. Both refer to Holden:

> The second in command, . . . was a man of gigantic size called "Judge Holden" of Texas. Who or what he was no-one knew but a cooler blooded villain never went unhung; he stood six feet six in his moccasins, had a large fleshy frame, a dull tallow colored face destitute of hair and all expression. His desires were blood and women, and terrible

stories were circulated in camp of horrid crimes committed by him . . . and before we left Fronteras a little girl of ten years was found in the chapperal, foully violated and murdered. The mark of a huge hand on her little throat pointed him out as the ravisher as no other man had such a hand, but although all suspected, no one charged him with the crime.

Holden was by far the best educated man in northern Mexico; he conversed with all in their own language, spoke in several Indian lingos, at a fandango he would take the Harp or Guitar from the hands of the musicians and charm all with his wonderful performance, and out-waltz any *poblana* of the ball. He was "plum center" with rifle or revolver, a daring horseman, acquainted with the nature of all the strange plants and their botanical names, great in Geology and Minerology, in short another Admirable Chrichton, and with all an arrant coward.[28]

The second passage to which McCarthy refers states that on encountering strange formations of weathered sandstone:

Judge Holden mounted a rock for a rostrum and gave us a scientific lecture on Geology. The Scalp Hunters, grouped in easy attitudes, listened to the "Literati" with marked attention. . . . Holden's lecture was no doubt very learned, but hardly true, for one statement he made was "that *millions* of years had witnessed the operation producing the result around us," which Glanton with recollections of the Bible teaching his young mind had undergone said "was a d--d lie."[29]

. . . To my question as to 'how he knew all this,' this encyclopaedian Scalp Hunter replied, 'Nature, these rocks, this little broken piece of clay, (holding up a little fragment of painted pottery such as are found all over the desert), the ruins scattered all over the land, all tell me the story of the past.'[30]

McCarthy's Holden is immediately recognizable from the above.

Another evident McCarthy source is John Bourke's *On the Border With Crook*, an account of regular service with the Cavalry under General Crook during the Indian wars of the 1870s and '80s and essentially a historical work. Bourke begins each of his chapters with an outline of its contents, as was common in texts of the nineteenth century.

Chapter VI is headed:

Tucson Incidents—The "Fiestas"—The Ruined Mission Church of San Xavier del Bac—Governer Safford—Arizona Mines—Apache Raids—Camp Grant Massacre—The Killing of Lieutenant Cushing.[31]

Other lists are much longer. McCarthy adopts the same practice: his chapter XVIII begins:

The return to camp—The idiot delivered—Sarah Borginnis—A confrontation—Bathed in the river—The tumbril burned—James Robert in camp—Another baptism—Judge and fool.[32]

Imitating the histories of the period also encourages the view of those who read *Blood Meridian* as a realist text. My contention is that it is in fact akin to Eudora Welty's mythic *The Robber Bridegroom*; Welty observes that ". . . you historians and scholars would be the first to recognize that this is not a *historical* historical novel."[33] Bourke was a talented writer with a broad education and an elegant literary style. Some idea of tone of his text can be gathered from his ironic account of the gambling halls of Tucson:

The flare of the lamps was undimmed, the plinkety-plunk of the harps was unchecked, and the voice of the dealer was abroad in the land from the setting of the sun until the rising of the same, . . .[34]

Bourke's account is very much a record of Crook's career and of the author's admiration for his commander. At the same time it contains a number of passages that may be considered significant for McCarthy. Bourke's initial base is at Camp Grant, Arizona. He reports that "Here one stumbles at almost every step upon the traces of former populations of whom little is known, . . ."[35] He describes the location as "our waste land on the frontier . . ."[36] He notes that "The title "Jedge" on the frontier does not always imply respect, . . ."[37] He records the words of a Mexican song in Spanish without translation—"No me mires con esos tus ojos, . . ."[38] He makes reference to the activities of scalphunters, recorded in the histories of the day:

Drawing nearer to our own days, we read the fact set down in black and white, that the state governments of Sonora and Chihuahua had offered and paid rewards of three hundred dollars for each scalp of an Apache that should be presented . . . the Irishman Glanton—entered into contracts . . . to do such bloody work. . . .

. . . Glanton was a blackguard, and set out to kill everything in human form, whether Indian or Mexican. . . .[39]

He also refers to Glanton's demise at the hands of the Yuma Indians at the crossing of the Colorado River. It is expressive of the dominant ideology of the day that so erudite and civilized a man as Bourke should write of General Crook's ". . . absolute integrity in his dealings with representatives of inferior races."[40] These extracts from just two of the books used as sources by McCarthy emphasize the overt eclecticism of his approach, an eclecticism that has been apparent in all his previous novels and which lies behind his comment in the line "And so these parties divided upon that midnight plain, each passing back the way the other had come, pursuing as all travelers must inversions without end upon other men's journeys."[41]

If McCarthy's ability to "make you see" deflects a mythic reading of *Blood Meridian*, a consideration of judge[42] Holden, the text's dominant figure, makes its true character absolutely clear. If Chamberlain's account of Holden should be taken "with a pinch of salt," how much more so should McCarthy's own? Holden first appears in the Reverend Green's tent meeting at Nacogdoches:

> An enormous man dressed in an oilcloth slicker had entered the tent and removed his hat. He was bald as a stone and he had no trace of beard and he had no brows to his eyes nor lashes to them. He was close on seven feet in height and he stood smoking a cigar even in this nomadic house of God and he seemed to have removed his hat only to chase the rain from it for now he put it on again.[43]

The scalphunters' first encounter with the judge is described by Tobin, the ex-priest:[44]

> Then about the meridian of the day we come upon the judge on his rock there in the wilderness by his single self. Aye and there was no rock, just the one. Irving said he'd brung it with him. I said it was a merestone for him to mark out of nothing at all. He had with him that rifle you see with him now, all mounted in German silver and the name he's give to it set with silver wire under the checkpiece in latin: *Et in Arcadia Ego*. A reference to the lethal in it.[45]

This is a manifestation rather than an appearance. It deliberately precludes rational explanation. It is clearly a reference to Natty Bumpo as encountered in *The Prairie*:

The sun had fallen below the crest of the nearest wave of the prairie, leaving the usual rich and glowing train on its track. In the centre of this flood of fiery light a human form appeared, drawn against the gilded background as distinctly, and seemingly as palpable, as though it would come within the grasp of the extended hand. The figure was colossal, the attitude musing and melancholy, and the situation directly in the route of the travelers. But embedded as it was in its setting of garish light, it was impossible to distinguish its just proportions or true character.[46]

Fennimore Cooper's mythic hero represents the fusion of idealized white hunter and pristine American nature. McCarthy refers to this myth in order to invert it in ways which I shall attempt to make clear in what follows. Like Natty Bumpo, Holden has come down like a demi-god to take his place in the ranks of those gigantic heroes (and villains) of American mythology (the "tall tales") and indeed of Western mythology as a whole. The impression is reinforced by the account of the judge's superhuman size and strength:

. . . a grown man with not a hair on his body and him weighin twenty-four stone which he did then and does now.[47]

. . . a small sturdy man named Pacheco . . . had for an anvil an enormous iron meteorite shaped like a great molar and the judge on a wager lifted it over his head. Several men pushed forward to feel the iron and to rock it where it stood, nor did the judge lose this opportunity to ventilate himself upon the ferric nature of heavenly bodies and their powers and claims. Two lines were drawn in the dirt and a third round of wagers was laid, . . . The judge seized that great slag wandered for what millennia from what unreckonable corner of the universe and he raised it overhead and stood tottering and then lunged forward. It cleared the mark by a foot.[48]

In my view the mythic nature of the judge, and therefore of *Blood Meridian* as a whole, is made clear by these passages alone. A reading of the text thus becomes an exercise in interpreting the myth, in decoding the metaphor; and this means interpreting the judge. He could simply be a refutation of the notion that the white man brought "civilization" to the wilderness, an anti-myth to the pretensions of "Manifest Destiny" and a counter to the often vainglorious accounts of the history of the Southwest in general and Texas in particular, the whole colored by American angst over the experience of the Vietnam war. All of these ideas have some validity as I have argued already. However I suggest that McCarthy in fact has far greater ambitions than these alone and that they do indeed centre on the figure of the judge. If the kid ventures into the American West in a state of nature, the judge is his opposite. He is a man of science; in chapter ten we read that he saves the scalphunters from their Apache pursuers on the Malpais by manufacturing gunpowder from ingredients naturally to hand—saltpetre crystalized from a solution of bat guano—charcoal from wood burned in a clay-built kiln—sulphur from the mouth of a volcano—all crystallized from a solution in the urine of the scalphunters themselves and evaporated by the sun. "We hauled forth our members and in it went and the judge on his knees kneading the mass with his naked arms and piss was splashin about . . ."[49] The judge is also an Enlightenment encyclopedist:

> . . . there was willow and alder and cherry growin out of the rock, just little trees. The judge would stop and botanize them and then ride to catch up. My hand to God. Pressing leaves into his book.[50]

> He roamed through the ruined kivas picking up small artifacts and he sat on a high wall and sketched in his book until the light failed.[51]

> . . . the judge, triangulating from known points of the landscape, reckoned anew their course.[52]

The judge traverses the landscape as did Lewis and Clarke, those men of the Enlightenment who surveyed the interior at Jefferson's behest, recording all in their notebooks, from surveyed measurements to sketches of the flora.[53] He is the very figure of a Renaissance man:

> God the man is a dancer, you'll not take that away from him. And fiddle. He's the greatest fiddler I ever heard and that's an end on it. The greatest. He can cut a trail, shoot a rifle, ride a horse, track a deer. He's been all over the world. Him and the governor they sat up till breakfast and it was Paris this and London that in five languages . . .[54]

He is a master of the complexities of law:

> The lieutenant came again in the evening. He and the judge sat together and the judge went over points of law with him. The lieutenant nodded, his lips pursed. The judge translated for him latin terms of jurisprudence.

He cited cases civil and martial. He quoted Coke and Blackstone, Anaximander, Thales.[55]

Characteristically this display of erudition is calculated to deceive. The judge himself was present at the murder that the lieutenant is investigating, a murder committed by black Jackson, and of which the judge denies all knowledge both for himself and for his companions. He is also a philosopher:

> Words are things. The words he is in possession of he cannot be deprived of. Their authority transcends his ignorance of their meaning.[56]

To all these accomplishments may be added the skills and knowledge of the archeologist,[57] psychologist,[58] art historian,[59] conjurer,[60] taxidermist,[61] magician,[62] paleontologist,[63] and military tactician.[64] This comprehensiveness indicates that the judge may be read as a metaphor for culture[65] itself, or rather for a specific kind of culture, a culture developed from a particular set of assumptions. As the judge sits writing up his findings regarding the flora and fauna of the day, Toadvine "asked him what was his purpose in all this?"[66]

> The judge wrote on and then he folded the ledger shut and laid it to one side and pressed his hands together and passed them down over his nose and mouth and placed them palm down on his knees. Whatever exists, he said. Whatever in creation exists without my knowledge exists without my consent.
>
> He looked about the dark forest in which they were bivouacked. He nodded towards the specimens he'd collected. These anonymous creatures, he said, may seem little or nothing in the world. Yet the smallest crumb can devour us. Only nature can enslave man and only when the existence of each last entity is routed out and made to stand naked before him will he be properly suzerain of the earth. . . .
>
> The judge placed his hands on the ground. He looked at his inquisitor. This is my claim, he said. And yet everywhere upon it are pockets of autonomous life. Autonomous. In order for it to be mine nothing must be permitted to occur upon it save by my dispensation.[67]

In this passage the judge's extremism is exposed at its root. What motivates the judge is terror, the terror of human insignificance, the terror that stalks the pages of every McCarthy text. The judge personifies the extreme of anthropocentrism, of Enlightenment hubris. He writes his *ledger* and makes his *claim*. This is the language of the accountant; it expresses the notion of knowledge as power, of the earth as commodity. It is the language of quantity rather than value. It holds out the false promise of progress through empirical investigation and the use of reason alone. *Blood Meridian* is McCarthy's *hommage* to *Moby Dick*. Melville wrote of America's hubristic drive to dominate nature; Ahab pursued the whale and it destroyed him. The kid, in his "cultureless" state of nature travels the deserts of the southwest in search of meaning; he finds the judge and is destroyed.[68] Try as he might he cannot escape the culture of his day, that overweening, hubristic culture that believed that reason could solve all ills and usher in endless progress. It is the hermit on the prairie that poses the fundamental question, "But where does a man come by his notions?" The answer is, of course, from his culture. What McCarthy attacks in *Blood Meridian* is gnosis, the faith in systems of knowledge and belief that claim a validity that cannot ever exist. This is another of his consistent themes, the notion that the intellectual grids, including language itself, that we deploy in order to mediate our experience of the world are incomplete, provisional, mythic, distinct from the world that they purport to define. The judge himself knows that his own quest for complete and certain knowledge is in vain:

> Even in this world more things exist without your knowledge than with it and the order in creation which you see is that which you have put there, like a string in a maze, so that you shall not lose your way.[69]

Such is the complexity and breadth of intellectual vision expressed in *Blood Meridian* that the text itself expresses the opposite extreme to the judge's megalomaniac anthropocentrism:

> The very clarity of these articles belied their familiarity, for the eye predicates the whole on some feature or part and here was nothing more luminous than another and nothing more enshadowed and in the optical democracy of such landscapes all preference is made whimsical and a man and a rock become endowed with unguessed kinships.[70]

George Guillemin expands on this notion of "optical democracy" in his interpretation of *Blood Meridian*. He points out that the novel is radically allegorical in character, a quality that it shares with *Outer Dark*, and that allegorical form confers existential equality on man, beast and rockform. ". . . landscape and characters in McCarthy's pastoralism share fate and status as existential equals."[71] Contemporary theory denotes this as ecopastoralism, what I have referred to as the myth of the anti-pastoral. Ecopastoralism also expresses a radical rejection of anthropocentrism; not just the extreme form represented by the judge, but anthropocentric epistemology per se, the "posthuman." Quite how such a paradoxical position may be located is not my concern. As I have noted throughout my analysis of McCarthy's work, his texts assert defiant contradiction of humanity's existential insignificance. Guillermin also relates McCarthy's variations of prose style to this ecopastoralism. He interprets the "run on" passages in which many read the influence of Faulkner (and Joyce) as denying distinctions between human and animal, animate and inanimate, a technique he labels parataxis. This is amply illustrated in the "death hilarious" passage, already quoted on p.161. For Guillemin this style is the vehicle for the allegorical mode; by contrast McCarthy's more "realist" prose, eidetic in its ability to "make you see," is mimetic in character.

As a further comment upon the depiction of the judge we may recall that, as we saw in *The Gardener's Son*, for McCarthy only fiction can begin to reflect the complex truth of human events. And the judge writes no fiction.

Of all the characters in *Blood Meridian* only James Robert, the idiot child, survives his relationship with the judge. James Robert has no language and is therefore immune to the judge as culture. The fate of the kid himself is the final element of the tale. Those who read the text in realist terms assume that the kid is murdered by the judge. Some presume that he is raped also. But despite McCarthy's propensity for making us "see" all the action and his complete lack of squeamishness in depicting the endless catalogue of outrage that constitutes the novel, we do not "see" the kid's fate. After taking his turn with the whore in the Griffin brothel the kid goes outside to the jakes:

> Then he opened the rough board door of the jakes and stepped in.
>
> The judge was seated upon the closet. He was naked and he rose up smiling and gathered him in his arms against his immense and terrible flesh and shot the wooden barlatch home behind him.
>
> . . . In the muddied dogyard behind the premises two men went down the boards towards the jakes. A third man was standing there urinating in the mud.
>
> Is someone in there? the first man said.
>
> The man who was relieving himself did not look up. I wouldn't go in there if I was you, he said.
>
> Is somebody in there?
>
> I wouldn't go in.

> He hitched himself up and buttoned his trousers and stepped past
> them and went up towards the lights. The first man watched him go
> and then opened the door of the jakes.
> Good God almighty, he said.
> What is it?
> He didn't answer. He stepped past the other and went back up the
> walk. The other man stood looking after him. Then he opened the door
> and looked in.[72]

And that is all. Of course it is quite in keeping with the judge's previous
conduct to assume that the kid is both raped and murdered. The point is
that we are not shown this, the final act of the kid's short and violent life.
In my view this can only be because McCarthy does not wish to show us
this event since its full meaning is metaphorical. Culture is—there can be
no human existence outside it. Thus the kid is finally "gathered against that
immense and terrible flesh" as the closing of the metaphor. His fate has been
to have his experience mediated by a culture that feeds the very impulses
it should restrain and feeds them by denying their existence. If the judge's
words represent the extreme of Apollonian rationality, the murderous eroticism of his deeds illustrate the fact that Dionysus also must have his due. The
judge appears in Dionysian mode on a number of occasions: "Someone had
reported the judge naked atop the walls, immense and pale in the revelations
of the lightning, striding the perimeter up there and declaiming in the old
epic mode."[73] In the morning a naked boy is found with his neck broken.
The culture that places all its faith in reason both ignores the fact that human
beings are far from being purely rational beings and also overestimates its
power to know man, the world and all that is in them.

But the fate of the kid in the jakes is not in fact the last passage of the
text. Back in the Griffin brothel the dance continues and the judge is its
leader:

> And they are dancing, the board floor slamming under the jackboots
> and the fiddlers grinning hideously over their canted pieces. Towering
> above them all is the judge and he is naked dancing, his small feet lively
> and quick and now in doubletime and bowing to the ladies, huge and
> pale and hairless, like an enormous infant. He never sleeps he says. He
> say's he'll never die. . . . His feet are light and nimble. He never sleeps.
> He says that he will never die. He dances in light and in shadow and he
> is a great favourite. He never sleeps, the judge. He is dancing, dancing.
> He says that he will never die.[74]

The appeal of gnosis, of the desire to know all, is the Faustian hubristic flaw of Enlightenment man, and once set in train it can never end. But the image of the dancer recalls another nineteenth century reference of significance in this context:

> Zarathustra the dancer, Zarathustra the light, who beckons with his wings, ready for flight, beckoning to all birds, prepared and ready, blissfully light-hearted:

> Zarathustra the prophet, Zarathustra the laughing prophet, no impatient or uncompromising man, one who loves jumping and escapades; I myself have set this crown upon my head!

> Lift up your hearts, my brothers, high! higher! And do not forget your legs! Lift up your legs, too, you fine dancers: and better still, stand on your heads![75]

Nietzsche saw that Enlightenment reason, having led man to the conclusion that "God is dead"[76] had also led him to the dead end of nihilism. The judge represents the endless futile quest of empirical reason to replace God. Nietzsche realized that the void can only be endured through positive assertion. He opposed the void by the assertion of life itself. Thus Zarathustra's is the dance of life and the judge's the dance of death. McCarthy contrasts the two attitudes in much of his fiction. I have characterized this as a dialectic of vitality and insignificance and argued that the ardenthearted McCarthy hero opposes cosmic insignificance, but only in the terms that his American culture permits. This dialectic is seen clearly in *The Orchard Keeper* and *Suttree* and becomes more apparent in The Border Trilogy. But in *Blood Meridian* the dance of death abides. In this, McCarthy's most highly wrought text, Nietzsche's myth is inverted and the result is a tale of such all encompassing pessimism that even the glories of its language and the realized ambition of its author's imagination cannot fully overcome the sense of crisis that it seems to express. It is a commonplace of interpretation that "historical" novels refer as much to the period in which they are written as to the past in which they are set and I have suggested that *Blood Meridian* reflects the angst of America's experience of violence, both at home and in Vietnam, during the period of the books gestation. What the nature of any personal crisis may have been, or if indeed any such existed, must remain a matter for speculation. However I have referred repeatedly to the theme of father/son conflict in McCarthy's work and have speculated on two possible meanings, the personal and the literary. It is perhaps possible that McCarthy felt himself driven to ever greater extremes in order to outdo his literary "fathers"—Melville, Faulkner et al. He is also preoccupied with questions raised and answered by his lost religious faith. Whatever the case may be, *Blood Meridian* expresses the oedipal theme in its most extreme form. I have quoted already that the kid's father ". . . has been a schoolmaster. He lies in drink. . ." and that the kid's childhood has bred in him "a taste for mindless violence."[77] The kid, abandoning his rudimentary home, ". . . sees a parricide hanged in a crossroads hamlet and the man's friends run forward and pull his legs and he hangs dead from his rope while urine darkens his trousers."[78] There is a sense in which the judge becomes a surrogate father to the kid, but, as in *A Drowning Incident*, this father is on the side of death in the matter of puppies: ". . . the judge had set forth, dogs dangling. He crossed the stone bridge and he looked down into the swollen waters and raised the dogs and pitched them in."[79] The judge himself expounds on the matter of oedipal conflict with regard to the son whose father dies before he is born:

> Now this son whose father's existence in the world is historical and spec-
> ulative even before the son has entered it is in a bad way. All his life he
> carries before him the idol of a perfection to which he can never attain.
> The father dead has euchered the son out of his patrimony. For it is the
> death of the father to which the son is entitled and to which he is heir,
> more so than his goods. . . . He is broken before a frozen god and will
> never find his way.[80]

Whatever the personal significance of this theme may be there is no doubt that it loses its intensity in the later texts which also exhibit a return to a more balanced expression of the dialectic between the forces of life and death. If there was a crisis in McCarthy's life, and who has not encountered such, then it passed with the creation of *Blood Meridian*.

I have attempted to demonstrate that this text shares the radical mythoclasm of McCarthy's other works. It should be clear however that it goes much further in this direction than have the Tennessee novels. In taking the arid Southwest in the nineteenth century as his chronotope, McCarthy extends the scope of his fiction and challenges a wider and more significant segment of exceptionalist mythology. His representation of the "waste land" is more extreme and the intensity of unrelieved violence in the novel's action reflects the aridity and deathliness of his chosen landscape; these factors are related to the almost total absence of the female from the world that he depicts. Patriarchal epistemology is represented by this arid vision and by the extreme intensity of the father/son conflict that is so characteristic of McCarthy's texts to this point. But in creating the judge he widens his critique to encompass the Faustian extreme of Enlightenment gnosticism and challenges the optimism of belief in the power of reason to generate "progress." He creates an anti-myth to Nietzsche's Zarathustra and portrays a world that has not learned to assert the primacy of life in the nihilistic void.

The majority of critics, some of them very distinguished, regard *Blood Meridian* as McCarthy's finest work. It is difficult to set oneself against such a broad and authoritative body of opinion. To my mind *Blood Meridian* is certainly a work of great intellectual power, erudition and linguistic virtuosity. But it lacks the qualities of human emotion that characterize most of McCarthy's other works. The Tennessee novels thus have a dimension that *Blood Meridian* lacks for all its undoubted brilliance. It is for this reason that I have characterized it as a novel of crisis. If the texts of the Border Trilogy lack the spectacular literary virtuosity of this novel, they display a greater sense of dramatic form, are couched in language of great beauty and power and recreate the human dimension that *Blood Meridian* has sacrificed. *The Crossing* combines all these qualities with great creative imagination and deals with philosophical concerns that are as profound as those focused in the judge. To my mind therefore *Blood Meridian* is a brilliant but troubled and troubling novel which provides a bridge between the young McCarthy of Tennessee and the mature artist who goes on to recover the humanity that it seemed his writing might have lost.

The Border Trilogy

Chapter Twelve
All the Pretty Horses

Between the wish and the thing the world lies waiting.

All the Pretty Horses is the first of the sequence of novels commonly known as "The Border Trilogy." Each of the three texts is set in the region that provided the setting for *Blood Meridian*; the trilogy may be read as a comment on the twentieth century consequences of those nineteenth century events, of the failure of modernity to take root in Mexico and of the deeply troubling consequences of its all too profound success in the United States. All three texts depict young American men crossing the border from a modern American present that cannot provide the satisfactions they desire, to a Mexico of an imagined past in which they hope that they will be able to fulfill the mythic roles by which their culture has structured their sense of identity. Octavio Paz writes:

> In general, Americans have not looked for Mexico in Mexico; they have looked for their obsessions, enthusiasms, phobias, hopes, interests—and these are what they have found. In short the history of our relationship is the history of a stubborn deceit, usually involuntary though not always so.[1]

This is, of course, a continuation of the mythoclastic project that I suggest unifies all McCarthy's work. The domestication of the wilderness was an aspect of the nineteenth century version of America's exceptionalist mythology and the cowboy became its romantic hero. John Grady Cole and Billy Parham, cowboys in the 1940s and '50s, learn the bitter lesson that modern America has become a waste land that has no place for either cowboys or heroes and whose Faustian pursuit of ultimate knowledge has presented man with the means of his own destruction.

The cowboy surely provides the single image that most directly represents the mythic American West. The power of this image is out of all proportion to the significance of the historical phenomenon from which it sprang. The cattle industry of the American Southwest enjoyed a brief heyday in the latter half of the nineteenth century, stimulated by the appetite of the growing cities of the east and the coming of the railroad that carried southwestern cattle to the Chicago stockyards. A combination of severe winter conditions and extended drought dealt the industry severe blows in the 1880s, blows from which it never recovered.[2] Never-the-less the mounted herdsman of the period, the precise equivalent of the vaquero of the Spanish American tradition, became the icon of the West. The initial vehicle of this mythicization was the dime novel. The cinema created a genre of its own from this literary source. Perhaps the best example of the cowboy movie is Howard Hawks' *Red River*,[3] which makes clear the fact that the Texas cattle industry was created on land acquired by force from the Indians and Mexicans alike. The female influence is absent from Hawks' pioneering West, and the mythic cattle drive, the first to follow the Chisholm Trail, is also a quest to re-establish a female presence in this patriarchal world. The film also features a fierce conflict between father and adopted son, as the autocratic power of Dunson the patriarch is challenged by his more "democratic" heir. The popularity of the "western" movie both exploited and promoted the cowboy myth. This popularity went far beyond the confines of America itself, since it drew on values that originated in and still informed European culture. The cowboy as herdsman represented an aspect of the myth of the pastoral in his role as a domesticator of the wilderness. His peripatetic life on the "open range" made him an image of freedom from the confines and restrictions of urban existence. His self-sufficiency in isolation made him a rugged individualist. As an armed horseman he could take on the role of the warrior, the conqueror of the "wild and savage" Indian, the bringer of civilization; in this latter role he was also invariably white[4] and thus a bulwark against racial otherness. In all these roles the cowboy could be easily identified as engaged in the ageless struggle between good and evil. Sara L. Spurgeon goes so far as to assert that "The icon of the sacred cowboy is one of our most potent national fantasies."[5] Of course this courageous warrior is readily identifiable as the romantic hero. Gail Moore Morrison writes that *All the Pretty Horses* is "imbued with an archetypal aura of romance,"[6] and for Spurgeon, "John Grady Cole seeks a return to the imagined innocence of the sacred cowboy of the mythic past."[7]

It is this romantic myth that McCarthy addresses in *All the Pretty Horses*. In so doing he resorts to his characteristic eclecticism. The armed horseman on his mythic quest is a figure of Arthurian romance. The forbidden love of John Grady and Alejandra, a betrayal of the master of the mythic realm,[8] reflects that of Lancelot and Guinevere. It is "Sweeter for the larceny of time and flesh, sweeter for the betrayal."[9] I have already mentioned *My Confession*. Chamberlain's autobiographical text is associated with *Blood Meridian* due to its references to Holden and the scalphunters. In my view his text is of greater significance for *All the Pretty Horses*. An American youth, his imagination fired by the romanticism of "Scott's immortal works"[10] leaves home and travels to Mexico in search of a chance to "emulate his heroes."[11] He describes himself as "always . . . a dear lover of horses"[12] He has a passionate love affair with a beautiful young Mexican woman but this is ended by the Mexican conflict. The historical events of *My Confession* inform *Blood Meridian* but its spirit is that of the subsequent novel.

McCarthy uses typically lyrical prose to create an atmosphere of romance in the first two parts of the text:[13]

> When the wind was in the north you could hear them, the horses and the breath of the horses and the horses' hooves that were shod in rawhide and the rattle of lances and the constant drag of the travois poles in the sand like the passing of some enormous serpent and the young boys naked on wild horses jaunty as circus riders and hazing wild horses before them and the dogs trotting with their tongues aloll and footslaves following half naked and sorely burdened and above all the low chant of their traveling song which the riders sang as they rode, nation and ghost of nation passing in a soft chorale across that mineral waste to darkness bearing lost to all history and all remembrance like a grail the sum of their secular and violent lives.[14]

As John Grady and Lacey Rawlins leave home for Mexico,

> . . . they rode out on the round dais of the earth which alone was dark and no light to it and which carried their figures and bore them up into the swarming stars so that they rode not under them but among them and they rode at once jaunty and circumspect, like thieves newly loosed in that dark electric, like young thieves in a glowing orchard, loosely jacketed against the cold and ten thousand worlds for the choosing.[15]

Despite the intense lyricism of these passages they both contain hints that the romantic vision is an illusion that will lead these young men astray. The

Comanche are "lost to all history" and the boys are only "loosely jacketed against the cold." The meeting of John Grady and Alejandra is described in terms that are almost a romantic cliché: "John Grady didn't answer. He was still looking down the road where she had gone. There was nothing there to see but he was looking anyway."[16]

This is compounded at their second encounter:

> She passed five feet away and turned her fineboned face and looked full at him. She had blue eyes and she nodded or perhaps only lowered her head slightly to see what sort of horse he rode . . . He'd half meant to speak but those eyes had altered the world forever in the space of a heartbeat.[17]

Of course a writer as serious and self-aware as McCarthy resorts to such an apparent cliché with deliberate irony; John Grady's world has been altered in a manner that will destroy it. McCarthy leaves us in no doubt of the sexual reality that lies behind this "romance." The parallel between the mating of the stallion with the mares and the passion that unites the human lovers is expressed in far and away the most erotically charged passages that he has produced. John Grady speaks to the stallion,

> . . . in spanish, in phrases almost biblical. . . . Soy commandante de las yeguas, he would say, yo y yo sólo. Sin la caridad de estas manos no tengas nada. Ni comida ni agua ni hijos. Soy yo que traigo los yeguas de las montañas, las yeguas jóvenes, las yeguas salvajes y ardientes.[18]

John Grady rides the stallion bareback and bootless, after it has mated, "leaning low along his wet hide and talking to him softly and obscenely. It was in this condition that all unexpectedly one evening he came upon her returning on the black Arabian down the ciénaga road."[19] Alejandra's response is both willful and an unmistakable *double entendre*: "I want to ride him she said."[20] When the two first make love the atmosphere is intensely romantic:

> . . . She was so pale in the lake she seemed to be burning. Like foxfire in a darkened wood. Like the moon that burned cold. Her black hair floating on the water about her, falling and floating on the water. She put her other arm about his shoulder and looked toward the moon in the west do not speak to her do not call and then she turned her face up to him. . . . .

Me quieres?[21] she said. Yes, he said. He said her name. God yes, he said.[22]

But Alejandra's willfulness means that her love, although deeply felt, is also an act of rebellion against the authority of her father and her passion for John Grady is pursued with deliberate audacity:

> The following night she came to his bed and she came every night for nine nights running . . . Saying I dont care I dont care. Drawing blood with her teeth where he held the heel of his hand against her mouth that she not cry out.[23]

The commercial success of *All the Pretty Horses* is surely due in some measure to this "aura of romance," not to mention its compelling eroticism. However those seduced by these powerful attractions, and the language in which they are expressed, can only have ignored the subversion of romantic assumptions that characterizes the text from the very beginning. John Grady sets out for Mexico because he has lost everything that might have kept him in Texas. His beloved grandfather has just died. The old man's funeral is irre-deemably bleak:

> A norther had blown in and there were spits of snow in the air with blowing dust and the women sat holding onto their hats. They'd put up an awning over the gravesite but the weather was all sideways and it did no good. The canvas rattled and the preacher's words were lost in the wind. When it was over and the mourners rose to go the canvas chairs they'd been sitting on raced away tumbling among the tombstones.[24]

John Grady longs to own and run his Grandfather's ranch, the place that has been his home; but, as his mother points out, "This place has barely paid expenses for twenty years." His father, defeated by his experiences in the Second World War and the ravages of disease, has signed the whole property over to his mother as part of a divorce settlement and she, hating the place, is determined to sell it. She has already left the ranch for a number of years and John Grady has been brought up by his grandfather and the Mexican servant Abuela. His mother's lawyer speaks with the voice of realism:

> Son, not everbody thinks that life on a cattle ranch in west Texas is the second best thing to dyin and goin to heaven. She just don't want to live

out there, that's all. If it was a payin proposition that'd be one thing. But
it aint.[25]

John Grady's attitude is expressed in the unspoken values that he shares with
Don Héctor, "that God had put horses on earth to work cattle and that other
then cattle there was no wealth proper to a man."[26] But this world is about to
disappear as impoverished Texas ranch land yields a new source of wealth in
the form of oil, and the old "natural" way of life gives way to industrialism.
John Grady's dispossession is complete when his girlfriend, Mary Catherine,
tells him she no longer cares for him. As he and Rawlins plan their "escape"
to Mexico John Grady makes his alienation clear:

> If I dont go will you go anyways?
>
> John Grady sat up and put his hat on. I'm already gone, he said.[27]

John Grady's flight to Mexico is therefore a romantic quest to regain
the lost world of the cowboy. The culture that has informed his understanding of the world has left him bereft of any alternative to that of romantic
cowboy mythology. He has been ill-prepared for life in modern Texas. McCarthy makes references to the inadequacy of John Grady's formative culture,
the culture of America's most powerful myth. The painting of horses on his
grandfather's wall is of "picturebook horses" that his grandfather regards as
irrelevant "as if he'd never seen it before."[28] The play in which John Grady's mother acts reveals nothing to him: ". . . he watched the play with great
intensity. He'd the notion that there would be something in the story itself
to tell him about the way the world was but there was not."[29] He shares with
Lester Ballard the fate of having his identity dependent on a set of conditions
that no longer exist—on a mythology that can no longer sustain existence in
a changed world.

McCarthy expresses this sense of the doomed quest for a lost world
with characteristic eclecticism. It is clear that he is increasingly concerned
to depict the racial and cultural variety of the southwest. He has recalled
the lost world of the Comanche, reminding us of their part in the history of
this place. He renders sections of dialogue in Spanish, acknowledging that
the culture of the region has Spanish and Mexican roots. For the quest of
the two modern cowboys he draws on the inspiration of the first novel,[30]
(Spanish of course): John Grady and Lacey Rawlins are Don Quixote and
Sancho Panza. John Grady is the man of ideals, the "ardenthearted" adven-
turer declining to count the cost of actions compelled by his romantic

impulses. Rawlins is the worldly pragmatist who counsels against foolhardy idealism. John Grady refuses to abandon Blevins; Rawlins sees clearly the inevitable outcome of continuing to associate with the "dangerous man" of the text:

> Ever dumb thing I ever done in my life there was a decision I made before that got me into it. It was never the dumb thing. It was always some choice I'd made before it. You understand what I'm sayin?
>
> Yeah. I think so. Meanin what?
>
> Meanin this is it. This is our last chance. Right now. This is the time and there won't be another time and I guarantee it.
>
> Meanin just leave him?
>
> Yessir.
>
> . . .
>
> They sat. Rawlins smoked. John Grady crossed his hands on the pommel of his saddle and sat looking at them . . . After a while he raised his head.
>
> I cant do it he said.[31]

Rawlins also understands the implications of John Grady's passion for Alejandra:

> I know the old man likes you, said Rawlins. But that don't mean he'll set still for you courtin his daughter.
>
> Yeah, I know.
>
> I dont see you holdin no aces.
>
> Yeah.
>
> What I see is you fixin to get us run off the place.[32]

After their release from the Saltillo gaol Rawlins advises John Grady against returning to La Purísima. "Dont go down there, he said."[33] Like that of Sancho Panza, his advice falls on deaf ears. McCarthy reinforces the reference to Cervantes in characteristic ways. On their journey south through Texas, "They watered their horses at a steel stocktank under an old F W Axtell windmill that creaked slowly in the wind."[34] John Grady's horse is called Redbo; Don Quixote rode Rosinante.[35] Don Hector philosophises over his game of billiards with John Grady:

> Beware gentle knight. There is no greater monster than reason.[36]
>
> He looked at John Grady and smiled and looked at the table.

That, of course is the spanish idea. You see. The idea of Quixote. But even Cervantes could not envision such a country as Mexico.[37]

E.C.Riley writes of *Don Quixote*,

> One of the great features of the novel is the dialogue, especially between the Knight and the Squire but also involving many others. On this scale, the conversations are unprecedented in previous prose fiction for their realism, as vehicles for characterization, and for the way they are used to gloss, enlarge upon, distort, and substitute for 'straight' narration. Never in literature had verbal discourse been shown as so integral to experience before.[38]

This emphasis on dialogue is one of the most striking features of *All the Pretty Horses*. It is one of the principal differences between the later novel and *Blood Meridian* and is, in part, the means by which McCarthy re-emphasizes the humane dimension of his work. All the functions of dialogue mentioned by Riley have already been exemplified in the examples quoted of exchanges between John Grady and Rawlins and in Don Hector's remarks on reason; other examples follow. This powerful use of dialogue is a feature of all the texts of The Border Trilogy.

However the principal significance of the parallel between the *All the Pretty Horses* and *Don Quixote* lies in their shared mythoclasm. Don Quixote rides out as a knight of chivalry in search of occasions to prove both his honor and his valor. His is a quest for the vanished world of the Middle Ages, a world dispelled by humanism and reason. His experience of the world is mediated by an outmoded culture, an irrelevant mythology. He has been led astray by what he has read in "the books that had occasioned his madness."[39] John Grady and Rawlins suffer the same fate for the same reason. The world of the cowboy, idealized in the myth created by the dime novels and the western movie, no longer exists in modern Texas, so they journey to Mexico, a *terra incognita*,[40] in the hope that it may still exist "down there." At first it appears that they have succeeded. Dialogue expresses their illusion with characteristic economy:

> This is some country, aint it?
> Yeah. It is. Go to sleep.
> Bud?
> Yeah.
> This is how it was with the old waddies, aint it?

Yeah.

How long do you think you'd like to stay here?

About a hundred years. Go to sleep.[41]

The hacienda is given a mythic dimension both in its name and its setting. La Hacienda de Nuestra Señora de la Purísima Concepción associates this mythic realm with the Virgin and hence by association with the Goddess and the female principle through which the waste land may become fertile. The ranch is portrayed in paradisal terms:

> ... the ranch occupied part of the broad barrial or basin floor of the bolsón and was well watered with natural springs and clear streams and dotted with marshes and shallow lakes or lagunas. In the lakes and in the streams were species of fish not known elsewhere on earth and birds and lizards and other forms of life as well all long relict here for the desert stretched away on every side.[42]

Gail Moore Morrison alludes to this aspect of the tale as the title of her essay indicates: "*All the Pretty Horses*: John Grady Cole's Expulsion from Paradise."[43] Deborah Madsen points out that the Edenic nature of the place of escape from harsh reality is a characteristic of the mythic "western" and cites *Riders of the Purple Sage* as an example.[44] She also draws the parallel between the western hero and the Arthurian knight, with *The Virginian* as the classic example, quoting Wister himself to this effect.[45] John Grady's genius with horses wins him a special place in this regained paradise:

> The boy ... sat on a horse not only as if he'd been born to it which he was but as if were he begot by malice or mischance in some queer land where horses never were he would have found them anyway.[46]

But the hacienda is not the location of a recovered cowboy paradise, but rather an alien world that John Grady's culture, couched in terms of an American mythology, renders him unable to understand. As ever some critics are disinclined to read McCarthy in any but realistic and naturalistic terms. Patrick Shaw writes:

> More perplexing than the thoughtless acts themselves is that they do not induce behavior modification in the protagonists. Cognitive thinking does not seem to be part of their masculine psychology.[47]

If such "behavior modification" were a trope of western culture then the canon would be diminished indeed. Shaw's concern with "masculine psychology" seems to ignore the point that it is John Grady's American culture that betrays him, not his psychology. Brock Clarke, writing in the same collection as Shaw, expresses ideas that indicate the other "school" of thinking about McCarthy's southwestern texts:

> *All the Pretty Horses* implies that one cannot write a Western without a certain self-consciousness about the genre itself: about its mythic origins, its historical confusions, its prejudices, its contemporary relevance. By contesting these generic norms, McCarthy shows that through his self-consciousness, the contemporary Western has the potential to analyze and close the rifts it has produced and maintained, while still honoring its own important literary history. The Western has rarely explored the possibility of shared social space, but by challenging the division between art and experience, McCarthy suggests that the Western might travel over the boundaries as well.[48]

It will be clear that Clarke is expressing ideas that closely correspond to significant aspects of my own analysis.

Whereas Cervantes' great satire achieves its effect through comic means, McCarthy's version is darkly serious. I have already drawn attention to the distinctly unromantic circumstances that prevail in the opening passages of John Grady's story. Other events could have warned a more sophisticated or less foolhardy hero of the fallen nature of the world. The encounter with Blevins is only the first of these. His age associates him with the notorious William Bonney,[49] Billy the Kid, aged fourteen when he killed his stepfather. Blevins' scant account of his own history reinforces the association:

> I told that son of a bitch that I wouldnt take a whippin off of him and I didn't.
>
> Your daddy?
>
> My daddy never come back from the war.
>
> Your stepdaddy?

Yeah.

Rawlins leaned forward and spat into the fire. You didn't shoot him did you?

I would of. He knowed it too.[50]

He has already established his credentials as the "dangerous man" by putting a hole in Rawlins' billfold after the manner of the sharpshooters of movie mythology. On learning that the wax-makers wished to buy the boy, Rawlins asserts "Somethin bad is goin to happen."[51] The text contains other intimations of the illusory nature of the riders' romantic quest. In consequence of drinking cider they are both drunk and sick:

> In the gray twilight those retchings seemed to echo like the calls of some rude provisional species loosed upon that waste. Something imperfect and malformed lodged in the heart of being. A thing smirking deep in the eyes of grace itself like a gorgon in an autumn pool.[52]

The natural world is no more romantic than the metaphysical:

> By and by they passed a stand of roadside cholla against which small birds had been driven by the storm and there impaled. Gray nameless birds espaliered in attitudes of stillborn flight or hanging loosely in their feathers. Some of them were still alive and they twisted in their spines as the horses passed and raised their heads and cried out but the horsemen rode on.[53]

A literary reference completes the compass of McCarthy's depiction of the deception inherent in a romantic view of existence. Blevins brings disaster to the three Americans in the pueblo of Encantada. This refers to Melville's story *The Encantadas:*[54] the eponymous "Enchanted Isles" drew deluded adventurers to their shores with a false promise of pirate fortune, only for them to be reduced to the most abject and depraved condition by the true situation on the islands. Blevins' "mindless violence"[55] results in his own death and the ruin of the two companions who have declined to abandon him, against Rawlins' better judgment. They suffer the degraded hell of the goal at Saltillo. Rawlins is probably raped[56] by the Mexican captain; he and John Grady have to fight to survive the daily conflicts with the other prisoners:

Underpinning all of it like the fiscal standard in commercial societies
lay a bedrock of depravity and violence where in an egalitarian absolute
every man was judged by a single standard and that was his readiness to
kill.[57]

John Grady and Rawlins are both severely wounded. John Grady is indeed
forced to kill in self-defense.

When John Grady finally realizes that he has lost Alejandra, and that
his romantic dreams are illusions, he is left without cultural or emotional
sustenance:

He saw clearly how all his life led only to this moment and all after
led nowhere at all. He felt something cold and soulless enter him like
another being and he imagined that it smiled malignly and he had no
reason to believe that it would ever leave.[58]

This is the final betrayal of John Grady, in so many ways an admirable and
ideal American man—chivalrous, resourceful, passionate, ardenthearted,
courageous, intelligent, considerate, loyal, honest, a master of horses, and,
above all, idealistic. The romantic idealism he has imbibed from his American culture has rendered him fit only for an imaginary world. It is the Dueña
Alfonsa who expresses the central notion of McCarthy's mythoclasm in the
words that John Grady cannot accept:

In the end we all become cured of our sentiments. Those whom life does
not cure death will. The world is quite ruthless in selecting between the
dream and the reality, even where we will not. Between the dream and
the thing the world lies waiting.[59]

Octavio Paz, whose ideas are so consistently reflected in McCarthy's work,
expresses the same notion: ". . . the liberal movement [in Mexico] was an
attempt to create a utopia, and thus provoked the vengeance of reality."[60]
The "something cold and soulless" that enters into John Grady is the disil-
lusioned nihilism that turns his "ardenteartedness" towards the pursuit of
death, the fate of the inverted romantic. In returning south to reclaim "all
the pretty horses" he becomes a Blevins-like desperado, a man of death:

He was determined to get the four horses out of the stable yard if he
died in the road and beyond that he had not thought much.[61]

And as he tells the Mexican captain, now his captive, "You just keep smilin. When I die you die."[62] He has already had a vision of his own death after a drunken brawl:

> He saw a vacant field in a city in the rain and in the field a wooden crate and he saw a dog emerge from the crate and into the slack and sallow lamplight like a carnival dog forlorn and pick its way brokenly across the rubble of the lot to vanish without fanfare among the darkened buildings.[63]

The meaning of this vision only becomes clear in *Cities of the Plain*. John Grady dies in the wooden crate, alone and bereft, his only companion the stray dog, his only friend the Rawlins-like Billy Parham. This passage makes clear the extent to which McCarthy conceived of his Trilogy as a related sequence of texts. The dog, symbol of lost fatherly and familial love, is a further example of the extent to which all his texts are united by common themes and imagery.

In the final passage of *All the Pretty Horses* John Grady rides the Texas plains alone, seeking the "real owner" of Blevins' magnificent bay:

> There were few cattle in that country because it was barren country indeed yet he came at evening upon a solitary bull rolling in the dust against the bloodred sunset like an animal in sacrificial torment. The bloodred dust blew down out of the sun. He touched the horse with his heels and rode on. He rode with the sun coppering his face and the red wind blowing out of the west across the evening land and the small desert birds flew chittering among the dry bracken and horse and rider and horse passed on and their long shadows passed in tandem like the shadow of a single being. Passed and paled into the darkening land, the world to come.[64]

It will come as no surprise to learn that "the world to come" is indeed barren for John Grady and that his romantic quest leads only to the darkness. That his has been a mythic quest is made clear by the reference to the sacrificial bull, itself an emblem of Spanish culture and a relic of the archaic religion of the Goddess. John Grady's quest for the female has failed and his life is a barren waste land as a consequence: his failure has been occasioned by the necessity of challenging the authority of the patriarch, a challenge he is not able to accomplish. As Don Hector says with conscious irony, "Who am I? A father. A father is nothing."[65] McCarthy's oedipal theme is present in a less extreme form than in *Blood Meridian*. John Grady never loses his love for his own father, a love that is returned. But the symbol of that love, the gift of the "brand new Hamley Formfitter saddle,"[66] is a product of the mythic cowboy culture that informs John Grady's undoing.

As is always the case with McCarthy the text contains a number of passages that are of interest although they do not contribute directly to the development of its principal themes. The Mexican captain's advice to John Grady is both an example of what Riley referred to in his remarks on the use of dialogue,[67] and a brief discourse on what might be seen as either political cynicism or postmodern cultural relativism:

> We can make the truth here. Or we can lose it. But when you leave here it will be too late. Too late for truth. Then you will be in the hands of other parties. Who can say what the truth will be then? At that time? Then you will blame yourself. You will see.[68]

After his return to Texas John Grady seeks the "true" owner of Blevins' horse. A claim is made in the town of Ozona and the case is heard before the local judge. John Grady tells his story and the judge discerns that what he says is true.[69] His judgment is succinct. "The constable is instructed to return the property in question to Mr Cole. Mr Smith, you see that the boy gets his horse." The Ozona judge is a direct contrast to judge Holden, and the proceedings of his court are in stark contrast to John Grady's experience with the Mexican captain. The irony is that the Ozona proceedings get no nearer to the truth of the *ownership* of "Blevins'" horse than did those in Saltillo. McCarthy makes it clear that we do not discover the truth of Blevins, neither his name nor his horse, because we cannot always find the truth, even of the world of material possessions and human identity. There is a sense in which the judge becomes, briefly, a surrogate father figure for John Grady. His real father is dead and Don Hector, the surrogate he found in the romantic realm, did not accept him as a fitting heir. The judge reassures him in his "American" values, particularly over his failure to save Blevins and his guilt at the killing of the cuchillero. But he cannot reverse the verdict of the Dueña Alfonsa concerning the fate of romantic illusion. Hers is another of Riley's significant discourses; it covers the better part of fourteen pages and is possibly the longest such passage that McCarthy has written. In it she gives an account of aspects of her own personal history and that of revolutionary Mexico. She makes clear the manner in which Mexico's fate is rooted in its utter poverty: "When I was a girl poverty in this country was very terrible. What you see today cannot even suggest it."[70] She tells of the efforts and downfall of the Moderos, pointing out that, "His [Francisco's] trust in the basic goodness of humankind became his undoing."[71] She points out that politics cannot be "scientific," that "In history there are no control groups. . . . What is constant in history is greed and foolishness and a love of blood . . ."[72] She expresses the feminist notion of the nature of patriarchal society: "The societies to which I have been exposed seemed to me largely machines for the suppression of women."[73] Ultimately she rejects the idea of fate:

> At some point we cannot escape naming responsibility. It's in our nature. Sometimes I think we are all like that myopic coiner at his press, taking the blind slugs one by one from the tray, all of us bent so jealously at our work, determined that not even chaos shall be outside of our own making.[74]

It is this sense of responsibility that John Grady cannot escape and that his romantic values will not enable him to discharge. The Dueña's is the voice of an educated aristocratic woman with experience of the bitter lessons of the world. She is Sancho Panza and Lacey Rawlins in another guise. She inverts the myth of the knight saving the imperiled lady. It is her power and money that saves John Grady, but at a price. Her great discourse has profound significance in the context of a series of texts that depict America as a waste land made barren by its patriarchal rejection of the female principle, the mythic source of fertility and life itself.

In *All the Pretty Horses* McCarthy adopts a literary style that reflects a change in the mood and atmosphere of his work. His extensive use of dialogue creates a heightened sense of realism and a closer concern with the humanity of his characters. He still creates passages of intense lyrical beauty but he pays less attention to landscape and its metaphorical associations and more to the depiction of human action and interaction.[75] Character and emotion become of primary importance and the tale features a number of complex and sympathetic characters with whom the reader can identify. The relation between the text and the culture of the cinema is also discernable. The prose is sparer and more economical than before. There are few of the complex "run on" sentences and lengthy rhetorical passages of the kind that occur in *Suttree* and *Blood Meridian* and upon which Guillemin has commented:[76] metaphysical and philosophical passages are rare. These changes of style make the text more readily accessible. Nancy Kreml draws on linguistic theory in her very fine and revealing analysis of the style(s) of *All the Pretty Horses*, an analysis that can be applied to McCarthy's work more generally in my view.

She identifies a "transparent" and an "opaque" style and demonstrates how these communicate different emotional states and levels of meaning to the reader. A brief outline of her ideas would not do them justice. I very strongly recommend a careful reading of her article in full.[77]

The theme of conflict between father and son features much less intensely than previously, although it has not completely disappeared. Despite these changes of style and mood *All the Pretty Horses* retains the chief characteristics of the texts that have preceded it. It has a mythoclastic form rooted in broad cultural eclecticism. It attacks the romantic myth of the cowboy, using conventions of the "western" cinematic genre to subvert what it depicts as an outmoded role and delusive set of values. John Grady Cole is a consummate horseman, the "All American Cowboy," in a modern Texas that will run on oil rather than beef. This reinforces the sense of America as a waste land, rendered barren by its patriarchal separation from the female. John Grady's journey to Mexico is a romantic quest for an idealized pastoral realm and an idealized female lover, but "between the dream and the thing the world lies waiting," and patriarchal power remains undiminished. It is within the context of what I have called McCarthy's "dialectic of vitality and insignificance" that John Grady's fall into nihilism attains its most poignant aspect. McCarthy's literary eclecticism, as powerful and significant as ever, serves two primary functions in this text. The parallel with *Don Quixote* reinforces the mythoclastic meaning of John Grady's romantic quest and the part played in it by Lacey Rawlins. It also draws attention to the fact that the history and culture of the Border region owes as much to Spanish and Mexican influences as it does to those of Anglo-American origin, an aspect of the text emphasized by the inclusion of dialogue in Spanish. This, together with the colloquial speech of the Texans, the ironic philosophizing of Don Hector, the strangely expressive imperfect English of the Mexican Captain and the powerful formal discourse of the Dueña Alfonsa, invest the novel with that polyglossia that Bakhtin regarded as fundamental to the fully developed form. The change in style evident in *All the Pretty Horses* provides McCarthy with fresh literary impetus. Like his cowboy heroes he faces the prospect of moving on from the influences of the literary past, Melville, Faulkner, Joyce, to confront issues raised by the cinematic culture of the present. McCarthy himself has crossed a literary border in embarking on the creation of his Border Trilogy. Ironically he chooses as his inspiration an even older text. Cervantes, the original novelist, was also a mythoclast, and raises in his satire the question that has been present in all McCarthy's texts but which becomes the predominant theme of *The Crossing*; the role of narrative in structuring culture and thus the mediation of our experience of the world.

Chapter Thirteen
The Crossing

Yo no soy un hombre del camino.

The Crossing is at once the most overtly philosophical and profoundly human of all McCarthy's works. None of his other characters suffers a more grievous fate than Billy Parham. None of his other novels addresses more directly the question of the role of culture, language and narrative in the mediation of our experience of the world.

I have argued that McCarthy is a consciously eclectic writer and have indicated some of his sources. I have also quoted his "regret" at this inevitable indebtedness to the past[1] and have suggested that the oedipal theme, so strongly present in all the texts up to and including *Blood Meridian*, can be read as a metaphor for the author's struggle to emancipate himself from Bakhtin's "voice of the fathers." In my view the narrative voice of *The Crossing* is most distinctly McCarthy's own. Both the eclecticism and the theme of oedipal conflict are much less overt in this novel than in any of his previous texts. This is a profound irony since the fundamental theme of the novel is the manner in which the narratives that structure culture also structure lives thereby. The strength and power of the novel lies in part in the organic relationship between structure and meaning. All three novels of the trilogy derive their dramatic impetus from the crossing of the border between the United States and Mexico. In each case this involves crossing a border between cultures. In each case these crossings make clear the role of culture in the mediation of experience. In each case it is the culture of the United States that is shown to be informed by a mythology that cannot sustain a satisfying existence. If Mexico is a land of disorder, poverty and revolutionary violence, the United States is a spiritual waste land from which its sons inherit a profound sense of the *unheimlich*.

The Crossing takes the same form as *All the Pretty Horses*. It comprises four sections, each of which contains a distinct part of the narrative. There are no separate chapters, each section comprising a sequence of passages of varying lengths, some of less than a page, others of several pages. The focus of the tale is on Billy Parham throughout. The range of characters is considerable, greater than in *All the Pretty Horses*, but none of them is conveyed with the force or depth of the minor characters of that novel. We do not get to know Billy's brother or Quijada, the "gerente of the Nahuerichic division of the Babícora"[2] in anything like the same intensity or detail as we do Lacey Rawlins or the Dueña Alfonsa. This reflects the isolation of Billy himself. The poignancy of the novel lies in Billy's failure to overcome this isolation, despite the heroic nature of his efforts to do so. In much of the text Billy is completely alone. When he is in human company he says little. As a consequence *The Crossing* does not feature dialogue as *All the Pretty Horses* has done and *Cities of the Plain* will do. What it does feature are interpolated tales. These are rendered in such a way as to illustrate the main theme of the text, and perhaps McCarthy's most insistent notion: "All is telling."[3] Wherever he goes Billy meets people who tell him stories. These stories combine with McCarthy's tale of Billy himself to make up the complex web of the narrative and serve as an illustration of the way in which a multitude of narratives make up the matrix of what we call "culture." *The Crossing* presents not only the structure of the matrix but also the manner in which it functions—not only how the tales are told but why, and therefore how they may be read. It also illustrates the fact that the tale may predate the events that it supposedly depicts.

I have already suggested that *The Crossing* is the least eclectic of McCarthy's novels, but that does not mean that his text has no literary antecedents at all. The most obvious of these are Jack London's *White Fang* and *Call of the Wild*. London anthropomorphizes his wolves in order to make them the subjects of his work. The very crux of McCarthy's tale is that the wolf is unreachably "other." Thus it may be argued that McCarthy inverts London's wolf-myth. Billy's quest to know as the wolf knows may be related to Whitman's aspiration:

> I think I could turn and live awhile with the animals . . . they are
> so placid and self-contained,
> I stand and look at them sometimes half the day long.[4]

It may perhaps be doubted whether Whitman had the wolf in mind but this also is an aspect of McCarthy's mythoclasm. A number of critics draw attention to the fact that the trapper Echols, whose traps and "matrix" are used to catch the wolf, was a real person who did indeed contribute much to the eradication of the wolf from the border country. Dianne Luce lists a number of sources for the history of the wolf and its hunters in an article that gives an environmentalist reading of *The Crossing*: she avers that "In most respects, McCarthy's references to Echols are based in fact."[5] Few critics write of *The Crossing* without mentioning the many interpolated tales told to Billy Parham on his wanderings. Just as *Don Quixote* served as an inspiration for *All the Pretty Horses* so its influence is present in second book of the trilogy. Riley points out that,

> Two forms of discourse within the overall narrative are particularly prominent and look like digressions. One is the literary discussions . . . The other is the 'interpolated' or 'extraneous' stories.[6]

McCarthy uses such tales in a manner that fulfils both functions. Jarrett comments that ". . . these interpolated tales . . . inquire into the purpose, form and craft of narrative art itself, construed as a dialogue between teller and listener, writer and reader."[7] A number of the tales that Billy hears on his wanderings have a discursive, metaphysical character that the young American seems ill equipped to understand, none more so than that told by the keeper of the ruined church of Huisichepic. Twenty-one pages in length, it takes the form of the history of the earthquake that destroyed the church, and the death of a wife and son. It deals in metaphysical speculation and philosophical discourse: "To see God everywhere is to see Him nowhere."[8] "What counsel had he to give, this man of words? He'd no answers to the questions the old messenger had brought from the capital. The more he considered them the more knotted they became."[9] It also contains one of McCarthy's most significant passages, expressing his notion of the nature and function of narrative:

> The task of the narrator is not an easy one, he said. He appears to be required to choose his tale from among the many that are possible. But of course this is not the case. The case is rather to make many of the one. Always the teller must be at pains to devise against the listener's claim—perhaps spoken, perhaps not—that he has heard the tale before. He sets forth the categories into which the listener will wish to fit the narrative as he hears it. But he understands that the narrative is itself in fact no category but is rather the category of all categories for there is nothing that falls outside its purview. All is telling. Do not doubt it.[10]

Billy is here cast as the "wedding guest" confronted by the Ancient Mariner. He listens passively to the doleful tale. Of course McCarthy declines to make so simple and direct a parallel. Billy himself has become the desolate wanderer. He has already committed his mythic act against the nature he wished to espouse in the wolf:

> . . . a hawk passed before the sun and its shadow ran so quick in the grass before them that it caused the horse to shy and the boy looked up to where the hawk turned high above them and he took the bow from his shoulder and nocked and loosed an arrow and watched it rise with the wind rattling the fletching slotted into the cane and watched it turning and arcing and the hawk wheeling and then flaring suddenly with the arrow locked in its pale breast.[11]

The reference to Coleridge is obvious: "With my cross-bow / I shot the Albatross,"[12] There are other such references. Shooting the bird disrupts the natural order; the mariner's voyage begins in cheerful optimism:

> The Sun came up upon the left,
> Out of the sea came he:
> And he shone bright, and on the right
> Went down into the Sea.[13]

Immediately on the shooting of the albatross the "order" is reversed:

> The Sun came up upon the right,
> Out of the sea came he;
> And broad as a weft upon the left
> Went down into the sea.[14]

Immediately after Billy shoots the hawk he experiences a similar disorientation:

> Two days later he sat the horse on a promontory overlooking the Bavispe River and the river was running backwards. That or the sun was setting in the east behind him. . . . in the morning when day broke . . . he realized that he had crossed back through the mountains to where the river ran north again along the eastern side of the sierras.[15]

Coleridge's poem finds other echoes in McCarthy's text. It speaks of border crossings and concerns both the teller and hearer of the tale:

> I pass, like night, from land to land;
>   I have strange power of speech;
> The moment that his face I see
> I know the man that must hear me;
>   To him my tale I teach.[16]

Billy passes "from land to land" but cannot relieve his isolation by telling his tale. His alienation and despair matches that of the Ancient Mariner himself:

> So lonely 'twas, that God himself
> Scarce seemed there to be.[17]

McCarthy's rejection of scientific gnosticism and its hubristic drive to dominate nature is predated by Romanticism's vision of the natural world and the threat to it of industrial modernity:

> He prayeth well who loveth well,
>   Both man and bird and beast.[18]

The image of the sun rising contrary to nature as a consequence of this hubris, recurs in the reference to the atomic bomb test at Alamagordo:[19]

> He woke in the white light of the desert noon and sat up in the rank-smelling blankets. The shadow of the bare wood windowsash stenciled onto the opposite wall began to pale and fade as he watched. As if a cloud were passing over the sun. . . . when he looked again at the road which lay as before yet more dark and darkening still where it ran on to the east and where there was no sun and no dawn and when he looked again towards the north the light was drawing away faster and that noon in which he'd woke was now become an alien dusk and now an alien dark and the birds that flew had lighted and all had hushed once again in the bracken by the road.[20]

> He sat there for a long time and after a while the right and godmade sun did rise, once again, for all and without distinction.[21]

McCarthy's choice of Coleridge as a source is appropriate since the English poet is one of the sources of the romantic inspiration that sends Billy on his "doomed enterprise" to save the wolf. At the same time the scientific hubris which both McCarthy and the romantics reject is one of the characteristics that gives his texts a relevance that goes beyond the confines of the United States.

The very notion that "All is telling" carries with it different levels of significance, all of which have been present by implication in McCarthy's previous texts but which are foregrounded in *The Crossing*. There have been various references to the notion that epistemologies are intellectual grids that we impose on the world rather than clear, direct apprehensions of reality. It has been implied that the veracity of human witnessing cannot be taken for granted and that in some cases no witness exists; herein lies the problem of historical truth. McCarthy's travelers repeatedly encounter traces of vanished cultures in the form of signs for which no known signification remains. The very eclecticism of McCarthy's literary method makes clear his acceptance of the "ugly fact" that "Always the teller must be at pains to devise against the listener's claim—perhaps spoken, perhaps not—that he has heard the tale before." The Huisachepic church-keeper's notion that ". . . the narrative is itself in fact no category but is rather the category of all categories, for there is nothing that falls outside its purview," expresses the belief that culture and thus identity are structured by narratives. McCarthy's choice of mythic form for his own texts acknowledges that this is the most powerful narrative mode for this structuring function. The "many" narratives combine to make the "one" culture—the matrix from which the telling must be derived and to which it also contributes. This is mirrored in Echols' "matrix," a mixture of what he had learned were the most significant smells for wolves in apprehending the world, and which Billy uses to try to attract the wolf to his traps. Of course if "All is telling" then *The Crossing* is itself a tale and must be read accordingly. It is a product of the very same cultural matrix within which it seeks to locate itself. In this respect we can recognize McCarthy's acknowledgement of contemporary ideas regarding literary reflexivity, intertextuality and deconstructive purpose. It also raises the question of the interpretation of certain McCarthy tropes; for instance is the representation of the female a deliberate literary and mythic metaphor or the unconscious expression of misogyny.[22] The question of how the tale is shaped by the purpose and culture of the teller is made clear in the gypsy's tale (or rather tales). Within the main part of the narrative (ie not the interpolated tales) we encounter contrasted aspects of the cultural matrix. The lyrical passage that describes Billy's childhood encounter with the wolves reflects the mythic nature of that aspect of the tale; it describes the experience that leads Billy on his "doomed enterprise" with all its associated consequences. This may be contrasted with the account of the Mexican doctor's tending of the wounded Boyd. The doctor applies his knowledge to good effect and the passage is expressed in clear, precise language and in the minutest detail. McCarthy implies that the discourse of scientific medicine may be different in kind to that of mythic or historical narrative. As to the wolf itself, McCarthy suggests that Billy is attracted to the notion of unmediated experience, but this can also be seen as a tale, since the wolf's experience of its sensations of the world cannot be knowable for human beings. There is a sense in which all these varying notions are so implicit in each aspect and stage of the text that it seems necessary to deal with them individually and this is what I attempt to do throughout this chapter.

The Crossing confronts the reader with the need to engage more and more deeply with the culture of the border country and of Mexico itself. It emphasizes the Spanish and Mexican elements of the culture of the region. Billy's grandmother was Mexican and he has learned Spanish from her. A considerable proportion of the text's dialogue is rendered in Spanish. The artificial nature of the boundary between Mexico and the USA[23] is emphasized as Billy returns from his final quest: "He rode past the first of the three white obelisks marking the international boundary line west of Dog Springs . . ."[24] McCarthy makes deliberate use of the traditional Mexican folk song form, the corrido, in a way which exactly reflects his depiction of romantic myth in *All the Pretty Horses*. Billy's wanderings involve him in events of Mexican history, the conflicts between different factions of the Mexican revolution. He is entirely divorced from the history of the United States, unaware of the beginning of the Second World War and rejected for service in the US army. The people he meets on his journeys are of many different classes and races; peasants and merchants, overseers and laborers, vaqueros and bandits, doctors, performers, gypsies, Indians. Many have tales to tell; each tale reflects the teller. Each tale bears on the relation between history and truth, narrative and reality, language and the world. Thus in this text McCarthy focuses attention on the very interrogation of myth that structures all his work. Billy Parham is a victim of the cowboy version of the myth of the pastoral; at the end of the tale and in spite of all his losses, he is still convinced by it: "I been more fortunate than most. There aint but one life worth livin and I was born to it. Thats worth all the rest."[25]

Other characteristic McCarthy's themes are prominent in *The Crossing*. The inevitable relationship between life, death and blood is given a particular intensity and form by placing so much of the action in the context of Mexican culture. The "dangerous man" appears in various forms and locations on Billy's journeys. Billy's tragedy lies in the fact that he is not "ardenthearted." This failing is given a physical equivalent: he has a heart murmur. He is reflective without being perceptive, a dreamer who wishes to run with the wolves and who comes to the end of his tale in the complete isolation in which he has spent so much of what has gone before. Billy is the most important McCarthy character who fails to combat his cosmic insignificance by means of inherent vitality. The "heroes" in this sense are Boyd and the nameless girl who is instinctively drawn to him, each recognizing the fiercely burning spark in the other. McCarthy's insistence on the inadequacy of systems of knowledge and belief[26] is clearly present, implicit in the notion of the cultural matrix as the mediator of experience. The related theme of the danger of modernity's utopian gnosis is present in Billy's unwitting experience of the false dawn of the atomic bomb test in the final pages of the tale. This is the pass to which modernity has brought not just America, but the world; it is the source of the ultimate image of the waste land, an image associated with the absence or loss of the female.[27] It is in *The Crossing* that McCarthy most clearly extends his cultural critique beyond the confines of the New World, to challenge the West as a whole. Against this he provides an intensely detailed, gripping and moving account of a man carrying out his craft with meticulous loving care, in the person of the Mexican doctor who tends Boyd's wound for no other reason or reward than that this is what he has sworn to.[28] It restates McCarthy's evident belief in the saving power of work well done,[29] and indicates that the fatal gnosis lies not in science itself, (an essentially skeptical and empirical discipline and the very foundation of the doctor's craft) but in its social and political deployment, its "mythology." The doctor's unhesitating response to Boyd's need for healing is an aspect of the other value that McCarthy's asserts against nihilism and death, that of human solidarity. Throughout his journeys, both north and south of the border, Billy receives hospitality freely given, often by the poorest of the poor, and invariably "para el camino."[30] The Mexican doctor also manifests this solidarity; Billy voices the best of epitaphs, "He said that the doctor had been a good man . . ."[31] The fact that we never learn the circumstances of the Doctor's death is an example of McCarthy's characteristic insistence that the facts cannot always be known, in individual lives, in history, even in fiction.[32]

As noted above *The Crossing* is structured in four sections, Billy and the wolf, Billy and Boyd in search of their parents' killers and the horses, Billy alone, and Billy's quest for his brother's bones. The mythic nature of each aspect of the tale is clear, but, as is invariably the case, McCarthy inverts the myth, creating the anti-myth. As Campbell suggests the mythic quest involves a journey into an alien place, a descent into the underworld, in order to obtain some boon, some special knowledge that confers maturity and ensures the continuity of life.[33] Billy Parham captures the wolf and attempts to save her. In returning her to Mexico he brings about her death. He also loses parents and home in his absence. The second quest fails to avenge the parent's death or bring back the stolen horses; instead Billy's beloved brother is also lost. The third and final quest alone is successful, but consists of returning with death rather than life. Billy's desolation is complete as he drives away the old crippled dog from his shelter in the ruined waystation east of Alamagordo:

> It tottered away up the road in the rain on its stricken legs and as it went it howled again and again in its heart's despair until it was gone from all sight and all sound in the night's onset.[34]

The contrast with Billy's initial quest to save the wolf brings home to him the full extent of his loss and failure: "He took off his hat and held his head in his hands and wept."[35] McCarthy combines the mythic form with deep human emotion in a manner that gives *The Crossing* its particular power. As Campbell writes "The myths of failure touch us with the tragedy of life, but those of success only with their incredibility."[36]

Billy's first encounter with wolves occurs in childhood. He wakes to hear them and leaves the house at night to see them pass:

> They were running on the plain harrying the antelope and the antelope moved like phantoms in the snow and circled and wheeled and the dry powder blew all about them in the cold moonlight and their breath smoked palely in the cold as if they burned with some inner fire and the wolves twisted and turned and leapt in a silence such that they seemed of another world entire. . . .
>
> There were seven of them and they passed within twenty feet of where he lay. He could see their almond eyes in the moonlight. He could hear their breath. He could feel the presence of their knowing that was electric in the air. They bunched and nuzzled and licked one another. Then they stopped. They stood with their ears cocked. Some with one forefoot raised to their chest. They were looking at him. He did not breathe. They did not breath. They stood. Then they turned and quietly trotted on. When he got back to the house Boyd was awake but he didnt tell him where he'd been nor what he'd seen. He never told anybody.[37]

Typically McCarthy "makes us see" the wolves; the description could almost have been written with a view to cinematic realization. The aesthetic appeal of the excerpt would be enough to justify its creation but McCarthy is always at pains to imbue key passages with multiple meanings. Its imaginative power has to be sufficient to motivate Billy's later quest to save the wolf, the key to the whole unfolding of the complex tale "toward a reckoning whose ledgers would be drawn up and dated only long after all due claims had passed, such is this history."[38] The silent, moonlit spectacle creates an atmosphere of myth; it has a fairytale quality that reflects Billy's perception of the scene, for he is only a child and his fate is to remain so throughout the tale.[39] Billy fails to return from his quest with the hero's boon of manhood in maturity. The depiction of the landscape of the valley below the Animas peaks creates a sense of what this land might have been; this is to be contrasted with the bleakness of the final "waste land:" "The country was all catclaw and creosote and on a gravel plain there were no fences and little grass."[40] The passage also refers to the question of perception and the mediation of experience. The wolves experience the world by sight, sound and smell. Their perception is direct. They communicate by dancing and gesture. Billy experiences a sense of this communication: "He could feel the presence of their knowing that was electric in the air."[41] It is this glimpse of their means of experiencing the world that he will seek to emulate when he returns the wolf to Mexico. Finally we learn at the very outset of Billy's inability to communicate. In a tale in which "All is telling," Billy "never told anybody."

As already mentioned Billy's fate is in part due to his crossing of a cultural border, of his failure to appreciate the meanings that will be mediated by Mexican culture. McCarthy's text draws on that culture. Octavio Paz writes of the Mexican cult of death: "Death is present in our fiestas, our games our loves and our thoughts."[42] "The cult of life, if it is truly profound and total, is also the cult of death, because the two are inseparable."[43] Billy does not realize the role the wolf will have to play in a Mexican town's fiesta and thus delivers it to the death from which he sought to save it. Billy's final and complete isolation reflect Paz's own conclusion: "Solitude is the profoundest fact of the human condition."[44] The Mexico of Billy's journeys struggles with the aftermath of the failed revolution described by the Dueña Alfonsa. The two factions in that aftermath seem to be characterized by the macho individualist and the generous men and women "of the people" with their tradition of automatic hospitality towards the poor traveler, their philosophy of solidarity expressed in the simple phrase "Es para el camino."[45] Paz writes,

> The *macho* represents the masculine pole of life. The phrase 'I am your father' has no paternal flavor and is not said in order to protect or guide another, but rather to impose one's superiority, that is, to humiliate.[46]

This is the type from which the unnamed girl has to be rescued: "He said that if they were old enough to bleed they were old enough to butcher."[47] The gerente of La Babicora, his back broken in the fall under his horse; the eye-sucking torturer of the blind man; the bandit who stabs Niño, Billy's horse; the belligerent drinker in the Janos bar and even Boyd himself, are all *machos.*[48] It is Boyd whose unexplained conflict with his father maintains the theme of oedipal conflict within the text, albeit in a greatly diluted form, and it is his speed of instinctive reaction that saves the girl but provokes the disaster of the death of the gerente. Juan Rulfo's novel, *Pedro Páramo,* is a powerful allegory of the destructive influence of the cult of *machismo* in Mexican culture and history. In his review of *The Crossing* Paul Quinn points out its relation with Rulfo's text and the similarity between the names Parham and Páramo.[49] The doctor's *mozo,* on returning Billy's horse, asks "for señor Páramo."[50] In her introduction to Rulfo's novel Susan Sontag points out that "Páramo means in Spanish barren plain, wasteland."[51] I have identified the waste land as one of McCarthy's recurrent metaphors and drawn attention to his habitual use of significant names. His use of the *corrido,* the traditional Mexican folk ballad, is not simply for the sake of authenticity. He shows how ". . . the poor man's history"[52] is a narrative that structures events and then relates them as myths. Américo Paredes has written extensively on the form and on the culture and history of the Border region. In *Folklore and Culture on the Texas-Mexican Border*[53] he points out that from a Mexican point of view the history of the area is one of usurpation. The Texas Rangers, heroes of so many Hollywood movies, are seen as racist bullies and the Mexican hero is a lone fighter, celebrated in the *corrido,* facing the Anglos "with his pistol in his hand," and fighting for his rights, as in *The Corrido of Gregorio Cortez.*[54] McCarthy makes very clear the way in which the poor of Mexico immediately mythologize the wounded Boyd's part in the death of the gerente according to the sentiments of the *corrido* tradition. In vain Billy explains that what occurred was an accident that he had witnessed personally. For the Mexican poor such a death can only be accounted for in terms of the revolution. The *corrido* is the tale that already exists as a narrative for Boyd's "exploit" and their culture admits of no possibility outside its compass. They tell Billy the tale of "How the güerito had risen from his blood in the dust to draw his pistol and shoot the manco dead from his horse."[55] This illustration of the manner in which narrative predates action, and culture mediates experience, is central to the meaning of *The Crossing* and is one of McCarthy's consistent themes, the root of his mythoclastic intent. That the analysis applies as much to the political culture of the contemporary

United States as it does to that of the rural poor of nineteen-thirties Mexico is precisely his point.

The "Mexican aspect" of The Border Trilogy has been largely neglected by critics, exceptions being Daniel Cooper Alarcón and John Wegner. Alarcón points out the manner in which American narratives have characterized Mexico as an "Infernal Paradise", and suggests that "McCarthy's novel (*All the Pretty Horses*) does little to challenge the conventions of the Infernal Paradise tradition."[56] McCarthy certainly portrays Mexico as both paradisal and infernal. John Grady finds and loses paradise in *All the Pretty Horses*. The Saltillo goal is hellish. The infernal is also encountered in the Juarez brothel of *Cities of the Plain*.[57] However it should be born in mind that McCarthy writes in a self-consciously mythic manner. He depicts the American side of the border as an arid wasteland, a sterile limbo, home to a myth that has lost its power. His Mexico is a mythic and exotic other that is increasingly shown to be as much the product of American fantasies as of indigenous reality. The depiction of Mexico is to be taken no more literally than that of Sevier County, Tennessee. That the US is complicit in the fate of Mexico is made quite clear in the reference to the ownership of La Barbicora by William Randolph Hearst.[58] Wegner writes of the historical background that plays such a significant role in McCarthy's text. He pays particular attention to Mexican history and draws attention to American involvement in the creation of ". . . Mexican people's economic weakness, a weakness caused, in part, by Americans, who have controlled Mexican capital, . . ."[59] He points out that "The map of existence McCarthy creates within this Border Trilogy fuses history and fiction and reminds us that our choices are limited by all choices made before us, whether with our consent or not."[60] The same remark concerning "all choices made before us" could, of course, apply to the creation of literary texts.

Although the preceding paragraphs indicate a range of influences from a variety of cultures, I suggest that the degree to which McCarthy deploys direct literary intertextuality is less intense than in previous texts. Coleridge is quoted pretty directly. Whitman and London are little more than shadows in the literary background. *Pedro Páramo* is referred to perhaps in *hommage*. McCarthy is much more concerned with his own activity as a writer of narrative and he uses the interpolated tales to foreground the nature of the teller's art. At the same time he suggests both the significance and limitations of that art. He makes clear the role that narrative plays, not only in structuring accounts of the past, as in the case of the *corrido*, but also in creating our sense of personal identity. This is, of course, a common enough notion. Joan Didion writes that "We tell ourselves stories in order to live."[61] Paz declares that "... we are inseparable from our fictions, our features. We are condemned to invent a mask and to discover afterward that the mask is our true visage."[62] Penn Warren's Amanda Starr remarks, "Oh, we are nothing more than the events of our own story, ..."[63] The idea has been a commonplace at least since Jaques declared that "All the world's a stage ..." McCarthy will express the idea directly in the epilogue to *Cities of the Plain*:

> Each man is the bard of his own existence. This is how he is joined to the world. For escaping from the world's dream of him this is at once his penalty and his reward.[64]

Most of the people Billy meets on his travels tell him stories. In each case these take the form of histories; they are narratives of witnessing. In the ruined church at Huisachepic an old man, once a priest, recounts the story of the earthquake and of his life wrestling with the problem of suffering in a world created by a supposedly loving God. The primadonna of the itinerant *comedia del arte* tells the story of the death of the "mule with theatrical experience"[65] and the company's consequent immobilization as if she herself can have played no part in causing these events, in contrast to the role that she portrays on the stage. But Gaspar, her companion, expresses Paz's notion of the "reality" of the chosen mask: "El secreto, he said, es que en este mundo la mascara es la que es verdadera."[66] And the primadonna suggests the same notion as Jaques, "The actor has no power to act but only as the world tells him. Mask or no mask is all one to him."[67] The blind man's tale, told in part by his wife, makes plain the horror of the violence of war in revolutionary Mexico. Significantly his blindness does not prevent him from continuing to experience the world, nor does it prevent him from creating his narrative. The man who helps him from the too shallow river in which he had sought to drown himself explains: "Toca, he said. Si el mundo es illusión la perdida del mundo es illusión también."[68] This expresses the fundamental idea explored in *The Crossing*: the illusion lies in our apprehension of the world rather than in the world itself, in our notion that experience is direct rather than culturally mediated. The blind man must learn a new means of perceiving the world, via touch rather than sight. As a consequence, "The world unfolded to him in a way it had not before in his life."[69] The tale takes on a level of complexity when he interprets the words of the sepultero,[70] spoken to the girl who was to befriend the blind man and become his wife. He will not have heard these words himself and will only have the version that she has told him. These he invests with meanings drawn from his own experience of the world, and which, by placing them within his narrative, he adds to

Billy Parham's stock of possible narratives, to his cultural matrix, his means of mediating experience. The sepultero, a man who lives at the boundary of life and death, is said to understand the nature of evil, but the blind man suggests that what he describes is the nature of language and epistemology:

> This man (the eyesucker) of which we speak will seek to impose order and lineage upon things which rightly have none. . . . he may seek to indemnify the world with blood for by now he will have discovered that words pale and lose their savor while pain is always new.

> . . . the picture of the world is all the world men know and this picture of the world is perilous. That which is given him to help him make his way in the world has power also to blind him to the way where his true path lies. The key to heaven has the power to open the gates of hell.[71]

These are ideas that have been encountered in McCarthy's previous texts but in *The Crossing* they are expressed with great power and directness. Their place in the structure of the text gives them an organic relationship with the overall narrative itself and, as I suggest above, are a fundamental theme of the novel.

This theme is, of course, inseparable from the question of veracity, of historical truth. The corrido has a version of Boyd's wounding, and the death of the gerente, that is at odds with "the facts." But even McCarthy's account of "the facts" does not enable us to answer certain other crucial questions. Who killed Billy's parents? What part, if any, did the menacing Indian play in the murders? As in the matter of the identity of Blevin's, horse we cannot say. Some facts are not known. Some "known facts" are not so. Some histories have the powerful character of myths that predate the events depicted. The wolf has its place in mythic tradition as the people of Morelos make clear:

> An old woman said that the wolf had been brought from the sierras where it had eaten many school-children. Another woman said that it had been captured in the company of a young boy who had run away naked into the woods. A third said that the hunters who had brought the wolf down from the sierras had been followed by other wolves who howled at night from the darkness beyond their fire and some of the hunters said that these wolves were no right wolves.[72]

This is the meaning of the enigmatic trio of tales told by the gypsy leader concerning the aeroplane they are transporting along the Santa María River.

"Con respecto al aeroplano, he said, hay tres historias. Cuál quiere oír?"[73] Billy, of course, wishes to hear the "true history." But his wish is accompanied by a smile, indicating that he has begun to learn that the truth of a tale is not such a simple matter. The gypsies are followed by the American horseman to whom Billy reveals his newfound insight:

> You think most of what a man hears is right?
> That's been my experience.
> It aint been mine.[74]

His conclusion is confirmed at once.

> It aint been mine neither. I just said that. I wasn't over yonder like I said neither. I'm a four-F. Always was, always will be.[75]

The horseman also denies the historical veracity of all the "tres historias." Of course none of this gets us any nearer the "truth" of either the aeroplane or the American horseman. We must, like Billy, learn that the tale must be read for what it tells us about the teller. The gypsy is aware that this is, for him and his folk, the whole purpose of the tale. The history of the aeroplane is of no consequence to them. Each of the "three histories" is constructed in order to tell something of the gypsies themselves, of their values, of heroic strength, resourcefulness and courage in the face of danger and deprivation in the gorge of the Pachigogic River; of the grief and desire for solace of a father who has lost his son; of the inability of modernity's frozen image of a photograph to represent life. The gypsy's histories are deliberate fictions, "histories" in the manner of *The Iliad* or *She Wore A Yellow Ribbon*. Like all the tales Billy hears they are there to be heard *and* "read."[76] In refusing to answer all the questions that the narrative of *The Crossing* implies, McCarthy acknowledges that his tale too must be "read."

A number of critics have commented on this aspect of the text. Dianne Luce is perhaps the most perceptive of these in her essay in *Perspectives on Cormac McCarthy*. She writes that,

> McCarthy is concerned with the role or function of story in human experience of life, not only our own stories, our autobiographies, but our biographies of others, our witnessing. These concerns are manifested in the folk ballad or *corrido* (literally, the running or flowing) associated with Boyd, and in the many stories told Billy by the people whose paths cross his on his journeys in Mexico.[77]

She expresses the notion of the role of narrative in the creation of cultural matrix:

> *The Crossing* is indeed a matrix of intersecting stories, partial or complete, often competing, with varying relationships to truth, cutting across and interwoven with the apparently simple linearity of the road narrative of Billy's life.[78]

She sees clearly the meaning of "The World as Tale":

> The *gitano's*[79] narrative, however, is the primary locus of McCarthy's treatment of the authority of competing narratives and the complex relationship of experience, witness, and tale. Together with the earlier diva's tale, it comments on the role of fiction in our lives and on the validity of our lives as fictions.[80]

My initial reading of *The Crossing* was informed by Luce's analysis. If I have developed her thesis it is with respect to the importance of myth for McCarthy and the fatal nature of the pastoral mythology that informs America's erstwhile cowboys, themes which Luce does not directly address.

As I have already suggested Billy's fascination with the wolves lies in his sense that they apprehend the world directly. He attempts to emulate this ability, to gain the wolf's direct sensory apprehension of the world, an experience unmediated by a cultural matrix and needing no structuring narrative:

> He lay awake a long time thinking about the wolf. He tried to see the world the wolf saw. He tried to think about it running in the mountains at night. He wondered if the wolf were as unknowable as the old man said. He wondered at the world it smelled or what it tasted.[81]

It is with this in mind that he embarks on his mythic quest to save the wolf, a quest given added significance in the American waste land by the fact that the wolf is both female and pregnant. We may also note that the wolf could be read as a dog, with all that this signifies as a McCarthy metaphor; Billy loses both wolf and family. McCarthy does devote one short section of the narrative to an account of the wolf's activities. He indicates the nature of her means of experiencing her surroundings and what has occurred there prior to her arrival:

> She circled the set for the better part of an hour sorting and indexing
> the varied scents and ordering their sequences in an effort to reconstruct
> the events that that had taken place there.[82]

Billy's fascination with this process is made very clear:

> He sat trickling water between her teeth and looking into her eye. He
> touched the pleated corner of her mouth. He studied the veined and
> velvet grotto into which the audible world poured. He began to talk to
> her.[83]

Of course his desire for unmediated experience can never be fulfilled. His
journeys will lose him the wolf, his family and his home. He will learn that
the matrix of tales and the ability to read them is our only source of meaning
in life, both for our selves and for our experiences. His learning will not be
complete until the very end of the tale. He will tell the gypsies, "Yo no soy
un hombre del camino."[84] Only after returning with Boyd's bones, wandering the American waste land and finally driving the crippled dog out of his
shelter does he realise with grief that this is exactly what he is, what he has
been all along:

> Standing in that inexplicable darkness. Where there was no sound any-
> where save only the wind. After a while he sat in the road. He took off
> his hat and placed it on the tarmac before him and he bowed his head
> and held his face in his hands and wept.[85]

Female characters are more frequent and more ubiquitous in *The Crossing*
than in McCarthy's other works. As ever they are associated with the lost
fertility of the waste land. The pregnant wolf has no place in either Mexico,
New or Old. The rescued girl is associated with life-giving water. Immediately before first meeting her, the brothers encounter an image of the life-
giving quality of the water that can transform the waste land:

> Late in the day from the crest of a rise in the road they halted the horses
> and looked out over the broken plats of dark ground below them where
> the sluicegates had been opened into the newplowed fields and where
> the water standing in the furrows shone in the evening light like grids of
> burnished barmetal stretching away into the distance. . . .

> By and by they overtook in the darkening road a young girl walking barefoot and carrying on her head a cloth bundle that hung to either side like a great soft hat.[86]

John Wesley Rattner encounters Wanita Tipton in the creek.[87] Suttree finds love with Wanda by the French Broad. Sarah Borginnis baths James Robert in the Colorado.[88] John Grady Cole first makes love with Alejandra in the lake. Like John Grady, Billy's view of the world is changed by a vision of the female. The primadonna, standing in the Casas Grandes River, appears as Aphrodite to the young man's eyes:

> A hundred feet away in water to her thighs stood the primadonna naked. Her hair was down and clinging to her back and it reached into the water. He stood frozen. She turned and swung her hair before her and bent down and lowered it into the river. Her breasts swung above the water. He took off his hat and stood with his heart laboring under his shirt. She raised up and gathered her hair and twisted out the water. Her skin so white. The dark hair under her belly almost an indelicacy. . . . The sun rising over the gray ranges to the east lit the upper air. . . . he watched and as he watched he saw that the world which had always been before him everywhere had been veiled from his sight. She turned and he thought that she might sing to the sun. . . .[89]

His sight has been veiled by the patriarchal Puritan American culture that has mediated his experience, and that embarrasses Boyd when the girl sees little boys bathing naked. Unlike Boyd, Billy's heart lacks the ardor that will enable him to reach out to the female. When the primadonna is encountered abandoned on the road he is quite unable to offer himself to her service. This only intensifies his growing grief and alienation when he finds her humiliated as an attraction at a fairground peepshow, just as the wolf had been. He blames himself, as he must, and turns away, refusing the gift of a "free look" at that which he had seen in freedom but knows that he can never have. Feminist critics have characterized *The Crossing*, and McCarthy's work in general, as patriarchal, not to say misogynistic.[90] It will be clear that I am suggesting that McCarthy writes to subvert patriarchal myth and its traditional texts[91] from within. McCarthy depicts the female in mythic terms, as so much else in his fiction. The depiction is derived from what Paz refers to as the "dethroned feminine deities." The image of the Goddess remained in vestigial form in the Catholic culture of McCarthy's youth.

The Crossing therefore interweaves McCarthy's characteristic themes, myth and anti-myth, pastoral refusal of history and the vision of America as a patriarchal waste land, alienated from the life-giving female principle and standing as a metaphor for a modernity threatened by the consequences of gnostic utopianism and the hubristic deployment of scientific knowledge, as symbolized by the test at Alamagordo. It employs intertextuality to encapsulate pre-existing meanings, particularly Coleridge's *Rhyme of the Ancient Mariner*, but uses this technique more sparingly than heretofore. It uses landscape as metaphor, but less commonly and intensely than in all previous texts. It tells of the fate of one who is not ardenthearted in the face of the cosmic insignificance of human life and portrays with great intensity the sense of *unheimlich* to which this leads. It reiterates frequently, and with emphasis, McCarthy's belief in the fundamental value of human solidarity and of the way in which this is manifested in the traditional hospitality of the poor towards the penniless stranger, especially in Mexico and "para el camino." *The Crossing* provides repeated images of the inseparable relation of life and death, especially in the context of Mexican culture and history, a relation made clear by the use of blood as the emblem of both. The persistent emphasis on the youth of the main protagonists adds to the poignancy of their fate. Despite the severity of their experiences they are innocents abroad:

> They turned the horses off of the road and set out upon a treeless plain. The flat black mountains in the distance made a jagged hem along the lower reach of the heavens. The girl sat small and erect with one hand holding onto Billy by his belt. Trekking in the starlight between the dark boundaries of the mountain ranges east and west they had the look of storybook riders conveying again to her homeland some stolen backland queen.[92]

It is with passages such as this that McCarthy constantly reaffirms the mythic character of his own text. In this case the image is reflexive, these riders are indeed in a storybook. Reflexivity is a principal characteristic of *The Crossing*; this is a narrative about narrative. It uses interpolated tales to make this apparent and to provide opportunities to make clear the dialectic relation between narrative and culture. It provides a meditation on the manner in which the matrix so created inevitably mediates our experience of the world and is a clear attempt to add significantly to that matrix. These themes are shown more clearly by contrasting the mediated reading of experience by the human characters with the direct[93] experience of the wolf, and by the errors and confusions caused by the crossing of a border between cultures.

Passages of dialogue are given in Spanish without translation and in a manner that extends the sense of the use of that language, even though continuations are in English.[94] This has the effect of emphasizing the mixed nature of the culture of the area on both sides of the Texas-Mexico border. It provides McCarthy with the opportunity to incorporate into his text the notion of the corrido and to use this to demonstrate how mythic narrative structures both the action of men and the narrative of history. The manner in which this text differs most obviously from its predecessors lies in the comparative lack of dialogue. This reflects the isolation of the central character, and his tragic fate as "un hombre del camino." On his journeys into ultimate deprivation Billy encounters the story-tellers who are the sources of the interpolated tales that are central to the novel's meaning and purpose. He listens, even if he does not understand. He tells no tale of his own. His final realization that he is *unheimlich* in every sense of the word emphasizes the emotional depth that is the constant but paradoxical accompaniment to the text's literary and philosophical concerns. It is this organic complexity of intellectual and humane concerns, expressed with McCarthy's usual controlled linguistic virtuosity, that lead me to assert *The Crossing* as his finest work to date.

Chapter Fourteen
Cities of the Plain

There's hard lessons in this world.
What's the hardest?
I dont know.
Maybe it's just that when things are gone they're gone. They aint comin
back.

That *Cities of the Plain*, subtitled "Volume Three of the Border Trilogy," has received comparatively little critical attention is due to some extent to its comparatively recent date of publication.[1] However of much greater significance in this regard is the fact that most critics have tended to write of "The Border Trilogy" as a whole and in so doing to concentrate on *All the Pretty Horses* and *The Crossing* rather than "Volume Three."[2] This has tended to create a sense, perhaps unintended, perhaps implicit, that *Cities of the Plain* is a lesser work than the preceding texts, although few go as far as Peter Josyph who comments:

> I was saddened by *Cities of the Plain.* Same character doing much the same things, making much the same mistakes, but McCarthy had run out of energy; he had nowhere to go.[3]

Edwin Arnold, a consistent McCarthy apologist, provides a more considered and sympathetic judgment of the text, placing it in the context of the trilogy as a whole:

> *All the Pretty Horses* is a *bildungsroman* set on a foundation of philosophical and ontological speculation . . . A much denser, more demanding work, *The Crossing* is a painful and exhausting and finally devastating narrative whose purpose seems almost a corrective to . . . popular

readings of the first book. . . . Some will view *Cities of the Plain* as a
lesser work and certainly it is more constricted than either of the first
two volumes, . . . This is a diminished world McCarthy creates in *Cities
of the Plain*, a post-war West suffering through its final mockeries and
subtractions, . . . But *Cities of the Plain* is also a necessary work, the one
towards which the first two have journeyed in all their richness, and it
is not without its own quiet moments of splendor. It may, in fact, prove
ultimately to be the wisest of the books and, in its cumulative effect, the
one that in retrospect will move us most deeply.[4]

Those critics who comment seriously on *Cities of the Plain*, if only in the
context of the trilogy as a whole,[5] clearly reject Josyph's view by implication. Stacey Peebles analyses the Epilogue and Dedication in terms of Latin
American influence, a field that has been neglected so far in my view:

> One of the most significant influences on the epilogue, . . . is the genre
> of Latin-American literature known as "lo fantastico," . . . which is best
> represented in the writings of Jorge Luis Borges and Julio Cortázar.[6]

But criticism dealing exclusively with *Cities of the Plain* remains relatively
scarce.

Although I would concede that I do not regard *Cities of the Plain* as
highly as *The Crossing*, I do feel that it takes its place as a fitting completion
of the Trilogy and that it occupies a distinctive place in the McCarthy oeuvre.
It weaves together the tales of John Grady Cole and Billy Parham and draws
them to a logical conclusion; at the same time it is very different in both style
and content and has an individual character of its own that distinguishes it
from the previous two texts. It displays a number of the characteristics that I
have identified as unifying McCarthy's work as a whole. It also has an elegiac
quality that carries with it an air of finality, a sense that this aspect of the
author's work has been completed. The validity of this comment will depend
on one's judgment of the relation between the Trilogy and the later novel, *No
Country for Old Men*.[7]

Like the other texts of the Trilogy, *Cities of the Plain* comprises main sections rather than separate chapters. There are three of these and an epilogue.
Each of the main sections features a series of passages of varying lengths,
some of less than a page, others of several pages. Consecutive passages deal
with different aspects of the action, creating a structure of vignettes in the
same manner as a John Ford movie, for instance *My Darling Clementine* or

The Man Who Shot Liberty Valance. This is particularly appropriate since the novel is concerned with the West that Ford mythologised. As the title suggests the action of the tale is as much urban as rural; landscape features much less extensively than in the rest of McCarthy's work. The prose style is much plainer than has previously been the case but the eidetic quality remains as strong as ever. This reinforces the text's relation to the cinema.[8] As I have suggested previously the myth of the West upon which McCarthy comments received its most powerful and widely effective representation in the Hollywood western.[9]

Perhaps the novel's primary claim to distinction lies in its spare but powerfully effective use of dialogue. McCarthy has used dialogue in a manner that was both economic and suggestive of character and relationship throughout his career. In my view his mastery of this aspect of his craft is most apparent in this particular text, even going beyond the level achieved in *All the Pretty Horses*. This mastery of realistic dialogue[10] is combined with a straightforward temporal structure and a clearly defined and dramatic plot, to create a sense that *Cities of the Plain* adheres to the conventions of realism. There is no difficulty in following the action. The range and depth of characterization is both convincing and, at times deeply affecting. The "plain style" predominates—the poetic and rhetorical passages that punctuate his other texts are largely absent, as are the lengthy "run on" sentences in the paratactic style analyzed by Guillemin. Elements of intertextuality, although present, are such that the reader's response is more dependent on having an acquaintance with popular cinema than the literary canon; references to the latter do exist but failure to spot them would result in only minor diminution of the impact of the tale. However this late reversion to "realism" is less than complete in at least two ways. The text still carries an aura of the mythic; and the Epilogue dispels any notion that McCarthy has rejected the novel's potential as a vehicle for the representation of philosophical discourse.[11]

As in the previous two texts the action involves crossing the border into Mexico, in this case the urban Mexico of Ciudad Juarez. However, all that is involved in this case is the paying of a toll at the bridge over the Rio Grande that joins the twin cities of Juarez and McCarthy's adopted home, El Paso. Whereas both John Grady and Billy, in their earlier texts, crossed into an alien culture they did not understand, this later more "modern" crossing sees the young men exploiting a culture of cheap whiskey and prostitutes that they understand only too well and with which they are complicit.

I shall therefore argue in this chapter that *Cities of the Plain* has its own unique characteristics but also continues the McCarthy project of criticizing the myth of American exceptionalism; in so doing it completes his depiction of the mythic west as a waste land.

> They stood in the doorway and stomped the rain from their boots and swung their hats and wiped the water from their faces. Out in the street the rain slashed through the standing water driving the gaudy red and green colors of the neon signs to wander and seethe and rain danced on the steel tops of the cars parked along the curb.[12]

This first paragraph of the text, expressed in McCarthy's by now familiar eidetic fashion, has an immediate two-fold effect. It creates a sense of literary realism and, at the same time, reflects the visual style that classical narrative cinema employs to disguise its own mythic forms. The sense of realism is heightened by the dialogue:

> Damned if I aint half drowned, Billy said. He swung his dripping hat. Where's the all-American cowboy at?
>
> He's done inside.
>
> Let's go. He'll have all them good fat ones picked out for hisself.
>
> The whores in their shabby deshabille looked up from the shabby sofas where they sat.[13]

As ever McCarthy relates the female to water but, in this case, it has no mythic, life-giving significance; the cowboys work a land divorced from the female. Their sexuality is directed to sterile ends and the rain falls, not on the plains but in the streets of one of the "Cities of the Plain." The biblical allusion to Sodom and Gomorrah is appropriate. Those cities were destroyed by the patriarchal God of the Old Testament for the "sin of sodomy," another sterile form of sexual expression. The rain has a further significance; towards the end of Eliot's *Waste Land* there is ". . . a damp gust / Bringing rain."[14] Eliot implies that there is the possibility of relief from the spiritual drought that he perceives as afflicting modernity. McCarthy's rain comes at the very beginning of his text but heralds no relief. In none of McCarthy's other texts is the loss or absence of the female so strongly depicted. As this initial passage indicates, the all-male society of *Cities of the Plain* values camaraderie, humour and solidarity but is coarsened by a way of life from which the female is excluded. The reasons for this exclusion become apparent as the tale unfolds. The coarsening is very apparent when this whorehouse Billy Parham is compared to the quietly gracious young man of *The Crossing*: "Get that one I had. She's five gaited or I never rode."[15] Billy's reference to John Grady as "the all-American cowboy" carries a double significance: it reminds us of John Grady's mythic stature as the inheritor of the American cowboy tradition in its most romanticized and idealized form; and it makes clear the extent to which Billy admires him. In fact it becomes clear that Billy hero-worships John Grady, loves him in fact, and sees in him his lost brother Boyd. In *All the Pretty Horses* John Grady, the romantic hero, discovered that his American cowboy mythology could not sustain him after the loss of Alejandra and the killing of the Saltillo cuchillero. The "something cold and soulless" that entered his heart perverts his ardentheartedness and leads him to seek both love and death in true romantic fashion, while Billy is left once again to wander the western wasteland and to diminish into a bereft old age.

While the sense of realism remains dominant throughout the text there is no mistaking the overall mythic tenor of the tale; John Grady sets out to rescue the "damsel in distress." That his quest is illusory is suggested from the beginning. His first sight of Magdalena is a reflection rather than a direct encounter:

> . . . John Grady was studying something in the backbar glass. Troy turned and followed his gaze. A young girl of no more then seventeen and perhaps younger was sitting on the arm of the sofa with her hands cupped and her eyes cast down.[16]

The relation between the mirror image and both inversion and illusion are commonplace. There is also a suggestion of the fatal consequences of such romantic "reflection;" the Lady of Shalott was undone in just such a manner; Magdalena also ends her life on the river:

> She lay as the rushcutters had found her that morning in the shallows under the shore willows with the mist rising off the river. Her hair damp and matted. So black. Hung with strands of dead brown weed. Her face so pale. The severed throat gaping bloodlessly. . . .
> There was no blood for it had all washed away.[17]

Even in death the female remains associated with water. Magdalena is, of course, the name of the prostitute Mary Magdalene, of the New Testament. It is one of McCarthy's significant names and adds another dimension to the mythic nature of the apparently realistic text. The rescue of the lost female is a recurring theme of traditional patriarchal narrative. It received powerful cinematic expression in Ford's *The Searchers*; one of the finest of all western movies it concerns the epic quest to recover a female child taken captive by the Comanche in post Civil War Texas.[18] The same theme is reworked in Wim Wenders' *Paris Texas*, a deliberate *hommage* to the acknowledged master of the genre. Wenders' version is set in contemporary Texas and features the quest of a man and his son for the lost wife/mother who has left of her own volition to work for gangsters in a cat house. The similarity with *Cities of the Plain* illustrates the inherent significance of the myth, if not deliberate references on McCarthy's part. Both the cinematic quests end in the recovery of the female, although the male remains "outside," *unheimlich*, in the sense that informs all McCarthy's texts. His final textual anti-myth ends in death and defeat for male and female alike. In this his conclusion is as pessimistic as that of Conrad's *Nostromo*. Only Billy Parham finds some consolation but this at the end of a long and desolate life as "un hombre de camino."

In each of the examples quoted above the mythic is conjoined with intertextuality, either literary or cinematic. The same is true of the final mythic element of the tale. Magdalena's virtual prison is the White Lake brothel. This may be read as a reference to the lake of ice in Dante's *Inferno*.[19] Sayers interprets the image thus:

> . . . here at the centre of the lost soul and the lost city, lie the silence and the rigidity of the eternal frozen cold. . . . A cold and cruel egotism, gradually striking inward till even the lingering passions of hatred and destruction are frozen into immobility—that is the final state of sin.[20]

At the White Lake Billy encounters the sexually ambivalent Tiburcio, the man who will cut Magdalena's throat at Eduardo's command; the image is infernal: "When he looked in the backbar glass the alcahuete was standing at his left elbow like Lucifer."[21] Eduardo himself is the epitome of "cold and cruel egotism," even his passion for Magdalena frozen by cruelty, the right of property superseding the claim of love. He kills rather than lose her; or rather he orders his man to kill for him. He represents the extreme of the destructive macho that Paz describes.[22] Magdalena herself is chilled by the pnuema that signals the onset of her epilepsy. There are further characteristic ironies in McCarthy's anti-myth. Both John Grady and Billy are struck by first visions of the female; John Grady by Alejandra and her pale, reflected other, Magdalena, and Billy by the diva. Their visions are transforming, like

Dante's first sight of Beatrice. They represent patriarchy's vision of a plenitude that only completeness with the female can provide. This completeness
is denied in the American waste land.

I have argued throughout this book that McCarthy's texts display a
self-conscious concern with uniqueness of voice and the impossibility of ever
achieving it. I have suggested that this concern, treated metaphorically as
a conflict between father and son,[23] diminishes as his writing career develops and that in *The Crossing* he achieves a distinctive personal voice. This
continues in *Cities of the Plain* and yet it seems that McCarthy is unwilling
to let the shadow of Faulkner disappear from his fiction completely. In *The
Hamlet*, Houston lives for a number of years in El Paso. With him, as his
wife, is a woman, "whom he had taken seven years ago out of a Galveston
brothel."[24] Faulkner comments (in a manner that McCarthy would never
permit himself):

> Although she had never suggested it, he even thought of marrying her,
> so had the impact of the West which was still young enough then to put
> a premium on individuality, softened and at last abolished his inher-
> ited southern-provincial-protestant fanaticism regarding marriage and
> female purity, the biblical Magdalen.[25]

Virtually all of McCarthy's previous texts have depicted family relationships
in terms of conflict, much of it violent, since patriarchal culture implies an
inherent contest between father and son. Mothers are dead or otherwise
absent; traditional culture expressed the notion of *unheimlich* as "motherless
child," since home was centred on a mother. The prevailing attitude towards
marriage is expressed in the words of "old Uncle Bud Langford . . . 'It would
take one hell of a wife to beat no wife at all.' "[26] In *Cities of the Plain* the sus-
taining family is represented as a possibility, and the union of husband and
wife is of fundamental significance, a boon in its realization and a deep sadness in its loss. The same is true of relationships with other female figures—
daughters, sisters, lovers. Troy's brother Johnny was brought down by falling
in love with the wrong sort of woman: "Satan hath power to assume a pleas-
ing form. Them big blue eyes. Knew more ways to turn a man's head than
the devil's grandmother."[27] Troy's misogyny is a product of bitterness but his
other brother Elton has a good marriage and a daughter. His wife's reluctance
to be called "Mam" is a sign of a changing world, a world that will challenge the patriarchal values of the cowboys and will render their way of life
redundant. "What's a modern kind of woman? Eat your supper she said. If
your daddy had his way we wouldn't even have the wheel yet."[28] When John

Grady gets a lift into El Paso to pay his last and fatal visit to the White Lake and Magdalena lies dead in the Juarez morgue, it is raining once again. The irony is compounded when the driver speaks of his wife:

> There aint been a day passed in sixty years I aint thanked God for that woman. I never done nothin to deserve her, I can tell you that. I dont know what you could do.[29]

The ranch foreman Oren has "even been married once."[30] He makes it clear that it was not his wife's fault that the marriage did not last. Old Mr. Johnson never married:

> She wouldnt have me. . . . She went and married another old boy and she died in childbirth. It was not an uncommon thing in them days. She was a awful pretty girl. Woman. I dont think she'd turned twenty. I think about her yet.[31]

Although he had no children Mr. Johnson took his brother's daughter as his own. "Him and his wife both was carried off in the influenza epidemic in nineteen and eighteen."[32] It is her death that has begun to turn his ageing mind and will not let him sleep:

> In his time the country had gone from the oil lamp and the horse and buggy to jet planes and the atomic bomb but that wasnt what confused him. It was the fact that his daughter was dead that he couldnt get the hang of.[33]

He tells John Grady of "life's hardest lesson": "Maybe its just that when things are gone they're gone. They aint comin back."[34] As with Margaret so with the world of the cowboy. The blind maestro of the Moderno[35] is invariably guided by his young daughter whom he trusts implicitly: "Oh my, he said. No no. We have no secrets. An old blind father with secrets? No, that would never do."[36] The young female acts in place of the eyes that he has lost. Billy has lost his entire family: in his old age he recalls his sister:

> In the night he dreamt of his sister dead seventy years and buried near Fort Sumner. He saw her so clearly. Nothing had changed, nothing faded. She was walking slowly along the dirt road past the house. She wore the white dress her grandmother had sewn for her from sheeting and in her grandmother's hands the dress had taken on a shirred bodice

and borders of tatting threaded with white ribbon. That's what she wore. That and the straw hat she'd gotten for Easter. When she passed the house he knew that she would never enter there again and in his sleep he called out to her but she did not turn or answer him but only passed on down that empty road in infinite sadness and infinite loss.[37]

Throughout the tale there is an implicit notion of the possibilities for love between male and female. The examples given above are, for the most part, small details, distributed throughout the text and creating an ambience that is different to that of those that have preceded it. This sense of the necessity of mythic union between male and female has epistemological implications in McCarthy's work that are similar to those identified by Hughes in his analysis of Shakespeare.[38] Instead of identifying the split between male and female as that between new and old in people's souls, Protestant and Catholic, McCarthy takes up the secular meanings, the symbolic order, utopian gnosticism, science, technology, progress—rendered sterile by its divorce from the natural order and producing the waste land. The principal representation of the possibility of love, and the grievous consequences of its loss, concern Margaret; her absence haunts the book. Not only did her death deprive Mr. Johnson of his *raison d'être*, it also deprived MacGovern of a wife he regards as irreplaceable. John Grady aspires to the same felicity and MacGovern makes clear his feelings for his dead wife when he passes on her wedding ring to the impecunious John Grady:

> . . . put it in your pocket and come Tuesday you put it on that girl's finger. You might need to get it resized. The woman that wore it was a beautiful woman. You can ask anybody, it wasn't just my opinion. But what you saw wouldnt hold a candle to what was on the inside. We would like to have had children but we didnt. It damn sure wasnt from not tryin. She was a woman with a awful lot of common sense. I thought she just wanted me to keep that ring for a remembrance but she said I'd know what to do with it when the time come and of course she was right. She was right about everthing. And there's no pride in it when I tell you she set more store by that ring than anything else she ever owned. And that includes some pretty damn fine horses.[39]

In a deceptively simple passage McCarthy associates drought and the lost female together with a reference to the Virgin, the contemporary version of the Great Goddess:

A storm front had moved down from the north and it had turned off cold. No rain. Maybe in the eastern sections. Up in the Sacramentos. People imagined that if you got through a drought you could expect a few good years to try and get caught up but it was just like the seven on a pair of dice. The drought didnt know when the last one was and nobody knew when the next one was coming. He was about out of the cattle business anyway. He drew slowly on the cigarette. It flared and faded. His wife would be dead three years in February. Socorro's Candlemas Day. Candelaria.[40] Something to do with the Virgin. As what didnt. In Mexico there is no God. Just her. He stubbed out the cigarette and rose and stood looking out at the softly lit barnlot. Oh Margaret, he said.[41]

This passage concludes a section and the simple "Oh Margaret" expresses Mac's grief more effectively than any longer passage could.

We are not given the details of Margaret's death but it is clear that it was not sudden. This implies the possibility that she suffered from cancer: there is a suggestion that the couple were sterile. Mac's ranch, afflicted by drought and "right in the middle of . . . the sorriest land . . . the army could find . . . in seven states,"[42] is itself becoming sterile, a veritable waste land. Its location is to the south of Alamagordo; an abnormally high number of cases of cancer[43] were recorded in that area in the years following the atomic bomb test of 1945.[44] Given the references to the bomb test in *The Crossing* and *Cities of the Plain*,[45] and the association of nuclear science with the utopian gnosticism that McCarthy so consistently rejects, it seems reasonable to conclude that there is an intended connection between the test and all that it represents and the fact that *Cities of the Plain* is set within a landscape of death.

The other female figure associated with MacGovern's ranch is Socorro, the Mexican housekeeper. McCarthy gives her another of his significant names, socorro being Spanish for helper and associated with the English "succour." She is the unfailing provider of the endless round of meals that a working farm demands, both in the house and on the range. She is the only female remaining on the ranch and is never presented as more than a rarely seen background figure in this predominantly male world. But she has had a greater significance and her humanity is strongly, if briefly asserted; speaking of Margaret, Mr. Johnson relates that, "Socorro pretty much raised her. She spoke better Spanish than Socorro did. It's just awful hard. It like to have killed Socorro. She still aint right. I dont expect she ever will be."[46] Although it can be argued that Socorro is marginalized as both female and Mexican[47]

I suggest that she represents the last vestige of the life-giving female that remains on Mac MacGovern's ranch.

The ranch therefore can be read as a last refuge for a disappearing way of life. This largely all-male world is the final redoubt of America's pastoral realm. Texas cattle will give way to Texas oil. Agriculture will be superseded by industry and corporate capitalism. The text is set in the 1950s during which decade Eisenhower was to warn of the growing power of "the military-industrial complex." McCarthy was writing in the 1990s when the power of that complex seemed unchallengeable and dominated not just America but the world. The cowboys of *Cities of the Plain* begin to realize that their world has passed:

> John Grady ran the brush down the horse's loins. The horse shuddered.
>
> We'll all be goin somewhere when the army takes this spread over.
>
> Yeah, I know it.[48]

Billy is aware of the inevitability of change and of the need to accommodate it at the expense of illusion:

> When you're a kid you have these notions about how things are goin to be, Billy said. You get a little older and you pull back some on that. I think you wind up just trying to minimize the pain. Anyway this country aint the same. Nor anything in it. The war changed everthing. I dont think people even know it yet.[49]

Billy has become aware that the lost world cannot be recovered in Mexico:

> I went down there three separate trips. I never once come back with what I started after.
>
>   John Grady nodded. What would you do if you couldn't be a cowboy?
>
>   I dont know. I reckon I'd think of somethin.
>
>   Yeah.
>
>   You think you could live in Mexico?
>
>   Yeah. Probably.
>
>   . . .
>
>   Dont you think if there's anything left of this life its down there?
>
>   Maybe.

You like it too. Yeah? I dont even know what this life is. I damn sure
dont know what Mexico is. I think its in your head. Mexico.[50]

This reflects the view stated by Paz that Americans have sought themselves in
Mexico, rather than the reality of that country.[51] It is, of course, the lesson
that John Grady is unable to acknowledge. When Mac says goodbye to Billy
he knows that his ranch is doomed: "You've always got a job here. The army's
goin to take this place, but we'll find somethin to do."[52]

In the fading all-male world of the ranch the men find their satisfaction
and identity in their work and their camaraderie. They admire John Grady,
the young master of horses. His expertise is matched by his integrity as he
diagnoses the fault in Wolfenbarger's filly and refuses to have the horse on
the property. They seek his advice at the horse auction. This scene comprises
long sections of dialogue, perhaps the most brilliantly effective that McCarthy has produced. They convey the character of the men, their relationships,
their humor, their love of horses and of their work and their understanding of their fellow bidders. They also capture the accent and idiom of the
time and place in a particularly convincing manner. The following is a small
extract of a much longer passage:

> The stableboy brought out the roan four year old from McKinney
> and they bid the horse in at six hundred.
>   Where's that string at?
>   I dont know.
>   Well, we're fixin to get down to the nutcuttin.
>   He put one finger to his ear. The spotter raised his hand. The auction-
> eer's voice clapped back from the high speakers. I got six got six got six.
> Do we hear seven. Who'll give me seven. Seven now. Seven seven seven.
>   Yonder he goes with that hand.
>   I see him.
>   The horse went to seven and seven and a half and eight. The horse
> went to eight and a half . . .
>   Bidders all over the barn, aint they? said Oren.
>   All over the barn.
>   Well there aint nothin you can do about it. What's this horse worth?
>   I dont know. Whatever it sells for. John Grady?
>   I liked the horse.
>   I wish they'd of run that string through first.
>   I know you got a figure in mind.
>   I did have.

> It's the same horse out here that it was in the paddock.
> Spoke like a gentleman.[53]

This seemingly simple passage requires great mastery and confidence on the part of the writer since it omits much of what a lesser man would feel compelled to include; there is neither description of the scene to contextualize the dialogue and only occasional indications of the identity of any speaker. Never-the-less it succeeds in conveying the tension and rhythm of the auction as well as the relationship of the men to each other and their work.

The converse of this positive view of the all-male world has already been seen in the initial scene in the Juarez brothel. The absence of the female from the cowboys' world drives them to their mutually corrupting relationship with Mexico. There is a sense of the conflict between the principles of life and death that runs throughout the text, and the Juarez brothel provides the first intimation of this struggle. As Troy and Billy drive over a rabbit on their way to visit Elton, Troy tells the story of his drive to Amarillo:

> The Oldsmobile had this big ovalshaped grille in the front of it was like a big scoop and when I got round to the front of the car it was just packed completely full of jackrabbit heads. I mean there was a hundred of em jammed in there and the front of the car the bumper and all just covered with blood and rabbit guts and them rabbits I reckon they'd sort of turned their heads away just at impact because they was all lookin out, eyes all crazy lookin. Teeth sideways. Grinnin. I cant tell you what it looked like.[54]

Mac, who is John Grady's surrogate father, as was Don Hector at La Purísima, speaks of the boy's real father: "He was on the death march, wasn't he? Yessir. There was a lot of boys from this part of the country was on it. Quite a few of em was Mexicans."[55] The feral dogs kill calves and have to be killed in their turn. The method of catching them is thrilling, conveyed with all McCarthy's skill in depicting action, but their deaths are brutal; they are roped and dragged:

> ... he rode on dragging the dog a ways and then hauled the horse up short and jumped down and ran back to get his rope off the dog. The dog was limp and bloody and it lay in the gravels grinning with its eyes half started from their sockets. He stood on it with his boot and trotted back to the waiting horse coiling the rope as he went.[56]

The fate of the last dog is both bloody and spectacular in a way which is characteristic of McCarthy as he implicitly acknowledges man's love of action and his excitement at violent death. Both Billy and John Grady rope the dog simultaneously:

> The slack of Billy's catchrope hissed along the ground and stopped and the big yellow dog rose suddenly from the ground in headlong flight taut between the two ropes and the ropes resonated in a single brief dull note and then the dog exploded.
>
> The sun was not up an hour and in the flat traverse of the light on the mesa the blood that burst in the air before them was as bright and unexpected as an apparition. Something evoked out of nothing and wholly unaccountable. The dog's head went cartwheeling, the ropes recoiled in the air, the dog's body slammed to the ground with a dull thud.
>
> Goddam said Billy.[57]

During the dog hunt McCarthy strikes familiar notes. John Grady and Billy climb onto the mesa:

> They crossed gray bands of midden soil from ancient campsites washed down out of the arroyo that carried bits of bone and pottery and they passed under pictographs upon the rimland borders that bore images of hunter and shaman and meetingfires and desert sheep all picked into the rock a thousand years and more. They passed beneath a band of dancers holding hands like paper figures scissored out by children and stenciled on the stone.[58]

The frequent repetition of this image emphasizes the significance it must hold for McCarthy. Not only does it indicate the impermanence and insignificance of human societies and cultures within the timescale of the history of the earth itself, it also signifies the "kinship" between those ancient hunters and their contemporary equivalents whose savage expertise has so ruthlessly exterminated the feral dogs. It serves to remind America that its "history" is not exclusively white and did not begin in 1620 or 1492. The shaman and the pictographs indicate that art too is impermanent; McCarthy knows that his own work will come to dust. The "band of dancers holding hands" is a reference to Matisse's *La Dance*;[59] ancient and modern artists have kinship also. The other "familiar note" concerns the puppy rescued from the lair beneath the great rock. "John Grady held the dog up and looked into its small wrinkled face. I think I got me a dog, he said."[60] I have indicated the significance of the puppy or dog in McCarthy's work from the very beginning. The recovery of this pup can be read as the son gaining redress through his own will and action, an earnest of John Grady's desire to create his own family. The irony of the final outcome of his efforts is made the more poignant by the gentle and loving manner in which he cares for the pup, a caring which reinforces the profound meaning that the creature holds for John Grady and for the text:

> There were times he'd fall asleep in the chair and wake at some strange hour and stagger up and cross the yard to the barn and get the pup and take it and put it in its box on the floor beside his bunk and lie face down with his arm over the side of the bunk and his hand in the box so that it would not cry and then fall asleep in his clothes.[61]

This pattern of conflict between life and death is clearly discernible in these contrasting passages. McCarthy's critique of American modernity is such that the balance of the conflict is decided in favor of death; John Grady, Eduardo and Magdalena join Margaret and other lesser figures in the undiscovered country.

That this should be so reflects the principal theme of both the John Grady texts. He is an idealized figure, a truly gracious hero who has taken to heart the values that inform his culture. But that culture is structured on illusion, on the myth of the pastoral and the exceptionalism of which it is a function. John Grady is indeed a new Adam but the garden which his mythology has promised him cannot exist and the romantic ideal of love has involved him in conflicts of emotion, class and possession that he cannot accept or understand. The loss of the paradise he found at La Purísima has left him to endure a conflict within himself that leads to self-destruction. Life and death play out their contest not only in the American waste land but in the person of the American hero. He desires the idyllic "home in the west," a house in the hills which he will restore for himself[62] and which he will share with his beautiful young wife in the manner of so many romantic western movies. But the darkness is in his heart at the loss of Alejandra and his consequent self-destructiveness is evident throughout the text, overshadowing his virtues and isolating him from the advice of those who perceive his folly. Billy in particular is most concerned since he knows the object of John Grady' affection. He is perhaps jealous. He is certainly forthright:

> Do I think your crazy? he said. No. I dont. You've rewrote the book for crazy. If all you are is crazy then all them poor bastards in the loonybin that they're feedin under the door need to be set loose in the street.[63]

This self-destructiveness is apparent in John Grady's refusal to give best to the wild stallion that he tames. Already lame from a fall from the horse he insists on roping it in the barn at night despite the confined space and the fact that the horse is "crazed"[64] and racing madly up and down the barn in the dark. He also rides out to work with the cattle although barely able to walk. But his principal act of self-destructiveness is, of course, his decision to try to take Magdalena away from the White Lake. This is another of McCarthy's "doomed enterprises." The illusory nature of John Grady's passion for the unfortunate girl has already been pointed out.[65] He desires the comforts of hearth and home but his love is an *amour fou* and he attempts the mythic task of rescuing the fair maiden from imprisonment by the evil oppressor.[66] McCarthy subverts the myth and John Grady acts out the anti-myth. His antagonist, the epitome of the destructive macho, the extreme of masculinity, is the final representation of patriarchal oppression, rivaling judge Holden as McCarthy's ultimate "dangerous man".

As the theme of oedipal conflict has waned in McCarthy's later work as far as conflict with the natural father is concerned, so at the last the conflict focuses on the mythic surrogate whose paternal role encompasses not only the possession of the beloved female, her actual ownership,[67] but also the possession of the voice and even the power of "writing." This supports the notion that the oedipal conflict of these texts is a metaphor for the writer's own struggle to emancipate himself from "the voice of the fathers." John Grady sacrifices himself to revenge the death of Magdalena. In so doing he also stops that voice:

> He felt Eduardo's blade slip from his rib and cross his upper stomach and pass on. It took his breath away. He made no effort to step or parry. He brought his knife up underhand from the knee and slammed it home and staggered back. He heard the clack of the Mexican's teeth as his jaw clapped shut. Eduardo's knife dropped with a light splash into the small pool of standing water at his feet and he turned away. Then he looked back. The way a man might look getting on a train. The handle of the hunting knife jutted from the underside of his jaw. He reached and touched it. His mouth was clenched in a grimace. His jaw was nailed to his upper skull and he held the handle in both hands as if he would withdraw it but he did not.[68]

There is greater irony in this text than in McCarthy's other work. Eduardo has given fatherly advice. His vision of the world is bleak and without illusion, conditioned by the Mexico that corroded the idealism of the Dueña Alfonsa:

Your kind cannot bear that the world be ordinary. That it contain nothing save what stands before one. But the Mexican world is a world of adornment only and underneath it is very plain indeed.[69]

Billy knows that Eduardo's view of John Grady is only too true:

Your friend is in the grip of an irrational passion. Nothing you say to him will matter. He has in his head a certain story. A story of how things will be. In this story he will be happy. What is wrong with this story?
You tell me.
What is wrong with this story is that it is not a true story. Men have in their minds a picture of how the world will be. How they will be in that world. The world may be many different ways for them but there is one world that will never be and that is the world they dream of.[70]

This mythoclastic vision lies at the heart of McCarthy's fiction. The dream world to which Eduardo refers is that of America itself. This contrasts with the advice of the blind maestro, "I think you ought to follow your heart, the old man said. That's all I ever thought about anything."[71] "A man is always right to pursue the thing he loves. No matter of it kills him? I think so. Yes. No matter even then."[72] In this regard the maestro appears as the oracle, the mythic seer, dispensing fatal prophecy, accompanied by his female "priestess." But Eduardo has a darker, more penetrating vision and speaks further hard truths even as he cuts the life from John Grady. His advice is profound and goes to the heart of the matter; "Change your mind, he said. Go back. Choose life. You are young."[73] He expresses the conflict between life and death that informs the text as a whole. He perceives that John Grady's fatal choice has already been made:

In his dying the suitor will see that it is his hunger for mysteries that has undone him. Whores. Superstition. Finally death. For that is what has brought you here. That is what you are seeking.[74]

Not only does John Grady shut the mythoclastic mouth of the infernal speaker of truths, he also stills the writing hand. Eduardo's egotism leads him to sign his work, carving his initial on John Grady's thigh, one stroke at a time.[75] The final irony of the text is that only the egotist can write the world; in Eduardo we see both a mocking self-portrait and, also, the rival writer whose voice must be overcome, even at the expense of self-annihilation.

This final reflexivity is confirmed in the Epilogue to the text. The mysterious traveler that the aged Billy encounters on the road, and who he mistakes at first for death, engages the bewildered old man in another interpolated tale, after the manner of *The Crossing*. The dreamer who dreams of a dreamer occupies a position analogous to that of the writer who must enter into the world of his creation as though it had a life of its own. It is significant that this dream is peopled by those ancients whose relics and remains have occurred so regularly throughout McCarthy's work, reminding us of our cosmic insignificance and of the fact that our own artifacts are created from the "fragments" of those of other cultures from the past.[76] This section of the text veers away from the conventions of realism in a manner that recalls other McCarthy texts but is the exception here. That a passing *hombre de camino* should be a philosopher versed in literary theory owes more to magic realism than to the conventional American version. The two travelers sit by an Arizona turnpike and discuss perception and subjectivity:

> Did you see it or did you just think you did?
> The man smiled. Que pregunta, he said.[77] What would be the difference?
> . . .
> I think you see just whatever's in front of you.
> Yes. I dont think that.[78]

There is a sense that both speakers in this dialogue serve to express in dialectic form McCarthy's own beliefs about narrative. Billy perceives that the dreamer's dream could be a fiction: "You could still have made them up. . . . It's like the picture of your life in that map. . . . It aint your life. A picture aint a thing. It's just a picture."[79] The text expresses McCarthy's scepticism regarding maps, standing as they do for those intellectual grids that we impose upon the world, those myths that may both energize and deceive, those intellectual constructs that are the culture which, despite its limitations, is all we have:

> You aint said whether your map was any use to you or not.
> . . .
> For now I can only say that I had hoped for a sort of calculus that would sum the convergence of map and life when life was done. For within their limitations there must be a common shape or shared domain between the telling and the told. And if that is so then the

picture also in whatever partial form must have a direction to it and if it does then whatever is to come must lie in its path.[80]

The weakness of map and picture lies in their stasis, their removal from time:

> The picture seeks to seize and immobilize within its own configurations what it never owned. Our map knows nothing of time.[81]

To take account of time is to be involved in history:

> You may say that he (the traveler in the dream) has no substance and therefore no history but my view is that whatever he may be or of whatever made he cannot exist without a history. And the ground of that history is not different from yours or mine for it is the predicate life of men that assures us of our own reality and that of all about us.[82]

The dreams of the Epilogue are metaphors for fictive narrative and I have already argued that, for McCarthy, only fiction can effectively portray the complexity of the world and our actions within it. But the most powerful narratives of a given culture are its myths, and these do not present to us the reality of the world. Thus narrative must be sceptical of myth. But Paz reminds us of Lévi-Strauss's assertion: ". . . any deciphering of a myth is another myth."[83] That this is the essential structure of McCarthy's work as a whole is what I argue throughout this book. The passage expresses this central conviction:

> The events of the waking world . . . are forced upon us and the narrative is the unguessed axis along which they must be strung. It falls to us to weigh and sort and order these events. It is we who assemble them into the story that is us. Each man is the bard of his own existence. That is how he is joined to the world. For escaping from the world's dream of him this is at once his penalty and his reward.[84]

The pursuit of freedom involves the endless need for narratives:

> These dreams and these acts are driven by a terrible hunger. They seek to meet a need which they can never satisfy, and for that we must be grateful.[85]

Herein lies the vocation of the creator of narratives. Despite the fact that our myths deceive us and we are engaged in "The unmappable world of our journey,"[86] McCarthy asserts that our concerns must remain inescapably human:

> Every man's death is a standing in for every other. And since death comes to all there is no way to abate the fear of it except to love the man who stands for us. We are not waiting for his history to be written. He passed here long ago. That man is all men and who stands in the dock for us until our own time come and we must stand for him. Do you love him, that man? Will you honor the path he has taken? Will you listen to his tale?[87]

The echo of John Donne's humanism is very clear.[88] If McCarthy's concern is with narrative and myth what could be more human than these two means of placing order in the world?

The Epilogue does not conclude with the traveler's farewell. Instead it concludes the story of Billy Parham and in so doing confirms the text's vision of the American waste land, the significance of water in that mythic landscape, and the relation of both to patriarchy's life giving other—the female. Joan Didion reminds us of a definition of the American West: "'The West begins,' Bernard DeVoto wrote, 'where the average annual rainfall drops below twenty inches.'"[89] The waste land image is confirmed by McCarthy. Billy's grief at the death of John Grady drives him back on the road:

> In the oncoming years a terrible drought struck west Texas. He moved on. There was no work in that country anywhere. Pasture gates stood open and sand drifted in the roads and after a few years it was rare to see stock of any kind and he rode on. Days of the world. Years of the world. Till he was old.[90]

The rhythmic and emotive language of the final three short phrases of this passage serves to create a different atmosphere in this final section of the text. The tone has become elegiac. All that remains for Billy are grief and regret. After dreaming of his dead sister he acknowledges that his vision of the world has proved false:

> He woke and lay in the dark and the cold and he thought of her and of his brother dead in Mexico. In everything that he'd ever thought about the world and about his life in it he'd been wrong.[91]

But the possibility of consolation remains even in this arid landscape. Water and the female are the means of this mythic grace:

> He drank one evening from a spring beneath a cottonwood, leaning to bow his mouth and suck from the cold silk top of the water and watch the minnows drift and recover in the current beneath him. There was a tin cup on a stob and he took it down and sat holding it. He'd not seen a cup at a spring in years and he held it in both hands as had thousands before him unknown to him yet joined in sacrament. He dipped the cup into the water and raised it cool and dripping to his mouth.[92]

Unlike the rain outside the Juarez brothel at the beginning of the tale this water is associated with life rather than death. Billy is taken in by a family "just outside of Portales[93] New Mexico." Billy's wanderings are at an end; he stands at the final portal of his life. He receives at the last that freely given hospitality that has been one of the cardinal virtues in McCarthy's world. More than this; he is adopted by a family and finds a home at last—the only one of McCarthy's wanderers to do so. Billy experiences a deliverance of great significance in these final days. Throughout *The Crossing* he told no tales of his own. Now he can create his own narratives:

> In the evening after supper sometimes the woman would invite him to play cards with them and sometimes he and the children would sit at the kitchen table and he'd tell them about horses and cattle and the old days. Sometimes he'd tell them about Mexico.[94]

Within this family context patriarchal mythology is inverted—the lost male is rescued by the female:

> One night he dreamed that Boyd was in the room with him but he would not speak for all that he called out to him. When he woke the woman was sitting on his bed with her hand on his shoulder.
> Mr Parham are you all right?
> Yes mam. I'm sorry. I was dreamin, I reckon.
> You sure you okay?
> Yes mam.
> Did you want me to bring you a sup of water?[95]

Her greatest boon is simply to assure him that he has an identity, that he can be known, that he is witnessed:

She patted his hand. Gnarled, ropescarred, speckled from the sun and the years of it. The ropy veins that bound them to his heart. There was map enough for men to read. There God's plenty of signs and wonders to make a landscape. To make a world. She rose to go.

Betty, he said.

Yes.

I'm not what you think I am. I aint nothin. I dont know why you put up with me.

Well, Mr Parham, I know who you are. And I do know why. You go to sleep now. I'll see you in the morning.

Yes mam.[96]

The final fragment of the text is the Dedication: it is not clear to whom or what it is directed. It does reflect themes present in this text and throughout McCarthy's work.

> *I will be your child to hold*
> *And you be mine when I am old*
> *The world grows cold*
> *The heathen rage*
> *The story's told*
> *Turn the page.*

Billy Parham ceases to be a "motherless child" in his old age. As he wrote McCarthy himself approached the completion of his seventh decade, albeit with a new wife. He reminds us of his work's intertextuality by quoting Psalm 2. The heathen rage on the waste land and the psalm concludes with the oedipal warning "Kiss the son lest he be angry, and ye perish from the way, when his wrath is kindled but a little."[97] If this is related to the author's struggle to make his own voice heard then he can now, at last, assert that "the story's told." But the story would be nothing without the reader, so we must "turn the page." Many have found the dedication enigmatic. In my view it expresses ideas that recur throughout McCarthy's work. I suggest that it reinforces the elegiac tone of *Cities of the Plain*. Whether it is more than an elegy for the mythic west remains to be seen.

In this chapter I have tried to indicate that those critics who have consigned *Cities of the Plain* to a minor place in the McCarthy canon, either by forthright denigration or simply by ignoring it, have failed to discern the density of allusion and richness of theme that lies beneath its apparent realism. It contains some of the author's most effective depictions of action and his most convincing and effective use of dialogue. It completes his mythoclastic vision of the American west as a waste land. It strengthens his relation to Eliot in this respect, reiterating the crucial image of water in many forms.[98] It portrays the mythic landscape as both pastoral and infernal, rural and urban, homeland and other. Within this mythology is acted out the existential struggle between life and death. The excesses of patriarchy and the symbolic order lie at the heart of the waste land's aridity. Above all, this deathliness is associated with the loss of the female. Water and the female are linked throughout, in a manner that goes far beyond what Eliot expressed. *Cities of the Plain* also concludes the stories of the two heroes so sadly betrayed by the myth of the cowboy, that product of pastoralism and exceptionalism that leads them both to seek a world that no longer exists, if it ever did. The dynamism of the tales is provided by the ardenthearted romantic John Grady Cole. His first quest for the female is defeated by patriarchal power and his culture fails to provide him with the worldliness to learn from this experience. His ardentheartedness is turned inwards against himself. He becomes a divided and self destructive soul who seeks both love and death in the person of Magdalena, Alejandra's inverse.[99] Ironically it is Billy Parham, the existential wanderer, who finds repose at the last, albeit after a lifetime as "un hombre del camino." His defective heart "still rattled in his chest, no will of his."[100] It has served to sustain him, reminding us of McCarthy's use of this as a significant image of the spontaneity and inherent vitality that is all that we have with which to oppose our annihilating cosmic insignificance. Finally in *Cities of the Plain* McCarthy concludes with a last interpolated tale, an allegory for the task of creating narrative. Against the destructiveness of false epistemologies and mythologies that deny history he asserts the primacy of narrative for both writer and reader. This final assertion is humanistic in character; that this is an unfashionable position may help to explain the reaction of such as Josyph.[101] If McCarthy asserts that "all is telling" he also makes it clear that this "all" is a very great deal and *Cities of the Plain* represents a fitting conclusion to the author's literary and personal journey from the "old weird America" of the Appalachian mountains to the mythic West.

Chapter Fifteen

No Country for Old Men

This is a goddamned homicidal lunatic, Ed Tom.
Yeah. I don't think he's a lunatic though.
Well what would you call him?
I don't know.

The publication dates of the Border Trilogy spanned the six years from 1992 to 1998, indicating that McCarthy had spent an average of three years writing each of the latter two texts. The elegiac tone of *Cities of the Plain*, noted in the previous chapter, (mis)led some to suppose that it might be his last novel.[1] The passing of a further seven years without literary issue did nothing to dispel this supposition. McCarthy scholars and admirers learned that the author had married again and had another son, that he showed every sign of leading a settled and comfortable life and that he was taking an active interest in the doings of the Santa Fe Institute. In 2005 however conclusions regarding the possible cessation of literary creation on McCarthy's part were shown to be erroneous by the publication of his ninth novel, *No Country for Old Men*.[2]

As with all his previous novels critical reception was decidedly mixed. A number of his admirers privately expressed disappointment; others responded with enthusiasm to what they saw as a further addition to McCarthy's already impressive literary accomplishments. Literary magazines and newspapers were as divided as always in their responses: writing in the Times Literary Supplement, Michael Gorra saw the novel as lacking the stature of his earlier work, drawing a parallel with Graham Greene's distinction "between his novels and his entertainments" and suggesting that "Only those who expect more will be disappointed."[3] Joyce Carol Oates is one of several reviewers who suggest that the sheriff in *No Country for Old Men*, in expressing conservative views (in the current US sense) "speaks for McCarthy," a view which seems to misread both the character of the sheriff and the thrust of McCarthy's work in general.[4] It should be clear that my reading of the author's work as a mythoclastic assault on America's exceptionalist vision of itself categorises him as anything but "conservative" in the current political sense, although his vision of humanity as irredeemably "fallen" is, of course, conservative in an older sense of that much contested word. William Deresiewicz, writing in *The Nation*, compares *No Country for Old Men* to McCarthy's previous work and finds it "superficial and perfunctory."[5] J.M.White is altogether more admiring, claiming that McCarthy's "nine tomes . . . will stand, . . . as 'monuments of unageing intellect.'"[6] Roger D. Hodge pens the most positive remarks of all: in so doing he takes to task the novel's detractors: ". . . there is something about the rough treatment this novel has received that is symptomatic of the shallowness and haste that characterizes so much of our literary culture. It's hard to miss the malice that creeps into these essays but not so easy to explain it."[7] Various "easy" explanations do suggest themselves but Hodge is too prudent to mention any of them. My own view is that many find McCarthy impossible to categorise; his pessimistic essentialism regarding "human nature" together with his evident heroic literary seriousness place him outside the category that provides so much of the current language of literary criticism and that we call "postmodern." Thus McCarthy's fiction leads reviewers into territory whose maps they have ceased to trust or have never possessed—reflecting, ironically, McCarthy's own distrust of "maps" of all kinds.

If the publication of a new novel came as a surprise to many, this was compounded by what seemed an even less likely occurrence when R.B. Woodward published a second McCarthy interview.[8] However, one aspect of the novel itself does not cause surprise; its form is unlike those that have gone before. This is unsurprising because the same thing could be said of each new novel on its first appearance. The text features alternate chapters in italic print; sections in italics have featured in a number of previous novels, *The Orchard Keeper, Outer Dark, Suttree, Blood Meridian* (the Epilogue) and *Cities of the Plain* (the Dedication). In each case these sections were distinguished from the rest of the text for some specific purpose, although that purpose varied from text to text. In this case the italicised sections are much more extensive than any that have gone before and serve to differentiate the novel's two narrative threads in ways that are both structural and stylistic. These two threads, although interwoven, remain strictly separate in crucial ways and serve to give *No Country for Old Men* a literary form that is very different from that of previous works. At the same time its eclecticism and mythoclastic character are of a piece with these previous works in ways that I expand upon in what follows.

Throughout my preceding chapters I have traced the occurrence of oedipal conflict in McCarthy's work, interpreting it, in part, as a metaphor for the writer's struggle to emancipate himself from the "the voice of the [literary] fathers" and suggesting that the intensity of this conflict diminishes in the texts of the Border Trilogy, becoming distinctly muted in *Cities of the Plain*. This interpretation is supported by McCarthy's remark to Woodward concerning the "ugly fact . . . that books are made out of other books."[9] McCarthy's literary eclecticism might be construed as a contradiction of both this perceived "ugliness" and the lack of confidence in his own voice that it might seem to imply. However as I have tried to demonstrate in previous chapters McCarthy "quotes" other writer's work either to reflect their mythoclasm (Cervantes, Eliot, Melville, for example) or else to invert their meanings (the Gadarene Swine, the Western). In addition his "quotations" tend to be indirect or disguised, as in the use of the phrase "rock and no water and the sandy trace" in *Blood Meridian*.[10] In *No Country for Old Men* however the oedipal fire seems to have burned down at last.

I read the text in this manner for two reasons. Firstly, the literary eclecticism of the novel is announced in a very direct manner. Even those unfamiliar with the poetry of W.B. Yeats would be likely to recognise the title *as* a quotation and in the Google age researching the source occupies a matter of moments only. If we compare this with a previous "quotation" from Yeats, in *The Orchard Keeper*, the contrast is marked.[11] It requires an intimate knowledge of the poet's work to recognise that distinctly indirect first example; McCarthy's eclecticism is becoming more overt.

The generic roots of the novel are even more obvious; *No Country for Old Men* is a crime novel; its cars, automatic weapons, motel rooms, corporate offices and city locations are the province of the genre developed by Chandler, Hammett, Cain, Ellroy and given cinematic form as film noir and its derivatives. But the Sheriff and his deputies, the hunter Moss, the riders on horseback and the landscape of desert, plain and river are, of course, elements of the Western and the Southwest is the quintessential location of its mythic history. In this as in other respects the novel is a hybrid. That his eclecticism is now so overt suggests that McCarthy regards it as less "ugly" than was initially the case; consequently we may infer that he feels that he has made his own voice heard at last, a conclusion that many have reached long since.

If this were the only reason for drawing such a conclusion the argument would be weak, but the nature of the novel's central character reinforces the case; Sheriff Ed Tom Bell is no Oedipus, no wayward rebellious son, fleeing paternal authority and desperate to make his own way in the world. On the contrary, Bell is himself the father in this text and an aging father at that. In addition he has the father's voice and the narrative's italicised sections are in that voice. He speaks to us directly and in so doing reveals the other structural means of conveying the fading of the Oedipal theme. Bell speaks from the heart; he examines his own life, beliefs and values, measuring them against his experience of the world. In other words he conveys that new thing in McCarthy, the revelation of the inner man, of character, personality and belief. In previous texts only Suttree[12] has come close to being revealed from within in this way; indeed given the allegorical nature of so much of McCarthy's writing the inner lives of most of his characters are not revealed at all since they exist as types,[13] the power of their stories lying in the intensity of the narrative, the dynamism of the action, the convincing rendering of dialogue and the vivid use of language—lyrical, majestic and colloquial by turns. To this can be added the power of the allegorical meanings themselves and the multitude of other theories and ideas that McCarthy weaves into his works, works united by the conception of narrative as the "category of categories"[14] conveyed in the words of the ex-priest in the church at Huisiachepic in *The Crossing*, "Rightly heard all tales are one."[15]

What Bell expresses are the thoughts and emotions of an aging man, a father whose only child is dead: *"Me and my wife has been married thirty-one years. No children. We lost a girl but I wont talk about that."*[16] He knows a father's grief, none greater than that due to the loss of a child. The poignancy of this loss is subtly accentuated a full 195 pages later:

> *I could stand back off and smile about such thoughts as them but I still have em. I don't make excuses for the way I think. Not no more. I talk to my daughter. She would be thirty now. That's all right. I don't care how that sounds. I like talking to her. Call it superstition or whatever you want. I know over the years I have give her the heart I always wanted for myself and that's all right. That's why I listen to her. I know I'll always get the best from her.*[17]

Nothing could be further from the Oedipal rage of Suttree, the kid, Blevins or Boyd Parham. Of course the two passages here quoted contradict each other. Close reading of Bell's monologues reveals that this is a pattern that runs throughout the novel. Many of his early pronouncements, often expressing the confident simplicities of the 'good old boy' of Southwestern tradition, are contradicted by later passages revealing that Bell's simple faith has not stood the test of bitter experience. Like so many of McCarthy's protagonists he finds that the world deals harshly with the myths that his culture has provided as his guide through life. His impotence in the face of the drug wars, funded, as he rightly remarks *"with our own money,"*[18] forces him to decide to quit his life's work as Sheriff, but his meditation on this event concerns his life as a whole. He reflects on his 'cowardice' in deserting his comrades in action in World War Two,[19] his guilt at being forced to accept a decoration for this act and for allowing this mark of 'heroism' to count in his favour when running for sheriff in the first place. He complains that the country has gone from being a place where folks could live in peace to being a place of violence and insecurity but later acknowledges that *"this country has a strange kind of history and a damned bloody one too."*[20] He knows that *"there's peace officers along this border getting rich off of narcotics"* and that this *"is just a damned abomination."*[21] He has discovered with patriotic astonishment that Wells, somehow involved in the slaughter that has overwhelmed his world, was "a ex-army colonel . . . Regular army. Twenty-four years service."[22] He notes that the drug traders had found it prudent to assassinate a federal judge. But his act of acceptance of his own 'failure' expresses the wisdom of resignation rather than the folly of despair:

> *Part of it was I always thought I could at least someway put things right and I guess I just don't feel that way no more. I don't know what I do feel like. I feel like them old people I was talkin about. Which aint goin to get better neither. I'm bein asked to stand for something that I don't have the same belief in I once did. Asked to believe in something I might not hold with the way I once did. That's the problem. I failed at it even when I did. Now I've seen it held to the light. Seen any number of believers fall away. I've been forced to look at it again and I've been forced to look at myself. For better or for worse I do not know. I don't know that I would even advise you to throw in with me, and I never had them sorts of doubts before. If I'm wiser in the ways of the world it come at a price. Pretty good price too. When I told her I was quittin she at first didn't take me to mean it literally but I told her I did so mean it. I told her I hoped the people of this county would have better sense than to even vote for me. I told her it didn't feel right takin their money. She said well you don't mean that and I told her I meant it ever word. . . . And she smiled and she said: You aim to quit while you're ahead? And I said no mam I just aim to quit. I aint ahead by a damn sight. I never will be.*[23]

Bell's speech expands on Billy Parham's conclusion at the end of *Cities of the Plain*: "In everything that he'd ever thought about the world and about his life in it he'd been wrong."[24] Bell will survive because he has the consolation of his love for his wife, a love that he perceives to be returned; there is no Oedipal contest in relation to the faithful Loretta. The fading of the Oedipal structuring of McCarthy's texts is signified very powerfully in Bell's recollection of his father:

> *My daddy always told me just to do the best you knew how and to tell the truth. He said there was nothing to set a man's mind at ease like wakin up in the morning and not havin to decide who you were. And if you done something wrong just stand up and say you done it and say you're sorry and get on with it. Don't haul stuff around with you. I guess all that sounds pretty simple today. Even to me.*[25]

Bell understands the limitations of his father's notions. He acknowledges that he rebelled somewhat himself: "*I might have strayed from all of that some as a younger man . . .*" The crucial point is that now he sees things differently: "*. . . but when I got back on that road I pretty much decided not to quit it again and I didn't.*"[26] The contrast with Suttree's protestations could not be more vivid:

> In my father's last letter he said that the world is run by those willing to take the responsibility for the running of it. If it is life that you feel you are missing I can tell you where to find it. In the law courts, in business, in government. There is nothing occurring in the streets. Nothing but a dumbshow composed of the helpless and the impotent.
>   *From all old seamy throats of elders, musty books, I've salvaged not a word.* (my italics)[27]

This contrast is rendered conclusively in Bell's dream, recounted on the book's final page and symbolising the passing of the Oedipal turn in McCarthy's works:

> *. . . it was like we was both back in older times and I was on horseback goin through the mountains of a night. Goin through this pass in the mountains. It was cold and there was snow on the ground and he rode past me and kept on goin. Never said nothing. He just rode on past and he had this blanket wrapped around him and he had his head down and when he rode past I seen he was carryin fire in a horn the way people used to do and I could see the horn from the light inside of it. About the color of the moon. And in the dream I knew that he was goin on ahead and that he was fixin to make a fire somewhere out there in all that dark and all that*

cold and I knew that whenever I got there he would be there. And then I woke up.[28]

The phallic symbolism of the horn of fire stands in this case for life, continuity and civilization. Thus the novel closes with an image that is in contrast to its other phallic signifier, the ubiquitous gun, instrument of equally ubiquitous death.

What can this dying away of such a consistent theme mean for us in reading McCarthy's work? It is reasonable to suppose that it simply reflects the fact that he is himself now a man approaching old age. In biblical terms, always significant for McCarthy, he has passed his allotted three-score years and ten.[29] But the sense of McCarthy as a critic of his culture and his times remains as strong as ever. If my interpretation is correct, then, as I have already argued, we can assume that he has begun to feel that he no longer has to strive to usurp the voice of the literary fathers and that his own voice can now be heard clearly, even if he remains aware of his debt to "other books."

It should be noted also that these italicised passages, Bell's monologues, internal, and/or addressed to some assumed audience (ourselves), are realist in character. Their colloquial language and patterns of speech reveal that McCarthy has lost none of his gift for the creation of a convincing "speaking" voice. These sequences, unique in his oeuvre, are mimetic in character, intended to take us into the mind and emotions of a fully realised human personality. This mimetic and humanistic thread of the narrative is generically rooted in the "western" aspect of the novel's antecedents. When *No Country for Old Men* is associated with the previous Southwestern novels we may read the series as tracing the historical line from the mid-nineteenth century of *Blood Meridian*, through the mid and late twentieth century of the Trilogy and into the twenty-first century of the Border and the "drug wars" that have made it no country for old men such as Sheriff Bell.

It is generally accepted that the two quintessentially American genres are the western and the crime novel and that the latter takes the moral, political and psychological preoccupations and mythic forms of the former into the urban setting of the twentieth century. The hybrid nature of *No Country for Old Men* reflects this literary transformation, incorporating both genres in a single text, and providing the vehicle for the violent contemporary aspect of the narrative; it also provides the alternative narrative strand interweaved with Bell's internal monologue. The generic hybridisation thus created is matched by the contrast in the style and purpose of the two strands and between the characters who dominate each, Sheriff Bell and his implacable adversary Anton Chigurh. This second strand, not printed in italics and devoted to eidetic descriptions of action that specifically exclude considerations of character and psychology matches the bulk of McCarthy's previous writing. Its fierce pace and the tight, minimalist style of its action sequences make the book a compelling read. I completed it in two sessions, only interrupted by the need for sleep; many other readers have made similar claims. Although he seems to have largely abandoned the complex, highly wrought and often lyrical prose passages that punctuate his previous novels, in this latest work McCarthy continues to match form and content in a manner that produces a highly polished result; and like all highly polished things its glistening surface is raised on an adamantine base and those that feature Chigurh have the spare precision of the killer himself:

> The headlights picked up some kind of large bird sitting on the aluminium bridgerail up ahead and Chigurh pushed the button to let the window down. Cool air coming in off the lake. He took the pistol from beside the box and cocked and levelled it out the window, resting the barrel on the rearview mirror. The pistol had been fitted with a silencer sweated onto the end of the barrel. The silencer was made out of brass mapp-gas burners fitted into a hairspray can and the whole thing stuffed with fiberglass roofing insulation and painted flat black. He fired just as the bird spread its wings.[30]

It is significant that Chigurh does not know what kind of bird this is. The contrast with Bell is acute; the sheriff is happier on a horse than in a "prowler" and considerate even of a dead hawk found in the road.[31]

The hybrid nature of the novel has a further aspect that increases its complexity, in further contradiction of those who have found it superficial. As already noted this second narrative thread gives no indications of the motivation or psychology of the characters depicted. We encounter their actions and interactions and hear their conversations but in respect of their inner being we learn only what we can deduce from their acts. The contrast with the Sheriff Bell thread is complete. In order to interpret this second thread we must first distinguish its own nature and this means reading that of its dominant character. As Guillermin has noted the refusal of any consideration of motivation or inner life is a characteristic of allegory. In what follows I consider Anton Chigurh, arguing that he is another of those allegorical figures with which McCarthy has populated his mythoclastic texts. Interpreting Chigurh will complete my reading of the text and make clear the final significance of McCarthy's choice of hybrid literary form.

A comparison between *No Country for Old Men* and *The Big Sleep* (1939)[32] is appropriate here; representative of the "hard-boiled" crime novel, the whole of Chandler's narrative is given in the first person and in the voice of Marlowe. As ever McCarthy inverts the essence of a text which he has chosen as an intertextual reference. The detective Marlowe is another character drawn from American mythology. His journey down the "dark streets" of urban American night always concludes with revelation and closure; Marlowe remains untainted by the corruption of the world in which he moves. He brings light into dark places and ensures the destruction of the "corrupting female." He succeeds in his pursuit of the truth and is able to find and despatch the criminals who inhabit his world. However, if Sheriff Bell is no Oedipus, he is no Marlowe either and his quest ends in an acknowledgement of inadequacy and failure. But if McCarthy inverts the mythology of the masculine hero he also rejects Chandler's radical misogyny; there is no *femme fatale* in *No Country For Old Men*, quite the contrary.

In other respects however the two novels bear direct comparison. The economy of style is similar. Both portray a world of ubiquitous corruption and criminal violence; in each case the roots of this corruption lie in an ill-founded belief that human appetites can be controlled by a legal prohibition that large numbers of people find irrelevant to their own experience, a fact that Bell does not understand.[33] Finally we should note that the "big sleep" is that of death. In his second interview with Woodward, McCarthy made a remark as significant as that concerning the "ugly fact" mentioned in the first. In discussing the themes of his latest novel he pointed up the centrality of the fact of death. "Death is a major issue in the world. For you, for me, for all of us. It just is. To not be able to talk about it is very odd."[34] It can come as no surprise to learn that a man into his eighth decade should feel the need to contemplate mortality. We may presume that Sheriff Bell, himself well on in years (he was a young man in World War Two), is similarly aware; indeed given the circumstance of his profession as they are presented in the text he could not fail to be acutely so, even if he were a young man in his prime. It is reasonable to presume that this has been responsible in no small part for Bell's period of reflection and his decision to pass judgement upon the manner in which he has lived up to his ideals. But all McCarthy's works have featured death to a greater or lesser extent. In *Suttree* in particular Suttree himself is obsessed by the image of his stillborn twin sibling; life and death battle it out for him; life wins, but it is a close run thing as he almost succumbs to typhoid. Of course it is easy to see that *No Country for Old Men* features a great many deaths, most of them violent and not a few due to the relentless and unstoppable efforts of Chigurh. I will return to his significance later but first I want to consider other aspects of the text's representation of mortality. In fact death is mentioned very frequently throughout and in many different circumstances. The novel's first words, spoken by Bell, are "*I sent one boy to the gas chamber at Huntsville.*" The young man had murdered a girl-friend, "*. . . had been planning to kill somebody for as long a he could remember. Said if they turned him out he would do it again.*"[35] Moss tells Carla Jean "If I don't come back tell Mother I love her;" she rejects the joke: "Your mother's dead Llewelyn."[36] Moss's decision to take the money is clearly the result of a death-wish. As he returns bringing water to the wounded drug dealer (already dead of course), compounding his initial suicidal action, he feels himself "A trespasser. Among the dead. Don't get weird on me, he said. You ain't one of em. Not yet."[37] He remarks that he is "Too dumb to live."[38] As the killers search for him in the darkness he asserts "Now you're goin to die."[39] And shortly afterwards, "You need to be put out of your misery. Be the best thing for everbody."[40] Like Bell, Moss has seen death in war: "Waiting. He'd had this feeling before. In another country. He never thought he'd have it again."[41] When Carla Jean asks after the truck Moss answers "Gone the way of all flesh. Nothin's forever."[42] Bell speaks of attending an execution and opines that "*The ones that really ought to be on death row will never make it.*"[43] I have already noted that Bell's daughter is dead; how or why we do not know. As he meditates on his family history he states that "*. . . the dead have more claims on you than what you might want to admit to or even what you might know about and them claims can be very strong indeed.*" He goes on to relate a newspaper story: "*. . . this couple in California they would rent out rooms to old people and then kill em and bury em in the yard and cash their social security checks. They'd torture em first, I don't know why.*"[44] Carla Jean's mother has cancer; by the end of the book she is dead: "Her funeral was on a cold and windy day in March."[45] Bell relates his wartime trauma: "*I lost a whole squad of men. . . . They died and I got a medal.*"[46] He considers the social aspect of death as old men must: "*I've lost a lot of friends over these last few years. Not all of em older then me neither. One of the things you realise about getting older is that not everbody is goin to get older with you.*"[47] Moss tells his hitchhiker that he is wearing his wild boar's tush for "*. . . a dead somebody.*"[48] In warning his young companion he is actually describing his own death-haunted behaviour: "Most people'll run from their own mother to get to hug death by the neck. They cant wait to see him."[49] Bell's conversation with Ellis is punctuated by references to death. The man who shot Ellis "*. . . died in prison.*"[50] Harold was killed in the war "*. . . dyin in a ditch somewhere . . . Seventeen year old.*"[51] Uncle Mac "*. . . was shot down on his own porch in Hudspeth County.*"[52] "This country will kill you in a heartbeat and still people love it."[53] And all this excludes the slaughter carried out by Chigurh and the drug gangs: *No Country for Old Men* is indeed a death-haunted text. George Guillemin identifies McCarthy's texts as essentially melancholic. I have already referred to Poland's suggestion that "the landscape in much western writing functions more like a character in itself and imprints on the human characters its own qualities."[54] The desert landscape may be thought to have imprinted itself on Bell and Moss both, but with differing results. The desert's indifference to human life is challenged by Moss with fatal results: for the reflective Bell the consequence is ". . . defeat. It was being beaten. More bitter to him than death."[55] If McCarthy has shaken off the melancholy associated with the task of challenging the literary fathers he continues to express the twin griefs resulting from his vision of human insignificance in an indifferent universe and the consequences of his culture's overreaching gnosis. As ever he counters this melancholy by expressing it in vital and compelling literary form.

The ironic paradox of this vitality has been apparent throughout McCarthy's fiction. Much of what he written has been allegorical in character. Figures such as judge Holden and the "grim triune' of *Outer Dark* are diminished by attempts to read them mimetically; so we turn our attention at last to Chigurh. He is indomitable, all-seeing and entirely without humour or sexuality. He kills without emotion, men and women alike. Drug runners, other hit-men, policemen, motel desk clerks, corporate executives, someone who insults him in a bar, motorists encountered by chance, all are one to him. Chigurh is indeed the "dangerous man" of this text, in one sense the most dangerous American that McCarthy has created. The only way to survive an encounter with him is by the toss of a coin—in other words by chance. He (mis)understands his use of language to be absolute: "I don't have some way to put it. That's the way it is."[56] His eyes are "At once glistening and totally opaque. Like wet stones:"[57] no windows of the soul these. He is impervious to temperature: "It was cold out on the barrial and he had no jacket but he didn't seem to notice."[58] His weapon of choice is the humane killer used to slaughter animals; to him humans, birds and animals are equals.[59] Hurt in a shootout, he treats his own wounds: "Other than a little light sweat on his forehead there was little evidence that his labours had cost him anything at all."[60] When Wells tells him, "You're not outside of death," he speaks more than he knows. Chigurh replies truthfully, "It doesn't mean to me what it means to you."[61] He is equally truthful when he asserts that he is ". . . completely reliable and completely honest."[62] He is not boasting when he says "I have no enemies. I don't permit such a thing."[63] As he explains to Carla Jean, (Chigurh chooses to meet his victims face to face whenever he can, to engage with them in a discourse of life and death) once he has decided on a victim he cannot change his mind: "My word is not dead. Nothing can change that."[64]

> "You're asking me to make myself vulnerable and that I can never do. I have only one way to live. It doesn't allow for special cases. A coin toss perhaps. In this case to small purpose. Most people don't believe that there can be such a person. You can see what a problem that must be for them. How to prevail over that which you refuse to acknowledge the existence of. . . . When I came into your life your life was over."[65]

Although McCarthy gives Chigurh human form, he denies him human qualities. Chigurh's actions and words make his meaning abundantly clear; he is death personified.[66] This explains why it is that Moss does not kill him when he has him under his gun in the Eagle Pass motel.[67] You cannot kill death; even chance and irony fail to accomplish this. Chigurh walks away from the car crash in Midland; it is the drugged boys in the Buick who die. It also explains the constant references to chance and luck in the novel, for who knows when death comes?[68] A single example will suffice but there are many more. At the Eagle Pass motel by the merest chance (from his point of view) "The nightclerk got killed. About as bad a piece of luck as you could have I reckon."[69]

If *No Country for Old Men* has a weakness it lies in the one-dimensional quality of Chigurh. He holds a fascination for the reader that is possessed by all those monstrous figures whose actions are unrestrained by either moral scruple or limitations of intellect or physical resource. Our long repressed infantile appetites still desire omnipotence and find its fictional representations seductive. But Chigurh, although convincing in action and transparent in allegorical meaning remains strangely flat, in contrast to McCarthy's other monsters, the Grim Triune of *Outer Dark*, the all too human Lester Ballard and, above all, judge Holden. Chigurh fades from the text after his car-crash. It is Moss who holds our attention until his demise and Sheriff Bell who retains it to the novel's end. McCarthy has always known that it is the villains who are the most interesting characters of any tale but Chigurh must be read as an exception. It is as if McCarthy is expressing his view of Death by making this personification one of the least compelling of his many literary creations.

It is the generic and stylistic hybridity of *No Country for Old Men*, with its interwoven narrative threads and innovatory form, that give the novel its claim to serious consideration within McCarthy's canon. If the motif that runs through his work is what I have termed the dialectic of insignificance and vitality, Sheriff Bell manifests that dialectic by his acknowledgement of his own insignificance and of the inevitability of his own death, by refusing to "hug death by the neck"[70] and by insisting on facing the truth of his own life, accepting responsibility for that truth and resting on the life-giving support of his wife. If he comes to see the "country" that is his home as a veritable "waste land," it is his union with the life-giving female that enables him to endure. If his inability to apprehend Chigurh is a "failure" at the level of plot, allegorically it is a "success," for the sheriff "chooses life" by avoiding Death personified.

Thus McCarthy combines the mimetic and the allegorical as he weaves together the musings of the realistically human Bell and his one-dimensional opaque opponent. It is this interweaving that lifts the novel from being a simple but utterly compelling 'pulp fiction' read, relying for its success on a racy narrative and a spare, highly polished, minimalistic style and turns it into something more complex and satisfying. Bell is forced to contemplate the approach of the one certain thing in human life. His retrospective on his own life forces him to admit, like all McCarthy's 'heroes', that there are no heroes and that the culture that taught him to believe in them, and that he could become one of them, was false. Above all he has to contemplate what the American West has come to and to see the fate, allegorised in the persons of Moss and Chigurh, of that place that Mrs. Jorgensen, the pioneer wife in John Ford's *The Searchers*, claimed would one day be "A fine good place to be."[71]

Bell reflects on his life as soldier, citizen, lawman, husband and father, his musings prompted by the acknowledgement of life's only certainty, its defining other, held in balance through out McCarthy's work, despite that certainty. I suggest that we may read in the author's latest example of overt, unapologetic eclecticism a musing of his own. Yeats' *Sailing to Byzantium* provides not only the title for the novel but some intimations of that confidence on McCarthy's part that he has succeeded in matching the voices of his great literary forebears and that when he is gone his works will indeed remain, "Monuments of unageing intellect."[72]

Chapter Sixteen

Conclusion

These dreams and these acts are driven by a terrible hunger. They seek
to meet a need which they can never satisfy, and for that we must be
grateful.

—*Cities of the Plain*

In the preceding chapters I have attempted to sketch the literary, geographical, historical and personal context within which Cormac McCarthy has
worked. I have portrayed him as a southern writer, concerned with that
most southern of themes, the relationship between past and present. At the
same time I have suggested that his childhood environment, the Appalachian region of East Tennessee and the urban environs of 50's Knoxville,
have given him a perspective that differs from that of other southern writers
such as Welty and Faulkner. I suggest that he uses the southern gothic style
to express a unique vision of the woods, mountains and creeks of Sevier
County and the stews of urban Knoxville rather than racially divided Mississippi, demoralized sharecropper Georgia or sensual, sophisticated New
Orleans. In so doing McCarthy brings within the purview of contemporary
literature the "old, weird America," that previously expressed itself solely in
the almost lost folk music that Harry Smith helped to preserve. It is only
when McCarthy's personal and cultural journey takes him to the borderlands of the Southwest that he writes of a people and a territory already
made familiar—by the western and crime genres of the popular novel and
the Hollywood movie.

I have given each of McCarthy's available texts a chapter of its own[1]
with a view to treating each as an entity with its own separate existence.
My analysis of each text is intended to stand on its own, just as do the texts
themselves. At the same time my overall aim has been to identify unifying
ideas and common themes within McCarthy's work as a whole, to trace not

only its continuities but its development. I have attempted to give an impression of the range of critical opinion regarding McCarthy's work. The texts have been dealt with in broadly chronological order and this has led me to consider them as falling into two consecutive categories, those rooted in Tennessee and those set in the Southwest. Within this broad categorization I suggest that the novels comprise two trilogies linked by two novels of transition, namely *Suttree* and *Blood Meridian*. *No Country for Old Men* may be seen as a coda to the Southwestern novels. Few would dispute that McCarthy's novels are of much greater significance than his other texts although I claim that the short stories are more interesting than is generally allowed and provide a clear indication both of McCarthy's technical competence, and two of his most insistent themes. I also suggest that *The Gardener's Son* is a complex and evocative work that is worthy of more attention than it is likely to receive, given that the film is not commercially available.[2] Although technically flawed from a performative point of view, *The Stonemason*, which I have treated as a text, expresses McCarthy's oedipal theme in its most direct and intense form.

The central argument of my thesis has been that McCarthy's work can be read as a critique of the myth of American exceptionalism. I have suggested that each of the first five novels comments on a different aspect of this myth, which has itself evolved to take on different meanings as America has evolved. The Tennessee novels variously contest the south's myth of the pastoral and its refusal of history. They attack the religious fundamentalism of the bible belt—itself inherited from the Puritanism and Calvinism of the original settlers of the Eastern seaboard, particularly the Scotch-Irish in the South. They satirize Jefferson's ideal of the self-sufficient yeoman farmer and the mythic figures of the lone hunter of the mountain and forest and the heroic pioneer. They point out the fate of those who were drawn to America's promise of the "more abundant life" only to find Appalachia as deprived as the Irish croft or German ghetto. The southwestern novels contest the republican version of the myth; the political "missionaries" carrying "the last best hope of mankind" across the Mississippi are portrayed as self-destructive, obsessive homicides; their mission of "Manifest Destiny" an exercise in existential atavism. The Border Trilogy addresses the myth of the cowboy, itself a composite of various aspects of exceptionalist mythology. *No Country for Old Men* depicts the death-haunted Borderland that the Southwest has become.

Any thoughts that postmodernism's assertion of the end of the "grand narratives" of western culture might have undermined the power of America's identifying myth will have been dispelled by reactions to the attack on the significantly named World Trade Centre. The incomprehension that greeted this grievous event was clearly informed by the view that America is still the "City on the Hill" standing as an example that can redeem the world, albeit that redemption is now to be economic rather than spiritual. I have characterized McCarthy's fiction therefore as mythoclastic as Guinn has suggested. I have argued that this mythoclasm has involved McCarthy in the creation of his own mythic forms, his anti-myths. I have suggested therefore that attempts to read him in realist or naturalist terms mistake the essential nature of his work.

One of the principal characteristics of McCarthy's novels is their broadly based eclecticism and I have been at pains to try to identify incidences of intertextuality within his work. It has seemed clear to me that McCarthy has made deliberate and highly appropriate references in each of his texts. Many of these have been from non-American sources and this has been another aspect of his mythoclasm in my view, emphasizing the extent to which American culture, has been, and continues to be created from the cultures of the past and denying the possibility of national cultural exclusiveness.[3] Of all the many influences I have identified in McCarthy's work none seems more significant than that of T. S. Eliot. Eliot's image of modernity as a "waste land" recurs throughout McCarthy's work and the notion that "these fragments have I shored against my ruin"[4] seems to inform McCarthy's own eclecticism.

I have suggested that McCarthy has remained a religious writer in a Godless world. His repeated references to the ruined artifacts of lost cultures and the fossilized remains of creatures long extinct serve as reminders of the insignificance of human life within the time span of the life of the earth itself, an insignificance that is reinforced when he depicts the stars as indicators of the seemingly infinite extent of the universe as a whole. I have suggested that McCarthy addresses the potentially annihilating implications of this human insignificance, and, like Nietzsche, suggests that it must be opposed, not by belief in life's inherent meaning, but by man's inherent vitality, by his "ardenthearted" efforts to create his own meaning in an absurd world. For McCarthy existence is spontaneous and meaning is constructed through narrative. That McCarthy's heroes exist in a state of *unheimlich* is therefore due to the fact that their quest for meaning and identity is informed by the false narrative of American Exceptionalism. The family remains a primary element of that American mythology; family and home offer little in the way of comfort to McCarthy's wanderers. I have pointed out two principal characteristics of McCarthy's fictional families; they are either sources of the most severe conflict or else they are swept away by misfortune and violence. I have further suggested that it is an aspect of McCarthy's mythoclasm that the heroic vitality he values, this precious ardentheartedness, is frequently perverted by the harshness of American experience, and that this produces the mythic American "dangerous man," a volatile, unthinking individual whose violence is never far from the surface. Indeed violence is a constant feature of McCarthy's world, a reflection of the place of violence in American life and mythology, especially that of the West. All who write on McCarthy refer not only to the violence in his texts but also to the ubiquity of the image of blood. Most read this in purely negative terms, associating it with this violence, but I have argued that it signifies both life and death and indicates McCarthy's assertion that the two are but opposite sides of the same coin. Thus blood becomes an image of spontaneous vitality as well as death.

While the overall tenor of the texts is pessimistic I have identified two positives in McCarthy's world, two sources of value and identity. He consistently portrays the saving value of work well done—of the mastery of a craft; and he asserts the virtue of hospitality, often offered by the poor to the penniless "man of the road." This occurs throughout the texts and on both sides of the border. In a society that is driven by the dynamic of competitive individualism this representation of generous human solidarity is itself an aspect of his critique of America.

American mythology, like that of most of the rest of the world, remains profoundly patriarchal. It is therefore consistent with McCarthy's mythoclastic intent that his texts should depict the violence and alienation of the American scene through the absence of the female and of the life-giving fertility with which the female is associated. Eliot's image of the "waste land" becomes McCarthy's image of the West; the metaphor is intensified by the consistent association of the female with water. The deliberate and conscious manner in which McCarthy makes these references to the female and her mythic association with the life-giving water on which the arid West is so dependent, suggests that he sees this absence as a root cause of patriarchal culture's most profound shortcomings.[5]

Throughout McCarthy's work there is a concern with the nature of narrative and a sense of its central importance in the structuring of the cultural matrix whereby we mediate our experience of the world. I have traced this aspect of the texts as it has developed from the implicit complexities of voice in *The Orchard Keeper* to overt discussion of the nature of narrative in *Cities of the Plain*. I have noted McCarthy's skepticism concerning the validity of maps and of those intellectual systems by which we interpret the world, pointing out his view of them as mere arbitrary "grids" that we impose on reality whether they "fit" or not. This skepticism is particularly focused on the notion that recorded history can represent the complexity and infinite variety of the past. He suggests that only fictional narrative can represent the nature of this complexity and provide a model against which to assess the reductionism of historical accounts. In short McCarthy asserts the inevitability of myth and the consequent necessity of anti-myth.

His skepticism regarding systems of belief is paralleled by an evident concern with language. He combines the uncertainty expressed by the phrase "words are not things," with an evident love of language and what it can do in the service of narrative. His love of work well done is reflected in his own work with language and narrative creation. I have drawn attention to the very diversity of McCarthy's use of language; the formal rhetoric of the introduction to *Suttree*, the compelling representation of dialogue and dialect—including sections in Spanish, the extraordinary "run on" descriptive passages, the vivid accounts of action, the poetic depictions of landscape. McCarthy has seemed at times to be creating a language of his own, frequently ignoring formal syntax, forming neologisms, dispensing with formal indications of speech. All these techniques are at the service of a style by turns expansive and economical, but always eidetic. This evident concern to use language in as wide a variety of styles as possible is one of the characteristics that sets McCarthy apart from other contemporary American writers, most of whom strive to achieve a uniformity of style that expresses a firm authorial identity. McCarthy's variations in style seem to me to have a twofold significance; they indicate both his love of language and his wish to be free to use it in as many ways as possible. At the same time I have argued that his literary journey, informed by the texts of other ages and cultures, has matched his own personal journey from Catholic boyhood in East Tennessee to skeptical maturity in the Southwest. I have suggested that the theme of conflict between father and son, so strong in the earlier texts, running with diminishing power after the extremes of *Blood Meridian*, reasserted in the climax of *Cities of the Plain* and fading almost completely in *No Country for Old Men*, is a metaphor for his struggle to assert his own individual voice, for it to be heard distinctly against "the voice of the fathers."

In conclusion therefore I suggest that McCarthy's mythoclasm is double-edged. In constructing his own anti-myth against the myth of American exceptionalism he aligns himself with an American literary and cinematic tradition that includes Hawthorne, Melville, Twain, Faulkner, Fitzgerald, Ford and Peckinpah. But these are the characters in another myth, one from which he must free himself in order to create his own literary identity. In fact McCarthy does not so much free himself as use the fragments of his culture's inherited myths and texts to create mythoclastic narratives of his own. Within this context he speaks with his own voice, a voice characterized by its breadth of vocabulary, mastery of dialogue, use of vivid eidetic language and wide-ranging variations of style; this voice is identifiably American but speaks to both worlds, the Old as well as the New.

Appendix One
The Sunset Limited

> I gather it to be your belief that culture tends to contribute to human
> misery. That the more one knows the more unhappy one is likely to be.
> As in the case of certain parties known to us.

No Country for Old Men proved to be the first of three new McCarthy texts
to be published in the period ending in late 2006, the point at which this
manuscript was due for completion. *The Sunset Limited* and *The Road*[1] both
emerged in that year, leaving little time for contemplation of their place
within McCarthy's oeuvre; but this book's initial claim of comprehensive
coverage of that oeuvre dictated that some attempt be made to include these
latest texts in its purview: rather than recast the whole of the rest of the book
I have elected to append brief considerations of them. Thus the following
must be viewed as first thoughts rather than fully considered positions.
However since my readings are consistent with what has gone before, these
late additions do not modify my overall view of McCarthy as an American
mythoclast.

Both texts display McCarthy's seemingly limitless appetite for literary
experiment and his broad eclecticism. No two of his previous works have
the same form, although the three volumes of "The Border Trilogy" come
close to it. The author characterises *The Sunset Limited* as "a novel in dramatic form." Whatever such a thing might be the world has regarded it as a
play for the theatre, a view substantiated by the fact of its recent production
by the Steppenwolf Company.[2] I was not able attend a performance of the
play and must therefore base my reading on the text alone, as I have done
in the case of McCarthy's other stage play, *The Stonemason*. At the time of
writing, critical response to the play has been informed by the performance
and confined to the pages of the press. These brief reviews hardly warrant
extensive quotation; such is not their purpose. The general tenor of the play's

reception was of muted appreciation: its meaning was not considered open to doubt, a philosophical debate concerning the justification for continuing to live in a world of meaningless suffering. The limitations of the play's form were also regarded as self-evident. Martin Denton wrote that the play's "talk" was "compelling, provocative, and significant." He added: "But it finally is just talk; with no protagonist or antagonist and no dramatic journey, I'm not sure that this amounts to much more than a well articulated philosophical debate".[3] Les Gutman is of a similar opinion: "So *The Sunset Limited*, for all its literary achievement, isn't quite a play".[4] While I wish to consider the questions of the text's form and content, my main concern will be to place the work in the context created by McCarthy's previous texts.

As described in chapter 9, *The Stonemason* proved to be a play too complex in structure to be staged. One is tempted to suppose that McCarthy determined to avoid all such complexity in his second theatrical venture to the extent of writing something that could be easily staged but was not really a play, or at least not a play in the usual theatrical sense of the word. Two characters sit at a table in a New York tenement room and talk: their conversation is indeed in the form of a debate, a verbal contest of life and death. It transpires that one has attempted to kill himself by jumping off the station platform into the path of the Sunset Limited, coming through at eighty miles per hour; the other has prevented him from doing so and brought him back to his place. That such a play might be better suited to television, or better still the radio, is neither here nor there. Comparisons with Beckett have been made but there is no sense in which *The Sunset Limited* could be considered as 'theatre of the absurd'. Although its theme of the essential meaninglessness of human life in a Godless universe is Beckettian, McCarthy's expression of the existential dilemma is straightforward and quite without the indirection, nuance and mordant wit of, say, *Waiting for Godot*.[5] Beckett's texts are nothing if not theatrical; they can be surreal. *The Sunset Limited* is a hybrid of mimesis and allegory; it is rather like *No Country for Old Men* in this respect. Although its setting and dialogue are highly realistic, the latter being not just the play's main strength, but almost its entirety, a metaphorical level is established by two principal devices.

The first of these is the more obvious: the characters' names are Black and White. The fact that these 'names' correspond to their racial categories has led some to speculate on race as a theme of the play. This does not seem to me to be the case. Ethnicity is not an issue in *The Sunset Limited*: race is acknowledged by Black himself but with irony, as if to indicate that the real matter at hand is something else. Speaking of his prison experiences he uses the word "nigger": White objects:

White: I just don't see why you have to use that word.

Black: Well it's my story ain't it? Anyway I don't remember there bein
    no Afro-Americans or persons of color there. To the best of my rec-
    ollection it was just a bunch of niggers.[6]

If Black represents the ghetto he bears the privilege of standing for life itself,
whereas White, educated, affluent and privileged, is the man of death. As
in other McCarthy texts, allegory features types rather than realistic characters; this typology is emphasised by the author in his stage directions which
invariably refer to "the black" and "the professor".[7] He also comments on it
reflexively in the dialogue. White refers to a notional Cecil in the course of
an explanation; "Who's Cecil?" asks Black.

He's not anybody. He's just a hypothetical . . .

There's not any Cecil. He's just a person I made up to illustrate a
point.[8]

In addition, the metaphorical representation of opposed and clear cut
philosophical positions is, of course, one of the meanings of the phrase "black
and white" as the text itself reminds us:

White: You see everything in black and white.
Black: It is black and white.
White: I suppose that makes the world easier to understand.[9]

What the professor fails to appreciate is that the argument between life and
death is, indeed, "black and white" and easy to understand.

The phrase is also a reference to the printed page which is 'down in
black and white', a usage that draws attention to textuality itself; if McCarthy
intended the work to be both a novel and a drama then this textuality is one
of its concerns. The theme of the limitations of language has been evident in
novels such as *Blood Meridian* and *The Crossing*; this concern is reflected here
when Black questions his failure to save White by addressing his god: "If you
wanted me to help him how come you didn't give me the words?" Significantly he adds "You give em to him. What about me?"[10] Black lives *because*
he does not have the words; not having the words is his strength. I enlarge on
this aspect of the play's meaning below.

The second indication of allegory lies in the title of the piece. The Sunset Limited is a train that runs across the southern part of the USA, linking

New Orleans[11] to Los Angeles. It does not run through New York City, nor indeed anywhere remotely near it; but McCarthy cites it as the vehicle of White's intended self-destruction and places the event in the northern metropolis.[12] This can only be read as another deliberate avoidance of realism and prompts us to interpret the metaphor. I suggest three readings, one of which I have mentioned previously. Flannery O'Conner's referred to Faulkner as the 'Dixie Limited,' collision with which/whom was to be avoided by fellow southern authors for fear of annihilation. I have argued that McCarthy has ignored this warning, raised his own voice against that of his great forebear and survived the resulting collision. However there seems no reason to suppose that White will survive his collision and the discourse of the play is clearly concerned with the notion of suicide. In this context the 'sunset' referred to is final; it is death itself.[13] Both 'Black' and 'White' would be familiar with the deathly import of the image of the setting sun:

> I hate to see that evenin' sun go down.
> It makes me think I'm on my last go round.[14]

However it is when the text is considered in the context of McCarthy's work as a whole that a third significance suggests itself.

I have argued that what I have called the "dialectic of vitality and insignificance" is one of the structuring elements of all McCarthy's work. Again and again his protagonists defy the implications of humanity's inconsequentiality in the face of the vastness of time and space, confronting their inherent meaninglessness with the sheer desire to be that inhabits all animal bodies. This defiance is, of course, non-rational in essence. It is also resides most intensely within the "ardent-hearted" and its vitality is consistently signified by blood. In this respect, among others, *The Sunset Limited* refers back most closely to *Suttree*. "Black" could be a born-again Ab Jones[15] and White a professor from the university attended by Suttree himself. The sheriff who runs him out of town after his fight with his former family expresses distrust of the education that Suttree has received:

> I will say one thing: you've opened my eyes. I've got two daughters, oldest fourteen, and I'd see them both in hell fore I'd send them up to that university. I'm damned if I wouldnt.[16]

A rejection of gnosis and a broad refusal of the possibility of "explaining" either the world or human character and behaviour are consistent McCarthy tropes. The sheriff's views could be dismissed as redneck reaction were it not for his previous assertion of the need for existential heroism in everyday life: Suttree expresses his despairing nihilism: "No one cares. It's not important." The Sheriff's response is unequivocal:

> That's where you're wrong my friend. Everything's important. A man lives his life, he has to make that important. Whether he's a small town county sheriff or the president. Or a busted out bum. You might even understand that some day. I don't say you will. You might.[17]

In *The Sunset Limited* it is Black who is the existential hero; his ardenthearted devotion to life is not a matter of intellectual conviction, but of his essential nature. He has returned from the very portal of death on hearing the voice of god. As ever blood signifies the imbrication of the two principles: Black's brutal fight with another prisoner involves stabbings and beatings: "They told me I'd lost about half my blood. I remember slippin around in it but I thought it was this other dude's."[18] But Black has blood and spirit and vitality to spare and his religious conversion can be read as an adoption of a mythology that makes possible the diversion of his ardentheartedness away from violence and towards a path that affirms life.[19] It is clear that the professor represents the inadequacy of pure intellect as a basis for living; the play's dialogue makes this quite explicit, most obviously in his final decision to go back out in search of the Sunset Limited again. Books have not been his salvation:

> Black: . . . You think maybe you read four thousand books.
> White: Probably. Maybe more than that.

Like so many of McCarthy's heroes, White has found that his culture has played him false:

> White: Probably I don't believe in a lot of things that I used to believe in but that doesn't mean I don't believe in anything.
>   . . .
> Lots of things. Cultural things, for instance. Books and music and art. Things like that.
>   . . .
> Those are the kinds of things that have value to me. They are the foundations of civilization. Or they used to have value. I suppose they don't have so much any more.
>   . . .

> People stopped valuing them. I stopped valuing them. To a certain
> extent. I'm not sure I could tell you why. That world is largely gone.
> Soon it will be wholly gone.
>   . . .
>   . . . The things I loved were very frail. Very fragile. I didn't know that. I
> thought they were indestructible. They weren't.
>   . . .
>   . . . That's what an education does. It makes the world personal.[20]

In short White believes in ". . . the primacy of the intellect".[21] As I have
noted in previous chapters the notion that any human culture is indestruc-
tible has been challenged repeatedly in McCarthy's other texts; references
to representations, the meaning of which has been irrecoverably lost, occur
throughout his work.

The professor is at the other end of the cultural spectrum from the wanderer Billy Parham but he has learned the same lesson: "In everything that
he'd ever thought about the world and about his life in it he'd been wrong,"[22]
a sentiment that could be shared by Lester Ballard, John Grady Cole, Sheriff
Bell and all those other American would-be heroes who have come at last to
disillusionment or death or both.

This fatal over-valuing of the intellect, which is a failure to recognise
the absolute necessity of ardentheartedness, provides a further intertextual
link between the play and the image of sunset. McCarthy has consistently
quoted the poets in acknowledgement of our debt to the language and ideas
inherited from our literary past. Wordsworth is one of his sources; ". . . the
child the father of the man" appearing on the first page of that most un-
Wordsworthian novel *Blood Meridian*. In "The Tables Turned" Wordsworth
expressed the inadequacy of pure intellect as a basis for human existence:

> Up! up! my Friend, and quit your books;
> Or surely you'll grow double:
> Up! up! my Friend, and clear your looks;
> Why all this toil and trouble?

The image of approaching sunset is evoked in precisely the opposite sense to
that used here by McCarthy; but this kind of inversion is absolutely typical
of the novelist. Never-the-less the image inheres in the poem that expresses
Romanticism's challenge to Enlightenment's over-rational epistemology;
and for Wordsworth, ardentheartedness is not only informed by nature, it is
nature itself.

The sun, above the mountain's head,
A freshening lustre mellow
Through all the long green fields has spread,
His first sweet evening yellow.

Books! 'tis a dull and endless strife:
Come, hear the woodland linnet,
How sweet his music! on my life,
There's more of wisdom in it.

And hark! how blithe the throstle sings!
He, too, is no mean preacher:
Come forth into the light of things,
Let Nature be your Teacher.
. . .
She has a world of ready wealth,
Our minds and hearts to bless-
Spontaneous wisdom breathed by health,
Truth breathed by cheerfulness.
. . .
Enough of Science and of Art;
Close up those barren leaves;
Come forth, and bring with you a heart
That watches and receives.[23]

The ideals of Enlightenment informed the American Revolution and the implied critique of that rationality is consistent with what I have suggested is McCarthy's overall critique of American Exceptionalism; of course that critique could be applied to Western culture as a whole. At the moment the USA is its most powerful representative and Exceptionalism has re-emerged as a potent political idea. Its current form is labelled "the war against terror."

However *The Sunset Limited* does not appear to me to have any overt political comment to make; its debate takes place at a more fundamental level, at the most fundamental level of all—of the question of life and death. White answers it in the negative: Black may not understand the argument or have the words—but it is he who knows that the response to the storms of life is, "You don't say nothin. You just turn up your collar and keep walkin."[24] McCarthy's play may not have the haunting theatricality achieved by Beckett but Black expresses a characteristic Beckettian existentialism: ". . . you must go on, I can't go on, I'll go on."[25]

There is of course an inherent contradiction in writing a play/book that condemns the culture of books: but the objection applies as much to Wordsworth as to McCarthy. Both attempt to find ways of transcending the paradoxes of the insufficiency of books and the limitations of language. Both use poetic means to convey the contrary meaning though affect rather than intellect. White's language is cold and deathly: it expresses the emptiness that lies behind his despair:

> . . . Well, here's my news, reverend. I yearn for the darkness. I pray for death. Real death. If I thought that in death I would meet the people I have met in life I don't know what I'd do. That would be the ultimate horror. The ultimate despair. If I had to meet my mother again and start all of that all over, only this time without the prospect of death to look forward to? Well. That would be the final nightmare. Kafka on wheels.[26]

His language is plain, dull, ugly. He may understand words but he cannot use them with love. His imagery expresses this perfectly: it is drawn from the Western high literary canon in its reference to Kafka, but the attached "on wheels" debases the allusion, reducing it to the level of banal colloquialism devoid of poetic feeling.

Black, on the other hand, speaks in the rolling cadences of the south:

> You see I wouldn't be this rude under normal circumstances. Man come in my house and set at my table and me not offer him nothin? But with you I figure I got to strategise. Got to play my cards right. Keep you from slippin off into the night.[27]

He uses words with relish, "strategise"; and his imagery is rich; "slippin off into the night" has a metaphorical meaning that is of crucial import and which deepens his seemingly 'uneducated' speech; and his implied reference to the importance of hospitality is at one with his humanity.[28] I have drawn attention to McCarthy's use of different linguistic registers in my chapter 12, especially as analysed by Nancy Kreml.[29] In this instance the variation is not only inherent in the structure of the play through the social origin of the characters, but is also organic in that style and meaning are unified.

The Sunset Limited then is in some senses the bare bones of a play. It clearly depends almost exclusively on its dialogue, since its action is minimal.[30] But dialogue is one of McCarthy's great strengths. In this case he keeps the tension of the situation alive until White's final despairing departure and Black's uncomprehending grief. The battle of wits and words between the two is cleverly constructed as Black finds ways to fend off White's more intellectual arguments and neither gains any advantage over the other. Seasoned McCarthy readers will recognise the author's gift for capturing speech in much of what Black has to say; but the task of rendering White's arguments in harsh, unpleasant tones is accomplished with equal facility and it is this that gives the play the rhythm that alone can lift it out of the category of intellectual exercise.[31] The 'internal' setting of the play denies McCarthy access to natural landscape, one of his richest sources of metaphor. The image of the "waste land" has been used to represent the destructive consequences of American mythology throughout his oeuvre; in this case 'waste land' characterises the inner landscape of White's being, rendered sterile by his failure to balance the implications of thought and intellect with the imperatives of nature, feeling and the body. Black perceives this in a manner that indicates that McCarthy relates the theme of the play to aspects of his previous work: speaking of "heresy" he remarks, ". . . It aint as big a heresy as sayin that a man aint all that much different from a rock. Which is how your view looks to me."[32] This is a direct reference to the "optical democracy" passage in *Blood Meridian*,[33] one of the author's most celebrated notions, and taken by some critics as an indication of an eco-critical stance on McCarthy's part.

This is evidence of a retrospective intent in *The Sunset Limited*, and one which would seem to indicate a rethinking of some of the authors more extreme notions. This thoughtful retrospection is also an aspect of *No Country for Old Men*; in my opinion it informs *The Road* also. Although unlikely to be ranked as a major work *The Sunset Limited* does have a depth and coherence that lies in its unification of theme, form and style. It also shares its major concern with the rest of McCarthy's oeuvre and will perhaps come to be read as a form of authorial reflection on the thread that runs through all his work at a fundamental level—the "dialectic of vitality and insignificance".

Appendix Two
The Road

When your dreams are of some world that never was or of some world that never will be and you are happy again then you will have given up. Do you understand? And you cant give up. I wont let you.

The Road is Cormac McCarthy's tenth novel.[1] Its appearance has been greeted with acclaim by all and sundry, especially those who were less than impressed by *No Country for Old Men*. Press reaction has been enthusiastic and opinion in academic circles similarly positive, albeit only available in unpublished form at the time of writing. It is the only one of McCarthy's books to have been received with uniform approval. In every case this approval focuses on the book's stylistic qualities; McCarthy scholars read in it a return to the unapologetically rich and poetic rhetoric of *Suttree* and *Blood Meridian*; and to the author's willingness to address fundamental philosophical questions in a manner generally out of fashion in a culture that has lost faith in the very notion of the grand narrative. The Grand Narrative of Western culture may be considered to have been McCarthy's concern all along, focused in the main on that variant known as American Exceptionalism, but always presenting that variant within its broader cultural context, and also identifying it as a product of changing historical circumstances.[2] My reading of the novel is that it is indeed a return, but not simply to a former daringly ambitious style, since it would be an exaggeration to claim that McCarthy ever completely abandoned this mode of writing. In my view *The Road* is a literary return, a retrospective on the author's own previous works, a re-viewing of his own work that offers a different perspective to that of the young man whose vision was structured by the oedipal paradigm that we find in the aforementioned *Suttree* and *Blood Meridian*.[3] In this respect it continues the development that I have identified in *No Country for Old Men*, but in this latest case the author's eclecticism, so marked in that novel, has sources closer to home. The "other books" out of which McCarthy constructs *The Road* are his own; the road is that which he has trodden himself.[4]

I have already remarked on McCarthy's habit of structuring his texts in different ways, to the extent that no two of his novels have the same form. *The Road* is no exception; it consists of a continuous sequence of discrete paragraphs, some only a few lines in length, none occupying much more than a single page. There are no chapters; paragraphs are separated by spaces that would occupy three lines of text: occasionally a pause is hinted by the indication of an ellipsis at the beginning or end of a page.[5] This structure is clearly intended to reflect the nature of the journey that constitutes the action of the book. The journey itself is of a piece, a series of short stages, entirely on foot, and comprising a continuous whole. The movement of the travellers and the movement of the text are one.[6] The long, painful journey is punctuated by infrequent intervals of rest and shelter or by rare but violent encounters with other travellers. Such a form creates for the writer the problem of maintaining the reader's engagement with the text. McCarthy's way of dealing with this gives him ample opportunity to express in rich language that metaphysical profundity that so many commentators have enjoyed. His descriptions of place and landscape are characteristically eidetic, an effect that is produced by sentences that are rich in nouns but devoid of verbs. But the paragraphs tend to feature a double style of a kind I mention in previous chapters and the sparse descriptions tend to lead up to final passages that are linguistically and philosophically ambitious. This creates an inner rhythm that carries the reader forward, buoyed up by the pleasures of the text. For example:

> He tried to think of something to say but he could not. He'd had this feeling before, beyond the numbness and the dull despair. The world shrinking down about a raw core of parsible entities. The names of things slowly following those things into oblivion. Colors. The names of birds. Things to eat. Finally the names of things one believed to be true. More fragile than he would have thought. How much was gone already? *The sacred idiom shorn of its referents and so of its reality. Drawing down like something trying to preserve heat. In time to wink out forever.*[7] (My italics)

Passages like this cause the reader to pause, reflect, perhaps re-read. They contrast markedly with the headlong pace and action that so compels the reader through *No Country for Old Men*. The passage also illustrates another characteristic of the text: it is initially a representation of the inner voice of the main protagonist, but as the train of thought develops it seems to segue into that of the author. In this way McCarthy manages to imbue the text with a sense of his own presence without departing from the technique designed to elide it. A further passage illustrates the same point:

> He walked out in the gray light and stood and he saw for a brief moment the absolute truth of the world. The cold relentless circling of the intestate earth. Darkness implacable. The blind dogs of the sun in their running. The crushing black vacuum of the universe. And somewhere two hunted animals trembling like ground-foxes in their cover. Borrowed time and borrowed world and borrowed eyes with which to sorrow it.[8]

The sense of man's insignificance in a godless universe, one of McCarthy's constant themes, is powerfully conveyed here. The theme is addressed directly and the author's characteristic answer to the existential question is provided in the working out of the tale.

Both these passages convey the atmosphere of the novel as a whole. The "two hunted animals" are a father and son, cast adrift in a world in which civilization and its concomitants have been destroyed. Most commentators refer to this setting as post-apocalyptic and one can readily see why. A few brief passages are drawn from the father's memory; one of them would seem to describe a nuclear attack:

> The clock's stopped at 1:17. A long shear of light and then a series of low concussions. He got up and went to the window. What is it? she said. He didn't answer. He went into the bathroom and threw a lightswitch but the power was already gone. A dull rose glow in the windowglass.[9]

Given the reference to the atomic bomb in *The Crossing* (and possibly *The Orchard Keeper* and *Cities of the Plain*) this is, on the face of it, a not unreasonable interpretation. But the general scale of the destruction of not only a large area of the United States, but of the world as a whole, suggests the need for a more considered interpretation. There are no birds or animals left alive in this world. Most of the trees and many of the buildings have been burned. The air is filled with ash which necessitates the wearing of face masks in order to filter what is breathed in. This ash is present at all times despite the fact that it rains with great frequency; at the same time, "The weeds they forded turned to dust about them."[10]

Only human beings remain, and those few in number. Murderous feral gangs roam the country killing and eating their fellows, such is the reduced state of their being. Infants are roasted on spits and captives are locked in a cellar that is in effect a larder. These monstrous happenings signal to us that we are present in another of McCarthy's allegorical worlds. The impression is strengthened by the fact that neither father nor son is given a name. If this was a post-nuclear holocaust world then ubiquitous radioactivity, especially in the ash and dust, would have long since killed everybody, the "event" whatever it may have been, having occurred some years prior to the main action of the text. None of the characters encountered in the novel have any of the symptoms of radiation sickness. In this case the "nuclear holocaust" is itself a metaphorical explanation for the state of the world that McCarthy creates as his wider metaphor for the condition of man in the realisation of his cosmic insignificance, powerfully signified in quotation (8) above.

The image of the waste land is one that has recurred throughout McCarthy's previous novels and is an intertexual reference to Eliot. In *The Road*, this image is reasserted more powerfully than ever before. The ash, the dust, the ubiquity of death, especially the death of nature, all contribute to this image: "He . . . looked out over the wasted country."[11] Ash and dust recall the words of the funeral service. The imagery of the poem reverberates through the novel: "I will show you fear in a handful of dust." "I had not thought death had undone so many, . . ." "He who was living is now dead—We who were living are now dying."[12]

The Road is replete with passages that express the same deathly sterility:

> The city was mostly burned. No sign of life. Cars in the street caked with ash, everything covered with ash and dust. Fossil tracks in the dried sludge. A corpse in a doorway dried to leather. Grimacing at the day. He pulled the boy closer. Just remember that the things you put in your head are there for ever, he said. You might want to think about that.
> You forget some things, don't you?
> Yes. You forget what you want to remember and you remember what you want to forget.[13]

The father's reason for the journey—"They were moving south. There'd be no surviving another winter here"[14] echoes "I read, much of the night, and go south in the winter."[15] The ultimate challenge of cosmic insignificance arises in the contemplation of death. It is this challenge that the Professor fails to meet in *The Sunset Limited*. Suttree was a young man; he conquered the fear of death but fled death itself: Sheriff Bell was wise enough not to challenge the unchallengeable. But the father in *The Road* is marked for death; he knows it and so do we. ". . . he stood bent with his hands on his knees, coughing. He raised up and stood with weeping eyes. On the gray snow a fine mist of blood."[16] This signifier of the father's doom is encountered at an early stage of the journey and we know that the question the novel must answer is not what will happen to the father, but to the son? and how are they to confront the waste land and what I suggest it signifies? McCarthy's favoured answer, expressed in each of his texts to a greater or lesser extent, is that of the inherent vitality of the ardenthearted, for whom the significance of life is asserted existentially and in defiance of mere reason alone. So it is in *The Road*. At various points of the text and journey the pair speak of "carrying the fire;" one thinks of Sheriff Bell's dream of his father carrying fire in a horn at the end of *No Country for Old Men*, the fire that I suggest signifies civilization being passed from father to son. Here civilization is no more and this pair carry no fire in any literal sense; but the literal is not McCarthy's concern. At first we can only guess at the meaning of this image:

> We're going to be okay, aren't we Papa?
>
> Yes. We are.
>
> And nothing bad is going to happen to us.
>
> That's right.
>
> Because we're carrying the fire.
>
> Yes. Because we're carrying the fire.[17]

The phrase is repeated on page109 and again on page182, but it is not until we are almost at the end of the father's journey and his life that we learn its meaning. The father realises that the son must go on without him:

> I want to be with you.
>
> You cant.
>
> Please.
>
> You cant. You have to carry the fire.
>
> I don't know how to.

Yes you do.

Is it real? The fire?

Yes it is.

Where is it? I don't know where it is.

Yes you do. It's inside you. It was always there. I can see it.[18]

The fire signifies that vitality that burns within the ardent heart, the mystery that is the spark of life itself and that needs no reason to exist. McCarthy reinforces this idea in the last passage in which the dying father's inner voice becomes that of the author: "In that cold corridor they had reached the point of no return which was measured from the first by the light they carried with them."[19] I have argued that the oedipal character of McCarthy's early and middle period works is notably diminished in *No Country for Old Men. The Road* reverses the oedipal theme completely and it is this reversal that gives the text a unique place in the author's oeuvre. The entire novel is devoted to a journey motivated by the father's heroic quest for a place in which his young son can survive. And this quest, undertaken in the certainty of his own impending death, is motivated by paternal love, a love that the son returns:

> He held the boy close to him. So thin. My heart, he said. My heart. But he knew that if he were a good father still it might well be as she had said. That the boy was all that stood between him and death.[20]

His own tenuous hold on life means nothing when the boy's own life is threatened by sickness: "You have to stay near, he said. You have to be quick. So you can be with him. Hold him close. Last day of the earth."[21] Nothing could be further from the anguished conflict between father and son implied in *Suttree* and *Blood Meridian*. I have interpreted the oedipal trope in McCarthy's work in terms of his raising of his own voice against that of the literary fathers—Faulkner, Melville, Eliot; many more have fed his eclecticism. How then to account for this reversal? The eclecticism was so apparent in *No Country for Old Men* that I suggested it was no longer a cause for "the anxiety of influence," no longer an "ugly fact"[22] Jay Ellis suggests that McCarthy's latest work is indicative of his changed familial circumstances, his third marriage and his joy in his young and growing son.[23] One can well imagine that this might be the case. Indeed McCarthy mentions his son John in his second Woodward interview, describing him as: "the best person I know, far better than I am."[24] This idealisation of the child is reflected in *The Road*: the father's determined pragmatism in the face of potential danger is constantly challenged by the boy's assertion of the claims of conscience. When the father reclaims their belongings from the thief on the beach and leaves him naked and bereft of any chance of survival, the boy weeps, not only for pity of the doomed man, but also for what his father has become:

> Let's go, he said. And they set out along the road south with the boy crying and looking back at the nude and slatlike creature standing there in the road shivering and hugging himself. Oh Papa, he sobbed.[25]

As his death approaches McCarthy gives the father words close to those quoted by Woodward: "You have my whole heart. You always did. You're the best guy. You always were."[26]

However, the evident allegorical nature of the text suggests a further, more generalised and literary interpretation, best approached by a consideration of the novel's location in fairly specific geographical spaces and the previous literary texts with which McCarthy himself has associated those spaces. The tropes of location, landscape and movement have been interpreted in previous chapters in relation to both individual novels and groups thereof. The "journey" of McCarthy's work, commenting as I suggest it does on the United States' sense of its own identity, has traced the path of the mythic representation of that identity, a path that has led from east to west. The road followed by father and son in this latest novel runs to the south however and its starting point is located in an area of woods and mountains where the winters are too cold to survive without shelter. As they journey they encounter features that gradually convey a sense of identifiable place:

> What is that Papa?
>
> It's a dam.
>
> What's it for?
>
> It made the lake. Before they built the dam that was just a river down there. The dam used the water that ran through it to turn big turbines that would generate electricity.[27]

This immediately suggests Appalachian East Tennessee as a possible location, a suggestion strengthened by "A log barn in a field with an advertisement in faded ten foot-letters across the roofscape. See Rock City."[28] Such advertisements are not uncommon in East Tennessee. They refer to a tourist feature associated with Lookout Mountain, near Chattanooga, in the Great Smoky Mountains, part of the Appalachian range. Any remaining doubts as to the generalised location of the start of this journey are soon dispelled:

> Three nights later in the foothills of the eastern mountains he woke in the darkness to hear something coming. He lay with his hands at either side of him. The ground was trembling. . . . It was an earthquake.[29]

This area of East Tennessee is the location of frequent earthquakes. McCarthy's latest novel features a journey that commences where his own literary journey began, together with oblique reminders of those early texts. On the very first page the father wakes with his son beside him, just as Culla Holme wakes beside his sister in *Outer Dark*. Like Culla, he has a had a nightmare:

> In the dream from which he'd wakened he had wandered in a cave where the child led him by the hand. Their light playing over the wet flowstone walls. Like pilgrims in a fable swallowed up and lost among the inward parts of some granitic beast. Deep stones where the water dripped and sang. Tolling in the silence the minutes of the earth and the hours and the days of it and the years without cease.[30]

We are at once in the McCarthy world of Appalachian allegory: father and son are indeed "pilgrims in a fable," their progress will be the substance of this tale. The dreamer's cave recalls Lester Ballard's womb-like underworld in *Child of God*. When the father lies in the dark, deliberately waking so as not to dream of ". . . a flowering wood where birds flew before them . . . with the uncanny taste of a peach from some phantom orchard fading in his mouth,"[31] we recall the worlds of *Wake for Susan* and *The Orchard Keeper*. The image of idyllic boyhood is recalled by the father standing on a bridge over a stream, "Where once he'd watched trout swaying in the current, tracking their perfect shadows on the stones beneath."[32] The small boy of *A Drowning Incident* watched minnows in such a stream. The more horrific images of *The Road* recall the later works, those set in the southwest:

> People sitting on the sidewalk in the dawn half immolate and smoking in their clothes. Like failed sectarian suicides. Others would come to

help them. Within a year there were fires on the ridges and deranged chanting. The screams of the murdered. By day the dead impaled on spikes along the road.[33]

In *Blood Meridian* we read that,

> The way narrowed through rocks and by and by they came to a bush that was hung with dead babies. . . . In the afternoon they came upon a village in the plain where smoke still rose from the ruins and all were gone to death.[34]

As my epigraph for my chapter on *The Crossing* I quote Billy Parham's vain assertion "Yo no soy un hombre del camino"[35] In this latest text father and son are "men of the road" in more senses than one.

I have already noted the way in which the author's own voice seems to speak through that of the father in *The Road*. This trope is also reinforced by other aspects of the novel. East Tennessee is indeed the area in which McCarthy grew up and the father revisits his own boyhood places. "What is this place Papa? It's the house where I grew up."[36] The dam mentioned above would have been created by the TVA.[37] Thus in this novel there is a complex imbrication of previous work revisited, fictional and authorial voices and the author's own distant past. If the last two of these must remain speculative to some degree the literary intertextuality seems clear. And like all such intertextuality, the interest lies not only in the similarities between texts, but in the differences—the re-visions. I wish to conclude my analysis by considering both differences and similarities, for although the former are radical the latter remain of fundamental significance.

Certain characteristic McCarthy tropes are to be found in *The Road* and these maintain a sense of continuity with his previous work. I have already mentioned the use of poetic language and the expression of profound ideas, often in the form of a coda to a descriptive passage. Detailed and precise descriptions of activities requiring skill occur in all the texts, expressive of the value the author places on work well done—an attitude that he surely adopts regarding his own literary work. In such a passage we read of the father's efforts to repair the trolley's wheel mount:

> They collected some old boxes and built a fire in the floor and he found some tools and emptied out the cart and sat working on the wheel. He pulled the bolt and bored out the collet with a hand drill and resleeved it with a section of pipe he'd cut to length with a hacksaw. Then he bolted

it all back together and stood the cart upright and wheeled it around the floor. It ran fairly true. The boy sat watching everything.[38]

This passage comprises one of the separate paragraphs of which the text is comprised. The care with which the actions are described matches the care taken over the actions themselves, a characteristic matching of style and meaning. The wording is technical and accurate; there are no missing verbs. The effect of the passage is to divert the reader's mind from the anxiety generated through identification with the protagonists in the extremity of their plight, just as it diverts the minds of the characters themselves to be absorbed in practical activity. A further level of meaning is added by the final phrase. The watching boy is learning both practical and moral lessons by observing his father's endeavours. The moral value that McCarthy associates with well-made things is asserted with painful irony when the father seeks salvage on the beached boat, itself ironically named "Pájaro de Esperanza" (Bird of Hope):

> Inside [the box] was a brass sextant, possibly a hundred years old. He lifted it from the fitted case and held it in his hand. Struck by the beauty of it. The brass was dull and there were patches of green on it that took the form of another hand that had once held it but otherwise it was perfect. He wiped the verdigris from the plate at the base. Hazzaninth, London. He held it to his eye and turned the wheel. It was the first thing he'd seen in a long time that stirred him. He held it in his hand and then he fitted it back into the blue baize lining of the case and closed the lid and snapped the latches shut and set it back in the locker and closed the door.[39]

That the father feels that he can only return the beautiful object to its case conveys a sense of poignancy that is intensified by the realisation that this is another action that signifies cultural demise, a further sinking towards that cultural entropy that the text identifies as the waste land. In the novels of the Border Trilogy McCarthy discourses on the question of maps. His general refusal to assign psychological motivation to his characters, who are for the most part types, is of a piece with his refusal of gnosis. His characters tend to assert that maps are false, simplifications that cannot signify the full complexity and variation of the changing world, fixed in time, representations of space, myths which lead astray those who think that they can be read. In *The Road* the case is otherwise: the travellers have a road map, fallen into pieces but still representing a world that is no longer. This map signifies not much less than exists in the world, but now much more. It is the world that will not suffice. Thus there is a profound sense of irony in the use of the map:

> Long days. Open country with the ash blowing over the road. The boy sat by the fire at night with the pieces of the map across his knees. He had the names of towns and rivers by heart and he measured their progress daily.[40]

In my reading the fragmented map, signifying a world that once was but is no more, can be seen as a metaphor for those texts that constitute McCarthy's own literary past, his former works now revisited.

I have consistently identified the overriding theme of McCarthy's work as a critique of American Exceptionalism in particular and Western gnosis in general. This trope is expressed in the father's reaction to books:

> Years later he'd stood in the charred ruins of a library where blackened books lay in pools of water. Shelves tipped over. Some rage at the lies arranged in their thousands row on row. He picked up one of the books and thumbed through the heavy bloated pages. He'd not have thought the value of the smallest thing predicated on a world to come. It surprised him. That the space which these things occupied was itself an expectation. He let the book fall and took a last look around and made his way out into the cold gray light.[41]

The books contain the "lies" that have led to this cultural demise and the faith in the future on which they based their validity has proved illusory. In this respect books and maps are alike.

One of the ways in which McCarthy draws attention to his narrative style is by employing occasional changes of voice. I have pointed this out in *Suttree* when the eponymous hero suddenly speaks of his "father's letter" in the narrative voice.[42] The same technique is used in *The Road*: the pair make camp in the woods:

> He held the child and after a while the child stopped shivering and after a while he slept.
>
> . . .
>
> The dog that he remembers followed us for two days. I tried to coax it to come but it would not. I made a noose of wire to catch it. There were

> three cartridges in the pistol. None to spare. She walked away down the
> road. The boy looked after her and then he looked at me and then he
> looked at the dog and he began to cry and to beg for the dog's life and I
> promised I would not hurt the dog.[43]

This quite radical departure from consistent technique seems to intensify the
poignancy of the scene as the father's emotion can be more powerfully imagined as he tells his own story. The affective quality of the passage is heightened
when one considers the significance of dogs in McCarthy's works generally:
they are frequently associated with friendship, family ties and affectionate
relationships in general.

It is abundantly clear that the great difference between *The Road* and
earlier texts lies in the loving nature of the relationship between father and
son, the complete reversal of the oedipal structure found previously. If I am
correct in interpreting this as McCarthy's assertion of his own voice against
that of the literary fathers and that his late departure from the paradigm is
evidence of his final confidence that his own voice can now be heard, then it
is not surprising that he should turn his critical attention to his own work.
Given his declared concern to write of death, it must also be the case that he
considers the possibility of the end of his authorial career.[44] This also must
cause such a thoughtful and self-aware writer to look back at his own work
and perhaps see some of it a different light, or perhaps through different
eyes, eyes made less pitiless by late experiences of love. The work on which
I wish to focus in this respect is both the most allegorical of the earlier texts
and also that which most directly relates to the myth of Oedipus, namely
Outer Dark. The parallels between the two texts are clear enough. Each novel
features a father and son; the father travels the road on a quest that will end
in a death. Violence and murder punctuate the action which takes place in
an identifiable but non-specific Appalachian mountain setting. The father of
the earlier text betrays a complete indifference to the fate of his infant son,
the son he abandoned at birth in the woods in the hope that he would die. In
what is surely McCarthy's most shocking and horrific literary moment Culla
Holme remains an impassive spectator:

> The man took hold of the child and lifted it up. It was watching the
> fire. Holme saw the blade wink in the light like a long cat's eye slant and
> malevolent and a dark smile erupted on the child's throat and went all
> broken down the front of it. The child made no sound. It hung there
> with its one eye glazing over like a wet stone and the black blood pump-
> ing down its naked belly. The mute one knelt forward. He was drooling

and making little whimpering noises in his throat. He knelt with his hands outstretched and his nostrils rimpled delicately. The man handed him the child and he seized it up, looked once at Holme with witless eyes, and buried his moaning face in its throat.[45]

There is cannibalism in *The Road* also but the loving father tries to comfort the son and the passage strikes a more restrained note:

He was standing [there] checking the perimeter when the boy turned and buried his face against him. He looked quickly to see what had happened. What is it? he said. What is it? The boy shook his head. Oh Papa, he said. He turned and looked again. What the boy had seen was a charred human infant headless and gutted and blackened on a spit. He bent and picked the boy up and started for the road with him, holding him close. I'm sorry, he whispered. I'm sorry.[46]

The comparison is completed, similarity and difference, when the boy's life is truly imperilled:

He was a big man but he was very quick. He dove and grabbed the boy and rolled and came up holding him against his chest with the knife at his throat. The man had already dropped to the ground and he swung with him and levelled the pistol and fired from a two-handed position balanced on both knees at a distance of six feet. The man fell back instantly and lay with blood bubbling from a hole in his forehead.

... He ... put the boy down in the ashes and leaves. He wiped the blood from his face and held him. It's OK, he said. It's OK.[47]

The similarity between the two texts is further emphasised in the person of the tinker, Deitch in *Outer Dark*. I find in him a parallel with the Wandering Jew of Christian mythology[48] In the later novel father and son encounter an ancient man, "A small figure distant on the road, bent and shuffling."[49] Deitch, having spent a "lifetime . . . strapped in front of a cart . . . couldn't stand straight to be hung."[50] He says his name is Ely—the only character in the novel to be given a name although he later says that the name is false. He it is who announces that "There is no God and we are his prophets."[51] Like Deitch, the old man has penetrating things to say:

Where men cant live gods fare no better. You'll see. It's better to be alone. So I hope that's not true what you said because to be on the road with the last god would be a terrible thing so I hope its not true. Things will be better when everybody's gone.

. . . When we're all gone at last then there'll be nobody here but death and his days will be numbered too. He'll be out in the road there with nothing to do and nobody to do it to. He'll say: Where did everybody go? And that's how it will be. What's wrong with that?[52]

The old man expresses the notion that when man goes his culture, capable of personifying death as McCarthy does in the person of Chighur in *No Country for Old Men*, goes with him, the extreme of cultural entropy encountered in the passage related to note 7 above. The relation of this old man to Deitch is reinforced in our final view of him:

When he looked back the old man had set out with his cane, tapping his way, dwindling slowly on the road behind them like some storybook peddler from an antique time, dark and spider thin and soon to vanish forever.[53]

Deitch was a "storybook peddler" and Rinthy Holme was associated with "an old dead time"[54] The relation between *The Road* and *Outer Dark* seems clear and intentional. The effect of the intertextuality is to confirm McCarthy's rejection of the intensely oedipal nature of his earlier work. Although the mythic image of the American waste land is taken to a new, all-encompassing extreme, this is done to provide a space in which a more individual, and perhaps personal eschatology is traced out. Although individual death must come at the end, collective continuity remains a possibility if the generations can pass on that ardenthearted vitality which is the inherent motor of life. Just as Eliot's "Waste Land" ends on a note of hope quite out of keeping with what has gone before, so McCarthy's Road runs not "from dark to dark"[55] but to a regaining of the lost female and the sense that the dead father's quest has been fulfilled, that the son will survive:

The woman when she saw him put her arms around him and held him. Oh, she said, I am so glad to see you. She would talk to him sometimes about God. He tried to talk to God but the best thing was to talk to his father and he did talk to him and he didn't forget. The woman said that was all right. She said that the breath of God was his breath yet though it pass from man to man through all of time.[56]

The question that the text leaves unanswered is that of the need for that revolt, oedipal or otherwise. If the oedipal paradigm passes with the patriarchal culture that generated it, what will take its place and how will the revolt of those who wish to make books, inevitably "out of other books," express itself in a mythic form that will carry the new writers against the voices of Fathers and Mothers alike? The authorial voice expresses the passing of the oedipal turn in a late interjected paragraph: "Do you think that your fathers are watching? That they weigh you in their ledgerbook? Against what? There is no book and your fathers are dead in the ground."[57] *The Road* expresses a sense of the passing of a culture. It contains no intimation of what might take its place.

Ultimately the novel goes beyond all of the above and expresses what we all know: that in the long end all things will pass and the pattern of movement that was set in being aeons ago will one day cease and days will be no more since there will be no-one to measure their passing. Or as *The Road*'s final paragraph has it:

> Once there were brook trout in the streams in the mountains. You could see them standing in the amber current where the white edges of their fins wimpled softly in the flow. They smelled of moss in your hand. Polished and muscular and torsional. On their backs were vermiculite patterns that were maps of the world in its becoming. Maps and mazes. Of a thing which could not be put back. Not be made right again. In the deep glens where they lived all things were older than man and they hummed of mystery.[58]

The mystery hums in the ardent heart but not for ever.

The Road expresses that paradox that lies at the heart of all serious pessimistic literature: its literary passion defies the very emptiness that it proclaims. It declares the inevitability of cultural entropy, but is itself an example of cultural vitality.

Appendix Three
Supplementary Bibliography

PRIMARY TEXTS

McCarthy, C. *The Sunset Limited* (New York: Vintage, 2006). *The Road* (New York: Knopf, 2006).

SECONDARY TEXTS

Beckett, S. *The Unnameable* in *Molloy* (London: Calder, 1959).
Denton, M. "The Sunset Limited." nytheatre.com review 28/10/2006.
Didion, J. *The Year of Magical Thinking* (London: Harper, 2006).
Ellis, J. *No Place for Home: Spatial Constraint and Character Flight in the Novels of Cormac McCarthy* (New York: Routledge, 2006).
Gutman, L. Curtain Up Review of *The Sunset Limited*. www.curtainup.com 23/11/2006.
Jagoe, E.A. "Pace and the Pampas in Argentine Travel Narratives" in *Bulletin of Hispanic Studies* 81.2 (2004): 361–377
Kellman, S.G. "Cormac McCarthy Imagines the End." *Texas Observer*, 20/10/2006. www.texasobserver.org/article.php?aid=2383
Mars-Jones, A. "Life After Armageddon" Review of *The Road*, *The Observer*, 26/10/2006.
Roth, P. *Everyman* (London: Cape, 2006).

FILMOGRAPHY

Children of Men. Dir. Alfonso Cuaron. Feat. Clive Owen, Julianne Moore, Michael Caine. UK/USA, Universal/Strike/Hit & Run/Quietus, 2006.
Night of the Living Dead. Dir. George Romero. Feat. Duane Jones, Judith O'Dea. USA, Image Ten/Laurel/Market Square/Off Color. 1968.

MUSIC

Handy, W.C. "Saint Louis Blues." 1914.

Notes

NOTES TO CHAPTER ONE

1. J. Conrad, *Lord Jim* [1900] (London: Penguin, 1975) p.163.
2. For qualification of this remark see note 1, p.302.
3. McCarthy makes this claim in a letter to an admirer of his work.
4. R.B.Woodward, "Cormac McCarthy's Venomous Fiction," *New York Times Magazine*, 19/04/92, 36.
5. C. McCarthy, *The Crossing* [1994] (London: Picador, 1995), p.135.
6. C. McCarthy, *The Orchard Keeper* [1965] (London: Picador, 1994), p.264.
7. C. McCarthy, *All the Pretty Horses* [1992] (London: Picador, 1993), p.6.
8. T.S.Eliot, "The Waste Land" [1922] in *Collected Poems, 1909–1962*, (London: faber, 1963), l.430, p.79.
9. C. McCarthy, *Blood Meridian* [1985] (London: Picador, 1990), p.62. and "The Waste Land," l.332, p.76. Quoting more fully from both sources makes both the intertextuality and the mythic meaning clear: the West is a waste land. "Climbing up through ocotillo and pricklypear where the rocks trembled and sleared in the sun, rock and no water and the sandy trace and they kept watch for any green thing that might tell of water but there was no water." (*Blood Meridian*, p.76.)
    Here is no water but only rock
    Rock and no water and the sandy road
    The road winding over the mountains
    Which are mountains of rock without water
    If there were any water we should stop and drink. ("The Waste Land," ll.331–5)
10. Guinn, M. "Atavism and the Exploded Metanarrative: Cormac McCarthy's Journey Into Mythoclasm," in *After Southern Modernism* (Jackson: U P of Mississippi, 2000), pp.91–109.
11. *The Crossing*, p.155.
12. For example, C.Kiefer, "The Morality of Blood: Examining the Moral Code of *The Crossing*" in *The Cormac McCarthy Journal* 1:1 (2000), pp.27–38.

13. C.Chollier, "Exposure and Double Exposure in Cormac McCarthy's Baroque Trilogy" in D.Holloway (ed) *Proceedings of the First European Conference on Cormac McCarthy* (Miami: Cormac McCarthy Society, 1998), pp.49–56.

14. "We had a three hour conversation on the way to New York on Hegel and the nature of narrative. . . . He talked about how narrative was basic to all human beings, . . . Verification of one's story to someone else is essential for living, he said; our reality comes out of the narrative we create, not out of the experiences themselves." (Conversation between Douglas Wager and McCarthy, Fall 1991: quoted by E. Arnold in "Cormac McCarthy's *The Stonemason*: the Unmaking of a Play" in R. Wallach (ed) *Myth, Legend, Dust* (Manchester: Manchester U P, 2000), p.145.

15. C. McCarthy, *Cities of the Plain* (London: Picador, 1998), p.134.

16. C. McCarthy, *Whales and Men*, unpublished manuscript quoted by E. Arnold, " 'Go To Sleep:' Dreams and Visions in the Trilogy," in *The Southern Quarterly*, XXXVIII:3, (2000), pp.34–58.

17. E. Arnold, "The Mosaic of McCarthy's Fiction" in W. Hall and R. Wallach (eds) *Sacred Violence: Volume 1, Cormac McCarthy's Appalachian Works* (El Paso: Texas Western Press, 2002), p.7.

18. Section II of *The Crossing* commences immediately after the death of the wolf with the words "Doomed Enterprises divide lives forever into the then and now." (p.129)

19. R. Barthes, *Mythologies* [1957] (St. Albans: Paladin, 1976), p.143.

20. R. Slotkin, *Regeneration Through Violence, the Mythology of the American Frontier* [1973] (Norman: U P of Oklahoma, 2000), p.5.

21. R. Gray, *Southern Aberrations: Writers of the American South and the Problems of Regionalism* (Baton Rouge, Louisiana U P, 2000), pp.442–3.

22. Ibid.

23. Welty herself wrote ". . . this is not a *historical* historical novel," in *The Robber Bridegroom* [1942] (London: Virago, 1999), p.vii. Mike Fink also appears in the story.

24. A number of critics remark on the similarity with the style of the Hemingway of *The Sun Also Rises* and *A Farewell to Arms*.

25. R. Wallach, "Three Dreams: The Bizarre Epilogue to *Cities of the Plain*," *The Proceedings of the First European Conference on Cormac McCarthy*, pp.57–61.

26. *All the Pretty Horses*, p.111.

27. *Blood Meridian*, p.245.

28. *The Crossing*, p.143.

29. *Cities of the Plain*, p.277.

30. V. Bell, *The Achievement of Cormac McCarthy* [1975] (Baton Rouge: Louisiana State U P, 1988), p.xii.

31. O'Connor is quoting Conrad's own preface to *The Nigger of the Narcissus*.

32. N. Campbell, *The Cultures of the American New West* (Edinburgh: Edinburgh U P, 2000), p.63.
33. Ibid. pp.67–8.
34. *Blood Meridian*, p.251.
35. *Cities of the Plain*, p.231.
36. The third history is this. It exists in the history of histories. It is that ultimately the truth cannot lie in anything but the speaking.
37. *The Crossing*, p.411.
38. R. Jarrett, *Cormac McCarthy* (New York: Twayne, 1997), p.134.
39. C. McCarthy, *Suttree* [1979] (London: Picador, 1989).
40. Encarta Encyclopedia, CD XO3-51821.
41. The character Tobin in *Blood Meridian* is the "expriest." The old man in the ruined church in *The Crossing* is also an apostate; he disputes with the priest and "sends him away." It is this old man who expresses the key idea in McCarthy—"All is Telling." (p.153).
42. J. Keats, "Ode To A Nightingale," [1820], ll.55–6. *The Works of John Keats* (Ware: Wordsworth, 1995).
43. C. McCarthy, *Outer Dark* [1968] (London: Picador, 1994).
44. *Cities of the Plain*, p.283.
45. H. Bloom, *The Anxiety of Influence: A Theory of Poetry* [1973] (New York: Oxford U P, 1997), p.xxii. One is tempted to think that Bloom does also.
46. R. Jarrett, *Cormac McCarthy*, p.23.
47. For instance at the climax of *Dead Man's Walk* the surviving rangers are led to safety in procession by the female European opera singer, who terrifies the invincible Indian chief Buffalo Hump by her combination of leprous features, pet snake and soprano aria. The historical context of *Dead Man's Walk* coincides with that of the ill-fated expedition led by Captain White in *Blood Meridian* (1985). Publishing in 1995, McMurtry cannot have been unaware of the McCarthy treatment of the subject. I would suggest that he deliberately writes the female into the text in the way that McCarthy has not. (L. McMurtry, *Dead Man's Walk* [London: Phoenix, 1996], pp.471–475.
48. "Heath" is sometimes defined as "waste land."
49. O. Paz, *The Labyrinth of Solitude*, trans. L. Kemp, Y. Milos, R.P. Belash [1961] (London: Penguin, 1969), p.104.
50. R. Jarrett, *Cormac McCarthy*, p.153.

NOTES TO CHAPTER TWO

1. As already indicated, McCarthy does his best to avoid having a public persona.
2. R.B.Woodward, "Cormac McCarthy's Venomous Fiction," *New York Times Magazine*, 19/04/92, p.36.

3. E. Arnold and D. Luce (eds) "Introduction," *Perspectives on Cormac McCarthy: Revised Edition* (Jackson: Mississippi UP, 1999), p.2.
4. C. McCarthy, *Wake For Susan* in *The Phoenix, University of Tennessee Magazine* (Knoxville: 1959) and *A Drowning Incident* in *The Phoenix* (1960).
5. L. McCarthy, "A History Minor at U.T. and Territorial Rights" in *Desires Door* (Brownsville: Storyline Press, 1991), p.61.
6. L. McCarthy, "Stories," Ibid. p.83.
7. Ibid.
8. "A History Minor and Territorial Rights," Ibid. p.62.
9. R. Jarrett, *Cormac McCarthy*, p.2.
10. D. Williams, "Annie DeLisle," *Knoxville Sentinel*, 10/10/90. Quoted in Jarrett, *Cormac McCarthy* p.3.
11. E. Hemingway, *The Sun Also Rises* [1926] (New York: Scribners, 1987), p.4.
12. For example the blacksmith sharpening the axe in *Child of God*, the gunsmith refusing to cut the barrels from the shotgun in *Blood Meridian*, the doctor treating Boyd in *The Crossing*, John Grady breaking the wild horses in *All the Pretty Horses* and, above all, Papaw Telfair as described by Ben in *The Stonemason*; these are all detailed in their appropriate chapters.
13. C. McCarthy, *Child of God* [1973] (London: Picador, 1989).
14. R. Jarrett, *Cormac McCarthy*, p.4.
15. R. Brickner, "A Hero Cast Out, Even By Tragedy," *New York Times Book Review*, 13/01/74. Quoted in *Perspectives on Cormac McCarthy*, p.5.
16. J. Yardley, "Alone, Alone, All, All Alone," *Washington Post Book World*, 13/01/74. Quoted in *Perspectives on Cormac McCarthy*, p.5.
17. C. McCarthy, *The Gardener's Son* (Hopewell NJ: Ecco, 1996). (The published text, not the TV film.)
18. R. Jarrett, *Cormac McCarthy, p.4*.
19. R. Marius, "*Suttree* as Window into the Soul of Cormac McCarthy," in *Sacred Violence Vol 1*. p.5.
20. R. Jarrett, *Cormac McCarthy*, p.5.
21. T. Nolan, review of *Blood Meridian, Los Angeles Times Book Review*, 9/06/85.
22. "Cormac McCarthy's Venomous Fiction."
23. Ibid. According to Woodward, McCarthy ". . . quit [drinking] 16 years ago in El Paso." This would mean that he did so immediately on leaving Knoxville. Like all the details of McCarthy's biography, this seems both plausible and impossible to verify. It is a truth of the kind "made" by the Mexican Captain in *All the Pretty Horses*, or by the Gypsy storyteller in *The Crossing*. The fact that McCarthy is still alive supports the thesis.
24. Symbolically attacked by Ather Ownby in *The Orchard Keeper*.
25. D. Holloway, "'A false book is no book at all:' the ideology of representation in *Blood Meridian* and the Border Trilogy," in *Myth, Legend, Dust*, pp.185–200.

26. There remains a division among McCarthy critics regarding the relative merits of the Tennessee and Southwestern novels. Despite this the overall regard for McCarthy's work has remained high in academic circles and interest in his work has continued to grow.

27. C. McCarthy, *The Stonemason* (Hopwell NJ: Ecco, 1994).

28. This remark requires qualification. For comment on a single performance of a modified version of the play see note 1, p.302.

29. P. Josyph, "Older professions: the fourth wall of *The Stonemason*," in *Myth, Legend, Dust*, p.119.

30. *All the Pretty Horses* was made into a film in 2001: *No Country for Old Men* is reported to be in production. These facts could account for the considerable change in McCarthy's material circumstances.

NOTES TO CHAPTER THREE

1. O. Paz, *The Labyrinth of Solitude* [1961] (London: Penguin, 1990), p.25.

2. *All the Pretty Horses*, p.168.

3. *The Labyrinth of Solitude*, p.398.

4. This is of course the version of American history that elides the Native Americans. It is the version addressed by McCarthy, rather than my own. It is the aspect of time-scale that is significant from my point of view here. It should be pointed out that American *people* of European origin have an ancient history; it happens not to have occurred in America. It should also be noted that, although my own usage is not consistent, "America" and "USA" are not coterminous.

5. There are parallels with what Britain was doing in the territories of its Empire, but I am concerned with events "at home." One must admit that "at home" did not include Ireland.

6. F. O'Connor, *Mystery and Manners* [1957] (New York: Noonday Press, 1999), p.203.

7. In McCarthy's case the migration is literal as well as fictional.

8. Given the tendency for Americans to date their culture from the Revolution.

9. Perry Miller is less comprehensive in his claim that "Without some understanding of Puritanism, and that at its source, there is no understanding of America." (*The American Puritans: Their Prose and Poetry*, p.ix). Miller published in 1956 and Bercovitch in 1975. There has been a growing movement in the subsequent decades to address the contribution to American culture of other racial, religious and political groups besides the "WASP." McCarthy's Southwestern novels are themselves both products of, and evidence of this change in perspective. Where they differ from much other revisionist writing is in their rejection of any romanticizing of minority or defeated groups such as the Native Americans.

10. J. Winthrop, sermon on board the Arbella, 1630, in P. Miller (ed), *The American Puritans: Their Prose and Poetry* (New York, Anchor, 1956), p.79.

11. This seems to be particularly true of American critics. East Tennessee in particular seems to be regarded as something of an American backwater.

12. The artificiality of these boundaries of Latitude is most marked, particularly when they are contrasted with the courses of the Cumberland and Tennessee Rivers, which might well have been chosen as the natural boundaries they actually were before the white man's arrival.

13. *Child of God*, p.127.

14. I argue subsequently that McCarthy deals with race implicitly in Suttree. Urban Knoxville would have had more black citizens than did the mountain communities.

15. M. Haun, *The Hawk's Done Gone, and Other Stories* (ed) H. Gower [1940–68] (Nashville: Vanderbilt University Press, 1995), p.98. Mary Dorthula White is the narrator of the stories in the first section of the book.

16. E.L. Ayers & B. Mittendorf, (eds), *The Oxford Book of the American South* (New York: Oxford University Press, 1997), p.126.

17. S. Watkins, *Co. Aytch* [1882] in *The Oxford Book of the American South*, p.126.

18. Ibid. p.129.

19. Murfree published initially under the name Charles Egbert Craddock. She adopted a male pseudonym for much the same reasons as did Marian Evans and the Brontes.

20. M.N. Murfree, *The Bushwhackers and Other* Stories [1899] (New York: Books For Libraries Press, 1969), p.16.

21. Ibid. p.17. Hillary's mother, herself "fur the Union" (p.78) relates that Hillary "jined the critter-company" (p.79). This is probably a reference to the cavalry regiment of Bedford Forrest which campaigned throughout Tennessee. Andrew Nelson Lytle's highly partial and romanticized account of Forrest's exploits in Tennessee and Georgia is entitled *Bedford Forrest and His Critter Company*.

22. M.N. Murfree, *The Panther of Jolton's Ridge* in *The Bushwhackers and Other Stories*, pp.119–213.

23. Murfree's tale can be read as prophetic of the coming and consequences of Prohibition, already a subject for political campaigning at the time (c.1880).

24. M.N. Murfree, *The Prophet of the Great Smoky Mountains* [1885] (Boston: Houghton Mifflin,1890), p.188.

25. Unlike McCarthy, Murfree was not a resident of the mountains. Her family were from Middle Tennessee; Murfreesboro is a few miles southeast of Nashville—and her stories of the mountains were inspired by her visits there on family holidays in her youth.

26. The location of most of the tales is the mountain area of Haun's native Cocke County, some 50 miles east of Knoxville and on the border with North Carolina. In this area lies Rag Mountain, rising to almost 4000 feet. The isolation of the area was increased by the combination of mountains and large river systems. This was especially true of the period 1910–1930 in which Haun's tales are mostly set.
27. *The Hawk's Done Gone and Other Stories*, p.39.
28. Ibid.
29. Ibid. p.42.
30. Ibid. p.118.
31. Mary Dorthula's name for the "horse."
32. Ibid. p.56.
33. *The Orchard Keeper*, p.227.
34. "*Suttree* As Window into the Soul of Cormac McCarthy", in *Sacred Violence*, Second Edition, Vol.1. p.117.
35. M. Gibson, "The White Cap Book" in *Knoxville Local History Magazine*, No. 26. June 29th 2000.
36. *Child of God*, p.165. This is quoted in more detail in the section on *Child of God* that follows.
37. "The White Cap Book," *Knoxville Local History Magazine*.
38. *The Hawk's Done Gone and Other Stories*, pp.124–44.
39. J. Agee, *A Death in the Family* [1938] (New York: Vintage, 1998), p.209.
40. G.W. Harris, *Sut Lovingood: Yarns Spun* [1864] (Chapel Hill: University of North Carolina Library Electronic Text, 1997, http://metalab.unc.edu/docsouth/harrisg/gharris.html), p.23.
41. P. Taylor, *In the Tennessee Country* (London: Chatto & Windus, 1994), p.82.
42. All the characters in *The Stonemason* are black.
43. *Suttree*, p.203.
44. Ibid.
45. A surely deliberate but inverted reference to the fate of Haze Motes' car in *Wise Blood*.
46. Will Rogers spoke for that culture when he remarked "Prohibition is better than no liquor at all." Quoted by E. Behr in *Prohibition, The Thirteen Years That Changed America* (London, BBC, 1997), p.174. A new Prohibition helps to fuel the violent destructiveness of *No Country for Old Men*, a novel with a contemporary setting.
47. The date of the repeal of the Volstead Act.
48. "*Suttree* As Window Into the Soul of Cormac McCarthy" in *Sacred Violence*, Second Edition, Vol. 1 p.114.
49. Ibid.
50. *Suttree*, p.366.

51. T.H Watkins, *The Great Depression* (Boston: Blackside,1993), p.154. James R. McCarthy was not related to Cormac's family. Arthur E. Morgan was the first chairman of TVA.
52. *The Orchard Keeper*, p.10.
53. "Suttree As Window Into the Soul of Cormac McCarthy," in *Sacred Violence*, p.1–2.
54. Marcus draws attention to the gothic atmosphere of the actual folk music of the people. The "folk revival" of the 60s was associated with a more optimistic vision of the world. It was transformed into a music of protest and, to the extent that it promoted notions such as racial justice and sexual liberation it had some impact on the world. It was however, also an example of a yearning for the myth of the pastoral, of a nostalgia for a pre-industrial world of rural simplicity that had never existed, and especially not in the mountains of Appalachia. It was also an understandable yearning for a world without "the bomb," the existence of which made the threat of universal annihilation all too real. I suggest that McCarthy was influenced by the old folk music rather than the new. He rejects the myth of the pastoral and accepts that all life forms come to dust in the context of geological time. The threat posed by the existence of nuclear technology is a clearly discernable theme in the Border Trilogy.
55. Black and white artists are featured indifferently.
56. G. Marcus, *Invisible Republic* (London: Picador, 1998).
57. All on *The Harry Smith Anthology of American Folk Music*, American Folkways Recordings, on CDs SFW 40090/A 28746–28751.
58. From Dock Boggs version of the traditional "Oh Death!" [1963] *Smithsonian Folkways Recordings*, CD no. SFW 40108, 1998.
59. C. Vann Woodward, *The Burden of Southern History: Third Edition* (Baton Rouge: Louisiana State University Press,1993), p.21.

NOTES TO CHAPTER FOUR

1. Rick Wallach of the Cormac McCarthy Society and the University of Miami was kind enough to send me copies of *Wake For Susan* and *A Drowning Incident* when he learned that I was working on McCarthy.
2. R. Wallach, "Prefiguring Cormac McCarthy: the Early Short Stories," in *Myth, Legend, Dust* p.15.
3. D. Luce, " 'They ain't the thing': Artifact and Hallucinated Recollection in Cormac McCarthy's Frame-Works", in *Myth, Legend, Dust*, p.21.
4. *Wake for Susan*, p.5.
5. S.E. Chamberlain, *My Confession* (New York: Harper's, 1956), p.7.
6. M. Twain, *Life on the Mississippi* [1883] (New York: Penguin, 1986), p.285.
7. See appendix p.54 below.

8. The reference has a double significance. There is a "Madge Wildfire" inciting the mob at the "Porteus riot" that Scott incorporates in his novel.

9. H. Bloom & L. Trilling (eds), *The Oxford Anthology of English Literature: Romantic Prose and Poetry* (New York: Oxford University Press, 1973), p.563.

10. W. Scott, *The Heart of Midlothian* (London: Adam & Charles Black,1893), p.416.

11. *Invisible Republic: Bob Dylan's Basement Tapes*, pp.87–126.

12. *Wake for Susan*, p.5.

13. Ibid. pp.5–6.

14. Ibid. p.6.

15. Ibid. p.4.

16. Ibid. p.3.

17. As Eduardo points out in *Cities of the Plain* (p.143), "What is wrong with this story is that it is not a true story." Eduardo refers to the romantic story that John Grady has told himself about how his life will be, the story inherent in the cultural matrix of John Grady's America.

18. D. Luce, "'They ain't the thing': Artifact and Hallucinated Recollection in Cormac McCarthy's Early Frame Works," *Myth, Legend, Dust.* p. 23.

19. *Wake for Susan*, p.4.

20. Ibid.

21. See Ch.1, p.25.

22. "'They Ain't the Thing': Artifact and Hallucinated Recollection in Cormac McCarthy's Early Frame Works", in *Myth, Legend, Dust*, p.25.

23. *Wake for Susan*, p.6.

24. Ibid.

25. Ibid. p.4. Faulkner uses the same word with the same purpose in, for example, *Absalom, Absalom!* as Quentin and Shreeve speculate regarding Charles Bon in New Orleans.

26. *Wake For Susan*, p.4.

27. W. Scott, "Proud Masie" [1818] in *The Oxford Anthology of Romantic Poetry and Prose*, p.563.

28. Ibid.

29. Ibid. p.5

30. The owl is the traditional "bird of death."

31. R. Wallach, "Prefiguring Cormac McCarthy: the Early Short Stories," in *Myth, Legend, Dust*, p.18.

32. *A Drowning Incident*, p.3.

33. Ibid. p.3.

34. Ibid.

35. A euphemism for outside lavatory; the old-fashioned "privy" consisting of a board with a hole in it giving on to a bucket or ditch.

36. Ibid.

37. Ibid.
38. Ibid.
39. Ibid.
40. Ibid.
41. Ibid.
42. Ibid.
43. Ibid
44. Ibid.
45. Ibid. p.4.
46. Ibid.
47. Ibid.
48. Ibid.
49. Obviously Freudian psychology should be considered one of these "systems of belief." Although there is some evidence of Freudian influence in this text it is perhaps less than comprehensive. I would argue that McCarthy does indeed reject all such systems in his later works. Even in this story the twin notions of father/son conflict and sibling rivalry do not require a belief in Freudian theory to explain their appearance. Father/son conflict is plainly inherent in any patriarchal epistemology, while overt sibling rivalry may be observed in small children as a commonplace.

NOTES TO CHAPTER FIVE

1. T.S. Eliot, "Burnt Norton I," in his *Collected Poems: 1909–1962* [1963] (London: Faber, 1974), p.190.
2. "Atavism and the Exploded Metanarrative: Cormac McCarthy's Journey into Mythoclasm," in *After Southern Modernism*, pp.96–7.
3. "'They Ain't the Thing': Artifact and Hallucinated Recollection in Cormac McCarthy's Early Frame Works," in *Myth, Legend, Dust*, p.23.
4. *The Orchard Keeper*, p.85. This detail is conveyed by including in the text the agreement written out by the storekeeper.
5. Ibid. p.131.
6. Ibid. p.32.
7. Ibid. p.225.
8. Ibid. p.245.
9. Ibid. p.67.
10. Ibid. p.82.
11. Ibid. p.164. Both these passages are printed in italics.
12. Ibid. p.3
13. *After Southern Modernism*, p.97.
14. Ibid.
15. *The Orchard Keeper*, p.246.
16. Ibid. p.51.

17. Ibid.
18. Ibid. p.156.
19. Ibid. p.155. Both printed in italics.
20. Ibid. p.55. Ather's words are a reference to Yeats's "The Lake Isle of Innisfree"

    I will arise now and go to Innisfree,
    And a small cabin build there of clay and wattles made:
    Nine bean-rows will I have there, a hive for the honey-bee,
    And live alone in the bee-loud glade.

    This characteristically modernist intertextuality connects Southern pastoralism to the mythic escapism of Yeats's brand of Irish nationalism and also to the wider American pastoralism of Thoreau.
21. Ibid. p.11.
22. Ibid. p.51.
23. Ibid. p.90.
24. Ibid. p.46. Ather is a product of the same pre-enlightenment Tennessee mountain culture that Mildred Haun portrayed in *The Hawk's Done Gone*. Her image of that world was even further removed from a vision of the pastoral than is McCarthy's.
25. Ibid. p.75.
26. Ibid. p.88.
27. R. Jarrett, "The Human Comedy of Cormac McCarthy," in *Sacred Violence*, p.59.
28. This episode is echoed by the exchanges between the authorities and the Weaver family in their mountain cabin at Ruby Ridge, Idaho.
29. *The Orchard Keeper*, p.98.
30. Ibid. p.141.
31. *The Pastoral Vision of Cormac McCarthy*, p.13.
32. Ibid. p.33.
33. Ibid. p.235. The same characteristics are displayed when Johnny Romines speculates on the identity of Rattner's killer: "Reckon it was somebody from around here? I doubt it was somebody from New York City, the constable said." (Ibid. p.236)
34. Seven is a number with many significations in many different cultures. In archaic mythology seven years is supposedly the duration of the reign of the sacred king. Ather makes frequent reference to seven year cycles when John Wesley visits him in the asylum.
35. Ibid. p.79. Printed in italics.
36. Sylder has "beaten up" on Gifford while the constable lay in the darkness in bed, hardly an honourable act in itself.
37. Ibid p.233.
38. Ibid. p.66.
39. See Ch.3. pp.46–50.
40. See Ch.3. pp.35–41.

NOTES TO CHAPTER SIX

1. Guillermin asserts that much of McCarthy's work is allegorical in nature; he points out that *Outer Dark* and *Blood Meridian* are most notable in this respect.
2. Albert Erskine, McCarthy's editor at Knopf.
3. *Outer Dark*, p.5.
4. D. Carr, "The Dispossessed White as Naked Ape and Stereotyped Hillbilly in the Southern Novels of Cormac McCarthy," *Midwest Quarterly: A Journal of Contemporary Thought.* 40:1 (1998), p.9.
5. *Outer Dark*, p.5.
6. F. Hopkinson Smith, *Colonel Carter of Cartersville* [1891] (Boston: Houghton Mifflin undated), p.82.
7. *Outer Dark*, p.14.
8. I have previously mentioned the deliberate use of significant names by McCarthy. I have also mentioned the representation of the state of *unheimlich*, particularly relevant to *Outer Dark* and mentioned by a number of critics including Gray (*Southern Aberrations*, p.443) and Bell (*The Achievement of Cormac McCarthy*, p.33).
9. P. Miller, *Errand Into the Wilderness* [1956] (Cambridge Mass: Harvard University Press, 1996), p.5.
10. *Outer Dark*, p.223.
11. T. Witek, " 'He's Hell When He's Well': Cormac McCarthy's Rhyming Dictions", in *Myth, Legend, Dust*, p.83.
12. R. Jarrett, *Cormac McCarthy*, p.17.
13. W.C. Spencer, "Cormac McCarthy's Unholy Trinity: Biblical Parody in Outer Dark", in *Sacred Violence*, p.69.
14. *Outer Dark*, p.3.
15. Ibid. p.129.
16. Ibid. pp.224–5.
17. It does not explain the failure to recognize this imagery on the part of a substantial number of scholars. One can only speculate as to why this should be, especially in America where even the ungodly can hardly be unaware of the continuing ubiquity of religious belief. Perhaps even some secular academics were so shocked by the extreme nature of the inversion—the supreme creator and redeemer of the world as pitiless murdering cannibal—that they repressed the obvious implication.
18. The Achievement of Cormac McCarthy, p.34.
19. J-J. Goux, *Oedipus Philosopher*, trans. C. Porter [1993] (Stanford: Stanford University Press). If, as I have suggested, Culla is "virtually without culture," then McCarthy has characteristically inverted the image: Culla is Oedipus without the philosophy.

20. The ubiquity of this ancient culture and the manner in which the image of the Goddess has evolved and been incorporated into the religious culture of later ages, including, of course, Christianity in the shape of the Virgin, is detailed in A. Baring, and J. Cashford, *The Myth of the Goddess, Evolution of an Image* (London: Arkana, 1993).

21. *The Labyrinth of Solitude*, pp.80–81. This was first published in 1961 and is in tune with so much that McCarthy has written that it is hard to believe that the latter has not read and been strongly influenced by the former. There is ample material for a full study of the correspondences between the two writers. Of these I shall have space to mention only a few.

22. Ibid.

23. Acts, XIX, 34–5.

24. J.M. Grammer, "A Thing Against Which Time Will Not Prevail: Pastoral and History in Cormac McCarthy's South," in *Perspectives on Cormac McCarthy: Revised Edition*, pp.35–36. Grammer does not comment on the theological parody of the triune.

25. Ibid. p.31

26. Ibid.

27. *Outer Dark*, p.45–6. The concentration on clock time is a further Faulknerian reference—as in *The Sound and the Fury*.

28. Ibid. p.47.

29. Ibid. p.126.

30. Ibid.

31. This is, of course, the significance of the snake in the Genesis myth of Eden, contra Freud. The bee was also a Goddess emblem; Culla encounters a beehiver on the road at the start of his journey. He is one of the more neighbourly inhabitants of that grim realm.

32. Ibid. p.141.

33. Ibid. p.143.

34. Ibid.p.148.

35. Ibid. p.151.

36. Ibid. p.98.

37. Ibid. p.113.

38. Ibid. p.237.

39. Ibid. The reference is to the Virgin, Catholicism's version of the Goddess, and to the Ave Maria, "Hail Mary, full of grace."

40. Ibid. pp.237–8.

41. Ibid. p.193. Both the indomitable Dietch and the unfailingly maternal Rinthy display that ardent-heartedness that McCarthy so values. The other aspect of the dialectic, human insignificance, is represented by Culla, the existential wanderer in the "outer dark" of a meaningless universe.

42. Ibid. p.238. Anti-Semitism was, of course, an aspect of the racial prejudice of the South. McCarthy gives the reader one characteristically oblique clue to this rather more esoteric aspect of his text. The hog-drover, finding Culla as limited a conversationalist as does everyone else, recounts that the bible says "a jew wouldn't eat hog-meat." Culla responds, "What's a jew?" (Ibid. p.215)

43. J. Grammer, "A Thing Against Which Time Will Not Prevail", in *Perspectives on Cormac McCarthy*, pp. 36–7. The "band of Marauders" also bear a strong resemblance to the three outlaws who threaten the pioneers in John Ford's *Wagonmaster*.

44. *Outer Dark*. p.218. The absence of conventional punctuation from the latter stage of the passage increases the dynamism of the account.

45. Matthew, VIII, 28–33. As ever McCarthy inverts the meaning of the passage he 'quotes'. Christ cast out 'evil spirits' into the swine and thus saved the man possessed thereby. The evil in this passage remains in the hearts of the drovers who blame Culla for their loss and seek to lynch him; the preacher urges them on to violence.

46. *Outer Dark*, p.144.

47. Ibid. p. 177. McCarthy is referring here to Wittgenstein's dictum, "Whereof we cannot speak, thereof we must be silent."

48. See p.4 above.

49. Outer Dark, p.88.

50. Ibid. p.95.

51. Ibid.

52. "Grove" has classical associations; "Rinthy" is presumably short for "Corinthians" the biblical source of the reference to "Faith, hope and charity, these three, but the greatest of these is charity" (I, Corinthians, XIII, 13), charity being the biblical term for selfless Christian love. It also contains the line "For now we see through a glass darkly." Ibid. v.12. The names of the texts themselves are also related: Faulkner's "Light" is Hightower's *ignis fatuus*. McCarthy transforms it into an uncompromising existential "Dark."

53. Ibid. p.88. See p.34 for absence of race issue in East Tennessee.

54. Ibid. p.236.

NOTES TO CHAPTER SEVEN

1. Although *Suttree* is set in East Tennessee, it is predominantly an urban novel and is centred on an educated and articulate protagonist, different in almost every way from the mountain people of Sevier County and environs.

2. *Child of God*, p.4. In the South the term "child of God" traditionally referred to the mentally handicapped or insane. In the discourse of Christianity we are all "God's children."

3. Ibid. p.81.

4. *Invisible Republic*, p.125.
5. *Child of God*, p.81. It is characteristic of McCarthy that these simple lines contain multiple significances in addition to those I have noted above. The reference to Adam, the use of the term out*strip*, the lack of an upper case 'g' for 'god'—all may be considered deliberate. Lester, like all McCarthy's "heroes" is cast out of his American "paradise"; "strip" has obvious sexual connotations; there is no God in McCarthy's universe.
6. D. Luce, "The Murderers Behind *Child of God*", Cormac McCarthy International Colloquy, El Paso, Texas, 1998. Quoted by N. Sullivan, "The Evolution of the Dead Girlfriend Motif in *Outer Dark* and *Child of God*" in *Myth, Legend, Dust*, p.77.
7. Not to mention Faulkner, Caldwell, Richard Wright, Hugh Selby Jnr. et al.
8. A rare book; my attempts to obtain a copy have so far been unsuccessful.
9. M. Gibson, "The White Cap Book," in *Knoxville Local History Magazine, No. 26*, 29/6/00, (Temporary internet site). See pp.53–4.
10. *Child of God*, p.165.
11. Ibid.
12. Gibson suggests that its roots lay in the tradition of charivari.
13. *The Orchard Keeper*, p.140. There is no explanation of what a White-Cap might be in this text, nor any other reference to the phenomenon. Only a local Sevier County reader would recognize the term.
14. *Child of God*, p.81. It must be added that even after reading *Child of God*, I had no idea what White Caps might have been. I assumed that they were a kind of Ku Klux Klan. Inquiry at the University of Tennessee in Knoxville produced no enlightenment. The internet proved the only productive source.
15. Ibid. p.48. The lawn is an antipastoral "gray."
16. Ibid. p.51.
17. Ibid. p.35.
18. Ibid. p.22.
19. Ibid.
20. Ibid. p.36.
21. Ibid. p.44–5.
22. T. Jefferson, "Notes on the State of Virginia: Query XIX, Manufactures" in N. Baym et al (eds), *The Norton Anthology of American Literature, Second Edition, Vol. 1* [1985] (New York: Norton), p.627.
23. J. Grammer, "A Thing Against Which Time Shall Not Prevail," in *Perspectives on Cormac McCarthy*, pp.29–44.
24. *Child of God*, p. 21.
25. Ibid.
26. Ibid. p.9.
27. Ibid. p.140. *Psycho*'s Norman Bates was also 'inspired' by a real serial killer—Ed Gein, of Plainfield, Wisconsin.

28. Ibid.
29. Ibid. p.127.
30. "The woods are lovely, dark and deep." Frost also is drawn to seductive death, but is held to life by his responsibilities: "But I have promises to keep, And miles to go before I sleep." R. Frost, "Stopping By Woods on a Snowy Evening," in E.C. Latham (ed), *The Poetry of Robert Frost* (New York: Holt, Rinehart & Winston, 1979), pp.224–225.
31. *Child of God*, p.132.
32. Ibid. p.69.
33. Ibid. p.194.
34. Ibid. p.168.
35. Barn burning is a feature of various Faulkner tales, not least *As I Lay Dying*. The flood is also a common feature, the river having to be crossed in spate.
36. As opposed to the eroticism that is such a feature of *All the Pretty Horses*.
37. *Child of God*, p.65.
38. Ibid. p.134–5.
39. Ibid. p.135. Like Ralph Ellison, McCarthy could also be said to have taken from Dostoevsky the image of the Underground Man. Unlike both predecessors, Lester lacks the language with which to articulate his alienation.
40. Ibid. p.136.
41. Ibid. p.141.
42. Ibid. p.156.
43. Christopher Lasch identified this freedom from restraint as the infantile desire for omnipotence and saw it as a symptom of the loss of clearly delineated identity in a narcissistic culture. C. Lasch, *The Minimal Self: Psychic Survival in Troubled Times* [1985] (London: Picador, 1985).
44. *Child of God*, p.74.
45. Ibid. p.67 Given the phallic significance of the rifle this passage can be read as representing masturbation, the culturally repressed aspect of the narcissistic sexuality of the isolated pioneer hero of the wilderness.
46. Ibid. p.128.
47. Ibid. p.105.
48. Ibid. p.152.
49. Ibid. p.86.
50. Ibid. The song is characteristically expressive of the "old, weird America."
    > Death is an angel sent down from above,
    > Sent for the buds of the flowers we love.
    > Truly a soul for in heaven's own way,
    > Each is a flower for the master's bouquet.

    ("Gathering Flowers For the Master's Bouquet" on C. Stanley & R. Stanley, *Too Late To Cry* [UK: Catfish Records KATCD 206, 2001]). The use of subtly erotic imagery to express religious attitudes to death adds to the disturbing quality of the song and makes it particularly appropriate for *Child*

of God. It is, of course, a commonplace to link Southern religious fundamentalism and sexuality.

51. Ibid. p.196. Seven maidens were sacrificed to the Minotaur.
52. Ibid.

NOTES TO CHAPTER EIGHT

1. Author's Introduction. J. Conrad, *Chance* [1913] (London: Penguin Modern Classics, 1974), p.10.
2. "Southern" here meaning, of course, the Southern United States.
3. D. Kiberd, Introductory Chapter in J.Joyce, *Ulysses* [1922] (London: Penguin Twentieth Century Classics, 1992), p.xiii.
4. *Suttree*, p.9.
5. *Ulysses*, p. 63. The two works are further linked by Eliot and the section of
   "The Waste Land" entitled "Death By Water." Eliot wrote of *Ulysses* "It is
   the book to which we are all indebted and which none of us can escape."
6. D. Kiberd, Introduction to *Ulysses*, p.lxxx.
7. O'Connor expressed this defensiveness in a celebrated remark: "The presence of Faulkner in our midst makes a great difference in what the writer
   can and cannot permit himself to do. Nobody wants his mule and wagon
   stalled on the same track the Dixie Limited is roaring down." (F. O'Connor,
   Mystery and Manners [1970] (New York: Noonday Press, 1999), p.45).
8. The term "nightmare" is used by both Joyce and Paz. I have already quoted
   Paz on p.19. "History, Stephen said, is a nightmare from which I am trying
   to awake." *Ulysses*, p.42. McCarthy does not give the impression that he
   considers such an awakening possible.
9. And shall continue to do throughout.
10. *Suttree*, pp.13–14.
11. Ibid.
12. Ibid. p.184.
13. Ibid. p.24. "Early Times," the destructive home-made whiskey drunk by
    the carousers of McAnally reflects the Southern myth of the "Old Times"
    that "are not forgotten". "Dixie" is the anthem of the South's refusal of
    history and the denial of death that fails to recognize that "lo, the thing's
    inside."
14. *Cities of the Plain*, p.283.
15. It is not beyond McCarthy to have deliberately chosen the name "Harro-
    gate" for its similarity to "surrogate".
16. *Suttree*, p.372.
17. Ibid. p.417.
18. Ibid.
19. *Suttree*, p.3. Characteristically Joycean word-pairs in combination are fre-
    quently used; "highshouldered," "sootblackened," "lightwire."

20. T.S. Eliot, "The Love Song of J. Alfred Prufrock" [1917], in *Collected Poems*, lines 1–7, p.13.

21. *Ulysses*, p.565.

22. *Suttree*, p.4.

23. Ibid. One is reminded of the decomposed corpse of the puppy in the creek in *A Drowning Incident*.

24. *Suttree*, pp.4–5. The "carder of souls" is a reference to "The Weaver God" of Melville's *Moby Dick*, an image of the interconnectedness of life and death.

25. "Nigger" tells of Irish Long: "He would mortally whip your ass if you messed with him, Irish Long would. And there wasn't nobody in McAnally Flats no betterhearted. He give away everything he owned. . . . He never turned down nobody, Irish Long never. *Suttree*, p.25. Characteristically we are given no clue as to Nigger's race. He is "a gray looking man in glasses." Race is not an issue for Suttree. Those who become too infirm to care for themselves seek out the care of Mrs. Long, "Good a woman as ever walked." Ibid. p.296.

26. McCarthy's pride in his Irish ancestry strengthens the autobiographical aspect of his choice of name for his principal protagonist.

27. Ibid. p.153.

28. Ibid. p.471.

29. F. Thompson, "The Hound of Heaven," opening lines. Quoted in J. Campbell, *The Hero With A Thousand Faces*, [1949] (London: Fontana, 1993), p.60. It is characteristic of McCarthy that he should invest a single image, the dog, with such a wealth of complimentary meanings.

30. *Suttree*, p.4.

31. Ibid. p.254.

32. *The Achievement of Cormac McCarthy*, p.69. Bell entitles the chapter "Death and Affirmation" and states that "*Suttree* is a novel about transcending death—not in fact of course, but in the mind and spirit."

33. See "Chaining the Rough Beast" in R. Gray, *Writing the South* [1986] (Baton Rouge: Louisiana State University Press, 1997), pp.62–74.

34. There are departures from the naturalistic but they are mainly presented as dreams or hallucinations.

35. If Suttree becomes at times the author of his own narrative he may also be associated with Faulkner's Thomas Sutpen.

36. *Suttree*, p.4.

37. Ibid. p.7.

38. Ibid. p.29.

39. Ibid. p.281.

40. Ibid. p.106.

41. Ibid. p.276.

42. Ibid. p.470.

43. N.O. Brown, *Life Against Death: The Psychoanalytical Meaning of History* [1959] (London: Sphere, 1970), p.251.

44. *Suttree*, p.14.

45. Ibid.

46. Ibid.

47. Ibid.

48. Ibid. p.13.

49. Ibid. p.203.

50. Ibid. p.287.

51. These twins resemble Thornton Wilder's Manuel and Esteban, for whom "telepathy was a common occurrence in their lives" (T. Wilder, *The Bridge of San Luis Rey* [1927] (London: Longmans, 1931), p.52.) McCarthy uses the expression "sinister isomer in bone and flesh" regarding the relation of Vern to Fern, sinister having two meanings that are both significant to Suttree. *Suttree*, p.361.

52. *Suttree*, p.283.

53. Ibid. p.285.

54. Ibid. p.12.

55. An example of McCarthy's literary humour: Hoghead's real name is "James Henry." Ibid. p.403.

56. Ibid. p.430. Suttree foresees this death in a waking dream.

57. Ibid. p.86.

58. Ibid. pp.457–8.

59. Ibid. p.203.

60. Ibid. p.332.

61. Ibid. p.353.

62. Ibid. p.355.

63. Ibid. p.327. Suttree takes the gorget to wear on a cord around his neck. When he leaves the city of death he discards it, symbolizing his freeing of himself from his terror of nothingness.

64. Ibid. p.354.

65. Ibid. p.276.

66. Ibid. p.295.

67. T.D. Young, "The Imprisonment of Sensibility: *Suttree*" in *Perspectives on Cormac McCarthy*, p.120.

68. *Suttree*, p.291.

69. Ibid. p.426.

70. Ibid. p.427.

71. Ibid. p.426.

72. Ibid. p.461.

73. Ibid. p.157.

74. Ibid.

NOTES TO CHAPTER NINE

1. An attempt was made to produce the play at the Arena Stage, Washington, in 1992. For a detailed account of the circumstances that led to the failure of this project see E. Arnold, "*The Stonemason*: the unmaking of a play." in *Myth, Legend, Dust*, pp.141–154.

    Since the time of writing a single performance of the play was given on October 12th. 2001, at The Arts Alliance Center, Clear Lake, Texas. For a short account of the strategy adopted for this production see E.T.Arnold, "A Stonemason Evening", *The Cormac McCarthy Journal*, Vol.2, No.1, Spring 2002, pp.7–11. It is clear that this production omits a great deal and that it would be of diminished relevance to the analysis of the published text contained in this chapter.

2. Stage direction in *The Stonemason*, p.5.

3. Ibid. All stage directions in the text are in italics. The heavy type emphasis is mine.

4. "Houston's Arts Center to Stage Multimedia Version of The Stonemason" in *The Cormac McCarthy Society Newsletter*, Summer Issue, 2001. See also endnote 1 above.

5. *The Stonemason*, p.6.

6. Ibid. My emphasis.

7. I was obliged to look up the meaning of this word. Webster's on-line dictionary defines it as:

    > An institution that flourished in the late 19th and early 20th centuries providing popular education combined with entertainment in the form of lectures, concerts and plays often presented outdoors or in a tent.

8. *The Stonemason*, p.6.

9. My emphasis.

10. Ibid. p.9.

11. Ibid. p.14.

12. Ibid. Act 1, Scene 2. pp.24–5.

13. Notice in *Cormac McCarthy Society Newsletter*, Summer, 2001.

14. Race does feature but only incidentally. Papaw relates the story of the death of Uncle Selman at the hands of a white man who went unpunished but this is not represented as being of great significance. It is perhaps an example of that powerlessness which promotes the belief that justification can be purely internal and that virtue is its own reward.

15. Such representations are a staple of popular culture—*The Waltons, Little House on the Prairie, Bonanza, Dallas*.

16. Ibid. Act 1, Scene 4. p.30.

17. Ibid. Act 1, Scene 2. p.14.

18. Ibid. Act 3, Scene 2. p.69.

19. Ibid. Act 3. Scene 4. pp.78–9.
20. Ibid. Act 1, Scene 2. p.13.
21. Ibid. Act 1, Scene 2. p.18–9.
22. Ibid. Act 5, Scene 5. p.120.
23. "Thomas Alva Edison: Hearing Impaired Inventor," in *20th Century History Guide*, Internet.
24. *The Stonemason*, Act 1, Scene 4. pp.32–3.
25. Ibid. Act 5, Scene 3. pp.111–2
26. Ibid. pp.112–3.
27. He is an insurance claims adjuster.
28. Ibid. Act 2, Scene 6. p.60.
29. Ibid. Act 5, Scene 4. p.116.
30. Ibid. Act 2, Scene 2. pp.44–5.
31. Ibid.
32. Ibid.
33. Ibid. Act 1, Scene 2. p.25.
34. Ibid. Act 5, Scene 1. p.104.
35. The name receives another layer of significance in its shortened form, "Ben", Hebrew for "son of."
36. The nickname expresses the dangerous nature of the conflict within the young man's life.
37. Ibid. Act 1, Scene 1. p.9.
38. Ibid. Act 3, Scene 3. p.74.
39. Ibid. Act 5, Scene 11. p.133.
40. Ibid. Act 5, Scene 2. p.110.

NOTES TO CHAPTER TEN

1. Since the "successfully completed" artefact was a film it must be acknowledged that its creation involved the efforts of a large team of people, for whom McCarthy and, more particularly Pearce, will have to stand as a synecdoche.
2. At the Society's Manchester Conference, June, 2000.
3. D. Luce, "Cormac McCarthy's First Screenplay: *The Gardener's Son*." in *Perspectives on Cormac McCarthy*, pp.71–96.
4. J. Huston, *Wise Blood*, Artificial Eye/Anthea/Ithaca, USA/Germany, 1979. From the novel by Flannery O'Connor.
5. It should be noted that the screenplay is not in any way a shooting script. It consists mainly of dialogue, but with directions that make both the action and its visual context clear.
6. In this case I am using the term to refer to both the screenplay as text and the film as text also. The two articles are "Cormac McCarthy's First Screenplay, *The Gardener's Son*" in *Perspectives on Cormac McCarthy*, pp.71–96, and

" 'They Ain't the Thing': Artifact and Hallucinated Recollection in Cormac McCarthy's Early Frame-Works", in *Myth, Legend, Dust*, pp.21–36.

7. "Cormac McCarthy's First Screenplay," in *Perspectives on Cormac McCarthy*, p.73.
8. The historical record comprises the 1928 account by Broadus Mitchell, contained in his "highly laudatory" biography of William Gregg; Pearce has interpreted this account with the aid of "Professor Tom Terrill, economic historian at the University of South Carolina" and "consulting historian for the film." Ibid. p.72.
9. *The Gardener's Son*, p.5.
10. She quotes *Outer Dark, Child of God* and *Blood Meridian*. I would add both *The Orchard Keeper* and *Suttree*. It is also a central concern of *The Crossing*, in which the *corrido* is seen as "the poor man's history." Luce's article was written before *The Crossing* was published.
11. Also held by the University of South Carolina.
12. *The Gardener's Son*, p.3.
13. Abbreviation for "off-stage."
14. Ibid.
15. Ibid. p.5. The name "Timekeeper" itself has ironic significance in this respect.
16. Ibid. p.90. The word dont is printed without the apostrophe. This kind of omission occurs frequently throughout this text and others. It appears to be a part of McCarthy's idiosyncratic use of punctuation. The usage is not applied consistently.
17. Ibid. p.34.
18. By this I mean its significance within McCarthy's work as a whole. His other texts do not deal explicitly with this aspect of cultural hegemony at the political/economic level.
19. "Cormac McCarthy's First Screenplay," *Perspectives on Cormac McCarthy*, p.72.
20. Ibid. p.73.
21. Ibid.
22. Ibid.
23. Ibid. p.6. Kalmia is the name of the Gregg home.
24. Ibid. p.7.
25. Ibid.
26. Ibid. p.9.
27. Ibid. p.16.
28. Ibid.
29. W. Gregg, *Essays on Domestic Industry*, quoted by Mitchell and by Luce in "Cormac McCarthy's First Screenplay," *Perspectives on Cormac McCarthy*, p.76.
30. *The Gardener's Son*, p.19.

31. Ibid. p.23.
32. Ibid. p.53. The text names the speakers as GREGG and McEVOY in this exchange between James and Robert. In previous passages they has been named as JAMES GREGG and ROBERT. As far as the text is concerned this style of naming matches the emotional tenor of the passage concerned.
33. Ibid. pp.25–6.
34. Ibid. p.48.
35. Ibid. p.53.
36. This remark has a double significance. The history of the period "called no female witnesses."
37. Ibid. p.61.
38. Ibid. p.59.
39. Ibid. p.56.
40. Ibid. pp.32–3.
41. Quoted on p.177 above.
42. Ibid. p.50.
43. Ibid. pp.43–4. McCarthy reverses Faulkner's outcome. The distraught, bereaved Rider, kills and is killed. As noted previously McCarthy himself claims to have avoided death by giving up drinking.
44. Ibid.
45. Ibid. p.69.
46. Ibid. p.80.
47. Ibid. p.84.
48. Ibid. p.29.
49. Ibid. p.30.
50. Psalm 2, verse 1. The reference is reiterated in the short verse at the conclusion of *Cities of the Plain*. See chapter on that text.
51. Ibid. verse 12.
52. *The Gardener's Son*, pp.30–31.
53. Ibid. p.33.
54. Ibid. p.38.
55. Ibid. The phrase also expresses Robert's feeling that "home" does exist but that it is elsewhere.
56. Ibid.
57. Ibid. p.70.
58. Ibid. p.18.
59. Ibid. p.50.
60. As previously noted, for a discussion of this aspect of the significance of East Tennessee see p.46. The choice of a black family as representative Americans in *The Stonemason*, as already mentioned, is itself a radical statement on race. But it is one thing to set such a representation in the Louisville of the 1970s and quite another to depict blacks as socially and educationally superior to whites in the South Carolina of the Reconstruction period.

NOTES TO CHAPTER ELEVEN

1. But what in 1830 was largely still Mexico. The filibusters' imperialist philosophy is expressed by Captain White: "What we are dealing with, he said, is a race of degenerates. A mongrel race, little better than niggers. And maybe no better. There is no government in Mexico. Hell, there's no God in Mexico. Never will be. We are dealing with a people manifestly incapable of governing themselves. And do you know what happens to a people who cannot govern themselves? That's right. Others come in to govern for them." (*Blood Meridian*, p.34.) McCarthy deals with these pretensions in short order. The filibusters are massacred: in the city of Chihuahua the kid encounters ". . . a trestle table whereon stood a large glass carboy of clear mescal. In this container with hair afloat and eyes turned upward in a pale face sat a human head. . . . It was Captain White. Lately at war among the heathen. (Ibid. pp.60–70) Nothing more is heard of filibusters in the text. The scalphunters are completely apolitical opportunists ". . . wholly at venture, primal, provisional, devoid of order." (Ibid. p.172)

2. *Suttree* may be considered as separate from these in scale, setting and form. As noted it is a long book, predominantly urban in setting and centred on an educated and self-aware individual.

3. T. Poland, " 'A relative to All That Is': The Eco-Hero in Western American Literature." *Western American Literature*, 26, no.3 (Fall 1991): pp.195–208, in *The Pastoral Vision of Cormac McCarthy*, p. 37.

4. To some extent this is an assumption. It is supported by the lines, "Outside lie . . . fields with rags of snow and darker woods that harbor yet a few last wolves," and that the child on first running away from home, ". . . wanders as far as Memphis." *Blood Meridian* pp.3–4.

5. Vegetation map of North America in *Bartholomew's Atlas of the World*, p.74

6. Bakhtin's term for the literary image that expresses a combined sense of time and place, defining both the subject and its author. c.f. Faulkner's Yoknapatawpha.

7. *Blood Meridian*, p.5.

8. In the account of the massacre of the Gilenoes, (Ibid. pp.155–159) we read that "Women were screaming and one old man tottered forth waving a white pair of pantaloons. The horsemen moved among them and slew them with clubs or knives." (p.156) The indiscriminate nature of this type of "warfare" reflects the same moral chaos that the Vietnamese war engendered.

9. Ibid. p.98. McCarthy deepens the mythic significance of the image by making the victim female. This demonstration of male power, emanating from the phallic colt revolver—an example of the high technology of the day—is a metaphor for the death-bringing consequences of the triumph of patriarchy over "the feminine deities." (*The Labyrinth of Solitude*, pp.80–81). See also p.79 above.

10. L. Daugherty, "Gravers False and True: *Blood Meridian* as Gnostic Tragedy" in *Perspectives on Cormac McCarthy*, p.172.

11. D. Phillips, "History and the Ugly Facts of Cormac McCarthy's *Blood Meridian*", *American Literature*, 68:2 (1996), p.433.

12. Bloom was in conversation with Peter Josyph: in "Tragic Ecstasy: A Conversation With Harold Bloom About Cormac McCarthy's *Blood Meridian*", *Southwestern American Literature*, 26:1 (2000), p.7.

13. D. Donoghue, "Reading *Blood Meridian*," *Sewanee Review*, 105:3 (1997), p.418.

14. McCarthy acknowledges the comic aspect of this surreal passage. ". . . the horsemen's faces gaudy and grotesque with daubings like a company of mounted clowns, death hilarious, . . ." It reflects the same sensibility as the "Mad Max" post-apocalypse movies of the 1980s.

15. *Blood Meridian*, pp.53–4. This is a part only of the passage, the whole of which takes up almost three pages.

16. The exception is Sarah Borginnis, a matriarchal figure and the only female character of the text. She is of no more than marginal significance, since the female principle has no place in the arid, infertile "waste land." Her motherliness is manifested in her attempt to care for the idiot, an attempt that fails. The idiot becomes companion to the judge.

17. There is one small exception to this, on the very first page of the text. "Night of your birth. Thirty-three. The Leonids they were called. God how the stars did fall. I looked for blackness, holes in the heavens. The Dipper stove. (*Blood Meridian*, p.3).

18. The only character to whom the "I" could refer seems to be the kid's father. He could not possibly be the narrator of the rest of the tale, since he is wholly absent thereafter. This is perhaps a last passing glimpse of a modernist reflexivity that is to be finally abandoned. A concern with literary antecedents and with the place of narrative within the cultural matrix is far from abandoned however and remains a primary concern of The Border Trilogy.

19. Ibid. The reference to Wordsworth expresses a typically ironic inversion of the spirit of the original.

20. Ibid.

21. Ibid. p.139.

22. S. Chamberlain, *My Confession* (New York: Harper, 1956).

23. Ibid. pp.7–8.

24. There is some debate regarding the authenticity of *My Confession*. However the Harper 1956 edition contains an introduction and notes by R. Butterfield and he points out a number of instances in which Chamberlain's account is supported by official military records. Given McCarthy's concern with myth, it is arguably of little consequence whether the account is authentic or not.

25. *My Confession* p.259.

26. Ibid. p.260.
27. Ibid. p.262.
28. Ibid. p.271–2.
29. Ibid. p.276.
30. Ibid. p.284.
31. J.G. Bourke, *On the Border With Crook* [1891] (Lincoln: University of Nebraska Press, 1971), p.96.
32. *Blood Meridian*, p.256.
33. E. Welty, From talk to the Mississippi Historical Society: in *The Robber Bridegroom* [1942] (London: Virago, 1999). Quoted in Introduction by Paul Binding, 1981. p.vi. I have already quoted Guillemin's assertion of the allegorical nature of *Blood Meridian*.
34. *On the Border With Crook*, p.83.
35. Ibid. p.2.
36. Ibid. p.7.
37. Ibid. p.67.
38. Ibid. p.90. McCarthy's habit in The Border Trilogy. The sense of sophistication thus engendered is somewhat undermined by Bourke's rendering of the song's musical accompaniment: "(Fluke—fluky—fluke; plink, planky—plink.)
39. Ibid. p.117.
40. Ibid. p.484.
41. *Blood Meridian*, p.121.
42. McCarthy commences the word "judge" with a lower case "j" so, when referring to his text, I shall do the same.
43. Ibid. p.6.
44. Tobin's former sacerdotal status is another of McCarthy frequent references to the failure of religion, or man's rejection of it.
45. *Blood Meridian*, p.125.
46. J. Fennimore Cooper, *The Prairie* [1827] (New York: Signet Classic, 1964), p.15.
47. *Blood Meridian*, p.128.
48. Ibid. p.240.
49. *Blood Meridian*, p.132. This recalls the kneading of the whale-sperm in *Moby Dick*, but the loving eroticism is transformed into an image of eroticised violence.
50. Ibid. p.127.
51. Ibid. p.139.
52. Ibid. p.251.
53. Recorded in *The Journals of the Lewis and Clarke Expedition, Volume Six, Scientific Data* [1804–6]. R.G. Thwaites (ed) (New York: Antiquarian Press, 1959).
54. *Blood Meridian*, p.123.

55. Ibid. p.239.
56. Ibid. p.85.
57. Ibid. p.139.
58. Ibid. p.145.
59. Ibid. p.173.
60. Ibid. p.192.
61. Ibid. p.198.
62. Ibid. p.246.
63. Ibid. p.251.
64. Ibid. p.275.
65. It is in this respect that McCarthy inverts the myth of Natty Bumpo, who fled culture to be at one with nature.
66. Ibid. p.198.
67. Ibid. p.198–9.
68. The judge may be likened to Melville's whale in his mythic form, his size and colouring, his destructive power and his multiple meanings. The whale symbolized both the creative and destructive power of nature, both life and death. Its whiteness reflected that nihilism that so haunted the nineteenth century imagination. The judge parallels these meanings, but as they inhere in culture. To the twentieth century it is culture that has the power to be monstrous. E.L.Doctorow writes, "It [architecture] can inadvertently express the monstrousness of culture." *The Waterworks* [1994] (Sydney: Picador, 1995), p.54.
69. Ibid. p.245.
70. Ibid. p.247. It is hard to see such a vision arising from the landscape of East Tennessee.
71. *The Pastoral Vision of Cormac McCarthy*, p.120.
72. Ibid. p.334.
73. Ibid. p.118.
74. Ibid. p.335.
75. F. Nietzsche, "Of the Higher Man" in *Thus Spake Zarathustra* [1885] (London: Penguin Classics, 1974), p.305.
76. This is in effect what the judge does when he wrecks the Reverend Green's tent meeting.
77. *Blood Meridian*, p.3.
78. Ibid. p.5.
79. Ibid. p.192.
80. Ibid. p.145. The account of father/son conflict outlined by the judge is not essentially Freudian in the psycho-sexual sense. Instead it expresses an aspect of the power relations inherent in patriarchal epistemology. It is consistent with McCarthy's critique of a power obsessed, death haunted culture that has lost its "female" aspect.

NOTES TO CHAPTER TWELVE

1. *The Labyrinth of Solitude*, p.358.
2. H. Brogan, *The Penguin History of the United States* [1985] (London: Penguin, 1990), p.434.
3. *Red River* was directed by Howard Hawks and released in 1948. The screenplay was written by Borden Chase and Charles Schnee. It was adapted from a Borden Chase story first published in the *Saturday Evening Post*.
4. In contrast to the historical cowboys who were, of course, of varied racial origin.
5. S.L. Spurgeon, "'Pledged in Blood:' Truth and Redemption in Cormac McCarthy's *All the Pretty Horses*", *Western American Literature*, 34:1 (1999), p.25.
6. G.M. Morrison, "John Grady Cole's Expulsion from Paradise", in *Perspectives on Cormac McCarthy*, p.175.
7. "'Pledged in Blood:' Truth and Redemption in Cormac McCarthy's *All the Pretty Horses*", p.25.
8. Don Héctor Rocha y Villareal; the hacendado has significant names. Hector was a tamer of horses on the plains of Troy. The Trojan war was occasioned by erotic transgression. Villareal can be translated as "royal house."
9. *All the Pretty Horses*, p.141.
10. *My Confession*, p.7.
11. Ibid. p.8.
12. Ibid. p.22.
13. The novel is in four parts: the journey to La Purísima, the sojourn there, the incarceration at Saltillo, the recovery of the horses and return to Texas.
14. *All the Pretty Horses*, p.5.
15. Ibid. p.30.
16. Ibid. p.94.
17. Ibid. p.109.
18. Ibid. p.128. "I am the commander of the mares. I and I alone. Without charity from my hands you have nothing. Neither food nor water nor children. I am the one who brings the mares from the mountains, the young mares, the savage ones, and the mares that burn with passion."
    Dylan sang "Spanish is the Loving Tongue."
19. Ibid. p.129. The passage suggests Whitman:

    > A gigantic beauty of a stallion, fresh and responsive to my caresses, . . .
    > His nostrils dilate . . . my heels embrace him . . . his well built limbs
    > tremble with pleasure . . . we speed around and return. ("Song of
    > Myself" in *Leaves of Grass* [1855] [New York: Penguin Classics,1986],
    > ll.702 & 706, p.56.)

> There is a sense in which John Grady Cole, the "All American Cowboy", is a Whitmanesque "representative man" misled by the romanticism of which Whitman was an American prophet.

20. Ibid. p.130.
21. Do you love me?
22. *All the Pretty Horses*, p.141.
23. Ibid. p.142. The passage contains a mythic reference. Myrrha visited her father's bed on nine consecutive nights. Like Alejandra she took the sexual initiative. From this union came Adonis, the corn god.
24. Ibid. p.4–5. The old man's death occurs in 1949, precisely one hundred years after the kid rides into Nacogdoches at the start of *Blood Meridian*.
25. *All the Pretty Horses*, p.17.
26. Ibid. p.127.
27. Ibid. p.27.
28. Ibid. p.16.
29. Ibid. p.21.
30. Depending on one's definition of the term "novel."
31. Ibid. p.79.
32. Ibid. p.138.
33. Ibid. p.211.
34. Ibid. p.41–42.
35. Rosa being Spanish for red. However, it must be admitted that this is, at best, a pun. The actual derivation is from rocin, meaning work-horse, a further satire on Don Quixote's chivalric delusions.
36. A reference not only to the values that informed Cervantes satire but also to judge Holden, the monster of *Blood Meridian*.
37. Ibid.146.
38. E.C. Riley: Introduction to M. de Cervantes, *Don Quixote* [c.1605] (Oxford: World's Classics, 1992), p.xiii.
39. *Don Quixote*, p.26. In his "Author's Preface" Cervantes indulges in an early exercise of literary reflexivity by remarking that his tale is "only an invective against the books of chivalry." Ibid p.19.
40. Their map shows ". . . roads and rivers and towns on the American side of the map as far south as the Rio Grande and beyond that all was white." This recalls the youthful Marlow's maps of Africa in *Heart of Darkness*. Even when John Grady produces a map of Mexico itself Rawlins remarks, "There aint shit down there." (*All the Pretty Horses*, p.34.)
41. Ibid. p.96.
42. Ibid. p.97.
43. In *Perspectives on Cormac McCarthy*, pp.175–194.
44. D. Madsen, *American Exceptionalism* [1998] (Jackson: University Press of Mississippi), p.129.

45. Ibid. p.126. She notes that in his essay "The Evolution of the Cow-Puncher," Wister wrote of the cowboy as the descendent of the Anglo-Saxon knight-at-arms.

46. *All the Pretty Horses*, p.23. There is a subtle irony in this passage. There were no horses in America until the Spanish introduced them. The whole episode involving John Grady and the wild horses recalls Flem Snopes' Texas horses in *The Hamlet*, but the implications are quite different. Flem's horses bring chaos as much as order.

47. P. Shaw, "Female Presence, Male Violence, and the Art of Artlessness in Cormac McCarthy's Border Trilogy," *Southwestern American Literature*, 25:1 (1999), p.19.

48. B. Clarke, "Art, Authenticity, and Social Transgression in Cormac McCarthy's *All the Pretty Horses*", in *Southwestern American Literature*, 25:1 (1999), pp.117–8.

49. Bonney gets an unexpected reference in J.D.Hart (ed), *The Oxford Companion to American Literature* (New York: Oxford University Press, 1995), p.68, where he bears the character ". . . desperado of the Southwest."

50. *All the Pretty Horses*, p.64.The fact that his conflict has been with his step-father rather than his natural father is an indication of the easing of the oedipal tension in McCarthy's work.

51. Ibid. p.77.

52. Ibid. p.71.

53. Ibid. p.73.

54. Literally "The Enchanted Ones." H. Melville, *The Encantadas* [1854], in *Billy Budd, Sailor and Other Stories* (London: Penguin English Library, 1979), pp.131–194. The reference is given added significance by the association with the Galapagos Islands and hence with Darwin and the distinctly unromantic notion of the survival of the fittest.

55. Blevins is incapable of thinking things through. His horse and pistol are his only property (if it is his horse). For him the only response to dispossession is to fight to reclaim what is "his." He is too naive to understand that he must make allowances for the customs of another land and for his own weakness and vulnerability. His actions are informed by the mythology of "a desperado of the Southwest." The Mexican captain speaks the truth when he says of Blevins, "He was no quiet boy. He was this other kind of boy all the time. All the time." (*All the Pretty* Horses, p.169.) I have already referred to the real Blevins, the murderous Georgian necrophiliac, who was the original for Lester Ballard. (See p.90 above.) McCarthy compounds the complex of references with conscious irony when he makes the "real" Jimmy Blevins of *All the Pretty Horses* a Texas radio evangelist. He even has him resident "in South Georgia" at one time. (p.296)

56. This is not made explicit but the implication is strong. Jay Ellis makes a convincing case for this interpretation. J.Ellis, "The Rape of Rawlins: a

Note on *All the Pretty Horses*", *The Cormac McCarthy Journal*, 1:1 (2001), pp.66–68.

57. *All the Pretty Horses*, p.182.
58. Ibid. p.254.
59. Ibid. p.238. The proprietor of the Los Picos cafe is scarcely more encouraging. He observes the celebrations of a local wedding from his window and says ". . . that it was good that God kept the truths of life from the young as they were starting out or else they'd have no heart to start at all." (Ibid. p.284.)
60. *The Labyrinth of Solitude*, p.167.
61. *All the Pretty Horses*, p.268.
62. Ibid. p.270.
63. Ibid. p.255.
64. Ibid. p.302.
65. Ibid. p.146.
66. Ibid. p.14. As in the case of Blevins, John Grady encounters conflict with his surrogate father, Don Hector, rather than his natural father. See p.192 above.
67. See p.186 above.
68. Ibid. p.168.
69. McCarthy inserts an ironic joke at this point. The judge says "I dont believe anybody could make up the story you just now got done tellin us." Ibid. p.288. This reflexivity could be read as another comment on the unrealistic nature of romantic values.
70. Ibid. p.231.
71. Ibid. p.237.
72. Ibid. p.239.
73. Ibid. p.231.
74. Ibid. p.241.
75. I am referring to a change of balance here. Landscape remains significant but less so than in previous texts; human concerns become more intense.
76. See p.247.
77. N. Kreml, "Stylistic Variations and Cognitive Constraint in *All the Pretty Horses*," in *Sacred Violence, Second Edition, Vol. 2. Cormac McCarthy's Western Novels* (El Paso: Texas Western Press, 2002), pp.37–49.

NOTES TO CHAPTER THIRTEEN

1. See quote from Woodward, p.5 above.
2. *The Crossing*, p.383.
3. Ibid. p.155. The passage is quoted more fully on p.197 above.
4. "Song of Myself" in *Leaves of Grass*, ll.684–5, pp.55–56.
5. D. Luce, "The Vanishing World of Cormac McCarthy's Border Trilogy" *The Southern Quarterly*, XXXVIII:3 (2000), p.130.

6. E.C Riley, Introduction to *Don Quixote*, p.xiii. For example the beautiful Marcela is excoriated by the local men for rejecting one who died for love of her. In her response to her accusers she delivers a perfectly argued rational and incontrovertible defense of her position. She thus becomes the voice of reason against the absurdities of romantic chivalry. *Don Quixote*, pp.100–102.

7. R. Jarrett, *Cormac McCarthy*, p.142.

8. *The Crossing*, p.153.

9. Ibid. p.157.

10. Ibid. p.155. The implication is that culture may be infinitely rich and varied but all narratives must be read in the same sense as the Gypsy's three histories of the same event; in other words the teller must be "read" as well as the tale. See p.209.

11. Ibid. p.129.

12. S.T. Coleridge, "The Rhyme of the Ancient Mariner" [1798], in J. Beer (ed), *Poems* [1995] (London: Everyman), ll.79–80, p.220.

13. Ibid. ll.29–33. p.216.

14. Ibid. ll.81–4. p.220.

15. *The Crossing*, p.130.

16. "The Rhyme of the Ancient Mariner", ll.619–623. p.252.

17. Ibid. ll.632–4. p.254.

18. Ibid. ll.645–6. p.254.

19. See p.224.

20. *The Crossing*, p.425. The "shadow of the windowsash stenciled onto the opposite wall" refers to the "shadows" of incinerated victims cast on the walls of Hiroshima on actual use of the atomic bomb. This oblique reference to a real horror is characteristic of McCarthy's dense and disciplined allusiveness.

21. Ibid. p.426. The phrase "godmade sun" is a final reference to "The Rhyme of the Ancient Mariner," in which the sun symbolizes God.

22. For discussion of this see p.16.

23. This is the boundary between Mexico and New Mexico. The "natural" boundary formed by the Rio Grande ceases at El Paso/Ciudad Juarez.

24. *The Crossing*. p.421.

25. Ibid. p.420.

26. See p.170–171.

27. The female is, in turn, associated with water, an essential of life, as in "The Waste Land."

28. The account covers no less than 15 pages (*The Crossing* pp.300–314).

29. The blacksmith sharpening the axe in *Child of God*; Old Ben Telfair's faith in the mason's craft in *The Stonemason*; John Grady Cole's mastery of the wild horses in *All the Pretty Horses*.

30. "For the road."

31. *The Crossing*, p.332.
32. We may speculate that the Doctor has been "disappeared" in the manner that has become a familiar aspect of the politics of the countries of Latin America, Mexico included. In ministering to Boyd, the Doctor has given succour to the revolutionary side, or to its mythology, which is the same thing.
33. *The Hero With A Thousand Faces*. This is one of the recurring themes of Campbell's analysis.
34. *The Crossing*, pp.424–5.
35. Ibid. p.426. Quoted more fully on p.211.
36. *The Hero With A Thousand Faces*, p.206.
37. *The Crossing*, pp.4–5.
38. Ibid. p.5.
39. And arguably throughout *Cities of the Plain* also. See the epilogue to that text.
40. *The Crossing*, p.422.
41. Ibid. p.4.
42. *The Labyrinth of Solitude*, p.58.
43. Ibid. p.60.
44. Ibid. p.195.
45. "It is for the road." The phrase occurs several times, always with the same import; for example p.367.
46. Ibid. p.81.
47. *The Crossing*, p.209.
48. The "dangerous men" of the text.
49. P.Quinn, "Crossing the Mountains of Mexico", *Times Literary Supplement*, 4968, 19/6/98, p.24. Billy is named after his father, Will Parham; his brother's name is Boyd. William Boyd was the actor who played Hopalong Cassidy, the cowboy hero of 1930's western movies typical of those that propounded the cowboy myth that informs Billy's values, that provides him with his "narrative."
50. *The Crossing*, p.315.
51. S. Sontag, Introduction to J. Rulfo, *Pedro Páramo* [1955], trans. M.S.Peden (London: Serpent's Tail, 1994), p.vi.
52. *The Crossing*, p.386.
53. A. Paredes, *Folklore and Culture on the Texas-Mexican Border* [1993] (Austin: University of Texas Press).
54. A. Paredes, *With His Pistol In His Hand: A Border Ballad and Its Hero* [1958] (Austin: University of Texas Press).
55. *The Crossing*, p.318. Güerito—young blonde one. Manco—one armed man.
56. D.C. Alarcón, *The Aztec Palimpsest* [1997] (Tucson: University of Arizona Press), p.88.

57. The appropriateness of the term "infernal" is emphasized in the chapter below on *Cities of the Plain*.
58. *The Crossing*, p.200. The reference reflects the celebrated remark by Porfirio Diaz: "Poor Mexico, so far from God and so near to the United States!" Alarcón writes on *All the Pretty Horses* but no other McCarthy text.
59. J. Wegner, "'Mexico Para los Mexicanos': Revolution, Mexico and McCarthy's Border Trilogy" in *Myth, Legend, Dust*, p.254.
60. Ibid.
61. J. Didion, *The White Album* [1979] (London: Flamingo, 1993), p.11.
62. *The Labyrinth of Solitude*, p.216.
63. R. Penn Warren, *Band of Angels* [1995] (New York: Random House, 1955), p.52.
64. *Cities of the Plain*, p.283.
65. *The Crossing*, p.228.
66. Ibid. p.229. "The secret is that in this world the mask is that which is true."
67. Ibid. p.230.
68. Ibid. pp.282–3. "Touch, he said. If the world is an illusion the loss of the world is an illusion also."
69. Ibid. p.285.
70. Sexton or gravedigger.
71. Ibid. p.293.
72. Ibid. p.102.The myths of the man eater, the wolf boy and the werewolf are all alluded to here. These inform three histories, as in the case of the aeroplane. Conversely, as with the wolf, myths have accrued to the aeroplane.
73. Ibid. p.404. "With respect to the aeroplane there are three histories. Which one do you want to hear?" "Historia" is Spanish for both story and history, a linguistic detail that is of particular significance in this case. I have chosen to interpret it as "history," but this is actually quite arbitrary.
74. Ibid. p.418.
75. Ibid.
76. "Read" in the sense of interpreted in the light of the culture that informs them and that we ourselves bring to the act of "reading." Other tale tellers include Don Arnulfo—source of Mexican wolf lore and information on Echols; the rescued girl who disappears into myth with Boyd; old Mr. Sanders, back in New Mexico and grieving for those lost in the war; the belligerent drunk (provoked by Billy) in the Janos bar—the scars of his wounds of honour on his chest; the woman of Janos who feeds him "para el camino"— who had lost three husbands and would take no other; the rider from whom the girl had been rescued—for whom ". . . the bitch was dead. The world rolled on." (p. 380); Quijada of Babicora, part Indian and the just man who had discerned the truth of Billy's ownership by observing the horses, and who tells him of Boyd's end.

77. D. Luce, "The Road and the Matrix: The World as Tale in *The Crossing*", in *Perspectives on Cormac McCarthy*, p.195

78. Ibid. p.196.

79. The gypsy leader.

80. Ibid. p.199.

81. *The Crossing*, pp.51–2.

82. Ibid. p.26.

83. Ibid. p.76.

84. Ibid. p.414. "I am not a man of the road."

85. Ibid. p.426. Both the derelict dog and the wolf are versions of the puppy, McCarthy's symbol of familial security.

86. Ibid. p.203.

87. *The Orchard Keeper*, p.70.

88. *Blood Meridian*, p.257.

89. *The Crossing*, p.220.

90. For example N. Sullivan, "Boys Will Be Boys and Girls Will Be Gone: The Circuit of Male Desire in Cormac McCarthy's Border Trilogy," *The Southern Quarterly*, XXXVIII:3 (2000), 167–185. Sullivan suggests that women are elided from McCarthy's fiction and that desire is projected onto other male figures in homoerotic terms. This recalls Fiedler's analysis in *Love and Death in the American Novel*. Sullivan further suggests that McCarthy's use of the imagery of blood is a patriarchal substitution for menstruation.

    Sullivan gives a feminist reading of two earlier novels in "The Evolution of the Dead Girlfriend Motif in *Outer Dark* and *Child of God*" in *Myth, Legend, Dust*, pp.68–77. However she does note that Jaqueline Scoones draws a different conclusion: "Scoones argues that the women in the Border Trilogy, especially Magdelena, are aligned with nature in an ethical system at odds with the masculine order." (J. Scoones, "McCarthy's "Girls" and the Ethics of Dwelling in *The Border Trilogy*", American Literature Association Conference, Baltimore. May 28, 1999.)

91. The "western" prominent among them.

92. *The Crossing*. p.213.

93. "Direct" here means by means of sensory experience, rather than experience mediated by the ambiguities of language and culture as noted on p.7.

94. See p.13.

NOTES TO CHAPTER FOURTEEN

1. 1998.

2. For example the Spring 2000 issue of *The Southern Quarterly* was headed "Special Issue: Cormac McCarthy's Border Trilogy." I have referred to a number of the ten essays in this collection. Contributors have clearly responded to the editorial brief. Reference has also been made to the 2000

collection *Myth, Legend, Dust,* part IV of which is devoted to "The Border tetralogy." (sic) This collection of 11 essays features one only devoted exclusively to *Cities of the Plain.* In C. Bailey, "The Last Stage of the Hero's Evolution: Cormac McCarthy's *Cities of the Plain*", Charles Bailey finds in the demise of John Grady Cole an assertion of Byronic romantic despair at the loss of belief consequent upon the discovery that the hero inhabits a degraded world. My reading of the novel is somewhat similar.

3. P. Josyph, "Tragic Ecstasy: A Conversation With Harold Bloom about Cormac McCarthy's *Blood Meridian*" in *Southwest American Literature,* 26:1 (2000), p.8.

4. E. Arnold, "The Last of the Trilogy: First Thoughts on *Cities of the Plain*" in *Perspectives on Cormac McCarthy,* pp.221–2. Arnold refers, I think, to the late emergence of an overt humanism in McCarthy's work. See p.234 below.

5. I have already referred to Alarcón's notion of the representation of Mexico as an "infernal paradise" (p.206 above) and to Wegner's analysis of the exploitive relationship of the US to Mexico. (p.206). I have also commented on Sullivan's feminist critique of McCarthy's representation of women, (p.317) suggesting an alternative reading. I have also referred to Luce's environmentalist reading. (p.197) Each of these critical articles referred to *Cities of the Plain* as well as to the other texts of the trilogy.

6. S. Peebles, "'Lo fantástico': The influence of Borges and Cortázar on the Epilogue of *Cities of the Plain,*" *Southwestern American Literature,* 25:1 (1998) p.105.

7. C. McCarthy, *No Country for Old Men* (London: Picador, 2005). At least one further novel is due to be published later this year (2006).

8. Arnold points out that McCarthy originally conceived the project as a screenplay and quotes Woodward to the effect that it had existed for ten years before *All the Pretty Horses* was published. This suggests that the trilogy was certainly conceived as a whole. Arnold states that, "A copy of what appears to be a late version of the screenplay can be found in the Cormac McCarthy Collection at Southwest Texas State University." ("First Thoughts on *Cities of the Plain*" in *Perspectives on Cormac McCarthy,* p.222.)

9. McCarthy consciously acknowledges this relationship to film culture and the western genre on at least two occasions, neither of them more than a small detail. Billy lies in his bunk reading "Destry," (p.59). Destry was a mythic cowboy hero of the dime novels that were the source for the cinema's westerns. As an old man Billy finds himself "working as an extra in a movie." (p.264) He is perhaps involved in the creation of a narrative of his own life, or a mythologising, after the manner of Suttree or John Wesley Rattner.

10. A proportion in Spanish as before.

11. As in *The Crossing.*

12. *Cities of the Plain*, p.3.
13. Ibid.
14. "The Waste Land," ll.393–4, p.78.
15. *Cities of the Plain*, p.6.
16. Ibid. The name Troy carries its own mythic connotations of the quest for the return of the lost female. The cutting of Magdalena's throat suggests the sacrifice of Iphigeneia in the same myth
17. Ibid. p.229. The Lady of Shalott whom "the silent isle embowers" also died in attempting to escape confinement. Her river ran below "willowy hills," "her blood was frozen" and she was "dead pale". The allusion compounds John Grady's association with Arthurian myth. McCarthy echoes Tennyson's language. The echo is ironic of course as befits the anti-myth. Juarez is no Camelot. (A. Tennyson, "The Lady of Shalott" in *The Works of Alfred Lord Tennyson* (London: MacMillan, 1894), pp.27–29.
18. John Grady tells Magdalena of his riding of the old Comanche trail that was described in *All the Pretty Horses*:

    . . . the Comanche trail that ran through the western sections and how he would ride that trail in the moonlight in the fall of the year when he was a boy and the ghosts of the Comanches would pass all about him on their way to the other world again and again for a thing once set in motion has no ending in the world until the last witness has passed. (*Cities of the Plain*, p.205.)

    The passage reverts to the poetic style of the former romantic text. It suggests that the past lives in the form of narrative, especially mythic narrative.
19.

    I turned and saw, stretched out before my face
    And 'neath my feet, a lake so bound with ice,
    It did not look like water but like glass.

    (Dante Alighieri, "The Divine Comedy: Hell", trans. D.L. Sayers [1949] [London: Penguin Classics, 1976], Canto XXXII, ll.22–24, p.271). I have already pointed out that John Grady first sees Magdalena's image in the glass of the mirror.
20. Ibid. p.275.
21. *Cities of the Plain*, p.128.
22. See p.101 above.
23. In *Cities of the Plain* this conflict has diminished to such an extent that the only reference to it concerns two characters absent from the action, (Troy's father and dead brother Johnny), their quarrel recalled by the elder brother, Elton. However there is a conflict with a surrogate father. See pp.230–231.
24. W. Faulkner, *The Hamlet* [1931] (New York: Vintage, 1990), p.234.
25. Ibid. p.235.
26. *The Crossing*, p.352.
27. Ibid. p.25.

28. Ibid. p.24.
29. Ibid. p.235.
30. Ibid. p.152.
31. Ibid. p.186.
32. Ibid. p.123.
33. Ibid. p.106.
34. Ibid. p.126.
35. Moderno, Spanish for modern, expresses the modernist trope of the past always already in the present: "The Moderno? It is a place where the musicians come. It is a very old place. It has always been there." (Ibid. p.87).
36. Ibid. p.191.
37. Ibid. p.265–6. Even the dream of the lost female is associated with water. In the preceding paragraph we read: "A rain had come down from the north . . ." (Ibid. p.265).
38. E. Hughes, *Shakespeare and the Goddess of Complete Being* (London: Faber, 1992). Hughes argues that Shakespeare's plays owed their contemporary power to their addressing at the mythic level the division in English culture between male and female, corresponding to Protestant and Catholic. Those plays which featured a complete rupture between male and female principles, *Hamlet, MacBeth, King Lear*, also featured a breakdown in the order of things. Those that depicted union of the sexes, *Much Ado About Nothing, A Midsummer Night's Dream, The Tempest*, led to order, resolution and plenitude. I have argued that McCarthy's texts operate at the same mythic level and that his challenge is to the patriarchal epistemology that underlies America's mythology of exceptionalism. In a broader sense McCarthy implies that the synthesis of the two principles is impossible under the epistemological conditions that pertain in Western modernity. That his mythic view is to some extent coloured by his background, raised a Catholic in a strongly Protestant milieu, adds weight to this analysis in my view. However I have made it clear that I do not read any specific religious meaning in this choice of mythic imagery, male and female symbolism having, of course, long since assumed purely secular significance.
39. *Cities of the Plain*, pp.215–6.
40. Candelaria (Candlemas, 2nd. February) is an ancient celebration that has been accommodated by many other cultures. Catholicism associates it with the Virgin. In the USA it is Ground Hog day—a celebration of the coming of spring. In Mexico it is a day celebrating the Constitution. The original significance was, of course, pagan. On this day the ancient Irish celebrated Brigid, the Celtic Goddess, who, in her triple aspect, was associated with Inspiration (poetry etc.), Smithcraft and Healing (medicine, fertility). The candle is a relic of the torchlight procession that formed part of the celebration. The significance for the (absent) female of *Cities of the Plain* is clear.

41. Ibid. p.116. Billy has already expressed Mac's reaction to Margaret's death: "He aint goin to be gettin over it. Not now. Not soon. Not never." (Ibid. p.12) This early intimation of mortality and grief sets the tone for the text as a whole, especially as it follows on directly from the first brothel scene. This tone is reinforced by the reference to Mr. Johnson: "JC says he aint been right since his daughter died. Well. There aint no reason why he should be. He thought the world of her." (Ibid.) Margaret is absent *in* the text rather than from it.

42. Ibid. p.11.

43. John Wayne was in the area at the time and it is thought that his fatal throat cancer could have been caused in this way. On his discharge from the army Troy took the bus from El Paso "and went up that evenin to Alamagordo." (Ibid p.22)

44. The exact temporality of the text is calculated as follows:—Billy is "twenty-eight years old" (Ibid. p.19). "In . . . the second year of the new millennium . . ." (Ibid. p.264) he is "seventy-eight years old" (Ibid. p.265). This means that he was born in 1924 and that the main action of the text is set in 1952. Therefore Margaret died in 1949, just four years after the test.

45. See the quote from p.199 above. The atomic bomb is also referred to arguably, if indirectly, in *The Orchard Keeper*.

46. Ibid. p.123. John Grady was also "pretty much raised" by a Mexican woman, Abuela, who ran the house on his Grandfather's ranch.

47. Female absence is the underlying principle of the text. Other Mexican characters are given major prominence, especially Magdalena of course.

48. Ibid. p.50.

49. Ibid. p.78.

50. Ibid. pp.217–8.

51. See quote from *The Labyrinth of Solitude* on p.191 above.

52. *Cities of the Plain*, p.264.

53. Ibid. p.110.

54. Ibid. p.22.

55. Ibid. p.214. Mac is a wholly supportive and positive father figure. John Grady does not come into conflict with him. Mac has no beautiful daughter whose affections John Grady could claim, neither is the ranch an item to be prized.

56. Ibid. p.162.

57. Ibid. p.167.

58. Ibid. p.165. The same image has been encountered earlier in the text: "He ate his lunch in an outcropping of lava rock with a view across the floodplain to the north and to the west. There were ancient pictographs among the rocks, engravings of animals and moons and men and lost hieroglyphics whose meaning no man would ever know." (Ibid. p.49).

59. Matisse was, of course, also influenced by the "savage" in art.

60. *Cities of the Plain*, p.177.
61. Ibid. p.178.
62. As McCarthy restored the farmhouse in which he lived with his second wife.
63. Ibid. p.137.
64. Ibid. p.17.
65. His first sight of her as a mirror image.
66. There is also a parallel with Orpheus' journey into the world of the dead, and his failure to bring back his Eurydice; or, since the setting is "the cities of the plain", with Lot and his petrified wife. In McCarthy's anti-myth male and female suffer the same fate.
67. Eduardo tells Billy that John Grady has coveted "another man's property." (Ibid. p.240).
68. Ibid. p.255.
69. Ibid. p.253.
70. Ibid. p.134. This is a key passage which I have quoted earlier. See p.7 above.
71. Ibid. p.188.
72. Ibid. p.199. This essentially romantic advice echoes that given by Stein to Jim in Conrad's *Lord Jim*. "Follow the dream." The consequences are similarly fatal.
73. *Cities of the Plain*, p.248.
74. Ibid. p.253.
75. It is perhaps fanciful to see the initial 'E' with which John Grady's thigh is "signed" as approximating to 'F'. Certainly *Cities of the Plain* is the least Faulknerian of McCarthy's texts in style. Jarrett suggested that Faulkner was dispatched as John Wesley's father in *The Orchard Keeper*. I suggest that he meets his demise again here.
76. Their intended sacrificial victim is, of course, female.
77. "What a question?"
78. Ibid. p.269.
79. Ibid. p.73.
80. Ibid. pp.273–4.
81. Ibid. p.274.
82. Ibid.
83. *The Labyrinth of Solitude*, p.334.
84. *Cities of the Plain*, p.283. Quoted in part on p.15 above.
85. Ibid. p.287.
86. Ibid. p.288.
87. Ibid. p.288–9.
88. "Any man's death diminishes me, because I am involved in Mankinde;" (J. Donne, "Devotions XVII" in J. Hayward (ed), *Donne: Complete Verse and Selected Prose* [London: Nonesuch Press, 1972].)
89. J. Didion, *The White Album* [1979] (London: Flamingo, 1993), p.65.

90. Ibid. p.264. The three simple phrases also encompass the passing of fifty years, an example of McCarthy's audacious literary mastery.
91. Ibid. p.266.
92. Ibid. p.290.
93. Portales is another significant name, being Spanish for portal or main door. It is an actual place of course.
94. Ibid. p.290.
95. Ibid. p.290–1.
96. Ibid. p.291–2.
97. Psalm 2,v.12. See also pp.190–191 above.
98. J. Douglas Canfield refers to the trilogy as being "set in a wasteland in the American Southwest, where modern technology and weaponry have corrupted the pastoral frontier. . ." He does refer to it as a "spiritual wasteland" and notes the relation to Heidegger's form of existentialism. He does not mention Eliot or "The Waste Land." J.D Canfield, "Crossing from the Wasteland into the Exotic in McCarthy's Border Trilogy", in *A Cormac McCarthy Companion: The Border Trilogy*, E.T. Arnold. & D. Luce (eds) (Jackson: University Press of Mississippi, 2001), p.256.
99. Alejandra first makes love with John Grady in the Lake at La Purísima. Magdalena is a captive at the White Lake. Both ask John Grady the same question, "Me quieres?" "Do you love me?" Alejandra at the lake and Magdalena at the Dos Mundos hotel. (*All the Pretty Horses*, p.141 and *Cities of the Plain*, p.205.) The hotel has another significant name: "Dos Mundos" is "Two Worlds." In the persons of the lovers two worlds meet.
100. Ibid. p.265.
101. See p.227 above.

NOTES TO CHAPTER FIFTEEN

1. Myself among them.
2. C. McCarthy, *No Country for Old Men* (London: Picador, 2005).
3. M. Gorra, "Journey into a land beyond the law: Cormac McCarthy's busted deal." in *Times Literary Supplement*, 28/10/05, p.21.
4. J.C.Oates "The Treasure of Comanche County" in *The New York Review of Books*. Vol.LII, No.16, 20/10/05, pp. 41–44. Oates is taken to task by David Cremean in his essay "For Whom Bell Tolls: Conservatism and Change in Cormac McCarthy's Sheriff from *No Country for Old Men*" in *The Cormac McCarthy Society Journal* Vol.5.
5. W. Deresiewicz "It's a Man's, Man's World" in *The Nation*, 281, (7) 12/09/05, pp.38–41.
6. J.M.White "Artifices of Eternity" in *Sewanee Review* 113 (2) Spring 2005, pp.xlix-li. White quotes Yeats' "Sailing to Byzantium" from which the novel's title is taken.

7. R.D.Hodge "Blood and Time: Cormac McCarthy and the Twilight of the West" in *Harpers Magazine* 01/02/2006. pp. 65–72.
8. R.B. Woodward "Cormac Country" in *Vanity Fair* August 2005, pp.98–104.
9. See p.5 and note 4, p.283.
10. See note 9, p.283.
11. See p.76 and note 20, p.293.
12. And Ather Ownby, to a very limited extent.
13. See Guillermin's analysis of various examples in *The Pastoral Vision of Cormac McCarthy*.
14. *No Country for Old Men* p.155.
15. Ibid. p.143.
16. Ibid. p.90.
17. Ibid. p.284–5.
18. Ibid. p.303.
19. As he sees it. He is hard on himself as Ellis remarks.
20. Ibid. p.284.
21. Ibid. p.216.
22. Ibid. p.216. We know, but Bell does not, that Wells and Chigurh are acquainted. This implies that they learned their skills as agents of the US government, as members of the "special forces" that operated in Vietnam and Latin America. Both are associated, one way or another, with the Metacumbe Petroleum Company of Houston. McCarthy makes clear the universal nature of the narcotics industry and its interpenetration of all aspects of life. The international drug trade reportedly has the second largest financial turnover in the world—after the oil industry.
23. Ibid. p.296.
24. *Cities of the Plain* p.266.
25. *No Country for Old Men* p.249.
26. Ibid. p.249.
27. *Suttree* p.13–4.
28. *No Country for Old Men* p.309.
29. The significance lies in the language and imagery of the King James Version rather than any religious interpretation.
30. Ibid. p.98–9.
31. See Ibid. p.44–5.
32. Many will be more familiar with the film version of *The Big Sleep* (1946). Hawks' version by no means preserves the pessimistic tone or grim misogyny of Chandler's novel, both of which would be inimicable to Hawks' characteristic filmic mood and values.
33. In this respect *No country for Old Men* refers back to *The Orchard Keeper*. Marion Sylder's job as a whiskey runner "had gone off the market December fifth 1933" (p.32) He was able to return to Red Branch and continue his vocation because Knoxville remained 'dry.'

34. "Cormac Country" p.104.
35. *No Country for Old Men* p.3.
36. Ibid. p.24.
37. Ibid. p.27.
38. Ibid.
39. Ibid.
40. Ibid. p.28.
41. Ibid. p.30.
42. Ibid. p.50.
43. Ibid. p.62.
44. Ibid. p.124
45. Ibid. p.253.
46. Ibid. p.195.
47. Ibid. p.216.
48. Ibid. p.225.
49. Ibid. p.243.
50. Ibid. p.267.
51. Ibid. p.268.
52. Ibid. p.269.
53. Ibid. p.271.
54. See p.170 for fuller version of Guillermin's quote from Poland and note 3, p.306.
55. *No Country for Old Men* p.306.
56. Ibid. p.55.
57. Ibid. p.56.
58. Ibid. pp.59–60.
59. The choice is ironic: Chigurh is anything but humane. The nature of the weapon suggests a further hint of grim, ironic humour: "Oh Death where is thy sting?"
60. Ibid. p.164.
61. Ibid. p.177.
62. Ibid. p.252.
63. Ibid. p.253.
64. Ibid. p.255.
65. Ibid. pp.259–60.
66. Death has made personal appearances before in McCarthy's work. He stalks the pages of *Suttree* and appears as the eponymous anti-hero escapes to the west:

    "Somewhere in the gray wood by the river is the huntsman and in the brooming corn and in the castellated press of cities. His work lies all wheres and his hounds tire not. I have seen them in a dream, slaverous and wild and their eyes crazed with ravening for souls in this world. Fly them." (Suttree p.471)

67. *No Country for Old Men* pp.112–3.
68. A further example of McCarthy's grim humour lies in the absence of a thirteenth floor in the building that houses the Metacumbe Petroleum Company. Supposedly a "security measure" it expresses the old Christian superstition regarding that number and is another reference to the importance of "luck." This aspect of corporate culture fails; the company executive does not survive his association with his Chigurh.
69. Ibid. p.136.
70. Ibid. p.243.
71. *The Searchers* Dir. John Ford. Feat. John Wayne, Jeffrey Hunter, Vera Miles. (Whitney/Warner, USA, 1956). Linda Townley Woodson notes the frequency of drug related killings, especially of police officers, in the Border region in her essay " 'You are the Battleground': Materiality, Moral responsibility and Determinism in *No Country for Old Men*" in *The Cormac McCarthy Society Journal*, Vol.5. pp.5–26.
72. W.B.Yeats "Sailing To Byzantium." See Appendix I below.

    The poem expresses Yeats belief that although flesh may die, art will live. He implies his belief that this applies to his own work. In choosing this as an intertextual reference McCarthy expresses the same hope for himself. Of course this hope has to interpreted in the light of his repeated references to artefacts of a distant past that have survived beyond our ability to understand their meanings. Steven Frye analyses in detail the relation between poem and novel in his essay "Yeats' 'Sailing to Byzantium' and McCarthy's *No Country for Old Men:* Art and Artifice in the New Novel," in *The Cormac Society Journal*, Vol.5. pp.27–41.

APPENDIX

Sailing to Byzantium

I

That is no country for old men. The young
In one another's arms, birds in the trees
—Those dying generations—at their song,
The salmon-falls, the mackerel-crowded seas,
Fish, flesh or fowl, commend all summer long
Whatever is begotten, born and dies.
Caught in that sensual music all neglect
Monuments of unageing intellect.

II

An aged man is but a paltry thing,
A tattered coat upon a stick, unless

Soul clap its hands and sing, and louder sing
For every tatter in its mortal dress,
Nor is there singing school but studying
Monuments of its own magnificence;
And therefore I have sailed the seas and come
To the holy city of Byzantium.

III
O sages standing in God's holy fire
As in the gold mosaic of a wall,
Come from the holy fire, perne in a gyre,
And be the singing-masters of my soul.
Consume my heart away; sick with desire
And fastened to a dying animal
It knows not what it is; and gather me
Into the artifice of eternity.

IV
Once out of nature I shall never take
My bodily form from any natural thing,
But such a form as Grecian goldsmiths make
Of hammered gold and gold enamelling
To keep a drowsy Emperor awake;
Or set upon a golden bough to sing
To lords and ladies of Byzantium
Of what is past, or passing, or to come.

NOTES TO CHAPTER SIXTEEN

1. Excepting the two short stories which share a chapter but are dealt with individually.
2. The text is available but receives little critical attention, Diane Luce's work excepted.
3. I am not claiming such an exclusiveness for any other culture either. There is a sense in which McCarthy is answering Emerson's call for the "American scholar" by being a distinctively American voice but pointing out that the language in which he speaks is itself the product of an inescapable and international cultural eclecticism.
4. "The Waste Land" l.430.
5. In the chapter on *Cities of the Plain* I suggest that the female is absent *in* the text rather than *from* it.

NOTES TO APPENDIX ONE

1. In fact *The Road* appeared in September, a little before *The Sunset Limited*, which became available in the following month. However the first *staging* took place in May and thus I feel justified in presenting this as a chronological order.

2. Steppenwolf gave the first performances of the play at Chicago's Garage Theatre. The four week run was repeated at New York's 59E59 Theatre in October-November. The play was directed by Sheldon Patinkin and featured Austin Pendleton and Freeman Coffey.

3. Denton, M. "The Sunset Limited" nytheatre.com review. 28/10/2006. Denton's failure to discern a protagonist and antagonist seems odd. The protagonist is surely Black and we identify with his vain efforts to save White from himself. Perhaps Denton failed to see himself in the role of the black ex-convict and could only think of himself potentially as the professor. His failure to identify in that case would be unsurprising.

4. Gutman, L. "The Sunset Limited" *Curtain Up Review*, www.curtainup.com, 23/11/2006.

5. I do not wish to imply that *The Sunset Limited* is without its moments of humour, but the source is always Black—White's lack of humour being of a piece with his despair—and Black's humour draws on sources that are quite different to those available to Beckett. He speaks of a friend run down by a taxicab: White asks "Was he killed?" Black replies "I hope so. We buried him." (p. 57) Black can laugh at death.

6. *The Sunset Limited*, p.47.

7. For example "*The professor leans back and studies the black.*" Ibid. p.135.

8. Ibid. p.11.

9. Ibid. p.105. It should be noted that Black and White represent absolute positions with regard to the existence of God and the claims of religion; the play resolutely refuses to endorse either of these positions. Black's faith in the efficacy of one book is no more valid than White's rejection of the value of many. Black's faith is as much a rationalisation as White's atheism. But Black is rationalising his desire to live whereas White, lacking that inherent vitality, rationalises his longing for death.

10. Ibid. p.142.

11. Formerly Orlando to Los Angeles but the railways have contracted in the US as elsewhere.

12. It does however call at El Paso, McCarthy's place of residence. This is one of several passing references to the author's own personal circumstances, which give the play a obliquely 'autobiographical' flavour. These images of North and South can be read as a framing device that encompasses the USA as a whole: the trope is reinforced in the speech of White—Northern educated liberal, and Black whose is happy to admit "That's just the old south talkin." (Ibid. p.70)

13. I have already argued that Chighur is the personification of death in *No Country for Old Men*. In my discussion of that novel I have pointed out that McCarthy, like a number of his distinguished literary peers, has reached the age at which mortality hoves into view. Philip Roth's most recent novel, *Everyman*, concerns itself with death and Joan Didion writes of the experience of bereavement in *The Year of Magical Thinking*.

    "The Sunset Limited" is a metaphor for death anyway in the traditional black culture of the South. For my previous reference to Flannery O'Connor's remark see note 7, pp.299 above.

14. Handy, W.C. "St. Louis Blues".

15. Ab Jones is recalled in Black's references to "niggers" (see note 6), when he tells Suttree that "Bein a nigger is a interesting life." *Suttree* p.203.

16. Ibid. p.158.

17. Ibid. p.157. As previously noted, McCarthy had two spells as an undergraduate at the University of Tennessee; he did not graduate. (See p.19 above.) However any suggestion that this apparent anti-intellectualism is a reflection of the author's own views would need to take into account his current association with the Santa Fe Institute.

    Suttree is a novel devoted to the contest between Life and Death, a contest won, narrowly, by Life.

18. *The Sunset Limited*, p.48.

19. McCarthy's stance seems always to have been that of a religious writer in a godless world. This rationalist interpretation of Black's conversion seems quite permissible in both the particular context of the play and in that of the author's oeuvre in general. However those of the faith, happy, like Black to dispense with the need for rationality, will interpret the matter accordingly. They can be comforted by the notion that McCarthy asserts the non-rational basis of ardenthearted living.

20. Ibid. pp.24–26.

21. Ibid. p.96.

22. *Cities of the Plain*, p.268.

23. Wordsworth, W. "The Tables Turned" vs 1, 2, 3, 4, 5, 8.

24. *The Sunset Limited*, p. 119. You "don't say nothing" since words do not serve when the only the ardent heart will suffice.

25. Beckett, S. *The Unnamable*, in *Molloy* (London: Calder, 1959) p.418.

26. *The Sunset Limited*, p.135. "Kafka on wheels" does not have the same 'ring' as the more usual "Hell on wheels." It also passes up the opportunity to relate the image more closely to the Sunset Limited itself, which is also "on wheels". The professor is no poet: he has nourished his intellect and starved his sensibility. His expressed desire not to see his mother again after death suggests that his failure to embrace life has its roots in familial conflict. His admission that he did not visit when his father was dying of cancer (p.32) hints at the oedipal conflict that is such an obvious characteristic of

McCarthy's work, but which, I have argued, appears to have lost much of its intensity in the later texts. The relationship between Black and White is not oedipal in character. White does mention that his father was a lawyer for the government and this, of course, was the case for McCarthy himself. (p.31) I have made little of possible correspondences between the author's life and his work; these are notoriously difficult to confirm in McCarthy's case; the general cultural significance of the works is more important from my point of view. Jay Ellis has speculated on these autobiographical correspondences in his recent book,* but he places the failure of family and the flight of young men from home at the centre of his analysis.

27. Ibid. p.80. Black has already acknowledged his southern mode of speech: see note 12 above.

28. Hospitality, especially to strangers, is one of the cardinal virtues of the bleak world of McCarthy's novels as I have argued throughout my previous chapters.

29. Kreml, N. "Stylistic Variations and Cognitive Constraint in *All the Pretty Horses*".

30. Of course the play's status cannot really be judged independently of its performance and of the interpretations achieved by its actors. This is a task that will have to be performed by others.

31. One suspects that the creation of White's unlovely language represents a higher technical achievement by McCarthy than that of the attractive speech of Black that seems to come so naturally to the author.

32. *The Sunset Limited*, p.95.

33. *Blood Meridian*, p.247. Although this passage expresses an extreme view it should be considered in relation to its opposite, as represented by the judge, that of extreme anthropocentrism.

NOTES TO APPENDIX TWO

1. Despite the author's claim I am not counting *The Sunset Limited* as a novel. Among the more considered, but still laudatory reviews of *The Road* is that of Steven Kellman who concludes that, Beckett-like, ". . . McCarthy offers a clear-eyed guide to how, though we can't go on. We go on. It is, despite everything, a bracing potion, one for the road." ("Cormac McCarthy Imagines the End"—Review of *The Road* for *The Texas Observer*, Oct. 20th. 2006.) Adam Mars-Jones writes, "*The Road* . . . [is] a thought and feeling experiment, bleak, exhilarating (in fact endurable) only because of its integrity, its wholeness of seeing." ("Life After Armageddon." Review of *The Road* in *The Observer*, 26/11/2006.

---

*(Ellis, J. *No Place for Home: Spatial Constraint and Character Flight in the Novels of Cormac McCarthy*, (New York: Routledge, 2006).

2. McCarthy's willingness to address 'ultimate' questions is exemplified in the old man's declaration that "There is no God and we are his prophets." (p.143) This is surely a characteristic McCarthy inversion of the Islamist claim "There is no God but Allah and Muhammad is his messenger," Muhammad being the Prophet of course. The apocalyptic tone of the novel reflects the mood of America following the destruction of the World Trade Centre (if not its religiosity), just as (I argue) *Blood Meridian* reflected the mood generated by the Vietnam War. See also note 33.

3. Together with all the other texts to a greater or lesser extent as I have argued in preceding chapters; up to but not including *No Country for Old Men*.

4. I am referring here to the quote from Woodward that I have mentioned several times in previous chapters. See for example p.283, Note 4, above.

5. These occur in a central position thus:

. . .

6. This relation between language and movement is explored in Eva-Lynn A. Jagoe's essay "Pace and the Pampas in Argentine Travel Narratives" in which she analyses the way in which narrative style reflects the motion that is described and also reveals ideologies inherent in the attitudes of the writers of the texts.

7. *The Road*, p.75. In this passage McCarthy expresses some of his habitual concerns; the relation between culture and the material world; the way in which signifiers become unreadable when the world that generated them disappears—the dependence of the signifier on the signified. What the passage describes is the onset of a cultural entropy against which McCarthy himself seems to fight ardentheartedly in his texts, especially in ambitious passages such as these.

8. Ibid. p.110. Faulkner uses the same technique to place in the consciousness of unsophisticated characters thoughts that they would not realistically be able to harbour. The father is not without sophistication but the narrative voice does seem to go beyond what he might possess in these metaphysical passages. McCarthy suggests that it is he himself who has "borrowed eyes" from his characters in order to "sorrow" the pain of the world.

9. Ibid. p.45. The wife and mother is driven to despair at the destruction of her world. To avoid her inevitable fate, as she sees it, as a victim of rape, murder and cannibalism, she commits suicide. The father's love for the son prevents him from joining her: his quest to enable his son to survive results in the recovery of the female at the tale's end. This is consistent with the structure of myths of the redemption of nature and the conquest of death to which both "The Waste Land" and *The Road* conform. The same trope is found in *Cities of the Plain*.

10. Ibid. p.6. The "Post Apocalyptic" can be regarded as a genre of its own. I have referred to its cinematic representations in Chapter 11 with respect to *Blood Meridian*, namely the "Mad Max" movies of the 1980s. (p.307) A

contemporary example is Alfonso Cuaron's *Children of Men*, itself an allegory of contemporary British paranoia regarding "otherness." The text itself extends the cinematic reference: "We're not survivors. We're the walking dead in a horror film." One thinks of Romero's *Night of the Living Dead*, a satire on contemporary consumerism, given added relevance by the traveller's use of a supermarket trolley to transport their meagre belongings.

Extreme images are also conjured by very real fears concerning global warming and climate change: the effects of Hurricane Katrina on New Orleans provided the USA with images drawn from everyday reality that were apocalyptic indeed. The war in Iraq is also such a source, not to mention the horrors associated with Abu Ghraib and Guantanamo Bay. I have mentioned the attacks on the World Trade Centre in note 1 above. *The Road* seems to reflect the mood of fear that has permeated the Western mind in the first decade of the twenty-first century.

11. Ibid. p.5.
12. "The Waste Land" ll. 30, 63, 328–9.
13. *The Road*, p.11.
14. Ibid. p.4.
15. "The Waste Land" l. 18.
16. *The Road*, p.26.
17. Ibid. p.70.
18. Ibid. p.234.
19. Ibid. p.236.
20. Ibid. p.25.
21. Ibid. p.210.
22. I have mentioned McCarthy's first Woodward interview and his reference to the "ugly fact that books are made out of other books" on a number of occasions (eg p.5). I have also referred to Harold Bloom's well known treatise on "influence." (p.15)
23. I mentioned the importance Ellis attached to McCarthy's personal circumstances in the previous appendix. See p.330, note 26.
24. "Cormac Country" in *Vanity Fair*, August 2005, p.104.
25. *The Road*, p.217.
26. Ibid. p.235.
27. Ibid. p.17.
28. "Seerockcity" is the tag of a website that advertises the location to the world at large.
29. Ibid. p.23–4.
30. Ibid. p.3.
31. Ibid. p.15–6.
32. Ibid. p.25.

33. Ibid. p.28. The reference to "failed sectarian suicides" is a further intimation of the text's association of an apocalyptic consciousness with current political violence. See also note 2.
34. *Blood Meridian*, p.57.
35. "I am not a man of the road." *The Crossing*, p.414 (and p.211 above).
36. *The Road*, p.21. His boyhood is also recalled in quote 32.
37. As noted previously McCarthy Senior was chief counsel for the Tennessee Valley Authority.
38. Ibid. p.14.
39. Ibid. p.192.
40. Ibid. p.181.
41. Ibid. p.157–8.
42. See p.159 above.
43. *The Road*, p.73–4.
44. There are rumours of another novel; they remain rumours only at the time of writing.
45. *Outer Dark*. p.236. In chapter 6 I interpret this as a parody of the mass. (p.87 above.)
46. *The Road*, p.167.
47. Ibid. p.56.
48. See p.83 above.
49. *The Road*, p.136.
50. *Outer Dark*, p.192.
51. *The Road*, p.143. "Ely" has Jewish connotations.
52. Ibid. 145–6. The old man paints a portrait of Anton Chighur out of a job.
53. Ibid. p. 147.
54. *Outer Dark*, p.98.
55. *The Road*, p.220.
56. Ibid. p.241.
57. Ibid. p.165.
58. Ibid. p.241. This final poetic passage marks McCarthy out as quite unlike anyone else writing today. As I claimed at the start of this book, he insists that literature must dare to address the serious questions. The reiterated image of the trout (see quote 32 above) once again recalls the boyhood scene of *A Drowning Incident*, linking the text's closing lyrical passage to McCarthy's earliest world and works. "Maps and mazes" are what he has been tracing in a writing career that has drawn on the culture of the USA and had its roots in the mountains and glens of East Tennessee.

Bibliography

C. MCCARTHY: PRIMARY TEXTS

Wake For Susan in *The Phoenix, University of Tennessee Magazine* (Knoxville: 1959).
A Drowning Incident in *The Phoenix, University of Tennessee Magazine*, (Knoxville: 1960).
The Orchard Keeper [1965] (London: Picador, 1994).
Outer Dark [1968] (London: Picador, 1994).
Child of God [1973] (London: Picador, 1989).
The Gardener's Son (Hopewell NJ: Ecco Press, 1996).)
Suttree [1979] (London: Picador, 1989).
Blood Meridian [1985] (London: Picador, 1990).
All the Pretty Horses [1992] (London: Picador, 1993).
The Stonemason (Hopewell NJ: Ecco Press, 1994).
The Crossing [1994] (London: Picador, 1995).
Cities of the Plain (London: Picador, 1998).
No Country for Old Men (London: Picador, 2005).

SECONDARY TEXTS

Arnold, E. "Cormac McCarthy's *The Stonemason*: the Unmaking of a Play," in Wallach (ed), *Myth, Legend, Dust*, pp.141–154.
—— " 'Go To Sleep,' Dreams and Visions in the Trilogy," in Arnold (ed) *The Southern Quarterly*, XVIII:3 (2000), pp.34–58.
—— "The Mosaic of McCarthy's Fiction," in Hall & Wallach (eds), *Sacred Violence*, 2nd. Edition, Vol.2. pp.17–24.
—— "The Last of the Trilogy: First Thoughts on *Cities of the Plain*" in Arnold & Luce (eds) *Perspectives on Cormac McCarthy*, pp.221–248.
—— "A Stonemason Evening," in Wegner, J. (ed) *The Cormac McCarthy Journal*, Vol.2, No.1, Spring 2002.

Arnold, E. & Luce, D. (eds) *Perspectives On Cormac McCarthy: Revised Edition* (Jackson: University Press of Mississippi, 1999).

—— *The Southern Quarterly. Special Issue: Cormac McCarthy's Border Trilogy*, XXXVIII:3 (2000).

—— *A Cormac McCarthy Companion: The Border Trilogy* (Jackson: University of Mississippi, 2001).

Bailey, C. "The Last Stage of the Hero's Evolution: Cormac McCarthy's *Cities of the Plain*," in Wallach (ed), *Myth, Legend, Dust*, pp.293–302.

Bartlett, A. "From Voyeurism to Archeology: Cormac McCarthy's *Child of God*," *Southern Literary Journal*, 24:3 (1991), pp.3–15.

Bell, V. *The Achievement of Cormac McCarthy* [1975] (Baton Rouge: Louisiana State University Press, 1988).

—— "The Ambiguous Nihilism of Cormac McCarthy," *Southern Literary Journal*, 15:2 (1983): pp.31–41.

Brickner, R. "A Hero Cast Out, Even By Tragedy," *New York Times Book Review*, 13/1/94, sec.7: pp.6–7, quoted by Arnold & Luce (eds) in their Introduction to *Perspectives on Cormac McCarthy*.

Canfield, J.D. "Crossing From the Wasteland Into the Exotic in Cormac McCarthy's Border Trilogy," in Arnold & Luce (eds) *A Cormac McCarthy Companion*, pp.256–269.

Cant, J. (ed) *The Cormac McCarthy Society Journal* Vol.5. 2006. Edition devoted to *No Country for Old Men*.

Carr, D. "The Dispossessed White as Naked Ape and Stereotyped Hillbilly in the Southern Novels of Cormac McCarthy," *Midwest Quarterly* 40:1 (1998), pp.9–20.

Chollier, C. "Exposure and Double Exposure in Cormac McCarthy's Baroque Trilogy," Holloway (ed), *Proceedings of the First European Conference on Cormac McCarthy*, pp.49–56.

Clark, B. "Art, Authenticity and Social Transgression in Cormac McCarthy's *All the Pretty Horses*," *Southwestern American Literature*, 25:1(1999), pp.117–123.

Cremean, D. "For Whom the Bell Tolls: Conservatism and Change in Cormac McCarthy's Sheriff from *No Country for Old Men*," in *The Cormac McCarthy Society Journal* Vol.5. 2006.

Daugherty, L. "Gravers False and True: *Blood Meridian* as Gnostic Tragedy," in Arnold & Luce (eds), *Perspectives on Cormac McCarthy*, pp.159–174.

Donoghue, D. "Reading *Blood Meridian*," *Sewanee Review* 105:3 (1997), pp.401–418.

—— "Dream Work" [Review of *All the Pretty Horses*], *New York Review of Books* IX:12 (1993), pp.5–10.

Ellis, J. "The Rape of Rawlins: a Note on *All the Pretty Horses*," *The Cormac McCarthy Journal*, 1:1 (2001), pp.67–69.

Ensor, A. " 'Knoxville's Sadder Regions': Places and Persons in Cormac McCarthy's *Suttree*," University of Tennessee Philological Society, 24/2/94.

Feld, R. "Timing and Spacing the As If: Poetic Prose and Prosaic Poetry" [Review of *The Crossing*] in *Parnassus, Poetry in Review* 20:1-2 (1995), pp.11–31.

Frye, S. "Yeats' 'Sailing to Byzantium' and McCarthy's *No Country for Old Men*: Art and Artifice in the New Novel," in *The Cormac McCarthy Society Journal*, Vol.5. 2006.

Gibson, M. "The White Cap Book," *Knoxville Local History Magazine*, No. 26, 29/6/2000.

Grammer, J.M. "A Thing Against Which Time Will Not Prevail: Pastoral and History in Cormac McCarthy's South," in Arnold & Luce (eds), *Perspectives on Cormac McCarthy*, pp.29–44.

Guillermin, G. *The Pastoral Vision of Cormac McCarthy* (College Station: Texas A & M University Press, 2004).

Hall, W. "The Human Comedy of Cormac McCarthy," in Hall & Wallach (eds), *Sacred Violence*, 2nd. Edn. Vol.1. pp.59–73.

Hall, W. & Wallach, R (eds), *Sacred Violence: 2nd. Edn. Vol.1. Cormac McCarthy's Appalachian Works* (El Paso: Texas Western Press, 2002) .

—— *Sacred Violence: 2nd. Edn. Vol.2. Cormac McCarthy's Western Novels* (El Paso: Texas Western Press, 2002).

Holloway, D. " 'A False Book Is No Book At All': the Ideology of Representation in *Blood Meridian* and the Border Trilogy," in Wallach (ed), *Myth, Legend, Dust*, pp.185–200.

—— (ed) *Proceedings of the First European Conference on Cormac McCarthy* (Miami: Cormac McCarthy Society,1998).

Iyer, P. "Leaning Toward Myth" [Review of *The Crossing*], *Partisan Review*, 62:2 (1995), pp.309–314.

Jarrett, R.L. *Cormac McCarthy* (New York: Twayne, 1997).

—— "Genre, Voice and Ethos: McCarthy's Perverse Thriller" in *The Cormac McCarthy Society Journal* Vol.5. 2006.

Josyph, P. "Older Professions: the Fourth Wall of *The Stonemason*," in Wallach (ed) *Myth, Legend, Dust*, pp.119–140.

—— "Tragic Ecstacy: A Conversation With Harold Bloom about Cormac McCarthy's *Blood Meridian*," *Southwest American Literature*, 26:1 (2000), pp.119–140.

Kerrigan, M. "Frontier Feelings" [Review of *The Crossing*], *Times Literary Supplement*, 4470 (1994), p.11.

Kiefer, C. "Examining the Moral Code of The Crossing," *The Cormac McCarthy Society Journal*, 1:1 (2000), pp.27–38.

Kreml, N. "Stylistic Variation and Cognitive Constraint in *All the Pretty Horses*" in *Sacred Violence: Vol. 2*. pp.37–49.

Lawson, L.A. "Ontological Uncertainties" [Review of Bell, *The Achievement of Cormac McCarthy*] *Sewanee Review*, 97:4 (1989), pp.110–112.

Longley, J.L. "Suttree and the Metaphysics of Death," *Southern Literary Journal*, 17:2 (1985), pp.78–90.

Luce, D. " 'They ain't the thing': Artifact and Hallucinated Recollection in Cormac McCarthy's Early Frame-Works," in Wallach (ed) *Myth, Legend, Dust,* pp.21–36.

—— "The Murderers Behind *Child of God,*" Cormac McCarthy International Colloquy, El Paso, 1998, quoted by Sullivan N. "The Evolution of the Dead Girlfriend Motif in *Outer Dark* and *Child of God,*" in Wallach (ed) *Myth Legend, Dust,* pp.68–77.

—— "Cormac McCarthy's First Screenplay: *The Gardener's Son,*" in Arnold & Luce (eds) *Perspectives on Cormac McCarthy,* pp.71–96.

—— "The Vanishing World of Cormac McCarthy's Border Trilogy," *The Southern Quarterly* XXXVIII:3 (2000), pp.121–146.

—— "The Road and the Matrix: The World as Tale in *The Crossing,*" in Arnold & Luce (eds), *Perspectives on Cormac McCarthy,* pp.195–220.

Lurie, M. "See the Child. The Fiction of Cormac McCarthy," *Meanjin* 54:2 (1995), pp.376–383.

Marius, R. "Suttree As Window Into the Soul of Cormac McCarthy," in Hall & Wallach (eds), *Sacred Violence,* pp.123–139.

Morrison, G.M. "John Grady Cole's Expulsion From Paradise," in Arnold & Luce (eds), *Perspectives on Cormac McCarthy,* pp.175–194.

Mosle, S. "Don't Let Your Babies Grow Up to be Cowboys" [Review of *Cities of the Plain*], *New York Times Book Review,* Vol.3. 1998, pp.16–18.

Peebles, S. " 'Lo Fantastico': The Influence of Borges and Cortázar on the Epilogue of *Cities of the Plain,*" *Southwestern American Literature,* 25:1 (1998), pp.105–109.

Phillips, D. "History and the Ugly Facts of Cormac McCarthy's *Blood Meridian,*" *American Literature* 68:2 (1996), pp.433–460.

Pitts, J. "Writing On: *Blood Meridian* as a Devisionary Western," *Western American Literature* 33:1 (1998), pp.6–25.

Quinn, P. "Crossing the Mountains of Mexico" [Review of *Cities of the Plain*], *Times Literary Supplement* 4968, 45:14, 19/6/98.

Scoones, J. "McCarthy's 'Girls' and the Ethics of Dwelling in The Border Trilogy," American Literature Association Conference, Baltimore, 28/5/99, in Wallach (ed), *Myth, Legend, Dust,* pp.68–77.

Scott, A.O. "The Sun Also Sets" [Review of *Cities of the Plain*], *New York Review of Books,* 45:14 (1998), pp.26–29.

Sepich, J. *Notes on Blood Meridian* (Louisville: Bellarmine College Press, 1993).

Shaw, P. "Female Presence, Male Violence, and the Art of Artlessness in Cormac McCarthy's Border Trilogy," *Southwestern American Literature* 25:1 (1999), pp.11–23.

—— "The Kid's Fate, the Judge's Guilt: Ramifications of Closure in Cormac McCarthy's *Blood Meridian,*" *Southern Literary Journal* 30:1 (1998), pp.102–119.

Smith, R.T. Review of *Cities of the Plain, Shenandoah* 48:3 (1998), pp.127–129.

Spencer, W.L. "Cormac McCarthy's Unholy Trinity: Biblical Parody in Outer Dark" in Hall & Wallach (eds), *Sacred Violence, 2nd. Edn. Vol.1.* pp.83–91.

Spurgeon, S.L. "'Pledged in Blood:' Truth and Redemption in Cormac McCarthy's *All the Pretty Horses*," in *Western American Literature* 34:1 (1999), pp.24–44.

Sullivan, N. "Boys Will Be Bad and Girls Will Be Gone: The Circuit of Male Desire in Cormac McCarthy's Border Trilogy," *The Southern Quarterly* XXXVIII:3 (2000), pp.167–187.

—— "The evolution of the dead girlfriend motif in *Outer Dark* and *Child of God*," in Wallach (ed), *Myth, Legend, Dust*, pp.68–77.

Sullivan, W. "About Any Kind of Meanness You Can Name," *Sewanee Review* 93:44 (1985), pp.649–656.

Wallach, R. "Three Dreams: The Bizarre Epilogue to *Cities of the Plain*," in Holloway (ed) *Proceedings of the First European Conference on Cormac McCarthy*, pp.57–61.

—— "Prefiguring Cormac McCarthy: the Early Short Stories," in Wallach (ed) *Myth, Legend, Dust*, pp.15–20.

—— (ed) *Southwestern American Literature: Special Edition on Cormac McCarthy*, 25:1 (1999).

—— (ed) *Myth, Legend, Dust: Critical Responses to Cormac McCarthy* (Manchester: Manchester University Press, 2000).

Wallace, G. "Meeting Mr. McCarthy," *Southern Quarterly* XXX:4 (1992), pp.134–139. Quoted by Arnold E. in "The Mosaic of McCarthy's Fiction," in Hall & Wallach (eds), *Sacred Violence, 2nd. Edn. Vol.1*. pp.17–24.

Wegner, J. " 'Mexico Para los Mexicanos' Revolution, Mexico and McCarthy's Border Trilogy," in Wallach (ed), *Myth, Legend, Dust*, pp.249–255.

—— "Whose Story Is It?: History and Fiction in Cormac McCarthy's *All the Pretty Horses*," *The Southern Quarterly* XXXVI:2 (1998), pp.103–110.

—— (ed) *The Cormac McCarthy Journal*, 1:1 (2000).

Wilhelmus, T. "Ranches of Isolation," *Hudson Review* 48:1 (1995), pp.145–152.

Williams, D. "Annie DeLisle," *Knoxville Sentinel*, 10/6/90; in Jarrett, *Cormac McCarthy*, pp.3–4.

Witek, T. " 'He's Hell When He's Well': Cormac McCarthy's Rhyming Dictions," in Wallach (ed) *Myth, Legend, Dust*, pp.78–88.

Woodward, R.B. "Cormac McCarthy's Venomous Fiction," *New York Times Magazine*, 19/4/92, pp.28–31, 36, 40.

—— "Cormac Country" in *Vanity Fair*, August, 2005, pp.98–104.

Yardley, J. "Alone, Alone, All, All Alone," *Washington Post Book World*, 13/1/74, p.1.

Young, T.D. Jr. "The Imprisonment of Sensibility: Suttree" in Arnold & Luce (eds), *Perspectives on Cormac McCarthy*, pp.97–123.

OTHER TEXTS

Abbey, E. (ed) *Cactus Country* [1973] (Amsterdam: Time-Life Books).

Alarcón, D.C. *The Aztec Palimpsest* (Tucson: University of Arizona Press, 1997).

Alinder, A. & Szarkowski, J. *Ansel Adams: Classic Images* [1985] (Boston: Bulfinch Press).

Agee, J. *A Death in the Family* [1938] (New York: Vintage, 1998).

Agee, J. & Evans, W. *Let Us Now Praise Famous Men* [1939] (London: Pan, 1988).

Alperovitz, G. *The Decision To Use The Atomic Bomb* [1995] (New York: Fontana, 1996).

Ayers, E.L. & Mittendorf, B (eds) *The Oxford Book of the American South* (New York: Oxford Univ. Press, 1997).

Baring, A. & Cashford, J. *The Myth of the Goddess, Evolution of an Image* (London: Arkana, 1993).

Barthelme, F. *Painted Desert* [1995] (New York: Penguin, 1997).

Barthes, R. *Mythologies* [1957] (St. Albans: Paladin, 1976).

Bass, R. *In the Loyal Mountains* (Boston: Houghton Mifflin, 1995).

—— *The Book of Yaak* (Boston, Houghton Mifflin, 1996).

Baym, N. et al (eds) *The Norton Anthology of American Literature, Vol. 1, Second Edn* (New York: Norton, 1985).

Behr, E. *Prohibition: The Thirteen Years That Changed America* (London: BBC, 1997).

Bercovitch, S. *The Puritan Origins of the American Self* (Newhaven: Yale University Press, 1975).

Betts, D. *Heading West* [1981] (New York: Scribner, 1995).

Bloom, H. *The Anxiety of Influence: A Theory of Poetry* [1973] (New York: Oxford University Press, 1997).

Bloom, H & Trilling, L. (eds) *The Oxford Anthology of English Literature: Romantic Poetry and Prose* (New York: Oxford University Press, 1985).

Bourke, J. *On the Border With Crook* [1891] (Lincoln: University of Nebraska Press, 1971).

Brogan, H. *The Penguin History of the United States* [1985] (London: Penguin, 1990).

Brown, N.O. *Life Against Death, The Psychological Meaning of History* [1959] (London: Sphere, 1970).

Caldwell, E. *Tobacco Road* [1934] (London: Pan, 1958).

Campbell, J. *The Hero With A Thousand Faces* [1949] (London: Fontana, 1993).

Campbell, N. *The Cultures of the New West* (Edinburgh, Edinburgh University Press, 2000).

de Cervantes, M. *Don Quixote*, [c. 1605]. Trans. Jarvis, C. Intro. Riley, E.C. (Oxford: Oxford University Press, 1998).

Chamberlain, S. *My Confession* (New York: Harpers, 1956).

Chesnutt, C.W. *The Conjure Woman* [1889] (Ann Arbor: University of Michigan Press, 1969).

Coleridge, S.T. "The Rhyme of the Ancient Mariner" [1798], in *Poems: Samuel Taylor Coleridge*, Beer, J. (ed) (London: Dent, 1995).

Conrad, J. *Lord Jim* [1900] (London: Penguin, 1975).

—— *The Nigger of the Narcissus and Other Stories* [1897] (London: Penguin Modern Classics, 1965).

—— *Chance* [1913] (London: Penguin Modern Classics, 1974).

—— *The Secret Sharer* [1912] in *Twixt Land and Sea* (London: Penguin, 1988).

—— *Heart of Darkness* [1902] (London: Penguin Modern Classics, 1973).

Dante Alighieri. *The Divine Comedy: Hell.* trans. Sayers, D.L. [1949] (London: Penguin Classics, 1976).

Dickens, C. *Hard Times* [1854] (Ware: Wordsworth Classics, 1995).

Didion, J. *Slouching Towards Bethlehem* [1968] (London: Flamingo, 2001).

—— *Play It As It Lays* [1970] (New York: Washington Square Press, 1978).

—— *The White Album* [1979] (London: Flamingo, 1993).

—— *Miami* [1987] (London: Flamingo, 1994).

—— *The Last Thing He Wanted* [1996] (London: Flamingo, 1997).

Doctorow, E.L. *The Waterworks* [1994] (Sydney: Picador, 1995).

Donne, J. "Devotions, XVII" in *Donne: Complete Verse and Selected Prose* [1972]. Hayward, J. (ed) (London: Nonesuch Press, 1972).

Dostoevsky, F. *Notes From the Underground* [1864], trans. Kentish, J. (Oxford: Oxford University Press, 1992).

Dugan, E. (ed) *Picturing the South: 1860 to the Present* [1996] (San Francisco: Chronicle Books).

Eagleton, M. (ed) *Feminist Literary Theory* [1986] (Cambridge: Mass: Blackwell, 1994).

Ellison, R. *Invisible Man* [1952] (London: Penguin, 1965).

Ellroy, J. *The Black Dahlia* [1987] (London: Arrow Books, 1993).

—— *The Big Nowhere* [1988] (London: Arrow Books, 1994).

—— *My Dark Places, An L.A. Crime Memoir* (London: Arrow Books, 1997).

Eliot, T.S. "The Waste Land" [1922], in *Collected Poems: 1909–1962* (London: Faber, 1963).

—— "The Four Quartets, Burnt Norton" [1935] in *Collected Poems, 1909–1962.*

—— "The Love Song of J. Alfred Prufrock" [1917] in *Collected Poems, 1909–1962.*

Faulkner, W. *Absalom, Absalom!* [1936] (New York: Vintage, 1972).

—— *As I Lay Dying* [1930] (London: Penguin, 1987).

—— *The Unvanquished* [1934] (London: Penguin, 1975).

—— *Light In August* [1932] (London: Penguin, 1970).

—— *The Hamlet* [1931] (New York: Vintage, 1990).

—— *The Mansion* [1959] (London: The Reprint Society, 1962).

—— *Pantaloon in Black* [1940] in *Go Down, Moses* (New York: Vintage, 1973).

Fennimore Cooper, J. *The Last of the Mohicans* [1826] (Ware: Wordsworth Classics, 1992).

—— *The Prairie* [1859] (New York: Signet Classic, 1964).

Fiedler, L. *Love and Death in the American Novel* [1960] (Normal Il: Dalkey Archive Press, 1997).

Filson, J. *The Adventures of Colonel Daniel Boone; Containing A Narrative of the Wars of Kentucky* [1784] (Electronic text, 2001, http://www.earlyamerica.com/lives/boone/).

Frost, R. "Stopping By Woods on a Snowy Evening" in Latham E.C. (ed), *The Poetry of Robert Frost* (New York: Holt, Rinehart & Winstone, 1979), pp.224–225.

Goux, J.J. *Oedipus Philosopher* trans. Porter, C. (Stanford: Stanford University Press, 1993).

Grammer, J.M. *Pastoral and Politics in the Old South* (Baton Rouge: Louisiana State University Press, 1996).

Graves, R. *The Greek Myths* [1955] (London: Penguin, 1978).

Gray, R. *Southern Aberrations: Writers of the American South and the Problems of Regionalism* (Baton Rouge: Louisiana University Press, 2000).

—— *Writing the South: Ideas of an American Region* [1986] (Baton Rouge: Louisiana State University Press, 1997).

Grey, Z. *Riders of the Purple Sage* [1912] (New York: Penguin, 1990).

Guinn, M. *After Southern Modernism* (Jackson: University Press of Mississippi, 2000).

Hannah, B. *Ray* [1980] (New York: Grove Press, 1994).

Harris, G.W. *Sut Lovingood's Yarns Spun* [1864] (Chapel Hill: University of North Carolina Library (Electronic Text, 1997, http://metalab.unc.edu/docsouth/harrisg/gharris.html).

Hart, J.D & Leninger, P.W. (eds) *The Oxford Companion To American Literature* (New York: Oxford University Press, 1995).

Haun, M. *The Hawk's Done Gone* [1940–68] Gower H (ed) (Nashville: Vanderbilt University Press, 1995).

Hopkinson Smith, F. *Colonel Carter of Cartersville* [1891] (Boston: Houghton Mifflin).

Hughes, E. *Shakespeare and the Goddess of Complete Being* (London: Faber, 1992).

Irving, W. *Rip Van Winkle* [1819] in *The Legend of Sleepy Hollow and Other Stories* (London: Penguin, 2000).

Jameson, F. *Postmodernism: or The Cultural Logic of Late Capitalism* [1991] (London: Verso, 1996).

Jefferson, T. "Notes on Virginia: Query XIX, Manufactures" in Baym et al (eds), *Norton Anthology of American Literature*, pp.627–628.

Joyce, J. *Ulysses* [1922] (London: PenguinTwentieth Century Classics, 1992).

Keats, J. "Ode to a Nightingale" [1819] in *The Works of John Keats* (Ware: Wordsworth, 1995), pp.230–232.

Kiberd, D. "Introduction" in Joyce, *Ulysses*, pp.ix-lxxxix.

Lasch, C. *The Minimal Self: Psychic Survival in Troubled Times* [1984] (London: Picador, 1985).

Lewis, M. *The Journals of the Lewis and Clarke Expedition, Vol. 6, Scientific Data* [1804–6] Thwaites R.G. (ed) (New York: Antiquarian Press, 1959).

Lilienthal. D. E. *TVA: Democracy on the March* (New York: Penguin Books, 1944).

Lytle, A.N. *Bedford Forrest and His Critter Company* [1931] (Nashville: J.S.Sanders & Co, 1992).

Madsen, D. *American Exceptionalism* (Jackson: University Press of Mississippi, 1998).

—— (ed) *Visions of America Since 1492* (London: Leicester University Press, 1994).

Marcus, G. *Invisible Republic: Bob Dylan's Basement Tapes* [1997] (New York: Picador, 1998).

McCarthy, L. *Desire's Door* (Brownsville: Storyline Press, 1991).

McMurtry, L. *Lonesome Dove* [1985] (London: Pan, 1990).

—— *Dead Man's Walk* [1995] (London: Phoenix, 1996).

Melville, H. *Moby-Dick* [1851] (London: Penguin Classics, 1986).

—— *The Encantadas* [1854] in *Billy Budd, Sailor and Other Stories* (London: Penguin English Library, 1979).

Miller, P. *Errand Into the Wilderness* [1956] (Cambridge Mass: Harvard University Press, 1996).

—— (ed) *The American Puritans: Their Prose and Poetry* (New York: Anchor, 1956).

Morris, P. (ed) *The Bakhtin Reader* (London: Arnold, 1994).

Murfree, M.N. *The Bushwhackers and Other Stories* [1899] (New York, Books for Libraries Press, 1969).

—— *In the Tennessee Mountains* [1885] (Knoxville: University of Tennessee Press, 1970).

—— *The Prophet of the Great Smoky Mountains* [1885] (Boston: Houghton Mifflin, 1890).

—— *The Panther of Jolton's Ridge* [1885] in *The Bushwhackers and Other Stories* [1889] (New York: Books for Libraries Press, 1969).

Nietzsche, F. *Thus Spake Zarathustra* [1883–5] (London: Penguin Classics, 1974).

O'Connor, F. *Wise Blood* [1949] (London: Faber, 1996).

—— *The Violent Bear It Away* [1955] (London: Faber, 1985).

—— *Mystery and Manners* [1957] (New York: Noonday Press, 1999).

Offutt, C. *The Good Brother* [1997] (New York: Scribner, 1998).

Paredes, A. & Foss, G. *The Décima on the Texas-Mexican Border*, No. 54 Offprint Series, Institute of Latin American Studies, University of Texas at Austin. Reprinted from *Journal of the Folklore Institute*, Indiana University, Bloominton, Indiana, III:2, (1996).

Paredes, A *The Anglo-American in Mexican Folklore*, No. 30 Offprint Series, Institute of Latin American Studies, University of Texas, 1963.

—— *With His Pistol In His Hand: A Border Ballad and Its Hero* (Austin: University of Texas Press, 1958).

—— *Folklore and Culture on the Texas-Mexican Border* [1993] (Austin: University of Texas Press, 1993).

Paz, O. *The Labyrinth of Solitude* [1961] (London: Penguin, 1990).

Penn Warren, R. *Band of Angels* (New York: Random House, 1955).

Porter, K.A. *Pale Horse, Pale Rider* in *Three Stories* [1939] (New York: Signet, 1967).

—— *Noon Wine* [1937] in *Three Stories* [1939] (New York: Signet, 1967).

Pritzker, B. (ed) *Ansel Adams* [1991] (New York: Crescent Books).

Rulfo, J. *Pedro Páramo* [1955] (London: Serpent's Tail, 1994).

Scott, W. *The Heart of Midlothian* [1818] (London: A. & C. Black, 1904).

Shaw, P.W. *The Modern American Novel of Violence* (New York: Whitstone Publishing, 2000).

Simms, W.G. *Tales of the South* (Colombia: University of South Carolina Press, 1996).

Simpson, L.P. *The Dispossessed Garden: Pastoral and History in Southern Literature* [1975] (Baton Rouge: Louisiana State University Press, 1983).

Slotkin, R. *Regeneration Through Violence: the Mythology of the American Frontier* [1973] (Norman: University of Oklahoma Press, 2000).

—— *The Fatal Environment: The Myth of the Frontier in the Age of Industrialization, 1800–1890* [1985] (Norman: University of Oklahoma Press, 1998).

—— *Gunfighter Nation: The Myth of the Frontier in Twentieth-Century America* [1992] (Norman: University of Oklahoma Press, 1998).

Smith, H.N. *Virgin Land: The American West as Symbol and Myth* [1950] (Cambridge Mass: Harvard University Press, 1970).

Sontag, S. Introduction to Rulfo, *Pedro Páramo*, pp.v–viii.

Tanner, M. *Nietzsche* [1994] (Oxford: Oxford University Press, 1996).

Tate, A. *The Fathers* [1938] (London: Penguin, 1969).

Taylor, P. *In the Tennessee Country* (London: Chatto & Windus, 1994).

Tennyson, A. "The Lady of Shalott" in *The Works of Alfred Lord Tennyson* (London: MacMillan, 1894), pp.27–29.

Thorpe, T.B. *The Big Bear of Arkansas* [1841] in Baym N. et al (eds) *The Norton Anthology of American Literature*, pp.1535–1544.

Turner, F.J. *The Frontier in American History* [1920] (Tucson: University Press of Arizona, 1992).

Twain, M. *Life on the Mississippi* [1883] (New York: Penguin, 1986).

—— *Mark Twain's Weapons of Satire: Anti-Imperialist Writings on the Philippine-American War*, Zwick, J. (ed) (New York: Syracuse University Press, 1992).

Vanderheide, J. "Varieties of Renunciation in the Works of Cormac McCarthy" in *The Cormac McCarthy Society Journal* Vol.5. 2006.

Vann Woodward, C. *The Burden of Southern History, Third Edition* [1960] (Baton Rouge: Louisiana State University Press, 1993).

—— *Origins of the New South: 1877–1913* [1951] (Baton Rouge: Louisiana State University Press, 1990).

Vidal, G. *Burr* (New York: Random House, 1973).

Watkins, S. *Co. Aytch* [1882] in Ayers & Mittendorf (eds), *The Oxford Book of the American South*, pp.126–139.

Watkins, T.H. *The Great Depression: America in the 1930s* (Boston: Little Brown, 1993).

Welty, E. *The Robber Bridegroom* [1942] (London: Virago Press, 1999).

—— *Delta Wedding* [1945] (London: Virago Press, 1986).

—— *One Time, One Place, Mississippi in the Depression* [1971] (Jackson: University Press of Mississippi).

Whitman, W. "Song of Myself" in *Leaves of Grass* [1855] (New York: Penguin Classics, 1986).

Wilder, T. *The Bridge of San Luis Rey* [1927] (London: Longmans Green, 1931).

—— *Our Town* [1938] (London: Longmans, 1966).

Wister, O. *The Virginian* [1902] (Oxford: Oxford World's Classics, 1998).

Woodson, L.T. "You are the battleground": Materiality, Moral Responsibility, and Determinism in *No Country for Old Men* in *The Cormac McCarthy Society Journal* Vol.5. 2006.

Yeats, W.B. "The Lake Isle of Innisfree" in Larkin, P. (ed), *The Oxford Book of Twentieth Century English Verse* [1973] (Oxford: Oxford University Press, 1978) p.75.

—— "Sailing to Byzantium" Ibid. pp. 82.

FILM

Coen, E. & Coen, J. *Oh Brother Where Art Thou?* [2000] (Universal/Touchstone).

Ford, J, *My Darling Clementine* [1946] (Fox).

—— *Wagonmaster* [1950] (Argosy/RKO).

—— *The Searchers* [1956] (Warner Bros).

—— *The Man Who Shot Liberty Valance* [1962] (Ford Productions).

Guercio, J. *Electra Glide in Blue* [1973] (Guercio/Hitzig).

Hawks, H. *Red River* [1948] (UA/Monterey: Howard Hawks).

Hitchcock, A. *Psycho* [1960] (Paramount).

Huston, J. *Wise Blood* [1979] (USA/Germany: Artificial Eye/Anthea/Ithaca,).

Wenders, W. *Paris, Texas* [1984] (Argos).

MUSIC

Dylan, B. "Spanish is the Loving Tongue," on *Dylan*, CBS Records, 1973.

Seeger, M (ed) *Dock Boggs, His Folkway Years*, Smithsonian Folkway Recordings, SFW 40108, 1998.

Smith, H. (ed) *Anthology of American Folk Music*, Smithsonian Folkways Recordings, SFW 40090 / A 28746–28751, 1997.

Stanley, C. & Stanley, R. "Gathering Flowers for the Master's Bouquet", trad. recorded c.1949, Columbia Records. Issued on *Too Late To Cry*, CD KATCD206, UK, Catfish Records, 2001.

Index